4 G 880

Londres
1799

Browne, William George

Travels in Africa, Egypt, and Syria, from the year 1792 to 1798

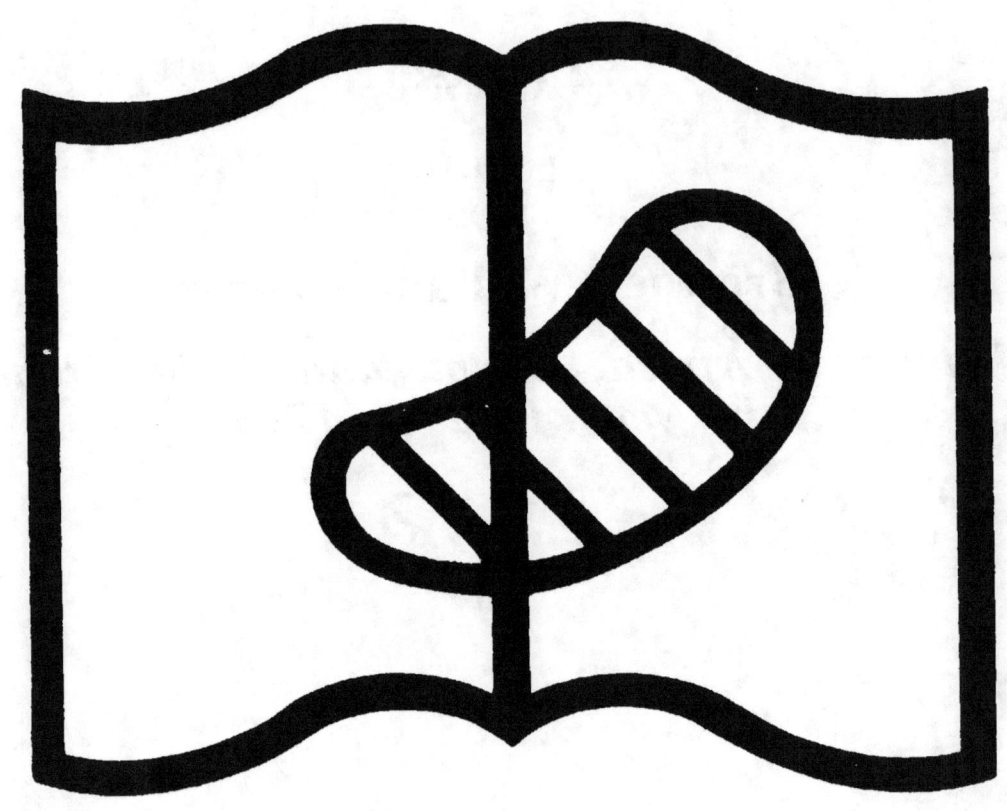

Symbole applicable
pour tout, ou partie
des documents microfilmés

Original illisible

NF Z 43-120-10

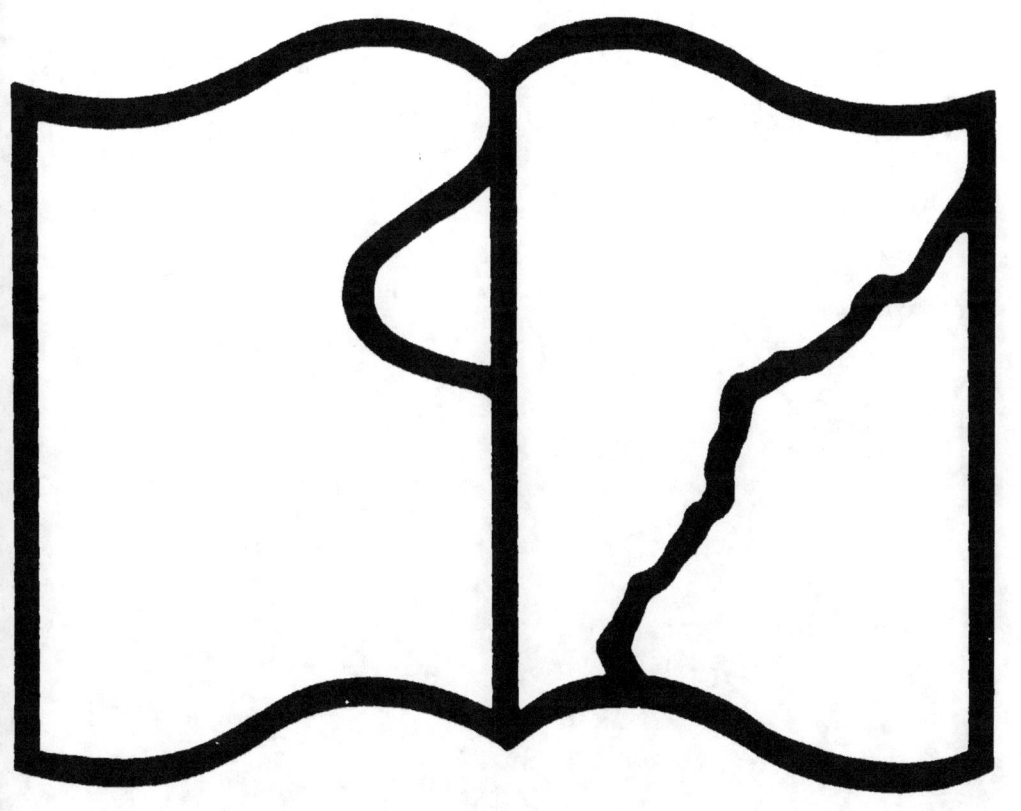

Symbole applicable
pour tout, ou partie
des documents microfilmés

Texte détérioré — reliure défectueuse

NF Z 43-120-11

TRAVELS

IN

AFRICA, &c.

PREFACE.

IF the defire of literary fame were the chief motive for fubmitting to public notice the following fheets, the writer is not fo far blinded by felf-love, as not to be confcious of having failed of his object. The fimple narrative of a journey is perhaps as little a proper fource of reputation for elegance of compofition, as a journey of the kind defcribed is in itfelf of the pleafures of fenfe. But the prefent, from various circumftances, comprehends fo fmall a portion of what might be expected from the obfervations of feveral years, that he has been often difpofed to give it a different title.

The retrofpect on the events of his life which are briefly mentioned in the enfuing pages, offers him a mixed sensation. The hopes with which he undertook the voyage, even without being very sanguine, contrasted with the disappointment with which he now sits down to relate its occurrences, allow him little satisfaction from what has been executed. He feels, however, some confidence of not experiencing severe censure when his design shall be understood. The work is not offered as elaborate or perfect. The account of Dar-Fûr fills up a vacancy in the geography of Africa; and of a country so little known, the information obtained should not be estimated by its quantity, but by its authenticity. Sitting in a chamber in Kahira or Tripoli, it is easy to give a plausible account of Northern Africa, from Sennaar and Gondar to Tombuctoo and Fez. It would not be difficult even to sanction it by the authority of the Jelabs. These people are never at a loss whatever question is asked them, and if they know not the name of the place inquired for, they recollect some other place of a name a little resembling it in sound, and describe what they never heard of by what they know. With regard to manners they are as little to be relied on. Ask but a leading question,

question, and all the miracles of antiquity, of dog-headed nations, and men with tails, will be described, with their situation, habits, and pastimes.

But their descriptions, when given without the smallest appearance of interested views, if verified on the spot, are constantly found defective or erroneous.

The writer is aware, that when the length of the time he passed in Dar-Fûr is considered, the short account here given will appear, to persons accustomed to the busy scenes of Europe, but very imperfectly to fill up the void. Confiding, however, that those of more reflection and experience in travelling, will be better pleased with a short and clear narrative of what really happened, than by frivolous anecdotes or remarks, inserted merely to swell the size of the volume, he has contented himself with extracting from his journal the principal occurrences during his residence there, and giving them the connection required; at the same time omitting nothing that could any way contribute to throw light on the state of the country, or character of the inhabitants.

A more creative imagination would have drawn more animated pictures; a mind more disposed to observation would have collected more facts and incidents; and a more vigorous intellect would have converted those facts and incidents into materials of more interesting and more striking investigation. The descriptions would have been more impressive, and the deductions more profound.

The present work has the merit of being composed from observations made in the places and on the subjects described. But the praise of fidelity, the only one to which the writer lays claim, cannot be received till another shall have traced his footsteps.

With respect to Egypt a greater number of persons may be found who are qualified to decide, and there is not the same reason for suspension of judgment.

Without

PREFACE.

Without pretending to any extraordinary sources of information, the writer hopes, that what is here said will afford some little satisfaction to those who wish for the latest information concerning that country. He arrogates not to himself the praise of augmenting greatly the sum of knowlege already to be found in books; but very widely dispersed, and within the reach of comparatively few persons.

Innumerable books have been written on Egypt, but none of them, in our language, can pretend to a popular plan. Those of Pococke and Norden are most known to ourselves—valuable works for all that concerns the antiquities, and they are by no means superseded. The form and price, however, at this time keep them out of the hands of the greater number.

Niebuhr's writings require not an additional testimony of their value; but the professed object of his voyage was Arabia; and the account of Egypt is only incidental.

Volney

PREFACE.

Volney and Savary are in the public hands, and no attempt shall be made to influence its judgment of their works. The talents of the former are well known; but he saw the East with no favourable eye; and his manner in speaking of Egypt will be found materially different from that here adopted.

Of Syria the Author could expect to say little that is new, after the numberless descriptions which have already been published, and he has accordingly used great rapidity in his narrative.

In Kahira, the sources of information are few and scanty. A traveller may remain there many months, without finding his ideas of the country, or its inhabitants, much more clear or precise.

The Europeans, there immured as prisoners, may be reasonably excused for hastening their commercial advantages, and, whenever unengaged by that object, for amusing themselves in trying to forget the place in which their ill fortune has obliged them to reside. Those who are found there, with every

disposition

PREFACE.

disposition to accommodate strangers, and receiving them always with complacency and kindness, are yet, with few exceptions, not of the order of men most able to generalize their ideas, and avail themselves to the utmost of the information which accident throws in their way.

The Greeks, whose inquisitive turn, and more intimate connection with the people at large and with the government, make them more familiar with characters and occurrences, rarely represent things as they really are, but as they feel them, or would have them to be. Where their report is not entirely imaginary, their portraits are like those of *Lely*, all adorned with nicely-combed locks and a fringed neckcloth. They mark no character, but as it appears to their prejudices; give no history that is not interlarded with their own fables; and describe no place but in the vague and superficial manner that satisfies their own ignorance.

The Copts who, it might be supposed, would be accurately informed of all that relates to the government

ment and history of the country, have no sentiment of antient glory, and are wholly immersed in gain or pleasure.

Settled in the composure of ignorance, they cannot conceive the motive of minute inquiries; and timid and reserved, they fear to discover even what they know.

The more liberal among the Mohammedan ecclesiastics, may be safely consulted for what concerns literature and the laws, and some few of them are communicative; but in general they despise strangers, and do not readily answer questions not of the most ordinary occurrence. On the whole, the most intelligent and communicative among the people of Kahira are the Mohammedan merchants, of a certain rank, who have visited various parts of the empire, and who have learned to think that all wisdom is not confined to one country or one race of men; and who having been led to mix, first by necessity and then by choice, with various nations, preserve their attachment to their own persuasion, without
thinking

thinking all the rest of mankind *dogs* and *accursed*.

The general design of the Writer, as will be seen in the sequel, was of such a nature, that, without being extremely sanguine, he might have hoped to execute a considerable part of it. His prospects the first year were darkened by an unexpected disappointment on his arrival at Assûan; concerning which he may say, without any disposition to complaint, that he felt it severely. Another winter furnished him with a little more information and more experience: but still, as he afterwards unfortunately discovered, by no means all that was necessary to his purpose.

He might have appeared in Dar-Fûr as a Mohammedan, if he had known that the character was necessary to his personal security, or to his unrestrained passage; but, from the accounts he received in Kahira, among the people of Soûdan no violent animosity was exhibited against Christians. The character of the converts to Mohammedism, among the

the black nations, was, according to the general voice of the Egyptians who travelled among them, mild and tolerant. A difpofition fo generally acknowleged, that the more zealous among the latter are little fcrupulous in honouring them with the appellation of *Caffre*. His furprife therefore was not inconfiderable at finding, on his arrival, that an unbeliever in the infallibility of the Korân was more openly perfecuted, and more frequently infulted, than in Kahira itfelf.

The information received, previoufly to his departure in 1793, taught the writer to expect, from having chofen the route of what is called the Soudân Caravan, the choice of a free paflage to Sennaar, which would, without much doubt, have fecured him an entrance into *Habbefh*, under the conduct of the Fungni, who trade there: for the Fûrian monarch, had his favour not been withdrawn in confequence of falfe infinuations, would readily have accorded a fafe-conduct through Kordofân, which was all that circumftances required. The being removed a few weeks journey too far to the Weftward, was no objection, when he reflected on the confufion

PREFACE.

confusion then reigning at Sennaar, and that in proportion as the road he took was indirect, the less suspicion would be entertained of him as a Frank, the greater experience he must acquire among the people of the interior, and the more easily he might be suffered to pass as a mere trader.

He had been taught, that the expeditions in quest of slaves, undertaken by the people of Fûr and its neighbourhood, extended often forty or more days to the Southward. This, at the lowest computation, gave a distance of five degrees on a meridian, and the single hope of penetrating so much farther Southward than any preceding traveller, was worth an effort to realize. He owns, he did not then foresee all the inconveniences of being exposed, on the one hand, to the band of plunderers whom he was to accompany, and on the other, to the just resentment of the wretched victims whom they were to enthral. Perhaps those very evils were magnified greatly beyond their real value by the Fûrians to whom he applied, and who were predetermined not to allow him to pass.

Another inducement to this route was, that part of it was reprefented to lie along the banks of the *Bahr-el-abiad*, which he had always conceived to be the true Nile, and which apparently no European had ever feen. To have traced it to its fource was rather to be wifhed than expected; but he promifed himfelf to reach a part of it near enough to that fource, to enable him to determine in what latitude and direction it was likely to exift. It is unneceffary to obferve, that, had either of thefe objects been realized, much interefting matter muft have occurred in the courfe of the route. He could not in the fequel difcover that the armed expeditions of the Fûrians extend to any high reaches of the Bahr-el-abiad.

Another object, perhaps in the eyes of fome the moft important of the three, was to pafs to one or more of the extended and populous empires to the Weftward. Africa, to the North of the Niger, as is certified from the late difcoveries, is almoft univerfally Mohammedan; and to have been well received among one of the nations of that defcription,

would

would have been a strong presumption in favour of future efforts. He expected in that road to have seen part of the *Niger*, and even though he had been strictly restrained to the direct road from *Dar-Fúr* through *Bernou* and thence to *Fezzan* and *Tripoli*, an opportunity must have offered of verifying several important geographical positions, and observing many facts worthy remembrance relative to commerce and general manners; or, if those designs had entirely failed, at least of marking a rough outline of the route, and facilitating the progress of some future traveller.

So fixed was his intention of executing some one of these plans, that near three years of suffering were unable to abate his resolution; and the pain he endured at being ultimately compelled to relinquish them, had induced him to neglect the only opportunity that was likely to offer of personal deliverance, till the destitution of the means of living roused him from his lethargy; and the ridicule of his Mohammedan friends, who, fatalists as they are, yield to circumstances, instructed him that to

despair

despair was weakness and not fortitude; and that the frail offspring of hope, nursed by credulity, and not by prudence, marks the morbid temperament of the mind that conceived it.

The following papers would perhaps have been something less imperfect, if what was originally committed to writing had been altogether within the reach of the writer, when he began to prepare them for publication. Two accidents, however, both equally unforeseen, rendered abortive his hope of compensating in some measure for the general failure in his design, by greater exactness and detail as to the particulars of what he had actually seen.

The losses he had sustained in Soudân, were not very important, comprising only some specimens of minerals, vegetables, and other cumbrous materials, which he designed to have brought with him. On his arrival in Kahira, he thought it would be an impediment, in his journey through Syria, to transport all he possessed thither, and therefore caused the greater part of his baggage to be sent to Alexandria;

dria; among which were copies of such papers as he thought least unfit for the use of a third person. In the number he regrets a register of the caravans which had arrived in Kahira from Fûr since the year of Hejira 1150, containing an account of their numbers, and many other curious particulars; copied from a book belonging to the shech of the slave-market in Kahira.

A kind of general itinerary, in the hand-writing of a Jelab of his acquaintance, containing the roads of Eastern Africa.

A vocabulary of the Fûrian language, compiled by himself.

Some remarks on natural history.

List of names of places both in Egypt and Fûr, written by an Arab.

The detail of particulars relating to the time and manner of his observations in Astronomy, with other remarks tending to illustrate the geography of his route.

To return to a few considerations on the present intercourse between Egypt and Abyssinia.

Towards

PREFACE.

Towards the close of the year 1796, I was told by the Coptic patriarch, that for the preceding nine years or more, no communication had taken place between Egypt and Abyssinia. Two men pretending to be priests of that country, came in 1793 to Kahira, but it was afterwards discovered that they were either not Abyssins, or fugitives, and without authority or commission. The interception of their intercourse by land might be caused by the unsettled state of *Sennaar* and *Nubia*. Slaves from Abyssinia are usually brought by the Red Sea from *Másuah* to Jidda, and many of them are sold in Mecca, though but few reach Kahira by way of Cosîr and Suez. Gold sometimes comes to market by the same route, and the Abyssins are thence supplied with such foreign commodities as they stand in need of.

To the slaves of Habbesh no very marked preference is shewn in Egypt. They are more beautiful than those of Soudân; but the price of the two kinds, *cæteris paribus*, is nearly the same.

A priest

PREFACE.

A priest of the Propaganda, a native of Egypt, and consequently possessing every advantage of language and local knowlege, during my absence to the Southward, had endeavoured to penetrate into Abyssinia. Having reached Sennaar, he was dissuaded by the people of that city from attempting to proceed. Unmindful of their representations he prosecuted his journey, but was assassinated between *Sennaar* and *Teawa*.

The Propagandists had a single missionary, a native of *Habbesh*, at *Gondar*, and styled *Bishop of Adel*, but concealing himself under the exterior of a physician. In 1796, the order at Kahira told me that they had received no authentic intelligence concerning him during several years preceding.

At Suez, March 1793, I met an Armenian merchant, who had formerly traded to Abyssinia, and seemed a man of intelligence. He told me that he was at Gondâr while Bruce was there, and that Yakûb was universally talked of with praise. This mer-

merchant narrated of his own accord the story of shooting a wax-candle through seven shields; but when I asked him if Bruce had been at the Abyssinian source of the Nile, he affirmed that he never was there. He observed that Bruce had been appointed governor of *Râs-el-Fîl*, a province in which Arabic is spoken. My informer added, that the Abyssins were a gross ignorant people, and often ate raw flesh.

In Dar-Fûr a Bergoo merchant, named *Hadji Hamâd*, who had long resided in Sennaar, and was in Bruce's party from Gondar to Sennaar, said that *Yakûb* had been highly favoured in the Abyssinian court, and lived splendidly. He was often observing the stars, &c. Both my informers agreed that he had been governor of Râs-el-Fîl; and both, that he had never visited the Abyssinian source of the Nile, esteemed the real one in that ignorant country.

An Englishman under the name of Robarts came to Alexandria in 1788, and after a short stay proceeded

ceeded to Kahira. His intention was, it is said, to have penetrated into Abyssinia by way of Massuah. While at Kahira he applied repeatedly to the Coptic Patriarch for a letter from him to the head of the Abyssin church; with which the latter, under various pretences, constantly refused to furnish him. He continued at Kahira several months, and afterwards found his way to *Moccha*. Repeated attempts were made by him to execute his projected voyage to the opposite territory, but all without success. The persons from whom I received this information, and who, as would seem, derived it from his own authority, assured me that he had encountered almost insurmountable obstacles, and been obliged to submit even to personal indignities. They allowed too that this gentleman was far from being unqualified for the enterprize, in judgment, experience, or physical force. The same persons acquainted me that he had afterwards advanced to the Mogul peninsula, and had accompanied the British troops, during two campaigns, against the usurper of Mysore, in various parts of the peninsula. He even returned to Alexandria after the treaty of Seringapatam,

patam; and at that place, being attacked by an acute difeafe, breathed his laft in the Francifcan convent there eftablifhed. More authentic and interefting materials refpecting this traveller, may poffibly have reached this country. Yet I thought it not improper to mention thefe few particulars, which may tend to illuftrate the nature of a voyage to Abyffinia.

The errors in African geography are numerous, and proceed from various caufes. Among thofe caufes, however, are particularly to be enumerated,

That the fame province has often one name in the language of that province, and another in Arabic. Of the places called indifcriminately *Fertit* by the Arabs, each little diftrict has an appropriate name.

Again, the name of a fmall province is occafionally taken for a large one, and *vice verfâ*. *Bahr* is applied to a great lake, as well as to a river. *Dar* is a kingdom, and is fometimes applied to a village, and often to a diftrict.

Fûr

PREFACE.

Fûr seems to be an Arabic name, signifying in that tongue a *Deer*; and, it may be conjectured, has been applied to that people in the same sense as *Towshán*, a hare, is by the Turks to the natives of the Greek islands—from the rapidity of their flight before the Mohammedan conquerors.

Nothing can well be more vague than the use of the word *Soudan* or *Súdan*. Among the Egyptians and Arabs *Ber-es-Soudan* is the place where the caravans arrive, when they reach the first habitable part of Dar-Fûr: but that country seems its eastern extremity; for I never heard it applied to Kordofán or Sennaar. It is used equally in Dar-Fûr to express the country to the West; but on the whole seems ordinarily applied to signify that part of the land of the blacks nearest Egypt.

An innovation as to the orthography of some proper names, it is supposed, will not appear affected or improper, when the reason is explained; as *Kahira*, *Damiatt*, *Rashîd*, for *Cairo*, *Damietta*, *Rosetto*. It is of some use in appellatives to approximate to the pronunciation of the natives, and there

can

can be as little reason for receiving Arabic names through the medium of the Italian, as for adopting the French way of writing Greek ones, as *Denys* for *Dionysius*, and *Tite-Live* for Titus Livius. Kahira and Rashîd have each of them their proper meaning in Arabic.—In Italian they have no meaning. The only rule observed has been, to bring back proper names to the original pronunciation, as far as might be done without obscurity.

Where a circumflex has been put over a vowel it is to denote its length, or something exotic in the enunciation. An approach to systematic regularity would have been attempted in expressing Arabic words by Roman letters, but the author freely owns that no rule, at once general in its use and simple and easy enough to be remembered, has yet occurred to him. He has therefore added the original word, wherever it could in any degree tend to illustration or precision.

The word *Turk* is never applied to signify a professor of Mohammedism, an indefinite mode of designation, that occasions perpetual confusion in speaking

speaking of the affairs of the East. The design was, to confine that term to the natives of Europe and Asia Minor. *Arab* is applied equally to the inhabitants of Syria, Egypt, and the coast of Barbary, as well as to those of Arabia Proper, whether villagers or wanderers. The wandering tribes are however more frequently marked by the terms *Bedouin* and *Muggrebin*.

The orthography of the word *Calif* conveys no idea of the strong guttural letter with which it commences; it is therefore here written *Chalif*, or more properly *Chalifé*. He is no stranger to the Turkish word *Bek* or *Beg*; but as those whose enunciation of that language is esteemed most correct, but faintly articulate the consonant which terminates it, he has retained the common orthography *Bey*. In general, the original language is esteemed the criterion of spelling; and if the same word be occasionally spelled in two different ways, it is only because they are both equally near to that original.

Weights and Measures.

One *oke* of Kahira = four hundred drams.
One *rotal* = one hundred forty-four drams.
One *rotal* silk of Syria = two hundred twenty-nine and a half drams.

The Cantar is rotals = 102—105—110—120—130, variable according to the commodity.

Jewels, Gold, and Silver.

One kerât = 4 grains.
One dram or dirhem = 16 kerâts.
One mitkâl = 24 kerâts.
One wekîé = 8¼ drams.

Measure of Cloth, &c.

Pike of Constantinople, called *Draa Stambuli*, Arab.; Turk. *Hindazi*, is used for selling cloth and silk. It amounts to twenty-seven inches.

Pike of Kahira, used for other articles = eighteen inches.

CONTENTS.

CHAP. I.
ALEXANDRIA.

Antient walls and ruins—The two ports—Reservoirs—Vegetation—Antiquities—Population—Government—Commerce—Manufactures—Anecdote of recent history. - Page 1

CHAP. II.
SIWA.

Attempt to penetrate to the Temple of Jupiter Ammon—Route and provisions—Animals of the desert—Occurrences on the road—Description of Siwa—Antient edifice—Intercourse with other countries—Produce and manners—Attempt to penetrate farther into the desert—Return. - - - 14

CHAP. III.
FROM ALEXANDRIA TO RASHID.

Abu-kir—Fertility of the country—Description of Rashid—Journey to Terané—Fué, Deirut, and Demenhúr. - 30

CHAP. IV.

TERANE AND THE NATRON LAKES.

Government of Terané—Carlo Rossetti—The trade in natrôn—Manners—Journey to the Lakes—Observations there—Remarks on natrôn—Coptic convents and MSS.—Proceed to Kahira.

Page 36

CHAP. V.

KAHIRA.

Topography—Government of Kahira and of Egypt—Pasha and Beys—Mamlúks—Birth, education, dress, arms, pay—Estimate of their military skill—Power and revenue of the Beys—The Chalige—The NILE—Mosques, baths, and okals—Houses—Manners and customs—Classes of people—Account of the Copts. - - - - - 45

CHAP. VI.

KAHIRA.

Commerce—Manufactures—Mint—Castle and well—Misr-el-Attiké and antient mosque—Antient Babylon—Fostat and Búlak—Jizé—Tomb of Shafei—Pleasure-boats—Charmers of serpents—Magic—Dancing girls—Amusements of Ramadán—Coffee-houses—Price of provisions—Recent history of Egypt—Account of the present Beys. - - - 74

CHAP. VII.

KAHIRA.

Brief abstract of the history of Africa in general, and Egypt in particular, under the domination of the Arabs.   Page 93

CHAP. VIII.

UPPER EGYPT.

Design to penetrate into Habbesh or Abyssinia—Voyage on the Nile—Description of Assiut—General course of the Nile—Caverns—Kaw—Achmim—Painted caverns—Jirjé or Girgi—Dendera—Antient temple—Kous—Topography of Upper Egypt—El-wah-el-Ghirbi—Situation of the Oasis parva.   120

CHAP. IX.

UPPER EGYPT.

Thebes—Site and antiquities—Painted caverns—Their discovery and plan—Manners of the people of Thebes—Isna—Fugitive Beys—Antiquities—Rain—Assüan or Syené—Obstacles to farther progress—Return to Ghenné.   134

CHAP. X.

JOURNEY TO COSSÎR ON THE RED SEA.

Inducements and danger—Route—Account of Cofsîr—Commerce—Return by another route—Granite rocks, and antient road—Marble quarries—Pretended canal—Earthen ware of Ghenné—Murder of two Greeks, and fubfequent report of the Author's death - - - - - Page 143

CHAP. XI.

OCCURRENCES AT KAHIRA.

Arrival of the Pafha—Death of Haffan Bey—Decline of the French factory in Kahira—Expulfion of the Maronite Chriftians from the Cuftom-houfe—Riot among the Galiongis—Obftructions of the canal of Menûf—Supply of fifh in the pools of Kahira—Expedition of Achmet Aga, &c. - 151

CHAP. XII.

ANTIENT EGYPTIANS.

Their perfons, complexion, &c. - - - 159

CHAP. XIII.

JOURNEY TO FEIUME.

Tamieh—Canals—Feiume—Rofes—Lake Mœris—Oafis parva—Pyramids—of Hawara—of Dafhûr—of Sakarra—of Jizé, or

CONTENTS.

or the Great Pyramids—Antient Memphis—Egyptian capitals. - - - - - Page 167

CHAP. XIV.

JOURNEY TO SINAI.

Route—Suez—Ships and ship-building — Trade—Scarcity of water—Remains of the antient canal—Tûr—Mountains of red granite—Description of Sinai—Eastern gulf of the Red Sea—Return to Kahira. - - - - 175

CHAP. XV.

JOURNEY TO DAR-FÛR,

A KINGDOM IN THE INTERIOR OF AFRICA.

Design to penetrate into the interior of Africa—Difficulties—Caravan from Soudan or Dar-Fûr—Preparations—Departure from Assiût—Journey to El-wah—Mountains—Desert—Charjè in El-wah—Bulak—Beiris—Mughes—Desert of Sheb—Desert of Selimé—Leghéa—Natrón spring—Difficulties—Enter the kingdom of Fûr—Sweini—Detention—Representations to the Melek—Residence—New difficulties—Villany of Agent—Sultan's letter—Enmity of the people against Franks—El-Fasher—Illness—Conversations with the Melek Misellim—Relapse—Robbery—Cobbé—Manners—Return to El-Fasher—The Melek Ibrahim—Amusements—Incidents—Audience of the Sultan Abd-el-rachmân-el-Rashid—His personal character—Ceremonies of the Court. - - - - 180

CHAP. XVI.

DAR-FÛR.

Residence with the Melek Mûsa—Dissimulation of the Arabs—Incidents—Return to Cobbé—Endeavours to proceed farther into Africa—Constrained to exercise medicine—Festival—Punishment of Conspirators—Art of the Sultan—Atrocious conduct of my Kabirine servant—At length an opportunity of departure is offered, after a constrained residence in Dar-Fûr of nearly three years. - - - - Page 216

CHAP. XVII.

DAR-FÛR.

Topography of Dar-Fûr, with some account of its various inhabitants. - - - - - 234

CHAP. XVIII.

DAR-FÛR.

*On the mode of travelling in Africa—Seasons in Dar-Fûr—*ANIMALS*—Quadrupeds—Birds—Reptiles and insects—Metals and minerals—Plants.* - - - 246

CONTENTS.

CHAP. XIX.
DAR-FÛR.

Government — History — Agriculture — Population — Building — Manners, Customs, &c. - - Page 276

CHAP. XX.
DAR-FÛR.

Miscellaneous remarks on Dar-Fûr, and the adjacent countries. - - - - - 305

CHAP. XXI.
MEDICAL OBSERVATIONS.

Psoropthalmia — Plague — Small-pox — Guinea worm — Scrophula — Syphilis — Bile — Tenia — Hernia — Hydrocele — Hemorrhoides and fistula — Apoplexy — Umbilical ruptures — Accouchemens — Hydrophobia — Phlebotomy — Remedies — Remarks — Circumcision — Excision. - - - - - 314

CHAP. XXII.
FINAL DEPARTURE FROM KAHIRA, AND JOURNEY TO JERUSALEM.

Voyage down the Nile to Damiatt — Vegetation — Papyrus — Commerce — Cruelty of the Mamlûk government — Voyage to Yaffé — Description

—Description of Yaffé—Rama—Jerusalem—Mendicants—Tombs of the kings—Bethlehem—Agriculture—Naplosa—Samaria—Mount Tabor. - - - Page 351

CHAP. XXIII.

GALILEE—ACCA.

Improvements by Jezzár—Trade—Taxes—White Promontory, and River Leontes—Tyre—Seide—Earthquake—Kesrawan—Syrian wines—Beirût—Anchorage—Provisions—River Adonis—Antûra—Harrise—Tripoli—Ladakia—Journey to Aleppo, or Haleb. - - - - - 366

CHAP. XXIV.

OBSERVATIONS AT HALEB.

Sherifs and Janizaries—Manufactures and commerce—Quarries—Price of provisions—New sect—Journey to Antioch—Description of antient Seleucia—Return to Haleb. - 384

CHAP. XXV.

JOURNEY TO DAMASCUS.

Entrance of the Hadjis—Topography of Damascus—Trade and manufactures—Population—Observations on the depopulation of the East—Government and manners of Damascus—Charitable foundations—Anecdotes of recent history—Taxes—Price of provisions—Sacred caravan. 394

CHAP. XXVI.

Journey from Damascus to Balbec—Syriac language—Balbec—Recent discoveries—Zahhlé—Printing-office—Houses of Damascus—Return to Aleppo.   Page 405

CHAP. XXVII.

Journey from Aleppo towards Constantinople—Route—Aintâb—Mount Taurus—Bostan—Inhabitants, their manners and dress—Kaisaria—Angora—Walls and antiquities—Angora goats—Manufactures—Topography—Journey to Ismit—Topography—General remarks concerning Anatolia or Asia Minor.   410

CHAP. XXVIII.

Observations at Constantinople—Paswân Oglo—Character of the present Sultan—State of learning—Public libraries—Turkish taste—Coals—Greek printing-house—Navy—Return to England.   419

CHAP. XXIX.

Comparative view of life and happiness in the East and in Europe.   425

APPENDIX.

No. I.	*Illustration of Maps*	Page 445
II.	*Itineraries*	451
III.	*Metereological Table*	473
IV.	*Remarks on the works of Savary and Volney*	481
V.	*Remarks on the recent French accounts of Egypt*	486
VI.	*Explanation of the plate facing page 286*	495

TRA-

TRAVELS
IN
AFRICA,
EGYPT, AND SYRIA.

CHAP. I.

ALEXANDRIA.

Antient Walls and Ruins—The two Ports—Reservoirs—Vegetation — Antiquities — Population — Government — Commerce — Manufactures—Anecdote of recent History.

THE transit from the coasts of Britain to those of Egypt was marked by nothing that can interest or amuse, unless it be the contrast between the phenomena of winter on the former, with those which strike the view on approaching the latter. A sea voyage is always tedious, except to the merchant and the mariner; and therefore, though our's was attended with every favourable circumstance, and occupied no more than twenty-six days, there is scarcely any thing relative to it that can afford entertainment in the recital. I arrived in Egypt on the 10th of January 1792.

Alexandria now exhibits very few marks, by which it could be recognized as one of the principal monuments of the magnificence of the conqueror of Asia, the emporium of the east, and the chosen theatre of the far-sought luxuries of the Roman Triumvir, and the Egyptian queen. Its decay doubtless has been gradual; but fifteen centuries, during which it has been progressive, have evinced its antient opulence by the slowness of its fall.

The present walls are of Saracenic structure, and therefore can determine nothing with respect to the antient dimensions of the city*. They are lofty, being in some places more than forty feet in height, and apparently no where so little as twenty. But, though substantial and flanked with towers, they could offer no resistance, unless it were against the Mamlûk cavalry, which alone the inhabitants fear, and accordingly keep them in some repair. They also furnish a sufficient security against the Bedouins, who live part of the year on the banks of the canal, and often plunder the cattle in the neighbourhood. The few flocks and herds, which are destined to supply the wants of the city, are pastured on the herbage, of which the vicinity of the canal favours the growth, and generally brought in at night, when the two gates are shut; as they also are whenever it is known that hostile tribes are encamped near them.

---

* Volney has considered the walls of Alexandria as of antient structure. But D'Anville had before rejected that idea, and the fragments of columns, &c. worked into the masonry, shew that he is right.

These

These Saracenic walls present nothing curious, except some ruinous towers: and the only remain of the antient city worth notice is a colonnade, near the gate leading to Rashîd, of which, however, only a few columns remain; and what is called the amphitheatre on the south east, a rising ground, whence is a fine view of the city and port. Of the singular suburb styled Necropolis, or " The City of the Dead," no remain exists.

It cannot be supposed that the antient city should have occupied only the small space contained within the present inclosure. The pristine wall was certainly far more extensive than the present: yet even of this only an inconsiderable portion between the two ports is now filled with habitations.—What remains is laid out in gardens, which supply such fruits and vegetables as are suited to the climate and soil, and the natives are most accustomed to use for food; or left waste, and serving as a receptacle for offal and rubbish; being in part rendered unfit for culture by the ruins which cover the surface to a considerable depth. For, though it be not now possible to determine the antient boundaries of the city, or to assign with precision the site of its more remarkable edifices, these vestiges of former magnificence yet remain. Heaps of rubbish are on all sides visible, whence every shower of rain, not to mention the industry of the natives in digging, discovers pieces of precious marble, and sometimes antient coins, and fragments of sculpture.

The harbour on the east, styled, I know not why, the new port, which in all appearance could never have been a very good one, from the rocky nature of the bottom, has the farther disadvantage of partaking in the agitation of the sea when certain winds prevail. The European vessels which frequent it are, however, enabled, with some precautions, to lie at anchor securely, to the number of about twenty. They are confined to this small space, which bears no proportion to the whole extent of the harbour, by the shallowness of the water, which seems in some degree the effect of great quantities of ballast, that from time to time have been discharged within its limits. The Government pays no regard to this practice, which yet in the end must render the port useless. It is currently reported in the place, and many marks yet exist to give credibility to that report, as well as the design of Norden, which so represents it, that the water, within the memory of persons now living, reached the gate of the old custom-house; which I now find removed many fathoms from the water's edge. So that it would seem the sea is retiring, and that nature, rather than any weaker agent, has effected the change. The old port, allotted to the Mohammedans, is spacious, though somewhat of less extent than the other. There is throughout a depth of five or six fathom; and in many places more: the anchorage is generally secure.

The city extends along a part of the isthmus and the peninsula; at the eastern extremity of which is situated a fort, where it would seem may formerly have stood the Pharos. This fort is now ruinous, and is joined with the continent by a mole built of stone, and in which are wrought arches, to weaken the effect of the water. It has been sheltered by a wall on the west side, now also ruinous. The houses, which are chiefly masonry, are

are commonly of more than one story, and well adapted to the mode of living among the inhabitants. Though rain occasionally fall in the autumn, a flat roof is found to answer every purpose of security from the weather, and accordingly it is the general form of the dwelling-houses.

Of the deep and capacious reservoirs, which preserved the water of the Nile during the annual subsidence of that river, and of which there was probably a series, continued from one to the other extremity of the city, not more than seven remain fit for use. From these the citizens are at this time supplied; and, as they are some way removed from the inhabited quarter, a few of the poorer class obtain a subsistence by drawing the water, and carrying it on camels from house to house; and for each camel's load they receive four or five *paras*, about twopence. The roofs of these cisterns or reservoirs are supported by massy timber. They have probably been thus constructed at the beginning, as it is difficult to suppose that the modern Alexandrians should entirely have changed so essential a part, and have chosen to substitute wood for stone, in a place where the former is extremely scarce, and the other very abundant.

The elevation of the city above the level of the sea is small; and it seems very difficult to render it capable of offering any formidable resistance to an external enemy.

The soil, wherever a vegetable mould is discoverable, is light, and favourable to any kind of culture; but it has apparently been brought there for the purpose, as the natural soil seems

wholly

wholly unfit for cultivation, being throughout either sand or stone. The orange and lemon are found in the gardens here, but not in great quantities. The dates are good, though not of the most esteemed kind. Yet they are found the most profitable article that the owner of the ground can cultivate. And accordingly these trees, with which the gardens are filled, not only relieve the eye from the dry whiteness of buildings, and the sandy soil; but well repay the owners for the trouble required to manage them, and for the space they occupy to the exclusion of almost every thing else. The greater number of esculent herbs, or roots, that are common among us, may be raised here, without any other difficulty than that of watering. The fruit trees that I have remarked as peculiar to the place, are the nebbek (*Paliurus Athenai*) and the kishné (*Cassia Keshta,*) the latter of which is also found in the West Indies. The former bears a small fruit like the cherry in size, and having a stone of the same kind; but very different in colour and flavour, which more resemble those of the apple.

The chief monuments of antiquity remaining in any degree perfect, are the column, usually but improperly termed of Pompey *, and the obelisk. On the former, not even so much of the inscription as Pococke copied is now to be distinguished. There is also a sarcophagus or chest of serpentine marble in the great mosque, which is used for a cistern. It is of the same kind with that so minutely described by Niebuhr, at Kallaat el Kabsh in Kahira, and seems to be almost as rich in hieroglyphics. It

* Now supposed to have been erected in honour of Severus.

has the additional advantage of being entire, and little if at all injured by time. It is said, that one of those who farmed the customs some years since, on retiring from Egypt, had negociated for the removal of this precious monument of antiquity, on board of an European vessel, with the intention of carrying it as a present to the Emperor of Germany. On the night when it was to be embarked, however, the secret being disclosed, the citizens clamorously insisted that the property of the mosque was inviolable. The projected removal was accordingly relinquished, and the chest has ever since been watched with uncommon vigilance, so that it is now difficult for an European even to obtain a sight of it; which must be my excuse for not having been more minute in my description of a monument that seems not to have been particularly observed by former travellers.

The population consists of Mohammedans of various nations; Greeks in considerable number, who have a church and convent, containing only three or four religious, but agreeably situated on the highest ground among the gardens; Armenians, who have also a church; and a few Jews, who have their synagogue. The whole, perhaps, may not amount to less than twenty thousand souls*; which, however, the length of my residence there did not enable me to decide. The Franciscans of Terra Santa have a church and monastery, in which reside three or four of their order. The habitations of the European con-

---

* There happened a plague in 1796, which it is said carried off one half of the inhabitants. This estimate is possibly exaggerated; but no doubt it thinned them much; so that at present they cannot be near so numerous.

suls and merchants are all near together, east of the city and close to the sea. They associate with each other, dress and live as in Europe, and, unless by their mutual animosities, are perfectly undisturbed. It is true, indeed, that the natives bear no very good character for their behaviour to strangers, but, I believe, when incivility has been experienced, it has generally first been provoked: and the natives are, perhaps, at least as often the dupes of the Frank merchants, as the latter are of the native brokers and factors, whom their commercial concerns oblige them to employ. The command of the fort, and of the few troops which are in the city, is vested in a Sardar, who is sometimes a Cashef, sometimes an inferior officer of the Beys. The internal government is in the hands of the citizens. The chief magistrate is the Cadi, an Arab, who receives his appointment from Constantinople; the others are, the Shechs of the four sects, and the Imâms of the two principal mosques. Here it may be observed, once for all, that the municipal magistrates in the east are always of the sacerdotal order.

The revenues of Alexandria, under the Ptolemies, are stated at 12,500 talents, which at 193l. 15s. the talent, is little less than two millions and an half sterling. At this time it is thought that they do not exceed four thousand five hundred purses, or 225,000l.

The commerce of Alexandria is more considerable than that of Damiatt. All exports to Europe, or imports from thence, are made at the former. The whole of the timber for house or ship building is brought from Candia, or the Archipelago. The copper,

copper, manufactured or rough, of which the consumption is large, from Constantinople. Coffee and rice, raw leather, &c. are exported to that and other places. The transit of all these keeps the inhabitants in that state of activity to which they are eminently disposed; and if various causes operate unavoidably to fetter and stagnate commerce, it cannot be said that they are in fault. The navigation from Alexandria to Rashîd is conducted in small vessels of from fifteen to fifty tons burthen, which deposit their goods at Rashîd, whence they are embarked in boats of another form, and conveyed to Kahira.

Among the articles of native produce, considerable quantities of which are taken by the Frank merchants in return for the goods of their respective countries, are saffranon, *Carthamus tinctorius*, which is cultivated in Egypt; and senna, which chiefly comes by way of Suez: but some portion of which is also produced in Nubia, and near the first Cataract.

The consumption of broad cloth in Egypt used to be about eight hundred bales; but it was greatly decreased when I left the country, owing to the war in Europe, which prevented a proper supply. The consequent high price constrained many to have recourse to the native manufactures. Red coral is imported from Leghorn, glass beads, &c. from Venice.

The Alexandrians are remarkable for the facility with which they acquire different languages. But their own Arabic is impure, being mingled with Turkish and other dialects.

Among the characteristic features of the people of this city, it is deserving of notice that they preserve the ancient character of perseverance and acuteness, especially ascribed to them by the historian of the Alexandrian war [*]. For example, suppose they wish to divide an antique column of three or four feet diameter, into two parts, for the purpose of securing the foundations of the houses near the shore from the encroachments of the sea, they make a line not more than half an inch deep, for the space of one twelfth of the circumference, then inserting two pieces of tempered steel, not larger than a dollar, at the extremities of the line, they drive a wedge in the midst. At the same time, small pieces of steel, like the former, are fixed at equal distances round the column, to the number of five or six, by means of small hammers, which strike quick, but with no violence. Thus the piece is cut off regular, and in a very short space of time.

Glass for lamps and phials is made at Alexandria, both green and white. They use natron in the manufacture instead of barilla: and the low beaches of the Egyptian coast afford plenty of excellent sand.

A dispute has lately arisen between the Alexandrians and the government, which originated in the conduct of the Syrian Christian, who has the management of the customs here. The people of Alexandria, it is to be remarked, are not among the most obedient and tractable subjects of the Mamlûk govern-

[*] Hirtius, Bell. Alex. prope init.

ment; and their situation, together with other circumstances, has favoured them in their opposition to public orders. The present Beys, especially, they affect to consider as rebels against the authority of the Porte. Thus mutually jealous, each party is constantly on the watch to profit by any oversight of the other: the Beys, in order to put the Alexandrians in the same unqualified subjection, with respect to them, as the rest of the Egyptians are; and the Alexandrians to perpetuate that qualified dependence, or imperfect autocracy, in which, by subterfuge and fertility of expedient, they have hitherto maintained themselves.

Affairs were in this state when an order came from Murad Bey, who had the jurisdiction of this district, to shut up the public warehouses, or *okals*, where commerce is chiefly carried on. A Cashef was sent to see it executed, but unaccompanied by any military force: he had also orders to arrest, and bring with him to Kahira, the person of Shech Mohammed el Missiri, one of the chief Mullas who had always been active in promoting opposition to the measures of the Beys; and who is remarkable, as I am informed, for eloquence both persuasive and deliberative. The greater part of the inhabitants assembled in the principal mosque, and came to the resolution of obliging the Cashef to quit the city. They also determined on sending away the superintendant of the customs, who by frauds of every kind had rendered himself hateful to them, and against whom unavailing complaints had already repeatedly been made to the Bey. Some of the body were deputed to inform both parties, that they must leave the city before night, under pain of death.

But the impatience of the people was too great to wait for night, and they were compelled to depart inftantly, the Cafhef by land, and the Chriftian by fea.

Orders were given to repair the walls, plant cannon, and put every thing in a ftate of defence. Shech Mohammed advifed the citizens to divide themfelves into diftricts; which being complied with, it was refolved that every man fhould provide himfelf with arms, who fhould be able to purchafe them; and that thofe who could not fhould be armed at the public expence. At the end of about a month, notice was brought that two Cafhefs were on their way, with a body of troops, to punifh the inhabitants for their contumacious behaviour. When their arrival at Rafhîd was known, the Alexandrians fent them word, that if they came without hoftile intentions, they would be peaceably received: but if it were their defign to have recourfe to violent meafures, the whole force of the city would be oppofed to their entrance. One of thefe Cafhefs afterwards proved to be the fame who had before been fent back. The other was a man of the firft rank, having formerly filled the office of Yenktchery Aga. They were in fact unattended, except by the domeftics of this latter, perhaps in all two hundred men, chiefly on foot. The Cafhef declared he had no view but to certify that the minds of the citizens were not alienated from the government, nor their intentions hoftile to it; which from the news, that they were putting themfelves in a ftate of defence, Murad Bey had been led to imagine. Yet he recommended it to them, in proof of their pacific difpofition, to depute three or four of the chief citizens to Kahira, who might have an opportunity of inform-

ing

ing the Beys concerning fuch grievances as they fhould have found reafon to reprefent, and might pave the way to a future good underftanding.

This was not complied with, and the Cafhef remained without propofing any alternative. After fourteen or fifteen days he left Alexandria, with a prefent of very fmall value from the citizens, and fome trifles given him, in refpect to the character he bore, by the European merchants. So ended this great turmoil, which I have mentioned perhaps at too great length; but which throws fome light on the fituation and character of the late government.

CHAP. II.

JOURNEY TO SIWA.

Attempt to penetrate to the Temple of Jupiter Ammon—Route and Provisions—Animals of the Desert—Occurrences on the Road—Description of Siwa—Antient Edifice—Intercourse with other Countries—Produce and Manners—Attempt to penetrate farther into the Desert—Return.

THE information I had obtained in Alexandria having induced me to resolve on attempting to explore the vestiges of the Temple of Jupiter Ammon from that place, I procured a proper person as interpreter, and made the necessary arrangements with some Arabs, who are employed in transporting through the desert, dates and other articles, between Siwa (a small town to the westward) and Alexandria, to convey my baggage and provisions, and to procure for me a secure passage among the other tribes of Arabs, who feed their flocks at this season in the vicinity of the coast. In this I was much assisted by Mr. Baldwin, who readily entered into my views, and used all the means in his power to promote their success.

When the Arabs had finished the business on which they came to the city, and had fixed on an hour, as they thought, auspicious to travellers, they made ready for departure; and on
Friday,

Friday, 24th February 1792, we left Alexandria. The inclinations of my conductors were in unison with mine, in the choice of a route; for they preferred that nearest the sea, for the sake of forage for their camels, which abounds more there than in the direct road; and I preferred it, as being the same that Alexander had chosen for the march of his army.

We travelled the first day only about eight miles*, in which space several foundations of buildings are discoverable; but so imperfect are the remains, that it is not possible to say whether they were antient or modern, or to what purpose they might have been applied. From that time till Sunday, 4th March, our route lay along the coast, and we were never long together out of sight of the sea. The coast is plain; and after having left the neighbourhood of Alexandria, where it is rocky, the soil is generally smooth and sandy. Many spots of verdure, particularly at this season, relieve the eye from the effect of general barrenness: and though the vegetation be very inconsiderable, the greater part of it consisting only of different kinds of th graffwort, or kali, it offers a seasonable relief to the f camel. For our horses we were obliged to carr supply of barley and cut straw.

There are several kinds of pref the orientals for long journie of salt provision by usir is called *mishli*, a brought fro

In the places where we generally rested are found the jerboa, the tortoise, the lizard, and some serpents, but not in great number. There is also an immense quantity of snails attached to the thorny plants on which the camels feed. These the Arabs frequently eat. Very few birds were visible in this quarter, except of the marine kind. One of our party killed a small hawk, which was the only one I saw. Near the few springs of water are found wild rabbits, which in Arabic they distinguish by the same name as the hare, (ارنب) and the track of the antelope and the ostrich are frequently discoverable. We passed no day without being incommoded with frequent showers; and generally a cold wind from north-west and north-west by north. Several small parties of Bedouins, who were feeding a few goats, sheep, and asses, were encamped in the road, and in the vicinity of the lake Mareotis, now dry. Such of them as were the friends of our conductor received us with every mark of hospitality and kindness; and regaled us with milk, dates, and bread newly baked. One party, indeed, became contentious for a present, or tribute on passing; but being in no condition to enforce their demand, it was after a time re-

4th, having travelled about six hours, we
was a copious supply of water; and
time to drink, we left the coast, and
direction. From Alexandria to this
motion was seventy-five hours
e to Siwa, there being little
use all possible diligence in
the

the route. Our arrival there happened on Friday the 9th, at eight in the evening. The space of time we were actually travelling from the coast, was sixty two hours and a quarter. The road from the shore inward to Siwa is perfectly barren, consisting wholly of rocks and sand, among which talc is found in great abundance. On Wednesday the 7th, at night, we had reached a small village called قارة ام الصغير Karet-am-el Sogheir: it is a miserable place, the buildings being chiefly of clay; and the people remarkably poor and dirty. It afforded the seasonable relief of fresh water, a small quantity of mutton, (for the Shech el Bellad was kind enough to kill a sheep, in return for some trifling presents which were made him,) and wood to dress pilau, from which we had been obliged to abstain since leaving the coast. This village is independent, and its environs afford nothing but dates, in which even the camels and asses of this quarter are accustomed to find their nourishment.

For about a mile and an half from Karet-am-el Sogheir the country is sprinkled with date trees, and some water is found. After which it again becomes perfectly desert, consisting of the same mountains of sand and barren rock, as before remarked, for the space of about five hours travelling. Then we were employed for more than eight hours in passing an extensive plain of barren sand, which was succeeded by other low hills and rocks. I observed, through a large portion of the road, that the surface of the earth is perfectly covered with salt.

We at length came to Siwa, which answers the description given of the Oases, as being a small fertile spot, surrounded on all sides by desert land. It was about half an hour from the time of our entrance on this territory, by a path surrounded with date trees, that we came to the town, which gives name to the district. We dismounted, and seated ourselves, as is usual for strangers in this country, on a *misjed*, or place used for prayer, adjoining the tomb of a *Marabút*, or holy person. In a short time the chiefs came to congratulate us on our arrival, with the grave but simple ceremony that is in general use among the Arabs. They then conducted us to an apartment, which, though not very commodious, was the best they were provided with; and after a short interval, a large dish of rice and some boiled meat were brought; the Shechs attending while the company was served, which consisted of my interpreter, our conductor, two other Bedouins our companions, and myself.

I should here mention that my attendants, finding reason to fear that the reception of a Frank, as such, would not be very favourable, had thought proper to make me pass for a Mamlûk. Not having had any intimation of this till it was too late, and unable as I then was to converse in Arabic, it was almost impossible to remain undiscovered. Our arrival happening before the evening prayer, when the people of the place disposed themselves to devotion, in the observance of which they are very rigorous, it was remarked that I did not join. This alone was sufficient to create suspicions, and the next morning my interpreter was obliged to explain. The Shechs seemed surprised at a Christian having penetrated thus far, with some expence and difficulty, and apparently without having any urgent business to transact. But all, except one of them, were disposed to conciliation;

ciliation; inclined thereto, no doubt, by a prefent of fome ufeful articles that had been brought for them. This one was, with the herd of the people, violently exafperated at the infolence of an unbeliever, in perfonating and wearing the drefs of a Mohammedan. At firft they infifted on my inftant return, or immediate converfion to the true faith; and threatened to affault the houfe, if compliance with thefe terms fhould be refufed. After much altercation, and loud vociferations, the more moderate gained fo far by their remonftrances, that it was permitted I fhould remain there two or three days to reft. But fo little were the chiefs able to keep peace, that during the two days enfuing, whenever I quitted my apartment, it was only to be affailed with ftones, and a torrent of abufive language. The time that had been allowed me to reft operated favourably for my intereft, at leaft with the chiefs, though the populace continued fomewhat intractable. For the former were contented on the fourth day to permit me to walk, and obferve what was remarkable in the place.

We left our apartment at day-break, before any great number of people was affembled; and having taken with me fuch inftruments as I was provided with, we paffed along fome fhady paths, between the gardens, till at the diftance of about two miles we arrived at what they called the ruins, or *birbé*. I was greatly furprifed at finding myfelf near a building of undoubted antiquity, and, though fmall, in every view worthy of remark. It was a fingle apartment, built of maffy ftones, of the fame kind as thofe of which the pyramids confift; and covered originally with fix large and folid blocks, that reach from one wall to the other. The length I found thirty-two feet in the clear; the height about eighteen, the width fifteen. A gate, situated at one extremity, forms the principal entrance; and two doors, also near that extremity, open opposite to each other. The other end is quite ruinous; but, judging from circumstances, it may be imagined that the building has never been much larger than it now is. There is no appearance of any other edifice having been attached to it, and the less so as there are remains of sculpture on the exterior of the walls. In the interior are three rows of emblematical figures, apparently designed to represent a procession: and the space between them is filled with hieroglyphic characters, properly so called. The soffit is also adorned in the same manner, but one of the stones which formed it is fallen within, and breaks the connection. The other five remain entire. The sculpture is sufficiently distinguishable; and even the colours in some places remain. The soil around seems to indicate that other buildings have once existed near the place; the materials of which either time has levelled with the soil, or the natives have applied to other purposes. I observed, indeed, some hewn stones wrought in the walls of the modern buildings, but was unable to identify them by any marks of sculpture.

It was mentioned to me that there were many other ruins near; but after walking for some time where they were described to be, and observing that they pointed out as ruins what were in fact only rough stones, apparently detached from the rock, I returned fatigued and dissatisfied. The Shechs had provided for us a dinner in a garden, where we were unmolested

molested by intruders; and the sun being then near the meridian, I took the opportunity of observing its altitude by means of an artificial horizon. They who are best versed in these matters will be far from thinking this the most accurate method of determining the latitude. But the result was not materially different, though in the sequel I repeated my observation. It gave N. L. 29° 12', and a fraction:—the long. E. F. 44° 54'.

The following day I was led to some apartments cut in the rock, which had the appearance of places of sepulture. They are without ornament or inscription, but have been hewn with some labour. They appear all to have been opened; and now contain nothing that can with certainty point out the use to which they may have been originally applied. Yet there are many parts of human sculls, and other bones, with fragments of skin, and even of hair, attached to them. All these have undergone the action of fire: but whether they are the remains of bodies, reposited there by a people in the habit of burning the dead, or whether they have been burned, in this their detached state, by the present inhabitants, it must now be difficult to affirm. Yet the size of the catacombs would induce the belief that they were designed for bodies in an unmutilated state; the proportions being, length twelve feet, width six, height about six. The number of these caverns may amount to thirty, or more.

Having found a monument so evidently Egyptian in this remote quarter, I had the greater hope of meeting with something more considerable by going farther; or of being able to

gain

gain some information from the natives, or the Arabs, that would fix exactly the position of the remains, if any such there were, of the far-famed Temple of Jupiter Ammon. The people of Siwa have communications equally with Egypt and Fezzan, and the wandering Arabs pass the desert in all directions, in their visits to that small territory, where they are furnished at a cheaper rate with many articles of food than they can be in the towns of Egypt. They pass thither from Elwah, from Feium, and the district of Thebes, from Fezzan, from Tripoli, from Kahira, and from Alexandria. It seemed therefore unlikely that any considerable ruins should exist within three or four days of Siwa, and unknown to them; still less so that they should be ignorant of any fertile spot, where might be found water, fruits, and other acceptable refreshments.

I therefore, by means of my interpreter, whom I had always found honest in his report, and attentive to my wishes, collected three of the Shechs who had shewn themselves most friendly to us, with my conductor, and two other Arabs who happened to be there. They entered freely into conversation about the roads, and described what was known to them of Elwah, Fezzan, and other places. But in the direction laid down for the site of the temple, they declared themselves ignorant of any such remains. I inquired for a place of the name of *Santrieh*, but of this too they professed their ignorance. Then, said I, if you know of no place by the name I have mentioned, and of no ruins in the direction or at the distance described, do you know of no ruins whatever farther to the westward or south-west? Yes, said one of them, there is a place called *Araschié*,
where

where are ruins, but you cannot go to them, for it is surrounded by water, and there are no boats. He then entered into an enchanted history of this place; and concluded with dissuading me from going there. I soon found, from the description, that *Araschié* was not the Oasis of Ammon, but conceiving it something gained to pass farther west, and that possibly some object might eventually offer itself that would lead to farther discovery, I determined, if it were possible, to proceed thither.

For this purpose we were obliged to use all possible secrecy, as the Siwese were bent on opposing our farther progress. An agreement was therefore made with two persons of the poorer class of the natives, for a few zecchins, that they should conduct us to *Araschié*; and if what we sought for was not there found, that they should, on leaving it, proceed with us to the first watering-place that they knew directly to the southward. The remainder of the time I stayed at Siwa was employed in combating the difficulties that were raised about our departure; and it was not till Monday, 12th March, that we were enabled to commence our journey west.

The Oasis which contains the town Siwa, is about six miles long, and four and a half or five wide. A large proportion of this space is filled with date trees; but there are also pomegranates, figs, and olives, apricots and plantains; and the gardens are remarkable flourishing. They cultivate a considerable quantity of rice, which, however, is of a reddish hue, and different from that of the Delta. The remainder of the cultivable land furnishes wheat enough for the consumption of the inhabitants.

inhabitants. Water, both salt and fresh, abounds; but the springs which furnish the latter are most of them tepid; and such is the nature of the water, air, and other circumstances, that strangers are often affected with agues and malignant fevers. One of those springs, which rises near the building described, is observed by the natives to be sometimes cold and sometimes warm.

I had been incommoded by the cold in the way, but in the town I found the heat oppressive, though thus early in the season. The government is in the hands of four or five Shechs, three of whom in my time were brothers, which induced me to suppose that their dignity was hereditary; but the information I received rather imported that, ostensibly, the maxim *detur digniori* was observed in the election, though, in fact, the party each was able to form among the people, was the real cause of his advancement. These parties, as well as the Shechs, are continually opposed to each other, which renders it difficult to carry any measure of public utility. The Shechs perform the office of Cadi, and have the administration of justice entirely in their own hands. But though external respect is shewn them, they have not that preponderating influence that is required for the preservation of public order. On the slightest grounds arms are taken up; and the hostile families fire on each other in the street, and from the houses. I observed many individuals who bore the marks of these intestine wars on their bodies and limbs. Perhaps too it is to the debility of the executive power that we are to attribute some crimes, that seem almost exclusively to belong to a different state of society. While I was there, a newly born

born infant was found murdered, having been thrown from the top of a house. I understood that these accidents were not unfrequent. It would seem an indirect proof of libertinism in the women, which, however, no other circumstance led me to suppose. Inquiry was instituted, but no means offering to identify the perpetrator of the crime, the matter was dropped. The complexion of the people is generally darker than that of the Egyptians. Their dialect is also different. They are not in the habitual use either of coffee or tobacco. Their sect is that of Malik. The dress of the lower class is very simple, they being almost naked: among those whose costume was discernible, it approaches nearer to that of the Arabs of the desert, than of the Egyptians or Moors. Their clothing consists of a shirt of white cotton, with large sleeves, and reaching to the feet; a red Tunisine cap, without a turban; and shoes of the same colour. In warm weather they commonly cast on the shoulder a blue and white cloth, called in Egypt *melayé*; and in winter they are defended from the cold by an *ihhram*, or blanket. The list of their household furniture is very short; some earthen ware made by themselves, and a few mats, form the chief part of it, none but the richer order being possessed of copper utensils. They occasionally purchase a few slaves from the Murzouk caravan. The remainder of their wants is supplied from Kahira or Alexandria, whither their dates are transported, both in a dry state, and beaten into a mass, which when good in some degree resembles a sweet meat. They eat no large quantity of animal food; and bread of the kind known to us is uncommon. Flat cakes, without leaven, kneaded, and then half baked, form part of their nourishment. The remainder consists of thin

sheets

sheets of paste, fried in the oil of the palm tree, rice, milk, dates, &c. They drink in great quantities the liquor extracted from the date tree, which they term *date-tree water*, though it have often, in the state they drink it, the power of inebriating. Their domestic animals are, the hairy sheep and goat of Egypt, the ass, and a very small number of oxen and camels. The women are veiled, as in Egypt. After the rains the ground in the neighbourhood of Siwa is covered with salt for many weeks.

Having left our temporary residence, we proceeded, myself and my interpreter on horseback, our original conductor on foot, and the two men we had hired each on an ass: but we had not gone far, before one of the latter told us that it would be necessary to return, as the people of the town were in pursuit of us, and would not permit us to go and disinter the treasures of Araschié.

We nevertheless continued our journey for two days, without any particular molestation; in constant alarm indeed, from the pretended vicinity of hostile tribes, but without actually seeing any. At the end of that time we arrived at the place described to us. It is not far from the plain of Gegabib*. I found it an island, in the middle of a small lake of salt water, which contained misshapen rocks in abundance, but nothing that I could positively decide to be ruins; nor indeed was it very likely that any such should be found there, the spot being entirely destitute of trees and fresh water. Yet I had the

* See Major Rennel's map.

curiosity

curiosity to approach nearer to these imaginary ruins; and accordingly forced my horse into the lake. He, from fatigue and weakness, or original inability to swim, soon found himself entangled, and could not keep his head above water. I fell with him, and was unable immediately to detach myself: at length, when I found myself again on dry ground, the circumstances I was under prevented me from making further observation on this island and lake.

After having visited this place, we continued our journey south, according to the agreement made with our guides, but found the pursuit equally fruitless. After having, at the end of the third day, arrived in lat. 28. 40. or nearly so, we became much distressed for water. We remained a whole night in suspense concerning our destiny, when at length a supply of this necessary refreshment was found. Not having, however, discovered any thing that bore the least resemblance to the object of our search, we were obliged to think of returning, as well from the importunity of the Arabs, as from our own fatigue and unpleasant sensations. We did so, and having fallen into the strait road from Siwa to Alexandria, we arrived at the latter place, without any new occurrence, on Monday, 2d April 1792.

I had been much indisposed with a fever and dysentery, apparently caused by drinking brackish water; and for the latter part of the time was utterly incapable of making observations, having been obliged to continue prostrate on a camel.

After leaving Siwa to go to Arafchié, at about six miles from the former, we passed a small building of the Doric order, apparently designed for a temple. There either has been no inscription on it, or it is now obliterated. But the proportions are those of the best age of architecture, though the materials are ordinary, being only a calcareous stone, full of marine spoils.

The ruin at Siwa resembles too exactly those of the Upper Egypt, to leave a doubt that it was erected and adorned by the same intelligent race of men. The figures of Isis and Anubis are conspicuous among the sculptures; and the proportions are those of the Egyptian temples, though in miniature. The rocks, which I saw in the neighbourhood, being of a sandy stone, bear so little resemblance to that which is employed in this fabric, that I am inclined to believe the materials cannot have been prepared on the spot. The people of Siwa seem to have no tradition concerning this edifice, nor to attribute to it any quality, but that of concealing treasures, and being the haunt of demons.

The distance between Siwa and Derna, on the coast, is said to be thirteen or fourteen days journey; from Siwa to Kahira, twelve days; and the same from Siwa to Charjé, the principal village of Elwah.

Since the above was written, an opinion has been communicated to me, that Siwa is the *Siropum* mentioned by Ptolemy, and that the building described was probably coëval with the Temple of Jupiter Ammon, and a dependency thereon*. The

* D'Anville with equal probability supposes Siwa to be Marcotis.

discovery

discovery of that celebrated fane, therefore, yet remains to reward the toil of the adventurous, or to baffle the research of the inquisitive. It may still survive the lapse of ages, yet remain unknown to the Arabs, who traverse the wide expanse of the desert; but such a circumstance is scarcely probable. It may be completely overwhelmed in the sand; but this is hardly within the compass of belief.

CHAP. III.

FROM ALEXANDRIA TO RASHID.

Abu-kir—Fertility of the Country—Description of Rashid—Journey to Terané—Fué—Deirut and Demenhúr.

AFTER a month, passed in recovering from the effects of the journey to the westward, I prepared for leaving Alexandria. For many days boats could not pass to Rashid from the contrary winds, and I constantly preferred going by land, as affording the means of more frequent and interesting observation. Reports were spread, of the road being infested by Bedouins; but I chose rather to encounter a slight danger, than omit seeing what might offer of the country. Accordingly, on the 1st of May, I commenced my journey to Rashid. We were near four hours in reaching the village called ابوقير Abu-kir, on horseback.

The road, for about two miles after leaving the gate of Rashîd, is marked by many vestiges of buildings, but nothing worth observing. There are also many date trees scattered round in the neighbourhood of the canal, and vegetation enough to serve for food for the small flocks of the city. About two miles from Abu-kîr are the ruins of a town, close to the sea, and a part of them under water. There are also some remains of columns. This is what has been remarked as the *Taposiris parva* of antiquity. Abu-kîr is a village, consisting of few inhabitants. There is near it, however, a small port, and on the point of land which forms it, a fortress, but of little strength. A Tsorbashi resides there, with a few soldiers. He collects a toll from those who pass the ferry near it. It is a place of no trade, and vessels that frequent it come there chiefly for the purpose of avoiding bad weather. We were eight hours and a half in reaching Rashîd, exclusively of the time taken up in crossing two ferries. The latter part of the road, from the seaside to Rashîd, has been all marked with short columns of burned brick, at certain distances from each other.

The beauty and fertility of the country round Rashîd deserves all the praise that has been given it. The eye is not, indeed, gratified with the romantic views, flowing lines, the mixture of plain and mountain, nor that universal verdure that is to be observed on the banks of the Rhine or the Danube. But his taste is poor who would reduce all kinds of picturesque beauty to one criterion. To me, after being wearied with the sandy dryness of the barren district to the west, the vegetable soil of Rashîd, filled with every production necessary for the sustenance, or flattering to the luxury of man, the rice fields covering the superficies with verdure, the orange groves exhaling aromatic odours, the date trees formed into an umbrageous roof over the head; shall I say the mosques and the tombs, which, though wholly incompatible with the rules of architecture, yet grave and simple in the structure, are adapted to fill the mind with pleasing ideas; and above all, the unruffled

weight

weight of waters of the majestic Nile, reluctantly descending to the sea, where its own vast tide, after pervading and fertilizing so long a tract, is to be lost in the general mass: these objects filled me with ideas, which, if not great or sublime, were certainly among the most soothing and tranquil that have ever affected my mind.

There are some few remains of antiquity in the neighbourhood of Rashìd, though the city itself be modern. The castle of Abu-Mandûr stands about two miles from it, higher up the Nile, in a situation very picturesque, as is seen by many drawings of it extant in Europe. Columns are frequently dug up here. My arrival at Rashìd happened in the month Ramadân, a time when it is particularly cheerful. The populace there are esteemed more quiet, and better disposed to civility than those of Alexandria or Kahira.

The city of Rashìd is built in an oblong irregular form. It has no walls nor fortress. Its population is considerable; among which are some Franks, and many Greeks. The commerce is principally the carrying trade between Kahira and Alexandria. There is a cotton manufacture, but confined to home consumption. Across the mouth of the Nile, below Rashìd, is a bar which renders navigation perilous, goods being obliged to be brought in boats of a particular form from Kahira, and embarked in others of a different description for Alexandria. Great damage is sustained by the boats striking on the banks in entering the river, in which case they are commonly overset and sunk; and it would be easy to institute an office of insurance

surance at Kahira, for goods coming by Rashîd. One half per cent. would be a sufficient rate; but it would be necessary that a person should inspect the jerms, or boats, at Rashîd, as the boatmen are such knaves that they will overset the vessel, on purpose afterwards to get at the goods under water.

It may not be improper here to observe, that though, during the rise of the Nile, the water runs through several small canals, yet the real mouths, presenting a constant stream, are but two, those of Rashîd and Damiatt.

Rashîd is governed by an inferior officer, appointed by the Beys. All this district is under the jurisdiction of Murad Bey. Property is secure from all plunderers, except the Beys.

At Rashîd are many learned men; that is, skilled in Mohammedan theology and casuistry. These Shechs pass their lives in great tranquillity, preserving an apathy completely stoical. Their chief amusement is to sit in their gardens, on the banks of the river, smoking and conversing.

After staying five days to see the place, May 6th, I embarked with a view of proceeding to Terané. It was my intention to have gone by land, but the persons to whom I had recourse for information could not persuade themselves that there was any security in that route at the moment.

The production called Natrôn, efforts to introduce which into general use in Europe have more than once been made, was at
that

that time becoming a confiderable article of export; and I felt fome curiofity to obferve the production in its nafcent ftate. Terané is the place neareft the lakes, and therefore I chofe it as a point of departure. We proceeded as far as the canal of Menûf with a fair wind. Beyond this a loaded boat of any fize cannot pafs, except by that canal; the water having left the main channel, and now flowing through the canal, which is more in a line with the courfe of the river above the Delta. No want of population appears in the villages of this quarter, which are very numerous; and the land adjoining them is clean and well cultivated. An unbounded plain on both fides ftrikes the view, but on the Weft there is no great extent of arable land. The peafants wear the appearance of poverty, which, indeed, under the prefent abufe of government, is neceffary to their perfonal fecurity; but they have abundance of cattle, and the frequent return of paffengers in the boats is to them a fource of much gain.

In many of the villages are women for the convenience of ftrangers, a part of whofe profits is paid to the government which tolerates them. I did not obferve, however, that the nature of their calling created any external levity or indecency of behaviour. Having taken a fmall boat from Menûf, in fix hours, the wind being either S. E. or calm, we arrived at Terané. I counted more than an hundred diftinct villages and towns between Rafhîd and Terané, as well on the Weft as the Eaft of the Nile. Among the moft confiderable of thofe on the Eaft is Fué, a place formerly more eminent in commerce than Rafhîd; but the latter has now in a great degree fuperfeded it,

and

and it is diminished in size and population. It is nevertheless one of the most agreeable situations on the Nile. Deîrût is the largest town on the West. For Demenhûr, which is more populous, is not visible from the Nile, being situated near the canal that conveys water to Alexandria. At Demenhûr is a garrison of Janizaries. The course of the Nile from its mouth to Terané is, with the exception of some curves, nearly N. W. and S. E. In that space are several islands, which are continually changing in place and number. From Rashîd to Damiatt, in a direct line, is computed to be about twenty-seven leagues.

CHAP. IV.

TERANÉ TO THE NATRÔN LAKES.

Government of Terané—Carlo Rossetti—The Trade in Natrôn— Manners—Journey to the Lakes—Observations there—Remarks on Natrôn—Coptic Convents and MSS.—Proceed to Kahira.

TERANÉ is a town situated on the left of the most western mouth of the Nile, at a very small distance from the river. Its latitude is 30° 24′. The buildings are chiefly unburned brick, but there are also some of stone. The town and district, containing several villages, belong to Murad Bey, who usually entrusts its government and the collection of its revenue to one of his Cashefs. But the person who now holds it, May 1792, is Carlo Rossetti, a Venetian merchant, recently appointed consul-general of the Emperor of Germany, and well known to those who have visited the country. Observing, as he thought, the demands for natrôn increasing in Europe, he supposed that by obtaining an exclusive right to collect and export it, he should secure to himself an immense and increasing revenue. Till now, indeed, this article had never been productive of any advantage to the Beys. The officers who successively obtained the government there, exacting, without any settled rule, whatever they thought themselves entitled to expect from the people, who brought the commodity from the lakes to the river: and

the

the European merchants obtained it by their agents at the cheapest rate they were able from the natives. The quantity supplied, the prime cost, and the contingent charges, were therefore variable and uncertain. It had never before, as I understood, been farmed by an European. S^{re} Rossetti wished for a clear and exclusive property in the produce of the lakes, on paying regularly an annual sum, to be determined by the quantity sold. He has attained, from long experience, a considerable local knowlege, and had, at that time, from various causes, great interest with Murad Bey. Pecuniary prospects singularly influence those regents, whose office being precarious, and at most for life, totally omit to reflect on any remote consequences, for the sake of an immediate advantage. The proposal was accepted, and Rossetti obtained over the district of Terané an authority almost equal to that exercised in former times by the Cashefs.

At that time the consumption was augmenting at Marseilles, Venice, and Leghorn, and the article had been tried with some success in Great Britain. Rossetti sent his nephew to reside at Terané as his deputy. But the young man, preferring the repose of his sofa to the Mamlûk exercises of arms, was little adapted to the government of a people accustomed to be ruled only by fear. He had a few Sclavonian soldiers, who could not prevent injuries being done to the little parties employed to fetch the natron. About three months after I left Terané the young man died, not without suspicions of poison; and S^{re} Rossetti has since sold a large share in the grant, which he now retains to little purpose.

During

During the year of the moſt extenſive export, the duty to government amounted, as was ſaid, to 32,000 patackes, which, at twelve piatres the pound ſterling, may be eſtimated at 6000l. Hence the quantity muſt have been from 3500 to 4000 tons, of which the greater part was ſhipped for Marſeilles. The preſent war exceedingly reduced the quantity exported.

On my arrival at Terané, my application to S͑ͬ Ferrari, nephew of Roſſetti, for whom recommendations had been given me, was attended with aſſurances from that gentleman of his co-operation in all I might wiſh to undertake, and an invitation to reſide with him. I paſſed a day in wandering over the adjacent ground, particularly that part of the Delta which is oppoſite the town, where are many columns and other conſiderable remains, which indicate the ſite of antient ſtructures. I could, however, find no inſcriptions, nor, indeed, any thing that was worth the ſearch.

S͑ͬ Roſſetti had made a very neat garden near his houſe, in which was cultivated a number of fruit-trees and uſeful plants. He had alſo attempted many other improvements, by planting trees, &c. in the ſuburbs; but in this laudable deſign he was far from being ſeconded by the natives, who refuſed even to water the trees he had been at the trouble of planting, and ſeemed to judge their forbearance remarkable in abſtaining from their deſtruction. A ſtriking leſſon to thoſe who would force refinement on any people, to which they muſt ever be ſtimulated by their neceſſities, or led by their perſonal conviction. Yet, perhaps, they had ſuſpicions which are unexplained, or

diſcontents

discontents at the appearance of novelty, concerning the sources of which we are ignorant. I have ever observed the Egyptians, as all the Orientals, passionately fond of trees and water; and if in this instance they preferred being without them, it might possibly be from distrust of bringing on themselves some real evil, by the pursuit of an imaginary advantage.

The ensuing night, when the Arabs were to go to the lake for a lading of natrôn, S^{re} F. appointed his company of five Sclavonians to attend me, and I set off at nine in the evening on horseback. We continued our march, chiefly in a western direction, till seven the following morning, at which time we came to a spring of fresh water, that rises among some rushes near the lake, which, though it afford no very copious supply of water, was yet a seasonable refreshment, as the heat of the sun was already inconvenient. The latitude at the eastern extremity of the most western lake I found 30°, 31′, north; but this is not decided by a single observation. The difference of time between Terané and the Convents of St. George, gave a distance, as nearly as I could compute it, of thirty-five miles.

The road from Terané is level, with very small exception, and generally firm and good, though with intervals of loose and deep sand.

The country we passed through, however, is destitute of water, and consequently barren, as is all that which borders on the lakes. The only buildings in the neighbourhood are three convents, inhabited by a few religious of the Coptic church;

two

two of which are about a mile and half, the third about six miles from the eastern lake. There are some vestiges of other buildings, which also seem to have been convents that have long since ceased to exist. The antelope and the ostrich are seen rarely here, and they appear to be the only wild animals that frequent that part of the country. No vegetation appears, except reeds on the margin of the lake, which is very irregular in its form; so that it is not very easy to say what may be the quantity of ground covered with water, nor to discern the extremities. It is higher in winter than in summer; and, at this period, I could no where observe that the breadth of it exceeded a mile: its length may be nearly four.

The Arabs told me, that the water during the last winter had been remarkably low. There seem to be marks of its having occasionally risen about four feet higher than at present; which must greatly change the appearance of the whole. Towards the end of the summer, it is said, these lakes are almost dry; and the space that the water has retired from is then occupied by a thick deposition of salt. Not far removed from the eastern extremity, a spring rises with some force, which much agitates the rest of the water. Close to that spring the depth was far greater than my height, in other parts it was observable that it did not generally exceed three feet. The thermometer near this spring stood at 76, while in the open air it was 87. The more western lake differs not materially from the eastern in size, form, or productions. The colour of the water in both is an imperfect red, and where the bottom is visible, it appears almost as if covered with blood. Salt, to the thickness of

five

five or six inches, lies constantly in the more shallow parts.

The surface of the earth, near the lake, partakes more or less generally of the character of natrôn, and, in the parts farthest removed, offers to the foot the slight resistance of ploughed ground after a slight frost. The soil is coarse sand. The water of the lake, on the slightest evaporation, immediately deposits salt. There is a mountain not far from the lakes, where natrôn is found in insulated bodies, near the surface, of a much lighter colour than that produced in the lake, and containing a greater portion of alkali. This kind more resembles the natrôn of Barbary, and what I have since observed in the road to Soudân.

How thick the substance of natrôn commonly is in the lake, I did not accurately determine, but those employed to collect it report that it never exceeds a cubit, or common pike; but it appears to be regenerated as it is carried away. The Arabs report that the natrôn country extends twenty days journey; and indeed I had remarked something resembling that substance near Siwa. I understood it was delivered at Terané for about a piaster the *cantâr*. But there are, probably, some other expenses attending it. Notwithstanding S*r* R.'s exclusive right, the Arabs carry off some of the commodity, which they sell wherever they can find a market. The quantity exported to Venice was much decreasing in 1792, as it had been found on trial inapplicable to many purposes to which it was supposed it might be converted. I know not how far correct their experiments

riments might have been; but if ever it should be brought to supersede the use of barilla, the quantity obtainable seems likely to answer every possible demand.

I detected much alkali in all the specimens which came into my possession; but not equal in all. And circumstances did not permit me to make an analysis so complete as to merit insertion here.

During my stay near the lakes, I visited two of the Coptic convents, that called the *Syrian*, and that of *St. George*; where I could observe no traces of any European traveller, but Baron Thunis, whom the Empress of Russia had sent, some years before, to negotiate a defection on the part of the Beys; but who having exhibited less prudence than courage, in the promotion of the designs of his mistress, had been privately put to death in Kahira, by order of the Beys, to avoid delivering him to the Porte, as had been required of them. These convents contain each of them several religious, who retain all the simplicity of the primitive ages.—They drink water, and eat coarse bread and vegetables; very seldom touching meat, wine, or coffee. They are ignorant indeed, but strangers to vice; and though their time is employed to no useful purpose, so neither is the application of it prejudicial to any.

They have each a small garden, which supplies common vegetables, and a breed of tame fowls, together with a well of water, within the walls; the rest of the necessaries of life are

are provided them by the voluntary contributions of the Chriſtians of their own perſuaſion; and as the buſineſs of artificers and menials is all performed by the monaſtics themſelves, their expenſes are not very extended. The entrance to each is by a ſmall trap-door, againſt which two great mill-ſtones are rolled within. The buildings appear to have laſted ſeveral centuries, and the walls are ſtill firm and ſubſtantial. No praiſe is to be given to the religious for cleanlineſs; but as the liſt of their furniture and apparel is very ſmall, they cannot be frequently renewed; human beings more ignorant of mankind and their tranſactions than ſome of thoſe whom I converſed with, are ſcarcely any where to be ſeen. But the ſuperiors in both were in a certain degree intelligent. One of them, when I was admitted, was mending his ſhoes, and ſeemed to think little of theological controverſies. The other attempted to prove to me the Eutychian tenet of monotheliſm, and on my expreſſing myſelf perſuaded by his arguments, he ſeemed highly gratified. Indeed I met with on their part every mark of hoſpitality.

I inquired for MSS. and ſaw in one of the convents ſeveral books in the Coptic, Syriac, and Arabic languages. Among theſe were an Arabo-Coptic Lexicon. The works of St. Gregory, and the Old and New Teſtament in Arabic. The ſuperior told me they had near eight hundred volumes; but poſitively refuſed to part with any of them, nor could I ſee any more. The monks are ſtrangers to all idioms but the vulgar Arabic.

Having thus spent two days and part of a third in the vicinity of the lakes, my attendants grew impatient, and I was obliged to return. After a short interval, having re-embarked for Kahira, I arrived there on the 16th May 1792 *.

* The water in the river between Terané and Kahira was so shallow, that with a very small boat (Canjia) we had great difficulty in passing.

CHAP. V.

KAHIRA.

Topography—Government of Kahira and of Egypt—Pasha and Beys—Mamlúks—Birth, education, dress, arms, pay—Estimate of their military skill—Power and revenue of the Beys—The Chalige—The NILE—Mosques, Baths, and Okals—Houses—Manners and customs—Classes of people—Account of the Copts.

A RESIDENCE in Kahira at distinct intervals, but extending in all to eleven months, may enable me to attempt some account of this celebrated city, with perhaps more advantages than have fallen to the lot of any recent traveller. A cursory glance of the manners and customs of a people is often fallacious, and a temporary exception is liable to be converted into a general rule.

The yet numerous population, the various nations with their several languages, dresses, and manners, conspire with the romantic fame of *Grand Cairo*, the second capital of the East, the metropolis of Africa, the scene of surprising events in history, and of yet more surprising incidents in Arabian fable, to impress the spectator with curiosity and admiration.

The

The city Kahira (مصر القهرة) is situated on the East of the Nile, which devolves its majestic flood at some little distance. The suburbs, however, Misr el attiké, and Bulak, or the port, form two points of contact with the river. To the South-East and East is a ridge of the extensive chain which runs along the course of the Nile to Upper Egypt, sometimes receding, and leaving a plain of about a league broad, at other places opposing its barrier to the stream. To the North a plain extends to the Delta, which it resembles in soil and productions. Immediately under the mountain is the castle, now incapable of defence, though esteemed of great strength, before the invention of artillery.

To an eye accustomed to the cities of Europe, their wide streets, and general uniformity, the view of the capital of Egypt might appear mean and disgusting. Yet it is termed by the natives " Misr without an equal, Misr the mother of the world." Convenience is comparative, and ideas of it must vary with manners and customs. The narrowness of the streets appears even necessary to a native, to protect him from the fierce effulgence of the meridian sun: a slight canopy, extended from house to house, affords him more pleasure than any architectural prospect could convey.

For about the space of three hundred years Egypt had been governed by the military aristocracy of the Mamlûks, when it was subdued by Sultan Selim, in the year 1517. Sensible of the distance, defended situation, and refractory spirit of the province, he thought it politic to enter into a compromise with its former

government

government and antient prejudices. It was likewise well known, that the secure situation of the country, little exposed to any external attack, would have favoured the ambitious designs of a rival Pasha.

By an institution still observed in some instances, he ordained, that the Pasha should be contented to share the power of the Beys, and that the duration of his authority should depend on their collective will. The Beys must necessarily have separate personal interests, which sometimes lead them to intestine outrage and bloodshed; yet, with regard to any external power or influence, their interests are universally the same. As allies or as enemies they form one body and one soul. Selim was too confident in the power and splendour of the Ottoman arms, and in his own character of chief of their religion, to entertain any suspicion that the commands of the Porte would ever be treated except with distinguished respect.

The power of the Pasha was at first very extensive; but has, by the intrigues and ambition of the Beys, been gradually reduced almost to a cipher.

His jurisdiction was rather civil than military. He was always president of the Diwan, which was held in the castle where he resided. But that council now commonly meets in the palace of one of the chief Beys, except when a firmân or mandate is received from Constantinople, when the Beys are summoned to the castle to hear the commands of the Porte. The few who attend, as soon as the reading is finished, answer,

as

as is usual, *Esmâna wa taâna*, " We have heard, and we obey."
On leaving the castle, their general voice is *Esmâna wa awsína*,
" We have heard, and shall disobey."

In the year 1791, Salah Aga, a slave of Murad Bey, was deputed from the government of Egypt to negotiate their peace with the Porte.—He carried presents of horses, rich stuffs, &c. A spontaneous tribute, which the Porte was in no condition to enforce, implied obligation on the part of the latter.—He was well received, and afterwards was appointed *Waquíl es Sultân*, " Agent or Attorney to the Sultan in Kahira." It is probable this office was given him to incline him to second the efforts of the Court in disuniting the Beys; but it was ineffectual. These had formerly experienced the evils of division, and now were united by common interest, grown rich, and well provided with slaves. So that, as I have understood, no tribute has since that time found its way to Constantinople.

As the Beys are chosen from among the Mamlûks, it may be proper to begin with some account of that extraordinary class of men. They remain, as they have ever been, military * slaves
imported

---

* The condition of slave is so very distinct in Egypt from what it is in other countries, that they who defend the practice of trading in human flesh by its antiquity, and the general consent of nations, should be well aware how they adduce the example of Egypt.—In Kahira, when a slave is legally purchased in the market, if after any length of time he feel discontented with his master, has only to say, " Carry me to the market," (Sûk-es Sultân,) and the master is legally compellable to offer him for sale.

It

imported from Georgia, Circassia, and Mingrelia. A few have been prisoners, taken from the Austrians and Russians, who have exchanged their religion for an establishment. The Beys give general orders to their agents at Constantinople, to purchase a certain number every year, and many are brought to Egypt by private merchants on speculation. When the supply proves insufficient, or many have been expended, black slaves from the interior of Africa are substituted, and if found docile, are armed and accoutred like the rest.

Particular attention is paid to the education of these favoured slaves. They are instructed in every exercise of agility or strength, and are in general distinguished by the grace and beauty of their persons. The gratitude of the disciples is equal to the favour of their masters, whom they never quit in the hour of danger. If they have a disposition for learning they are taught the use of letters; and some of them are excellent scribes: but the greater part neither can read nor write, a striking example of which deficiency is observable in Murad Bey himself.

The inferior Mamlûks constantly appear in the military dress, and are commonly armed with a pair of pistols, a sabre, and a

---

It can never be believed, that where a power so absolute as that of the proprietor over his slave, is supported by the sanctions of law, that no abuses of it should exist; but this single privilege greatly softens its asperity.

The child of a female slave, begotten by her master, is ipso facto free, and a slave may authorize a free person to purchase his emancipation.

dagger. They wear a peculiar cap of a greenish hue, around which is wreathed a turban *. The rest of their dress resembles that of other Mohammedan citizens, and is restricted to no particular colour: but another singularity is their large drawers of thick Venetian cloth, of a crimson colour, to which are attached their slippers of red leather. On horseback they add to their arms a pair of large horse-pistols, and the *Dubbûs* or battle-axe. In battle many of them wear an open helmet, and the antient ring armour of interwoven links of steel, worn under part of their dress, and thus concealed. These are dear, sometimes costing five hundred piastres, or about forty pounds. Some of them are made at Constantinople, others in Persia. Their horses are of the finest Arabian breeds, and are often purchased at three or four purses, 150l. to 200l. sterling.

They have no pay, as they eat at a table in the house of their master, the Bey, Cashef, or other officer. Any military officer may purchase a slave, who becomes *ipso facto* a Mamlûk. The name, from *Malek* to possess, implies merely a person who is the property of another. After a proper education, the candidate thus constituted a Mamlûk, receives a present of a horse

---

* The Mamlûks suffer not the beard to grow till they be emancipated, and hold some office, as Cashef, &c.—A similar practice obtains among the Osmanli. The Ytch oghlans, though free in their persons, yet exercising a kind of servitude, shave the beard: so that though it be not absolutely the mark of a slave, the want of a beard seems to denote a dependent situation. Among the Osmanli, (European Turks) the beard is allowed to grow rather in conformity to the precept and practice of the Prophet, than as a national fashion. The Tatars wear no beard; and the Arabs alone shew great respect to that ornament.

and

and arms from his master, together with a suit of clothes, which is renewed ever year in the month Ramadân. The generosity of their masters, and rewards or extortions from others, afford them supplies of money either for avarice or debauchery. Some of them, admitted to peculiar favour by the Beys, as chasnadars or pursebearers, &c. acquire great wealth. They are rather gay and thoughtless, than insolent; fond of shew, and unprincipled in their means of acquiring it. They seldom marry till they acquire some office.

Though born of Christian parents, they seem highly satisfied with their condition; which they have been known to refuse to exchange for freedom. The majority are regarded by the Arabs as little strict in the principles or duties of Mohammedism.

It is worthy of remark, that though the Mamlûks in general be strong and personable men, yet the few who marry very seldom have children. As the son even of a Bey is not honoured with any particular consideration, the women perhaps procure abortions. However this be, of eighteen Beys, whose history I particularly knew, only two had any children living.

Hardy, capable of every fatigue, of undaunted courage, and eminent skill in horsemanship and the use of the sabre, the Mamlûks may be regarded as by far the best troops in the East. But in a regular battle, conducted by manœuvres, and large or rapid movements, they are equally inferior to European troops.

Being distinguished by favouritism or merit, the Mamlûk becomes a Cashef, and in time a Bey. The chief cause of preference arises from political adherence to some powerful leader.

The government of Kahira, and Egypt in general, is vested in twenty-four Beys, each of whom is nominally chosen by the remaining twenty-three, but in fact appointed by one of the most powerful. The *Yenk-tchery aga*, and several other officers, are enumerated among the twenty-four Beys.

Besides being governors of certain districts of Egypt, several of the Beys receive other dignities from the Porte. Such are the *Shech el Bellad*, or governor of the city; the *Defterdar*, or accountant-general; the *Emir el Hadj*, or leader of the sacred caravan; and the *Emir es Saïd*, or governor of the upper Egypt*. These officers have also revenues allotted them by the Porte, ill-defined, and liable to much abuse.

Of the other Beys, each appoints all officers and governors within his district, putting into it some slave of his own, who is compelled to render an account of the receipts; of which a part passes to support the grandeur of his master. An opulent Bey may have from 600 to 1000 purses annually; the revenue of Murad Bey more than doubles that sum. The inferior Beys may have 300 purses or 15,000l.

The chief judicial authority in Kahira is delegated to a *Mulla*, who is annually appointed from Constantinople; but his

---

* The two last offices are annual.

jurifdiction is principally directed to cafes of doubt and difficulty. There are befides *Cadis*, in all the diftricts, or *parifhes*, if fo it may be expreffed, which, in this great city, amount to more than two hundred. There are Imâms, or priefts of the four fects, each having the direction of the adherents of that fect. The *Shech-el-Bikkeri* is an office of great refpect, having fpecial authority over the fhe-rîfs. There are other exclufive jurifdictions, which need not be fpecified.

The revenue of the Cadis arifes folely from a tenth of the value of the thing litigated. Juftice or injuftice is fpeedily adminiftered, but is often influenced by bribery.

Every Bey fits in judgment on cafes of equity. Thefe perfonages are very obfervant of their refpective jurifdictions; and no Bey will imprifon a man liberated by another. Though fometimes too impetuous, they neverthelefs difplay great acutenefs and knowlege of characters. This government at leaft poffeffes every advantage of publicity, as every Bey is a magiftrate.

But the juftice of the rulers is ever open to the omnipotent influence of gold. During my refidence at Kahira an inftance happened worthy of commemoration. Two Syrian Chriftians, of the Maronite perfuafion, had been fucceffively farmers of the cuftoms, and had acquired great wealth: a quarrel arifing between them, one made a reflection peculiarly grating on the other, who went to the Bey, and thus addreffed him: " This city is not wide enough for me and fuch a one. You muft muſt put one of us to death. If you will put him to death, here are ten thouſand ſequins." Said and done inſtantly.

Each Bey appoints his Caſhefs or lieutenants. Theſe officers preſide each over a town or village, collecting the revenues, and judging ſmall cauſes; but an appeal lies to the Bey. The Beys and Caſhefs are, from their ignorance, conſtrained to employ Copts as accomptants in adjuſting and receiving the revenues, that duty being of an intricate nature, and requiring great local knowlege. The authority of a Caſhef is as arbitrary as that of a Bey.

Revenue of Egypt.

THE more confiderable ſources of revenue, as well of the Porte at this day, as of the Chalifé while the ſovereignty remained with the Arabs, are nearly coëval in their inſtitution with Mohammediſm itſelf.

The innovations which have ſince had place derive their authority from the diſpenſing power of the ſovereign, or are reconciled with the primitive inſtitutes by the ingenuity of the legal profeſſors.

The moſt antient tribute due from the ſubject to government was the *zecchát*, a tenth of all the permanent productions of the earth. According to its original eſtabliſhment, this did not affect property under a certain value, and was exigible of an unbeliever in a twofold proportion. It was impoſed by Mohammed

hammed himself, and applied, as would appear, to the relief of the necessitous; the prophet expressly forbidding his own family to share in it, as unworthy of their rank, and, at the same time, allotting to them a fifth part of the plunder obtained in war. This impost continues to be levied, but is applied to needful expenses or unnecessary prodigality, rather than to soften the lot of the indigent, its original purpose. Ostentatious charities satisfy the scruples of the monarch, and blind the eyes of the people to this misapplication. The tax is not now applicable to land or houses, but to the merchandize imported into the country. The duties on these, when demanded of Mohammedans, are taken under the name of *zecchât*.

The second impost is the *charâge*, which signifies the product of lands. It is intended to denote, not only any tax on land, but also on the persons of *dhummies*, i. e. Christians and Jews; though in the latter case it receives the appellation of Jizie (جزية), the capitation tax, or *salvage* for their persons, which otherwise, according to the letter of the Korân, the true believer is not bound to spare.

In modern times, the public revenue of the Porte, which is derived from various sources, is known under the name of Miri; the private one of the emperor is supplied in a different way, and termed *Chafné*.

The nature of the revenue of each province depended at first, in a great measure, on the manner in which that province was originally acquired; and, even now, the same distinction in some cases operates. Irak was to be protected under one condition of tribute, Egypt under another. The immediate successors of Mohammed appear to have been guided in many instances by sound policy, and to have tempered the rage of fanaticism, by some attention at least to the well-being even of their heretical subjects. The imposts in Egypt, one of their earliest territorial acquisitions, and the inhabitants of which had many of them embraced Islamism, were not distinguished by any remarkable severity; and if that country have since been impoverished and depopulated, it appears not to result from the original institutions, so much as from the abuses which happened at an early period of the Egyptian Chalifat, and which may contaminate the mildest and most reasonable establishments. These abuses, which have long been gradually increasing, are now multiplied to a point, beyond which, consistently with the being of the peasantry, they cannot well be extended.

The principal local tribute is a tax on land of two patackes each *foddàn*, all over the country; which, whether the effect of a compact between the Arabian victor and the natives, or an impost in force under the former government, was continued by Sultan Selim. Taking the cultivable lands in Egypt at two million one hundred thousand acres, this should give the sum of twelve thousand nine hundred purses, or at the present exchange of 630,000l. sterling; but at this time only two-thirds of these lands are actually cultivated, which reduces the sum to 420,000l. On the other hand, however, the Beys are not contented with this legitimate revenue, but insist on receiving in many instances

five

five or six patackes per foddân*, which again raises this single branch of revenue to a million and a quarter, or even more. There are however some districts in the Upper Egypt always several years in arrear.

The other articles are, the customs of Alexandria, Damiatt, Suez, Cofsîr; and what is drawn from the commerce of Africa in its passage by Charjé, Assiût, and at Kahira itself. Of these it is difficult to form any correct idea. The caravan with which I returned to Assiût paid, in duties on the commodities it brought, a sum not less than 150 purses. I estimated the value of those commodities at nearly two thousand three hundred purses, or 115,000l. sterling.

The *Jizié* is much less considerable than it might be supposed, from the following considerations. 1. That though there be many entire villages of Copts in the Upper Egypt, several of them are rebellious, and pay nothing. 2. The same people is very numerous in the towns; but a great proportion of them consists of ecclesiastics, or of persons in the service of the Beys, and both these descriptions are exempt. The Greeks and Armenians are but few, and many of them pay the *Jizié* in other places, being only travellers. On the whole, I doubt whether that tax in Egypt amounts to more than fifteen hundred purses. The remaining revenue is made up of casualties;

---

* The patacke may be rated at from three shillings to three and four-pence. The foddân is a given measure, taking its name from the quantity that a yoke of oxen can plough in a day, roughly taken, equivalent to an acre.

as forfeitures, small imposts, and tolls, passing on the Nile, and other parts of the interior; and above all, the incalculable profit arising from continued plunder of all ranks and denominations. Five, ten, twenty to thirty thousand patackes are demanded, in one day, of the Christians engaged in commerce, at another of the Mohammedans, and at another of the Franks. Advantage was taken of the unprotected state in which the French merchants found themselves after the commencement of the war, and all, except three, were in consequence obliged to leave Kahira, and retire to Alexandria.

I never could learn that the wandering Arabs, or Bedouins, paid any regular tribute. They were often plundered and repulsed when they came in bodies too near the city; but in general the Beys appeared to be inclined to keep them in good humour, for their personal security, in case of being expelled from the government. The article of salt, for there are *salines* close to the sea, which supply all Egypt with culinary salt, pay a low impost in entering Kahira, and another at Assiût. All the prostitutes, the public baths, the places where brandy is sold, (*Chummari,*) &c. &c. are under a particular jurisdiction, and pay something to government.

In Kahira every trade or profession has its sheeh or leader, who has great authority over the rest of his order; and this circumstance tends much to the good order of the city. The gates no less, which are at the end of every street, and which, though not capable of resisting violence, impede the progress, and render difficult the escape of ill-intentioned persons. The

articles

The greater part of the lands in Egypt, is to be confidered as divided between the Government, and the religious bodies who perform the fervice of the mofques, who have obtained poffeffion of what they now hold by the munificence of princes and rich men, or by the meafures taken by individuals for the benefit of their pofterity. The property of the mofques is called *wakf,* a term fignifying, in its technical acceptation, the appropriation of a thing in fuch a way, that the proprietor's right in it fhall continue, but the profit belong to fome charitable eftablifhment.

From the right which the Government claims to inheritances, and the ruinous fines paid on readmiffion, thofe who have landed property frequently make this appropriation to the mofque, and their lands become part of the *wakf* of that eftablifhment. The Government then has no farther claim on them. But the appropriator takes care, at the fame time, that his next heir, or if a minor, truftees on his behalf, under the name of *Mutwálli,* fhall receive the rents, and fo on, as long as any heirs remain in the family. The individual continues in the fecure receipt of his income, paying however annually a fmall proportion of it to the adminiftrators of the mofque.

It will hence be obferved, that in Egypt, a large proportion of the tenants and cultivators hold either of the Government, or the procurators of the mofques. To the perfonal eafe of the cultivator, and the general good of the whole, it is of little confequence which. For there is one circumftance common to

them

them both, viz. that their lands, becoming unoccupied, are never let but on terms ruinous to the tenant. For as there is a number of bidders, and the managers of them are exorbitant in their demands, the tenant becomes acceſſory to his own miſery, by engaging to pay the owner ſo large a portion of the product, that his profits are abſolutely inſignificant.

Theſe contracts are of various forms, but commonly made for a given number of years, or for life, in the nature of leaſes. The occupier, aſſiſted by his family, is the cultivator; and in the operations of huſbandry ſcarcely requires any other aid. When the Nile riſes, thoſe who are employed to water the fields are commonly hired labourers. Volney * has ſaid generally, that the peaſants of Egypt are *hired labourers*. It will hence be ſeen to how ſmall a portion of them thoſe terms can be properly applied.

The hired ſervants of the great are paid chiefly by having their food provided for them, and receiving occaſionally preſents of clothes; excepting what they obtain by extortion, opportunities of which are given even to the loweſt menial, by the ſyſtem of terror eſtabliſhed in the country.

The tenant of land commonly holds no more than he and his family can cultivate, and gather the produce of. Yet he is far from being a villain, attached to the ſoil, having always the power of quitting his farm to obtain another in a different

* Engliſh edit. p. 188.

quarter.

quarter. It however often happens, that families are connected with a particular spot for a great length of time. I have met with persons of that description at *Ben-Ali* near Assiût, whose ancestors of the fifth remove had resided in the same spot. " I used to smoke tobacco," (said one of them, a very old man,) " but it cost me almost a para a-day, and times are always " growing worse, so now I am satisfied with a dry reed, till the " master (ربي) free me from these embarrassments."

I shall now return to the topography and population of this great city. It has been originally walled, but at present only fragments remain. The dimensions of the city from North to South * greatly exceed those from East to West. There are several open spaces, but the houses, generally speaking, are close to each other. The *Chalige*, which pierces the city from North to South, commencing near Misr-el-Attiké, assumes various aspects, according to the season of the year. Its most permanent character is that of a dunghill, a public receptacle for all kinds of offal. Before the rise of the Nile, it is cleaned, and becomes a street; it is then filled by the increase of the river, and exhibits the appearance of a canal covered with boats.

Here it may be remarked in general concerning that noble river, that its rise seems to remain the same as in the most antient times, namely, sixteen cubits, or twenty-four feet in perpendicular height. The medium increase is nearly four

* The length may be estimated at about three thousand five hundred yards.

inches a-day; and takes place, as is well known, from the end of June to the beginning of September, from which period to the following solstice it is gradually falling, again to rise. Those versed in antient astronomy know, that the rise of the river was indicated by the heliacal rising of Sirius, or the Dog-star, a few mornings before; whence that star was denominated, as resembling the fidelity of a dog, in warning his master to remove his effects from the ravages of the stream. It is asserted that Sihor, or Sihir, is an antient name of the Nile, as well as the Indus, whence *Siris*, corruptly *Sirius*, another appellation of the most brilliant of all the fixed stars.

Mr. Gray's well-known description of Egypt, as immersed under the influx of the Nile, is exquisitely poetical, but far from just. In Upper Egypt the river is confined by high banks, which prevent any inundation into the adjacent country. This is also the case in Lower Egypt, except at the extremities of the Delta, where the Nile is never more than a few feet below the surface of the ground, and where inundation of course takes place. But the country, as may be expected, is without habitations. The fertility of Egypt arises from human art. The lands near the river are watered by machines; and if they extend to any width, canals have been cut. The soil in general is so rich as to require no manure. It is a pure black mould, free from stones, and of a very tenacious and unctuous nature. When left uncultivated, I have observed fissures, arising from the extreme heat, of which a spear of six feet could not reach the bottom.

The

The greatest breadth of this majestic river may be computed at two thousand feet, or about a third of a mile. Its motion is even slower than that of the Thames, and does not exceed three miles an hour. The water is always muddy: in April and May, when it is clearest, it has still a cloudy hue. When it overflows, the colour is a dirty red. It is replete with a variety of fish; those I have chiefly observed are, *Bûlti*, Labrus Niloticus; *Kelb-el-bahr*; *Farbôn*; *Charmût*, a round fish about eight inches long, and said to be poisonous; *Tabân-el-bahr*, the eel, Muræna Anguilla; *Nefâsh*, apparently a species of salmon, and found of very large size. It seems not now determinable of what species, or whether of any now known, was the fish called *Oxyrynchus*, so famous in the antiquities of Egypt. D'Anville says it is the one now called *Kesher*. The best is the *Bûlti*, somewhat like the white trout, but sometimes attaining such a size as to weigh fifty pounds. Except good and large eels, none of the fish have a strict similitude of the European.

From Kâhira to Afsûan, a distance of about three hundred and sixty miles, the banks, except where rocky, present no natural plant; they somewhat resemble the steps of stairs, and are sown with all sorts of esculent vegetables, chiefly that useful plant the *Bamea*. It grows to a little more than three feet in height, with leaves like those of the currant-bush; and produces oblong aculeated pods, which lend a pleasant flavour to the repast.

Among several kinds of water-fowl which frequent the Nile, may be mentioned what is here called the Turkey goose, *Anas Nilotica*, Lin. a large fowl, the flesh of which is palatable and salubrious food.

Other striking and antient features of this distinguished stream, are the rafts of *Belasses*, or large white jars, used for carrying water; little rafts of gourds, on which a single person conducts himself with great philosophical dignity across the stream; and the divers, who, concealing their heads in pumpkins, approach the water-fowl unperceived, and seize them by the legs. Concerning the crocodile and hippopotamus so much has been said, that I despair of adding any thing new. The latter I never saw or heard of in Egypt; in Nubia they are said to abound. The crocodile itself seems reduced in number, and is confined to the district above Assiût, where he is dangerous to bathers. A young man bathing at Dendera, a day or two before I arrived, had his leg bitten off by one of those unwieldy animals.

Parallel to the *Chalige* * runs the principal street. It should be observed that the houses of the Europeans are all on the *Chalige*, the stench of which has been supposed to operate in producing the pestilence, to which that order of men is however the least subject. The mosques in Kahira are computed at more than three hundred; four or five of them far exceeding the rest in splendor. The *Jama el Az-her* is a very considerable eleemosynary establishment, supplying chiefly poor ecclesiastics, to the amount of some thousands, with broth and other articles. Most of the mendicants in Kahira are ecclesiastics, who urge their studies as an excuse for idleness. Blindness, I know not from what cause, affecting one or both eyes, is

---

* The city is still infested with the usual herds of dogs, and the kites still shriek wildly over the canal; while the turtle-doves, unmolested by men or children, breed in the houses, building their nests under the projecting beams.

extremely

extremely common among the Egyptian beggars. The mosque called *Jama el Az-her* is one of the most magnificent of Kahira, ornamented with pillars of marble, and Persian carpets. The property attached to this mosque is immense. A shech, being an ecclesiastic of the highest order, presides over the establishment; which also supports a number of persons distinguished for their profound skill in theology, and accurate knowlege of literal Arabic. It is furnished with an extensive collection of MSS. and lectures are read on all subjects which are here called *scientific*, being commonly removed farthest from science.

The other mosques most frequented are, that of *Sultan el Ghouri, el Hassanein*, and, of later date, that erected by Mohammed Bey Abudhahab. For the construction of the latter the most costly materials were provided, and it is esteemed a *chéf-d'œuvre* of oriental magnificence.

The Saracenic structure on the island *Rouda*, which contains the *Mokkias*, or Nilometer, has been represented in various designs, and repeatedly described. The graduation of it is confused, imperfect, and not to be depended on: so that they who would inform themselves correctly as to the Nile's increase, should make their observation on some smooth surface, washed by the river, and perpendicular to its plane; never depending on the public report, which the cryers are suborned to make agreable to the will of government; and which at the beginning of the increase generally exceeds the truth, and afterwards falls short of it.

Large and sumptuous reservoirs are found in various parts of the city, where water is given to passengers. Baths, adorned with marble, and provided with every possible convenience, and plenty of water, also abound. The attendants are extremely dextrous, and the charge very reasonable.

The Okals, or warehouses, are spacious, strongly built, commodious and clean. These are for wholesale goods. For retail, are the bazârs, as *Khân Chalil*, *Hamsâwi*, &c. extensive buildings, with convenient shops, each trade in its allotted quarter, and copiously supplied with every commodity.

Through the greater part of the city the houses are built with stone, two, or sometimes three stories high, with flat roofs. The windows of the upper stories are latticed, the ground floor being either a shop or having no windows to the street. Sometimes the lattices suffice; a few have paper windows, some of the rich have glass.

The houses of the great chiefly surround *Birket-el-fil*, a pool which receives the Nile water from the *Chalige*. The palace of a Bey contains a square court, one or two sides occupied by his Mamlûks. Apart is the Harem. The room in which the Bey generally sits in summer has a contrivance in the roof to admit a copious supply of fresh air. In Kahira fire is only employed in cookery, the effects of cold being sufficiently obviated by warmer clothing.

The

The apartments of the women are furnished with the finest and most expensive articles; but those of the men are only remarkable for a plain style of neatness. The houses in general are irregular, but substantial and commodious.

The Mamlûks breakfast before sun-rise, make their second meal at ten, and the third about five in the afternoon. Animal food abounds. A large dish of pilau appears in the middle of the table, surrounded with small dishes of meat, fish, and fowls. The meat is cut into minute pieces before it be dressed. Drink only water, and immediately after the meal, coffee is served. At the tables of the great *sherbet* is introduced. Egypt produces no wine; the Greeks and Franks procure that commodity from other quarters.

The Egyptians still make a fermented liquor of maize, millet, barley or rice, but it bears little resemblance to our ale. It is of a light colour, and in the hot season will not keep above a day; but it is sufficiently pleasant to the taste. It is drank in considerable quantities in Kahira and in Saïd. The native Christians mostly distil for themselves, from dates, a liquor called by the general name *Araki*; it is also made from currants, or the small grapes imported from Cerigo.

When brought into the houses, the water of the Nile is put into jars, called *hammam*, previously rubbed, in the inside, with a kind of paste, made of bitter almonds. Thus preserved, it becomes quite clear and limpid in two hours. But it is often drank in its most muddy state, without any ill effects.

The

The eyes and fingers are the only parts of a woman that are visible in public. In general, the women of Kahira are not tall, but well formed. The upper ranks tolerably fair, in which and in fatness, consist the chief praises of beauty in the Egyptian climate. They marry at fourteen or fifteen, and at twenty are passed their prime. For what reason the natives of hot climates ordinarily prefer women of large persons, I have not been able to discover. Nevertheless, the Coptic women have interesting features, large black eyes, and a genteel form.

The population of Kahira consists, 1. of the Arabs, or lower class of Mohammedans, who form the body of the people, and who pride themselves in the name of *ibn Arab*, son of an Arabian. 2. Of the Coptic Christians, who form a considerable number, here and in Upper Egypt; in the Delta they are rare. 3. Mamlûks. I was assured that, during the last eleven years, not fewer than sixteen thousand white slaves, of both sexes, have been imported into Egypt. A plague had carried off a thousand Mamlûks, and other causes had reduced their number to about eight thousand, so that there was a great demand for the article. Still I cannot venture to estimate the number of Mamlûks at more than ten or twelve thousand. 4. Greeks, Syrians, and Armenians; Muggrebîns, from Tripoli, Tunis, and Morocco, who have a quarter to themselves, are remarkable for industry and frugality, and are attracted hither by the great profits of trade. Other Mohammedans from Arabia Proper, and yet farther East. There are very few Turks established in Egypt, but

many

many come hither on bufinefs, and return to Conftantinople. Jews were once numerous, but are now on the decreafe. Exclufively of negro flaves in every houfe, there are blacks from Nubia, who act as porters at the gates of the rich, and fometimes fell *bouza* and eatables.

In general, the total population of Kahira cannot certainly be eftimated at lefs than three hundred thoufand fouls. Egypt may contain, in all, two millions and a half.

In fpeaking of the population of Egypt, and other countries under the fame circumftances, it may be remarked, that among ourfelves, to obtain a tolerably correct knowlege of the number of people in a town or city, it is fufficient to know the number of houfes, and the average number of inhabitants in each houfe. In Egypt the cafe is widely different. A large proportion of the people has no vifible dwelling. The flighteft fhelter fuffices to protect them from the inconfiderable variations of a regular climate, and obfcurity, under the falcon eye of power always a blefling, is here fought with peculiar avidity.

Of all thofe defcriptions of men, the Copts, or original inhabitants, moft intereft curiofity. There are fome peculiarities of feature common to all of them. I was not ftruck with any refemblance of the negro features or form. Their hair and eyes are indeed of a dark hue, and the former is often curled; but not in a greater degree than is occafionally feen among Europeans. The nofe is often aquiline, and though the lips be

fometimes

sometimes thick, by no means generally so; and on the whole, a strong resemblance may be traced between the form of visage in the modern Copts, and that presented in the antient mummies, paintings, and statues.

Their complexion, like that of the Arabs, is of a dusky brown; it is represented of the same colour in the paintings which I have seen in the tombs of Thebes.

The Coptic language may be considered as extinct. Numerous and minute researches have enabled me to ascertain this fact. In Upper Egypt, however, they unknowingly retain some Coptic words, such as *Boylini*, the name of a month.

Nevertheless, in the Coptic monasteries, the prayers are read in Arabic, and the epistle and gospel in Coptic; but the priest is a mere parrot, repeating a dead letter. Coptic manuscripts are found in some of the convents, and leave to copy them might be obtained from the Patriarch.

Their creed is the Monothelite, or Eutychian heresy. The solely divine nature of Christ, the procession of the Holy Ghost from the Father alone. The Copts embrace transubstantiation; in which, and other points, the Catholics of Kahira think they approach their faith nearer than the Greeks. Yet the Copts have adopted from the Mohammedans the custom of frequent prostrations during divine service, and of public individual prayer; of ablution after the conjugal rites, &c.

The

The Copts are an acute and ingenious people. They are generally writers and accomptants. In business they accumulate money steadily, without shew; long experience having taught them, what the other Christians have yet to learn, that, under an arbitrary government, obscurity is safety. Melancholic in their temperament, but when called into action, industrious and laborious. Otherwise, fond of their distilled liquor, and rather licentious in their amours. The Copts are zealous in their faith, and their ecclesiastics are numerous.

It is remarkable, that in Egypt the children of Europeans seldom survive their second or third year. This proceeds, it is likely, from the improper warmth of place and clothing, in which they are kept by the injudicious fondness of their parents, while the children of the natives run about almost naked, and enjoy a constitution firm and vigorous.

CHAP. VI.

KAHIRA.

Commerce—Manufactures—Mint—Castle and well—Misr attiké—Antient mosque—Antient Babylon—Fostat—Bulak—Jizé—Tomb of Shafei—Pleasure-boats—Charmers of Serpents—Magic—Dancing girls—Coffee-houses—Price of provisions—Recent history of Egypt—Account of the present Beys.

BEFORE the revolution in commerce, occasioned by the discovery of the passage to India by the Cape of Good Hope, that of Kahira was very extensive. It has since gradually declined, and is now restricted to the following articles.

From Yemen are imported coffee, odours, gems, and several useful drugs. From Surat, and other neighbouring parts of India, muslins and various articles of cotton manufacture, a portion of the spices of Ceylon; shawls from Cashmîr.

Kahira may still be regarded as the metropolis of the trade of eastern Africa, as Tripoli chiefly possesses that of the west. A few slaves are brought from Habbesh (Abyssinia) by the way of Jidda and Mecca. Caravans pass to and from Sennaar, Dar-Fûr, and Fezzan, bringing slaves, gold-dust, ivory, horns of Rhinoceros, Ostrich feathers, gum, drugs.

There

There is another uncertain caravan from Morocco, which employs five thousand camels for merchandise; part passes to Mecca, and part remains to transact business, and await the return of the pilgrims. The other caravans are merely for the carriage of goods; and the camels are supplied by the Arabs, who rove through the deserts which form the boundaries of Egypt.

The navigation of the Red Sea cannot be conducted upon worse principles than it is by the Egyptians and Arabs. The ships are constructed on a wrong plan, being sharp, while the shallows and rocks require vessels that draw little water; and they are overcharged with passengers and goods. Hence the passage would be dangerous, even if managed by able navigators; but the mariners here are extremely unskilful, and only pique themselves on avoiding the sunk rocks near the shore, in which it must be confessed they are very dextrous. The ships employed by persons residing in Egypt are thirty-seven in number, so far as I could learn from an agent at Suez, and so many are lost, that the continual building barely supplies the usual number.

European imports in general have been specified under the head Alexandria. From Tunis and Tripoli are brought oil, red caps, of a particular manufacture, for which Tunis is famous, and fine flannel, used for garments by the Bedouins and others. From Syria arrive cotton, silk, crude and manufactured, soap, tobacco, beads of glass. From Constantinople,

besides

besides white slaves, male and female, all kinds of brass, copper, and iron manufactures.

Proceeding to exports, those to Europe have been mentioned in treating of Alexandria, and those to Dar-Fûr shall be enumerated when we come to visit that kingdom. To Sennaar and Fezzan, the same with Dar-Fûr. Hedjas, in Arabia, is wholly supplied with grain from Egypt, but the trade to India and Jidda is carried on chiefly by money. To Constantinople, black slaves, chiefly eunuchs, great quantities of coffee, and some Indian goods, though these be for the most part conveyed thither by caravans.

Egypt was formerly the granary of Rome and of Constantinople. The exports of rice remain very great, with considerable quantities of wheat from Upper Egypt, in favourable years. No oats are seen in Egypt; and the barley is consumed by the horses.

To Syria are exported rice, crude leather, flax, and sometimes wheat.

The manufactures at Kahira are not numerous. The sugar cane being cultivated with ease in Egypt, it was manufactured in great quantities at Kahira, so as to supply Constantinople. But a capital being requisite, Government made demands on it which crushed the trade. The sugar, though of less strength than that of the West Indies, was nevertheless well refined, of a close a clofe texture, pure and of a light white. It is now extremely bad, and fo fcarce as to fell for fourteen pence the pound, retail.

The fal ammoniac made at Kahira is of a very good quality. Glafs lamps, faltpetre, and gun-powder, red and yellow leather, for home-confumption. There is a great manufacture of linen cloth made of the fine Egyptian flax.

The mode almoft peculiar to Kahira, of hatching eggs without incubation, has been very minutely defcribed by former travellers.—The practice is faid by the Egyptians to proceed from the experience that, at a certain feafon, the eggs foftered only by the hens are commonly unprolific. Of thofe hatched in the ovens, on the contrary, not quite one third is loft.—The ovens where thefe eggs are placed are of the moft fimple conftruction, confifting only of a low arched apartment of clay. Two rows of fhelves are formed, and the eggs placed on each in fuch a manner as not to touch each other. They are flightly moved five or fix times in twenty-four hours, and the whole time they are in the oven does not exceed twenty-two days, when the chickens free themfelves from the fhell. All poffible care is taken to diffufe the heat equally throughout, and there is but one fmall aperture, large enough to admit a man ftooping. During the firft eight days the heat is rendered great, and, during the laft eight is gradually diminifhed; till at length, when the young brood is ready to come forth, it is reduced almoft to the ftate of the natural atmofphere. At the end of the firft eight days, it is known which eggs will not be productive.

ductive. Those who have eggs to be hatched, bring them to the master of the oven, and contract to pay so much a hundred; and when the chickens appear, he receives his money on delivering them. Those which have not succeeded, are required to be produced. The oven is public property.

Kahira is the only mint for Egypt, where they strike in gold mahbûbs and half mahbûbs; the first about five shillings in value. In copper washed with silver the small coins worth about a halfpenny, and called in Turkish *paras*, in Arabic *diwani*, *fuddha*, or *maidi*: by European writers, *aspers*, and *medines*. On one side is the name of the reigning Sultan, on the reverse, *Misr*, and the date.

The mint is fixed in the castle, built by the celebrated *Yusfuf abu Moddafar ibn Aiûb*, whose title of honour was Salaheddîn, in the sixth century of Mohammedism. The people of the country, who are in the habit of confounding all history and chronology, attribute it to Joseph the son of Isaac, whose palace they say it was; but it is unnecessary to confute an opinion wholly unsupported by facts. Including the quarters of the Janizaries and Assabs (the latter of whom no longer exist), the building occupies a large space. But it is irregular, and the Pasha's apartments are mean and incommodious. The well is of great depth, and has been hewn with much labour through the solid rock, but as that rock is of a soft nature, the magnitude of the work is not comparable to that of some excavations which have been executed in several other places. The broken remains of the palace of Salah-eddîn, are indeed worthy of remark.

remark. An apartment of great length overlooks the city, the river, and the adjacent country; and several beautiful columns raise their heads out of the general wreck. In a chamber of this building is fabricated the embroidered cloth, which the munificence of the Porte annually devotes to the use of the *Kaba*.

Misr-el-Attiké, to the South of the present city, is pleasantly situated, and well inhabited. It can now only be esteemed a faux-bourg of the former. A mosque there, said, probably without reason, to have been built by order of the Chalifé Omar, was lately rescued from the oblivion to which it was hastening, by the mandate of Murad Bey. This mosque is a building of great extent; there may be thirty or thirty-five columns remaining in their original position. The rest have been reversed, and again set up without any regard to order. The most perfect remain is a small octagon building in the middle of the mosque, supported by eight Corinthian columns, the shaft, about ten feet high, of blue-and-white marble. In this small edifice is a chamber, which is said never to have been opened. Multitudes of columns appear around, to the number of more than a hundred, some in black marble, one has a small cavity, fabled an impression made by the hand of the Prophet. The cement is so hard as to evince that the Saracens were no strangers to the antient mode of preparing it. Many arches of an elliptical form remain, and some inscriptions, on the West, probably the place of the antient gate, as it is of the modern.

Antient Arabic books, some of them in the Kuphic character, have been recently discovered here, in a cellar, under lock and key, and inclosed in a sycamore chest. Some of them are on vellum, and very beautiful. Such a number was found as filled a very large chest. Murad Bey, being informed that treasures were hid under the antient mosque, had recourse to the finesse of pretending to rebuild it; he did rebuild part of a wall; and the cellar and books were discovered in clearing the foundations.

From the convent of St. George, one distinguishes clearly on the west the ruins of an antient city, ascertained to have been the Babylon built by the Persians. They constitute merely a heap of rubbish, already described by former travellers.

Fostât is a long street, running parallel to the river, and occupying part of the space between Kahira and its bank. It nearly joins Misr-el-Attiké on the South.

Bulak is a large irregular town, which has gradually risen around the place of embarkation. It is marked by an extensive and convenient okal, built by Ali Bey the Great, and called the Alexandrian okal, being chiefly used for goods brought from that city. Gardens, filling the fertile grounds between the houses, and betwixt Bulak and Kahira, afford an ample supply of fruits and vegetables. Boats croud the river at Bulak, which is the port of Lower Egypt, as Misr-el-Attiké is of the Upper.

An

An island is situated in the middle of the river, nearly opposite Bulak, where Murad Bey has a kind of summer-house, or place of retirement. Here are also several gardens. On the opposite coast is Embabîl, a village, where cows are kept, that furnish excellent butter.

Farther to the south, and nearly opposite Misr-el-Attiké, is Jiza, a considerable town, fortified by Ismaîl Bey, who also built a palace there, completed and since inhabited by Murad Bey, by whom has been established a foundery, constructed by a Zanthiote, who has embraced Mohammedism. I found six mortars and twenty-three cannon, some of them however almost useless. Three of the mortars and six of the field-pieces, cast by that Zanthiote, were excellent, considering the place, the instruments, and the workmen. The guns are twenty-four, eighteen, and twelve pounders. These are in reserve, and the Bey has a larger number mounted, in different parts of the fort. The walls of Jiza are of great extent, and have only one gate to the country; they are ten feet high, three feet thick, and have six half-moons: but are only fit to resist cavalry, the original intention in raising them. Murad Bey has suffered the iron work about the loop-holes, &c. to be plundered or ruined.

The palace is in the southern quarter of Jiza, close to the water. It has numerous apartments for the Mamlûks, and every convenience for ease or luxury.

Murad Bey has, of late years, thought it neceſſary to inſtitute a marine; to effect which, he has cauſed three or four veſſels to be built, and has purchaſed ſome from the Europeans. The whole has been attended with no ſmall expenſe, and promiſes no adequate advantage. The largeſt of theſe veſſels carries twenty-four guns. Six of them were moored before Jiza, whence they cannot be navigated, except during the time of the Nile's increaſe. They were well appointed, and had their full complement of mariners, chiefly Greeks of the Archipelago, moderately ſkilful in their art, and receiving every encouragement from the Bey. They were commanded by a native of Sagos named *Nikóla reis*, Admiral, or Captain Nicholas.

Not far ſouth of Jiza is *Geziret-ed-dahab*, a ſmall iſland, intended, as appears, by Diodorus Siculus under the name of *Venus aurea*.

North-eaſt of the city are gardens, and ſome ſpacious houſes, the property of the great, who occaſionally leave the city to divert themſelves in this retreat; and have there an open ſpace, where the Mamlûks perform their military evolutions, and exerciſe their horſes. The ground under the mountains to the Eaſt is filled with tombs. The mountain is of white ſand and calcareous ſtone, and deſtitute of verdure.

The tomb of the Imâm Shafei is without the walls of the city, near the caſtle. It is in a moſque of good architecture, and kept in complete repair. On Friday, the day of devotion among the Mohammedans, the women being at liberty to viſit
the

the tombs of their relations, crowd to this mosque to provide substitutes, the place being the Daphne of Kahira, and sacred to the blandishments of Venus.

There is a much more considerable canal, styled *Chalige ibn Menji*, which, from its opening to the Nile near Bulak, extends to *Bilbeis*, (according to D'Anville, the *Pharbæthus* of antiquity, which Herodotus, Pliny, and Ptolemy, make the capital of a *Nome*,) where it joins another canal, and passes to the lake *Sheib*.

The pleasure boats used by the great on the increase of the Nile are very numerous. They are light and of elegant form; rowers from four to eight. Those for the women covered with wainscot; such as are for the use of the men, are covered above, and open at the sides, or only latticed. Others are kept for hire, like the Venetian gondolas. They are used in the chalige, and upon the river.

The gates of Kahira are numerous; but the most striking are two at the northern extremity of the city, called *Bab-el-Nasr*, and *Bab-el-Fituch*, which present a splendid display of Saracenic architecture.

Romeili is an open place, of an irregular form, where feats of juggling are performed. The charmers of serpents also seem worthy of remark, their powers appearing extraordinary. The serpent most common at Kahira is of the viper class, and undoubtedly poisonous. If one of them enter a house, the charmer is sent for, who uses a certain form of words. I have seen three serpents enticed out of the cabin of a ship, lying near the shore. The operator handled them, and then put them into a bag. At other times I have seen the serpents twist round the bodies of these Psylli in all directions, without having had their fangs extracted or broken, and without doing them any injury.

The Egyptians pretend to numerous kinds of magic. The powerful influence of the name of the Divinity, *Ism Ullah*, an account of which is contained in the *Kitab-el-rihani*, is supposed to work various miracles. The mode of its application is divided into *halál*, lawful, and *harâm*, unlawful. Though the practice terminate in perpetual disappointment, the credulous, who still confide in it, are not few. There are three or four places on the mountain, above Kahira, to which the Arabs ascribe some influence of magic. *El Maraga*, where they say the earth trembles. *Bir-el-kuffár*, the well of the infidels.—*Cassaat el Molúk*.—*Ain el Siré*, a spring of salt water, to which they attribute medical virtues.

The dancing girls form a distinct class. They are always attended by an old man and woman, who play on musical instruments, and look to the conduct of the girls, that they may not bestow their favours for an inadequate reward; for, though not chaste, they are by no means common. Their dances exhibit all that the most luxurious imagination can picture—all the

the peculiar motions and arts for which Martial has remarked the Egyptians as celebrated,

Nequitias Tellus fcit dare nulla magis.

Their forms are elegant, their faces rather expressive than beautiful.

The following amusements are chiefly exhibited during the Ramadân:

After breaking the fast by some refreshments, the prayer commences, which is a long one. The principal meal then has place, and then the arrival of strangers to pay their respects to the Bey, or to transact business, occupies some time. The amusements then commence. The Gerîd and various other exercises are practised by day-light, but at night wrestling is commonly the first. In this the lower class of people in Egypt shew considerable vigour and activity at least, though perhaps not consummate skill. When the Bey and his company are tired of these exercises, singers (male) appear. The plaintive vocal music of Kahira, and the agreeable sensations occasioned by it, have been the subject of remark to many who have described Egypt. Then appear the story-tellers, who with wonderful readiness and rapidity of utterance go through the romantic adventures resembling the *Thousand and One Nights*, of which the varieties are innumerable. These are succeeded by wits, who with droll and unexpected similies often set the company in fits of laughter. The adversary brings some similitude equally unexpected.—Whoever holds out the longest is rewarded as conqueror.—" Methel Sire"—" Let us wrestle in similies;" the other answers, " Ma Methel-lak"—" What is your similitude?"

" You.

" You are like the city afs, look fleek and carry dung." Some of these have really a portion of wit, and it is almost the only occasion that I remember, when the Arabs exhibit any thing that can properly be so denominated. The place of these, when they have received a present according to the pleasure of the Bey, is often supplied by female singers, who frequently accompany their voices with an instrument, touched like the guitar. There are women who are highly valued for this talent of amusing the public; and if any judgment may be formed from the manner in which they are sometimes rewarded, the gratification of their auditors is far from being moderate. There are occasions when some of the *Harem* exhibit their vocal powers in the presence of select company; but this is not common; and in that case the performer is concealed behind a curtain or lattice.

The last are the female dancers or *ghawasie*. These, it may be supposed, if they are able to fascinate the eye of the multitude, in the public streets, with only ordinary exertions, neglect not to have recourse to the more laboured blandishments of their art in the presence of a prince.

Pehlawán, rope-dancers, &c. are introduced, whose exertions are not contemptible.

Chefs and the Polish drafts are the only games that are indulged in, and in these some of the Beys are skilled. They play remarkably quick, and apparently without much premeditation. But habit has given this facility. They practise daily, and their minds are occupied by few objects.

Convenient

Convenient markets appear in every part of the city. Coffee-houses are equally numerous, where the natives pass a great part of the day smoking and conversing. These commonly consist of one apartment, not very large. Only coffee and fire for the pipe are furnished. But at Damascus I afterwards saw coffee-houses remarkably large, some of them placed over running water. The furniture is however very simple, and unlike the splendid apartments, for the same purposes, to be seen in Constantinople. One, in particular, at Damascus, under the castle wall, is capable at a very moderate calculation of holding one thousand persons: it has no walls, but an extensive roof spreads over numerous benches, and it is encircled with trees and water.

The number of small imposts in Egypt is almost inconceivable; they are estimated to amount to three hundred and sixty. One is for all goods crossing from Jiza to Kahira; a poor woman bringing a basket of eggs, worth two paras, must pay the fifth part of a para for passing. Upon the whole, the revenue can hardly be raised to a greater amount than it is.

In May 1792 there was a famine, occasioned by various accidental circumstances; and wheat sold at 20 and 22 patackes the *ardeb*. In October 1796 it was at five patackes. When I made my inquiries at the latter period, the following prices of provisions were stated:

    Mutton, per rotal, 10 paras.
    Beef,   ditto,   8 ditto.

Sugar,

Sugar, per rotal, 20 to 25 paras.
Sweet oil, ditto, 12 ditto.
Milk, ditto, 4 ditto.
Tobacco of Ladakìa, per oke, 45 to 70 paras.
Fowls, small, 12 paras each.

The recent history of Egypt, till the time of Ismaîl Bey, is sufficiently known. On the death of Ismaîl, Hassan Bey succeeded him in his office of Shech-el-bellad, governor of the city, and implying the precedence among the Beys. Hassan was soon expelled by Murad Bey, who held the office till the Capitan Pasha arrived from Constantinople with a fleet, and drove him into Upper Egypt. The Pasha, after satisfying his avarice, withdrew, and the Beys returned. Ibrahim Bey, who had been a slave of Ali Bey the Great, had however acquired such authority, that Murad was constrained to share the government with him; and they have since ruled Egypt, Ibrahim as *Shech-el-bellad*, and Murad as *Defter-dâr*. Mutual jealousies prevail between them, each seeking the destruction of the other. They however conspire together to recruit the number of the Mamlûks, and to collect treasure from all quarters.

These are considered as usurpers by the Beys of Upper Egypt, who are favoured by the Porte; one of whom, named Ali, contrived to escape from Saïd into Syria, where he courted the nearest Pasha, Jezzâr of Akka, to support their interest; but that potent and able leader refused to listen to his suggestions, or amused him with false hopes.

The year before I arrived, there had been a pestilence which had destroyed great numbers of the Mamlûks. The next memorable event was the contest with Alexandria, before stated.

To strengthen his interest, Ibrahim Bey had negotiated a marriage between his daughter and another powerful Bey, of the same name, but no relation. The wedding-day, 30th of August 1792, was celebrated with great pomp. A splendid equipage was prepared, in the European form, of a coach, drawn by two horses, and ornamented with wreaths of artificial flowers, in which a beautiful slave from the *harem*, personating the bride, whose features were very plain, was carried through the principal streets of Kahira. The blinds of the coach were however drawn up, and the fair deputy sat concealed. The procession was attended by some Beys, several officers and Mamlûks, and ended at the house of the bridegroom, who received her from the carriage in his arms. The Beys have baths in their houses, otherwise this procession, on arriving at the house of the bridegroom, would have attended the female to the bath, and then returned thither. In general, at Kahira, the bride, completely veiled, walks under a canopy, and supported by two women, to the house of the bridegroom.

The fête had continued for three days preceding the marriage. In the evening, fire-works were exhibited at the houses of the husband and the father, and presents of shawls, caffetans, and other parts of dress and money were liberally distributed. After consummation the ensanguined cloth was shown to the relations of the bride, especially the mother. The virgin had been before instructed

instructed by matrons in what manner to receive the conjugal embraces, and the same women remained in an adjoining chamber during this final ceremony, to lend assistance if required. The Oriental virgins marry in such early youth that the marks of their purity are seldom deficient.

A curious circumstance occurred to mark the systematic rapacity of the Beys, which could not be lulled even by such a season of festivity. Ibrahim Bey, the father of the bride, having heard that a company of female singers, who usually attend on these occasions, had been employed in singing in Birket-el-fil, the chief open place in the city, not only during the day, but also most part of the ensuing night, and had in consequence collected donations to a considerable amount, sent for the leading woman to his house. She, supposing that she had been summoned to receive some reward, or that the charms of her voice had been made known to the Bey, readily obeyed the mandate. On entering the apartment, the first question was, "How many half sequins (*nusfiat*) did you collect yesterday?"—She replied, "About ten thousand."—"Pay me eight thousand, then," said the Bey, "and I will give you a note of credit on Ibrahim Jeuhari, my secretary." The money was paid, but the woman was turned out of the house without receiving any security whatever. She is said to have died of the disappointment a short time after.

Some negotiations took place that summer between the Beys here, and those in Upper Egypt (whom I afterwards found at Isna, attended by a small party of Mamlûks); the former were so powerful that they rejected the applications of the latter. All continued quiet till I went to Upper Egypt.

I shall now endeavour to give some idea of the most celebrated Beys, who at present have the sway in this unhappy country. Ibrahim Bey is upwards of sixty years of age, a tall thin man, with an aquiline nose. He is very avaricious, but by his treasures and connections has secured a large party. His Mamlûks may amount to about a thousand. Though reputed to manage the sabre with dexterity, he has nothing of enterprise in his character, which has the mean rapacity of the vulture, nothing of the daring flight of the eagle.

Murad Bey, once his superior, now his equal in power, has passed a life of tumult and activity. Originally a slave of Mohammed Bey Abu-dhahab, at the head of a detachment of his master's Mamlûks, he defeated and made prisoner Ali Bey the great, whose death shortly after ensued. Murad is detested by the Porte. He is an energetic character, and his profusion is supplied by his rapacity: about forty-five years of age, of a replete habit of body. His Mamlûks, in 1796, amounted to about seventeen hundred. His party, though not so numerous as that of Ibrahim Bey, is yet of a more decided and military stamp. Murad Bey is married to the widow of his master, the daughter of the celebrated Ali Bey.

Next in power is Mohammed Bey Elfi, a young man of not more than thirty-five years: his name imports that he was bought for a thousand patackes. His master was Murad Bey, just mentioned.

Quick in apprehension, impetuous in action. Mamlûks eight hundred. Power great and increasing.

Ibrahim Bey, *el Uali*, a name derived from the second military magistracy in the city, is a young man, about the same age with the last. He is married, as has been mentioned, to the daughter of the elder Ibrahim; and is firmly attached to his interests. Of a sedate, yet firm character. Mamlûks six or seven hundred.

Aiûb Bey, *el zogheir*, or junior, is another powerful leader, perhaps the most eminent in capacity among the whole, and on all occasions consulted by the rest. His age, between thirty and forty. Mamlûks not many. He is a prudent manager, and rarely accused of extortion.

Fatmé, now the aged daughter of the famous Ali, is held in much respect by all the Beys. Even Murad, her husband, stands reverently in her presence. When a Bey is appointed to a government, he never fails to pay a visit to this old lady, who lectures him on his duties; and will say, " Do not pillage the people; they were always spared by my father."

CHAP. VII.

Abstract of the history of Africa in general, and Egypt in particular, under the domination of the Arabs.

As this portion of history is little known, and may lend illustration to many topics discussed in these pages, I have been induced to insert a brief idea of it, abstracted chiefly, in what regards Africa, from the valuable work of Cardonne, a compilation which has saved me much research into the original writers *.

Syria and Persia had already fallen under the rapid progress of the followers of Mohammed, and it was so early as the 19th year of the Hejira, the 640th of the Christian æra, that the Chalif Omar commanded Amrû to subdue Egypt. Memphis, or Misr, submitted through the treason of the governor; but Alexandria stood a siege of fourteen months. The loss of the library has been much regretted; it was probably replete with the absurd philosophy and divinity of the times; and amid the

---

* Histoire de l'Afrique, et de l'Espagne sous la domination des Arabes; composée sur differens Manuscrits Arabes de la Bibliotheque du Roi, par M. Cardonne, &c. Paris 1765, 3 tomes 12mo. It is to be regretted that the learned author did not divide his work into epochs and chapters, and particularly separate the history of Africa from that of Spain.

number

number of libraries in the Greek empire, it is impossible to conceive, that the work of any truly valuable author should have existed only in one copy.

A. D. 643. A famine desolating Arabia, Amrû re-opened the canal, formed by the Romans from Memphis to the Red Sea. The capital seat of the Chalifs being soon after removed from Medina to Damascus, it was neglected and went to ruin.

A. D. 647. Abd-ullah, governor of Egypt, proceeds to the conquest of Africa. He vanquishes the Greek patrician Gregory in the battle of Yakûb.

PART I.

AFRICA.

THIS and the subsequent events are so ably narrated by Mr. Gibbon*, that it would be presumptuous to enter the same ground. It is sufficient to observe that the Arabs, alternately advancing and repulsed, were not complete masters of Africa, or rather that portion of this vast continent which extends along the Mediterranean Sea, till about the year 709 of our æra. They had not only been opposed by the Greeks, but by the *Berbers*, or natives of the West. These Berbers were, according to Cardonne, an ancient Arabian colony, which had

---

* Vol. ix. p. 448—466, 8vo.

migrated

migrated into Africa, and retained its native speech. They were divided into five tribes, which now amount to about six hundred lineages, partly dwelling under tents, and partly in towns and villages.

Mûsa ben Nasr had effectuated the conquest of Africa before he proceeded to that of Spain. Till this period Africa had remained an appendage to the government of Egypt, which was in quiet submission to the Chalîfs, successors of Mohammed. But Abd-el-aziz, governor of Egypt, having been guilty of great extortions from Hassan the general in Africa, the Chalîf, Walid I. had assigned to Mûsa an independent authority.

Mohammed-ben-Yezîd succeeded Mûsa in the government of Africa.

A. D. 721. Nechrên Seffran was appointed governor of Africa by the Chalîf Yezîd, and died in 727, after having made some incursions into the interior of that continent.

The natives soon after revolted against the Arabs, whom they defeated with great slaughter.

A. D. 741. Hantele-ben-Seffran, governor of Egypt, was sent against them by the Chalîf Hakim. He succeeded in his enterprise; subdued the insurgents with great slaughter, and regained possession of Cairoan, the Arabian capital of Africa, founded by Akbal, about A. D. 670, fifty miles to the south of Tunis.

The

The revolt reviving, Hantelé again conquered the rebels, whose vast army was conducted by Abd-el-wahhad. The exaggeration of the Arabian authors computes the insurgents slain at an hundred and sixty thousand; and Hantelé, in giving an account of his operations to the Chalif Hakim, reported that a more sanguinary contest had never been fought.

A. D. 749. The sceptre of the Chalifs passing from the Ommiades to the Abbassides, Abd-el-rachmân, governor of Africa, refused tribute, assembled the people in the mosque of Cairoan, tore his robe, and abjured the authority of the new Chalif.

Abd-el-rachmân being slain by his brothers, a civil war arose.

A. D. 772. The Chalif Abu-Mansùr Djafar sends Yezid with a strong army to regain Africa. He succeeds, re-establishes tranquillity, and attracts arts and manufactures to Cairoan the capital.

A. D. 786. On the death of Yezîd, the Chalif names Dawûd, son of that leader, to be his successor. Dawûd conquers the insurgent Berbers, and accepts the government of Egypt; his uncle, Ruhh-ben Chatem, succeeding him in that of Africa.

SECT.

SECT. I.

Dynasty of the Aglabites.

A. D. 800. It was under the reign of the famous Harôn-el-Rashîd, that Ibrahim ben-el-Aghleb, governor of Africa, finally threw off the yoke of the Chalif of Damascus. Ibrahim secured his authority by maintaining a regular body of troops; and died in 811, being succeeded by his son Abu-'l-abbâs.

Ziadet-Ullah, his successor, subdued Sicily.

837. Abu Akkal ascended the throne of Africa.

840. The next prince, Abu-'l-abbâs, reigned thirty-four years; humane, liberal, and a lover of justice. He was however too much addicted to the pleasures of the table; and it is related, that one day being in a state of intoxication in the town of Sût, he embarked for the isle of Kûssa, and when the fumes of the wine had evaporated, was not a little surprised to find himself in the open sea.

874. Abu-'l-Abbâs had obtained of his brother Ishak an open renunciation, in the chief mosque of Cairoan, of all claim to the crown; yet that prince seized it on his death, to the prejudice of the former's son. Ishak built a new town, called Rifadé.

A. D. 877. Iſhak ſends a fleet againſt Sicily. Syracuſe is beſieged for nine months, taken, ſacked, and all the inhabitants put to the ſword. The booty of that commercial city was immenſe.

The Egyptians invaded Africa, and beſieged Tripoli, but were forced to retire on the approach of Iſhak, with his regular negro troops.

878. A dreadful famine in Africa; corn at eight pieces of gold the buſhel.

Iſhak was a moſt cruel prince. It is reported that he put to death, in one day, ſixteen of his own natural daughters by various concubines. His mother preſenting him with two beautiful female ſlaves, he ſent her in return a platter covered with a napkin; on lifting it up, inſtead of jewels as ſhe expected, ſhe beheld the heads of the two ſlaves. He was ſucceeded by his ſon Abu-'l-Abbàs-Abd-ullah, murdered by his brother Ziadet-Ullah, who ſeized the ſceptre of Africa.

908. A revolt ariſing, the timid Ziadet-Ullah abandoned his dominions, and retired to Egypt, then governed by Baſi-el-Nùchiſi, in the name of Mûktadir-b'illah, eighteenth Chalif of the dynaſty of the Abbaſſides. With Ziadet-Ullah expired the dynaſty of the Aglabites, which had ruled Africa for an hundred and eight years [*].

[*] Their authority did not extend over the ancient Mauritania. The Edriſſite dynaſty ruled Ceuta, Fez, Tangier, &c. Fez was built by them in 788.

SECT.

SECT. II.

Dynasty of the Fatimites, or Ismaëlians.

Obeid-ullah, who had seized the authority, resigned it soon after to his son Abu-'l-Cassim. Though the new family was of Egyptian extract, it pretended to deduce its origin from Fâtmé, daughter of Mohammed, through Ismael the sixth Imâm of the posterity of Ali.

Abu-'l-Cassim assuming the style of *Mahadi*, or real successor of Ali, displayed talents that sanctioned his usurpation. In the first year of his reign he subdued the Edrissites of the West, and united all the Mohammedan part of Africa.

A. D. 912. Abu-'l-Cassim pours three armies into Egypt, intending to add that rich province to his other domains. The Chalîf Mûktadir, then reigning at Bagdad, had foreseen this design, which was frustrated by the defeat of the armies of Mahadi, though he took Alexandria. He built a city called Mehedié, now Mahdié, on the African shore, which he destined for the seat of his empire. He died in the sixty-third year of his age and twenty-sixth of his reign.

A. D. 933. His son Achmed was less fortunate. He died while his capital Mehedié was besieged by insurgents.

A. D. 945. Ismaïl his son defeated the rebels, and built Mansûrich in Africa.

952. Abu-Tammim succeeded Ismaïl his father. In 968, he sent Jeuhar, a Greek, at the head of a strong army to seize Egypt, and succeeded. The capital, then styled *Misr*, or *Fostat*, opened its gates. Jeuhar built a new capital, which he named *Kahira*, or the *Victorious*. Abu-Tammim, surnamed Moaz, in the twentieth year of his reign embarked for Sardinia, then subject to Africa, till Jeuhar should complete the new metropolis.

972. Abu-Tammim lands at Alexandria, where he is met by Jeuhar: advancing to Kahira he was welcomed by the acclamations of his new subjects. To this city he removed all his treasures, and even the bodies of his ancestors.

Jeuhar, the founder, had desired the building to be begun under the horoscope or ascendant of the planet Mars, called *Kahir*, or conqueror, by the Arabs; and hence it was styled Kahira.

The dynasty of the Fatimites, now transplanted to Egypt, ruled there till the year 1171, (Hejira 566,) when it was supplanted by Salah-el-din, the famous Saladin of the Christian authors.

SECT.

SECT. III.

Dynasty of the Zeirites.

To return to Africa. Abu-Tammim, before he proceeded to Egypt, had resigned the sovereignty of Africa, on condition of homage, to Yussuf-ben-Zeiri, of a family sprung from Arabia Felix.

The people of the province of Muggrib having rebelled, Yussuf defeated them; and Tremesen shewing a disposition to join the Muggrebins, it was razed, and the inhabitants transplanted to Aschir. Another revolt was equally unsuccessful: the chiefs were led in triumph through the streets of Cairoan, and then put to death.

979. Yussuf seized Fez and Sejelmas; and the Chalifs of Spain lost all their African possessions, except Ceuta.

983. Abu-'l-Cassim Mansûr succeeded his father. He built a palace in the city of Cairoan, which cost eight hundred thousand pieces of gold. His cruelty was shewn in the murder of Abd-ullah his minister, and even in the punishment of the ungrateful rebel Abu-'l-Fahm, whose heart this prince is said to have torn from his body and devoured.

996. His son Abu-Menad received the homage of his nobles in Sardinia, long subject to Africa. The Fatimite Chalif
of

of Egypt sent him the dress and sabre, the accustomed mark of their superiority over the African monarchy.

Moaz, his son and successor, displayed his rage against heretics, or those Mohammedans who differed from his own sect, by an universal massacre. A Roman Catholic prince, misled by his priests, could not have shewn more inveterate cruelty. Moaz was however so young, that the blame rests with his ministers.

A. D. 1050. An important war arose between Moaz and Mostansir, Chalif of Egypt, who wished to revive the absolute dominion of his house over Africa. The Egyptians entered the province of Muggrib, by the town of Zenata. Four years after they seized Tripoli. Mûnis, governor of the province of Cairoan, passed over to the enemy. Moaz lost a pitched battle, and took shelter in Mehedié. The Egyptians seized his capital Cairoan, stopped the springs, turned the course of the river, and destroyed the magnificent palaces and delicious gardens of the monarchs of Africa. Moaz, overwhelmed with his misfortunes, sunk into the grave, and closed a long and fortunate reign in the utmost misery.

1061. Tamîm, his eldest son, succeeded to the sceptre.

1088. The Greeks and Franks, equipping a fleet of four hundred sail, landed at the isle of Kûssa in Africa, which they ravaged. They then seized the town of Zawilé, but retired on
receiving

receiving a contribution of 200,000 pieces of gold. The conquest of Sicily by the Normans had given a military impulse, which Africa was often to feel.

A. D. 1107. Tamîm died, leaving the reputation of a just and generous prince. Having once purchased a slave, and her master, who was enamoured with her, deeply regretting the loss, Tamîm not only restored her, but sent him magnificent presents.

1108. Yaiah, his son and successor, put to death three alchymists, who had misled him by their vain pretensions.

1115. Yaiah died suddenly. Being addicted to astrology, he imagined a particular day would be fatal to him, and passed it in prayer. In the evening, happy that he had escaped the danger, he ordered a magnificent festival, and died as he sat down to table. His son Ali received the homage of his people at Mehedić.

1116. Ali suppressed the pirates of the isle of Gerbi, and received Tunis on submission. The people of Sebât, who robbed the caravans, were severely punished.

1121. Ali prepared a fleet of ten vessels of the first rank, and thirty of the second, against Sicily. Death prevented his designs.

His son Hassan being only in his fifteenth year, dissentions arose among the great.

1125. A Sicilian fleet ravaged the isle of Gerbi.

1146. The Sicilians seized Tripoli, which they held six months, and then retired.

A dreadful famine in Africa, so that even human carcases were devoured. Many of the inhabitants fled to Sicily.

Roger king of Sicily sent out a fleet of an hundred and fifty sail, loaded with soldiers and ammunition. Having captured an African ship, with some pigeons on board, Georgi the Christian admiral forced the captain to write a letter, importing that the Sicilian fleet had sailed to Constantinople. The pigeon flew back to Mehedié; and the inhabitants were exulting in the intelligence, when the hostile fleet appeared before the city. On landing, the Sicilians found the place totally abandoned, and the pillage lasted ten hours. Sfax and Sus were also taken; and the Sicilians became masters of all the coast from Tripoli to Tunis.

These events, accompanied with intestine commotions, terminated the rule of the Zeirite dynasty. Hassan-ben-Ali was the last prince.

SECT. IV.

Dynasty of the Marabûts, called by the Spanish authors Al-Moravides.

Marabût implies a saint; and this dynasty arose to power from a pretended zeal for religion. It originated in the West of Africa, about the year 1060. Yuſſuf the second prince, in the year 1069 founded Morocco; he conquered part of Spain, and died in 1106. His son Ali was less fortunate, and the short-lived dynasty of the Marabûts was followed by that of the Elmohâds or Unitarians.

SECT. V.

Dynasty of the Elmohâds.

This dynasty originated in Mount Atlas. Tomrût, its founder, was followed by his celebrated disciple Abd-el-mûmin, originally a doctor of theology, but who displayed such talents in war, that Ali, king of Morocco, after meeting with many defeats, died in despair.

Abd-el-mûmin aspiring to the universal sovereignty of the Mohammedans in Africa, besieged and took Oran and Fez, A. D. 1142. Tasfîn, son of Ali, hardly retained Morocco, which was taken by Abd-el-mûmin from Ishak his successor, the last of the Marabût dynasty.

1150.

1150. The Moors of Spain having suffered great losses, sent to Abd-el-mûmin to request his aid against the Christians. That ambitious prince eagerly seized the opportunity, and sent several armies into Spain. The following year he conquered Bugia in Africa.

1159. The Sicilians retaining Tunis, and other places on the coast in the Eastern part of Africa, Abd-el-mûmin equipped a fleet, and left Morocco at the head of one hundred thousand combatants. Tunis was taken by treason. Mehedié, surrounded by the sea, except one part which was strongly fortified, was bravely defended by the Sicilians, and their king sent a fleet to their assistance. It was defeated by that of the Mûslims, and famine forced the garrison to surrender.

Abd-el-mûmin, being acknowleged sovereign of all Mohammedan Africa, resolved on the conquest of Spain; but death unexpectedly seized him at Sallî in 1160. He was succeeded by Abu-Yakûb his son.

1180. Abu-Yakûb carried his arms into Spain, where he received the homage of several Arabian princes. He was constrained to return to Africa, on intelligence arriving that a horde of Turks, who had passed from Egypt, had seized Tripoli, and other places. Sfax had also revolted. These commotions were appeased; and, at Mehedié, Abu-Yakûb renewed the truce with Sicily for ten years.

1184.

1184. Abu-Yakûb invades Spain, is defeated, and killed. Yakûb his son succeeded him.

The El-Moravides, who had fled to Spain, endeavoured to regain their power in Africa. They were supported by the Turks of Tripoli; but Yakûb took that city, and razed its walls.

1195. Yakûb defeats Alfonso king of Castille at Rema near Cordova, and besieges Toledo. He makes other campaigns in Spain.

1199. Yakûb dies at Sallî, in his forty-eighth year. The sceptre passes to Mohammed-el-Nasîr his son.

Mohammed lost all that his ancestors had possessed in Spain.

1210. He attempts to recover his Spanish territories at the head of 600,000 men, according to the wonted exaggerations of the Arabs; but is completely defeated at the famous battle called *Akal* by the Arabs, and *Vanos-Tolosa* by the Spaniards. Mohammed died of vexation the following year. The Elmohâds had possessed Valencia, Seville, Carmona, &c.

1211. Yussuf, son of Mohammed, proved a voluptuous and feeble prince. He reigned twelve years, and died without posterity.

1223. Abd-el-wahhad, his great uncle, succeeded, or was chosen by the grandees. The same year the royal title was transferred to Abd-ullah his nephew, who was murdered by rebels.

1226. Edrîs-ben-Yakûb, brother of Abd-ullah, became king of Africa, and used great cruelties to establish his authority. After reigning five years, he died of an apoplexy.

1231. His son Abd-el-wahhad succeeded, and was drowned when bathing. Other princes of this dynasty were, Said-Abul, 1242; Umer, 1248; Wasîk-Abul, 1266. In this usurper closed the dynasty of the Elmohâds.

Upon the fall of this powerful dynasty, Africa was divided into those petty royalties which still subsist, with few variations.

The family of the *Merinis* became masters of Fez and Morocco, and were the most powerful of the successors of the Elmohâds.

The Abi-Hafs seized Tunis; and the Beni Ziân enjoyed Tremesen.

Abu-'l-Haffan, fultan of Morocco, became fovereign by conqueft, about A. D. 1347, of all the African ftates; but this power was only a momentary meteor.

About the year 1500 an ambitious *Sherif*, or defcendant of Mohammed, feized the fovereignty of Morocco; and his defcendants, under the ftyle of Sherîfs, retain the power to this day.

The kingdom of Tremefen, on the Eaft of Fez, contained Algier, Oran, &c. It was feized by the Beni Ziân about A. D. 1249. On the death of the laft of that race, A. D. 1560, it was united to the Turkifh Deydom of Algier.

The power of the Turks in Africa is very recent. It began in 1514, when the pirate Barbaroffa feized Algier; and piracy, as is too well known, has become an appendage of their dominion.

Tunis became fubject to the Abi-Hafs about A. D. 1240. Abu-Zekeria, the firft prince, is faid to have extended his contribution to the country of the negroes. A. D. 1270, St. Louis, attacking Tunis, perifhed by a peftilence.

In 1533 Barbaroffa feized Tunis. The expedition of Charles V. 1535, is well known; but the African marygold is its only permanent product. The race of the Abi Hafs terminated in 1570, when El-Wahhali, a defcendant of Barbaroffa, and Dey of Algier,

gier, took poffeffion of Tunis. The Mohammedan power, on the North and Weft of Africa, remains divided between the Sherifs of Morocco and Fez, and the Turks of Algier and Tunis.

PART II.

EGYPT.

EGYPT remained for a confiderable time in quiet fubjection to the Chalifs, fucceffors of Mohammed. But their power being on the decline, owing to the infolence of their Turcoman militia, the janizaries of that period, and other caufes, this fertile country began to throw off the yoke.

DYNASTY I.

The Tholonides.

In the year of the Hejira 265, A. D. 879, Achmed, fon of Tholon or Teilûn, governor of Egypt, ufurped the fovereignty from the Chalif Motamid-b'-illah. This fhort-lived dynafty expired in Sultan Harôn, grandfon of the ufurper, about thirty years after.

DYNASTY II.

The Fatimites.

The conqueft of Egypt by Abu-Tammîm, Sultan of Africa, has been already mentioned.

975.

EGYPT, AND SYRIA.

975. Abu-Tammîm or Moaz was succeeded by his son Aziz. He carried on several wars in Syria.

996. Hakim, his successor, is only famed for his cruelty.

1021. Daher, fourth Chalif of Egypt, conquered Aleppo, but was forced to abandon it.

1036. Abu-Tamîm Mostansir. In the reign of this Chalif most of the Egyptian possessions in Syria were lost.

1094. Mostali. This Chalif, in 1098, regained Jerusalem from the Turks; next year it was taken by the Franks, under Godefroy de Boulogne.

1101. Amer, a child. The Wizîr Afdhal exercised the sovereignty during his reign of thirty years.

1130. Hafed.

1149. Dafer. In his Chalifate the Christians took Ascalon.

1155. Fayez.

1160. Aded. The Fatimite race had before this period sunk into such imbecility, that the Wizirs held the whole executive power. Shawûr, the *reigning* Wizir, having been supplanted by the intrigues of Dargham, passed to Syria, to implore the

assistance

assistance of Nûr-el-dîn, Sultan of Damascus*. In 1164 his request was complied with. Shirakûk, called Syracon by the Christian writers, and his nephew, the famous Salah-el-dîn, or Saladin, were sent to re-establish Shawûr, who soon finding his associates too powerful, formed an alliance with the Franks. Shirakûk however defeated all his projects; and in 1169 procured an order from the Chalîf Aded for the decapitation of Schawûr, with the robe and firmân of wizîr for himself. He died in the same year, and was succeeded by his nephew Saladin.

1171. Saladin obliges the Franks to evacuate Egypt. An enemy of the Fatimites, from religious schism, he omits the name of Aded, in the public prayers, and substitutes that of the Chalîf of Bagdad. Aded died on the 13th of September 1171; and in him terminated the dynasty of the Fatimites. His successors renounced the title of Chalîf, and assumed only that of Sultans.

* The power of the Chalifs, successors of Mohammed, had fallen about the middle of the eleventh century. The Turks, a Tataric nation, seized Iconium, and most of Asia Minor, about 1074. Twenty years after, Aleppo and Damascus became separate sovereignties under the grandsons of Elf Arslân; the former city had been long subject to the Chalifs of Egypt.

DYNASTY III.

The Aiûbite Sultans.

Salah-ed-din, son of Aiûb, a Kurd, usurped the title of Sultan of Egypt in 1174. Not contented with that sovereignty, he extended his views to Syria. In 1177 he is defeated at Ramlé by Rainaud de Chatillon.

1182. More success attended his arms in Syria; and next year he seized Amida in Mesopotamia, and forced Aleppo to a capitulation.

1187. Saladin gains over the Franks his famous victory at Hittîn: the Christian power falls, and Saladin becomes master of Jerusalem on the 2d of October.

1189. The Franks besiege Akka, or Ptolemais, which did not surrender till after it had been invested for two years.

1192. Saladin concludes a truce with Richard king of England. Akka and Yaffa were almost the only places left to the Franks.

Saladin died on the 4th March 1193, aged only fifty-seven, leaving sixteen sons and a daughter.

1193. Malek-el-Azîz, second son of Saladin. He seized Damascus, and left to his brother only Samosata.

1198. Malek-el-Mansûr. His uncle Afdhal, prince of Samosata, was called by the Emîrs to rule the kingdom during the minority, by the title of Atabek.

1200. Adel-Seif-el-dîn, brother of Saladin, usurps the crown.

1209. The Franks penetrate into Egypt, and retire with considerable booty. Nine years afterward they returned, and seized the isle Pharos and Damiatt.

1218. Malek-el-Kâmel, son of Seif-el-dîn. The crusaders abandon Damiatt in 1221.

1228. Malek surrenders, by treaty, Jerusalem, Bethlehem, Nazareth, and Sidon, to Frederic II. the Emperor of Germany.

1239. Malek Adel deposed by his brother.

1240. Malek Salah. In 1244 he defeated the Franks and Syrians, who were about to penetrate into Egypt.

1249. St. Louis seized Damiatt; and in the same year Malek Salah died.

He

He had bought from the Tatars a number of Turkish slaves from Kaptchak, to form a guard and marine. These he raised to the highest employments; and they became the famous MAMLÛKS, who seized the sovereignty of Egypt.

1249. Turân Shah, son of Malek. Next year he captures St. Louis, and his army of 20,000. On the 1st May 1250, Turân Shah is massacred by the Mamlûks, who assign the sceptre to his step-mother, and afterwards to a boy of the Aiubite race, which in him closed its domination over Egypt.

MAMLUKS.

SECT. I.

Baharite Mamluks.

THESE were so styled, from having been originally employed as *mariners* on board the ships of the Sultan of Egypt. They were Turks.

A. D. 1254. Ezz-ed-dîn Moaz Ibegh was the first sovereign of this dynasty. He was assassinated.

1255. Nûr-ed-dîn Ali, son of Sultan Ezz-ed-dîn, followed.

It would be uninteresting to mark the names and short reigns of these princes, most of whom fell by assassination. The chief events alone shall be commemorated.

Bibars I. who reigned from A. D. 1260 to 1277, was an active prince, and seized most of the Christian possessions in Syria.

Kalil Ascraf, who ascended the throne in 1290, took Ptolemais, and terminated the power of the Christians in Palestine.

During successive reigns many contests took place in Syria, the possession of which was disputed by the Mamlûk Sultans and the Moguls.

Nazr Mohammed, who died in 1341, distinguished himself by the protection which he granted to agriculture and the arts.

In 1348 a pestilence appeared in Egypt, or perhaps originally in Syria, which spread over a great part of Europe.

A. D. 1365. In October, Peter de Lusignan, king of Cyprus, besieged Alexandria; but he was soon constrained to abandon it, for want of provisions*. Shabân Ascráf was then Sultan, and

---

* This expedition remains in considerable obscurity, though it may be regarded as the last dying spark of the crusades, as the adventurers seem to have been of several nations. Fordun, *Scotichr.* vol. ii. p. 488, mentions Norman Lesley,

and he was the first who ordered the Sherifs, or descendants of the Prophet, to wear a green turban.

SECT. II.

Borgite Mamlûks.

This race was of Circassian extract, and continued to rule Egypt till the French invasion.

1382. Barkûk-Daher, who had been Atabek in the minority of Hadgi Salah, deposed his pupil, and seized the supreme authority. Timûr invading Syria, Barkûk obtained two victories over the Moguls, and forced them to withdraw.

1399. Faradj, son of Barkûk. Few of these Sultans reigned above a year, till

1442. Bursbai, who reigned sixteen. He sent a fleet against Cyprus, which took Lymissos and Nicosia, and brought John II. and most of his nobility, captives. Syria remained almost a constant appanage to Egypt.

1461. Abu-'l-Fathe Achmed received tribute from Cyprus, and assigned the crown to James, natural son of John III.

Lesley, his countryman, as a prime actor. There was an old Scottish poem on the feats of Sir Walter, his brother, Duke of Leygaroch in France. *Ibid.* and Maitland's Poems.

Of the succeeding Sultans we find nothing remarkable; and the Mamlûk aristocracy began to render their station more and more precarious.

In 1501 Kansû El-ghûri was raised to the throne.

In 1516, Selim II. emperor of Constantinople, having declared war against him, defeated and slew him near Aleppo, and seized Syria.

Tomàn Bey was appointed his successor by the Mamlûks. On the 24th January 1517, he lost, at Rodania near Kahira, a great battle against the Othman troops. After another obstinate conflict, Tomàn Bey was again defeated by Selim, taken prisoner, and hanged at one of the gates of Kahira on the 13th April.

Selim was contented with abolishing the *monarchy* of the Mamlûks, but suffered their *aristocracy* to retain its former power, on certain conditions; the chief of which were, an annual tribute, obedience in matters of faith to the Mufti of Constantinople, and the insertion of the name of the Othman Emperors in the prayers, and on the coin.

Syria, its usual appanage, being withdrawn, Egypt has rarely intermeddled with foreign affairs, and the Beys have generally been contented with squeezing the people, and enjoying

ing in cafe the fruit of their extortions. During the pre-eminence of the Othman power, Egypt appears one of the moſt quiet and ſubmiſſive of the provinces: and the travellers of this and the two preceding centuries may ſupply what few materials ariſe, concerning its hiſtory, or rather its condition. The evening of the Turkiſh domination was marked by the appearance of that meteor, Ali Bey, who had ſcarcely dazzled the nations with his wild effulgence before he diſappeared.

CHAP. VIII.

UPPER EGYPT.

Design to penetrate into Habbesh or Abyssinia—Voyage on the Nile—Description of Assiut—General course of the Nile—Islands and villages—Caverns—Kaw—Achmim—Painted caverns—Girgi—Dendera—Antient Temple—Kous—Topography of Upper Egypt—El-wah-el-Ghurbi—Situation of the Oasis parva.

EVER eager to accomplish my proposed journey into Abyssinia, I was nevertheless not able to set out till Monday 10th of September, and, even then, not with all the advantages that might have been expected. I had indeed employed part of the summer, which was passed in Kahira, in learning the Arabic language; which is a task of difficulty to those who are unable to supply the utter want of books, and method and perspicuity in the teacher. My friends were forward in representing the dangers to be encountered, rather than in furnishing the means of avoiding them. I determined to adopt such a method as an imperfect knowlege of the country suggested as the least exceptionable, and leave the rest to fortune. Judging that I should yet have occasion for an interpreter, I took care to provide a Greek, who, besides his native language, was acquainted with the Turkish, Arabic, and Italian. I had also with me a Mohammedan of the lower class of Kahirines, who, as belongs

to

to that character, was prepared for every office. Thus provided, we commenced our voyage, and on the eighth day reached Affiût.

If we except some few inconveniences from the motley company that fills the boats, it is not easy to conceive a more pleasurable mode of travelling than that by the Nile when it overflows. The great body of water, perfectly calm and unruffled, the banks on each side covered with the rich product of the husbandman's labour, form a scene in every sense alluring. The passengers are protected by a simple awning of branches from the immediate action of the sun, and the great heat of the tropical latitude is assuaged by a gentle breeze, which generally continues during four or five meridian hours. The mariners chaunt responsive to the motion of their oars; and the vessel offers an apt emblem of smiling fortune in her most prosperous career.

I landed near Affiût, and went to an okal in that city to lodge. Here I suffered no kind of inconvenience.—A small room, dry and perfectly quiet, not infested with vermin, answered the purpose of security to property; and in this climate, at such a season, no shelter is required except from the sun's rays. Affiût is, at this time, by far the most considerable city in the higher Egypt. This character formerly belonged to Girgi, which is in effect still a place of note, but less so than Affiût. The situation is in all respects favourable, and the manner in which the water is conducted round the town is worthy of remark. A canal, dug probably from an early period, parallel to the Nile, in this part of the country laves the foot of the mountains which are near to Affiût, and having furrounded that city, and the villages adjacent, defcends again into the river. The water, however, is not admitted into it but at a certain period of its increafe, and then it overflows all the furrounding lands, and Affiût only communicates with the Nile, by a road, artificially raifed above the common level, which leads down to the point where the boats refort, and are laden and difcharged; and by two bridges, the one leading to this road, and the other towards the mountains.

It has become much more populous within a few years by the good government of Solyman Bey, who has alfo adorned it by planting many trees. Affiût was formerly known to the Arabic writers by the name of *bâut-es-Sultân*, the king's fifh, or fifh-pond, for حوض fignifies both. It would be curious to inquire from what circumftance; whether from having been appointed to fupply the king's table with fifh, or what other reafon? The mountains above Affiût abound with caverns which have probably originally anfwered the purpofe of fepulture, and then, in the Chriftian age, may have been the refort of perfons who fought religious retirement. There are fome hieroglyphic infcriptions, but nothing very remarkable, and they have been already defcribed by former travellers, fo that it is not neceffary to give a detailed account of them here. The principal antiquities between Kahira and Affiût, are at Shech Abade*, the

---

* This place takes its name from the tomb of a Chriftian ecclefiaftic, called *Ammon-el-abed*, or the devout; its other name is *Enfené*, evidently from that of *Antinous*.

antient

antient Antinoopolis, and at Ashmunein. In the former are two Corinthian columns, highly adorned, standing diagonally opposed to each other, and having each a Greek inscription. The first words of the one are as follow,

ΑΓΑΘΗ ΤΥΧΗ

ΑΥΤΟΚΡΑΤΟΡΙ ΚΑΙΣΑΡΙ ΜΑΡΚΩ ΑΥΡΗΛΙΩ.

The next word appears to be ΣΕΚΟΥΝΔΩ, but it is obliterated *.

Having passed about fourteen days in Assiût, waiting for a boat to go forward, which, in this season, when the corn is transported into the magazines, it is rather difficult to find, at length was able to hire one, of a moderate size, and entirely devoted to ourselves. We left Assiût on the 4th of October, and passed the night before a village called Mehâla. It has been built by a certain Osman Bey, within twenty years; and however destitute of any spirit of improvement persons of this description may be thought in Europe, this village is an evidence of some attention thereto; for the four streets of which it consists are at right angles with each other, built in right lines, and four times as wide as what is generally seen in places of the same kind. It is true, the materials are mean, and the number of houses inconsiderable.

The villagers of the Upper Egypt are at little expense for building. Clay and unburned bricks, the chief materials used

* The remainder might be easily copied, but circumstances did not then permit me to give the time necessary for that purpose.

in fabricating houfes, are to be had for the labour of collecting or forming them. The fame may be faid of the thatch; and the date tree, though perifhable, furnifhes the timber required. If a carpenter be employed, his time is not occupied in preparing ufelefs ornaments. In the towns however, as Ghenné, Affiût, Girgi, &c. the habitations are conftructed of better materials, with much more art, and are fome of them fumptuous.

Many confiderable iflands exift in the courfe of the Nile, but they are too frequently changing place, in confequence of new depofitions of mud, to admit of their being marked with permanent accuracy.

The number of towns and villages which I diftinguifhed on the Eaftern fide between Kahira and Affuân, amounted to about one hundred and fixty.

On the Weftern, where the cultivable lands are more extended, two hundred and twenty-eight. Yet they cannot be enumerated very accurately in paffing on the ftream; for there are many within the limits of the arable land on both fides, but principally on the Weft, which are not vifible from the river, and the names and numbers of which the circumftances then exifting did not permit me to learn from thofe to whom I could have recourfe for information.

The

The more populous of the towns seem to be those which follow:

East of the Nile.	West of the Nile.
1. Achmîm.	1. Benesoef.
2. Ghenné.	2. Mînié; city.
3. Kous.	3. Melawi.
4. Assuân.	4. Monfalût; city.
	5. Assiût; city.
	6. Tachta.
	7. Girgi; city.
	8. Bardîs.
	9. Bagjúra.
	10. Nakade.
	11. Erment.
	12. Isna; city.

In the mountain above Assiût are several remarkable caverns, very spacious, and adorned with hieroglyphics and emblematic figures. Some appear to have been sepulchral, as they contain fragments of the jars in which were deposited, not only the Ibis, but cats, dogs, and other animals, whether considered as sacred, or slain to attend their master or mistress in the other world. In one of these caverns, besides the entrance, there are three chambers hewn in the rock, which is free-stone, one sixty feet by thirty, another sixty by twenty-six, a third twenty-six by twenty-five. Farther up the mountain there are caverns yet more spacious than these.

In other parts of the mountain are numerous rough cavities, from which the stone has been extracted for the purposes of building, but they have afterwards been used for various objects; some for sepulture, as appears from the remains of jars curiously stopped with bitumen, others for summer retreats, as they are exposed to the North, and very cool.

Large quantities of fine flax are cultivated in the neighbourhood of Assiût: this article and wheat are transported from Upper to Lower Egypt. Salt and other articles are brought in return. From Mecca by way of Cosŝîr are imported Indian goods; but the European articles of broad-cloth, tin, &c. are here rarely seen. The Soudân caravans form a chief support of Assiût, which, with respect to them, serves as a midway station. Assiût is regarded as the capital of Middle Egypt; and in population exceeds all the towns to the South of Kahira. I should not be inclined to estimate the inhabitants at less than twenty-five thousand. The *Senjiak*, or Bey of Saïd, divides the year of his office between Assiût and Girgi; the internal government consists of the Cadi, assisted by other civil officers; and five Cashefs, mostly appointed by Soliman Bey, constantly reside there. It is the seat of a Coptic bishop, but the Copts are not very numerous, the people being chiefly Mohammedans.

So severely is female chastity guarded in this country, that instant death follows its violation. If tenderness of disposition should prevent the father, brother, husband from inflicting this punishment,

punishment, he is shunned by all his acquaintance, and becomes a stranger to society.

Provisions are considerably cheaper at Assiût than in Kahira.

Lentilles form a considerable article of food to the inhabitants of the Upper Egypt, who rarely enjoy the luxury of rice. The lentilles are so prepared as to be very palatable.

In Dar-Fûr are no lentilles.

The Egyptian onions are remarkably mild, more so than the Spanish, but not so large. They are of the purest white, and the *lamina* are of a softer and looser contexture than those of any other species. They deteriorate by transplantation; so that much must depend on the soil and climate. They remain a favourite article of food with all classes; and it is usual to put a layer or two of them, and of meat, on a spit or skewer, and thus roast them over a charcoal fire. The desire of the Israelites for the onions of Egypt is not to be wondered at.

About four hours from Assiût we had passed Monfalût, a city which I afterwards returned to view at more leisure. Monfalût is of considerable extent and population. Between it and Assiût stands Ben-Ali, a populous town. Those three places constitute, with Girgi, the chief marts of the trade of Upper Egypt.

October

October 4th, 1792. Continued our navigation up the Nile.

6th. Paſſed Kaw or Gaw-es-Sherkî, the Antæopolis of antiquity, where remains part of a curious temple, confiſting of ſeveral columns, built of large ſtones, as uſual in Egyptian remains, and covered with emblematical figures, interſperſed with hieroglyphics. Some of the ſtones in the temple are from eighteen to twenty feet in length. At How on the Weſt, ſuppoſed the ancient Dioſpolis, obſerved no ruins.

8th. Came to Achmîm, the antient Chemmis or Panopolis, on the Eaſt ſide of the Nile, now a pleaſant village or ſmall town. Heliodorus, in his celebrated romance, often mentions Chemmis, and ſpeaks of a diſpute between its people and thoſe of Beſſa or Antinoe. Many cities intervened between Beſſa and Chemmis, the latter of which he ſeems to place not far from a lake near the Heracleotic mouth of the Nile. The whole geography of that ingenious prelate forms one puzzle, though he was a native of the neighbouring country of Syria.

At Achmîm ſome fragments of columns ſtill remain, and in the adjacent mountain are caverns reſembling thoſe at Aſſiût. The hieroglyphics have been painted in diſtemperature, as uſual with all thoſe executed on the ſmooth ſurface of free-ſtone. A mummy had been recently taken out of the principal room, as appeared from the remains of prepared cloth, and human bones.

bones. The cielings of the chambers have been plaistered and coloured. Perhaps the antient Egyptians had a custom, not unknown to other Oriental nations, of annual visits to the dead*; and these chambers might be constructed for the reception of the relations on those occasions.

The neighbourhood of Achmîm abounds with sycamores.

This kind of sycamore, it is well known, bears a small dry fig, of a yellowish colour, adhering to the trunk of the tree. Many gardens are also seen, in which grow date and other trees.

11th October, arrived at Girgi, formerly the capital of Upper Egypt, now declining. There is a large market-place, with shops in abundance. At Menshié, antient Ptolemais, and at Girgi, observed several large pieces of granite, seemingly antique mill-stones. They are about six feet in diameter, and nearly three feet thick, with a perforation of one foot square in the centre, from which waving radii, about an inch deep, pass to the circumference.

The Senjiak, or Emîr-es-Saïd, passes half the year at Girgi, as already mentioned. His office is esteemed the third in importance, and is now filled by Soliman Bey, an honest and respectable character.

* That custom is still retained at Damiatt, notwithstanding the purer precepts of Islamism.

15th

15th October. Passed onward to Farshiût, a populous town, with many Christian inhabitants.

17th. Arrived at Dendera, the antient Tentyra. Saw the noted temple, the most perfect remain of Egyptian architecture. It is in the form of an oblong square, 200 feet by 150—Pococke says 145; is now almost buried in the sand. Ascending some steps in the middle of the wall, you come to a dark gallery, passing through all the sides. Many of the columns are standing. The inside of the *pronaos* and of the gallery is covered with painted hieroglyphics in all their original freshness. A Cashef, imagining treasures were concealed, was employed in the laudable work of blowing up part of the walls!

The same night, about twelve, reached Ghenné, the antient Cœne, or Cœnopolis. The navigation on the Nile is particularly delightful in the stillness of the night, diversified by the bright reflection of the moon on the water, or the clear sparkling of innumerable stars; among which the brilliant Canopus, unseen in European climates, is observable, except when some mountain conceals that part of the hemisphere.

19th. Came opposite to Coptis, now Kepht. The rubbish may fill a circumference of two miles, evinces its antient extent. Several small columns of grey granite lie on the ground, and some large stones, engraved with hieroglyphics. The distance from the Nile to Coptis is much smaller than has been supposed by European geographers.

A small

A small part of a bridge remains near Kepht or Coptis, sufficient to determine that there once was one, but it is impossible to say of what æra. There is nothing grand in the structure, which consists of small stones.

20th. Stopped at Kous, the Apollinopolis parva. Observed at a small distance on the North-east an antient gate, adorned with figures, and a deep cornice. Kous is a populous town, about a mile on the East of the Nile.

21st October 1792. Passed the night at Nakadé, where is a Catholic convent. On the following day came to Aksôr, the antient Thebes.

A brief general retrospect of the topography of Upper Egypt may here be given. The towns and cultivation are wholly confined to the banks of the Nile, but especially on the East. Mountains continue to present a regular barrier behind on both sides. Beyond this natural wall, on the West, is a vast sandy desert, traversed at times by the Muggrebin Arabs; here and there, at the distance of about a hundred miles or more from the Nile, are Oases or fertile isles, in the ocean of sand. On the East, between the river and the Arabian gulf, are vast ranges of mountains, abounding with marble and porphyry, but generally destitute of water, so that no town or village can be built. Among these ranges, however, some tribes of Bedouin Arabs, as the *Ababdi* and *Beni Hoffein*, contrive to find some fertile spots and diminutive springs, so as to furnish residences for about three or four thousand inhabitants. Even the shores of the Red Sea, corresponding with Egypt, contain but a small number of tribes; and the Arabs on the East in general are little formidable. The Muggrebîns are more ferocious, and might send forth thirty thousand men capable of bearing arms, could they ever be united, a thing almost impossible, their parties seldom exceeding four or five hundred, and the tribes being divided by intestine enmities. The Lesser Oasis, now *El-wah el-Ghurbi*, forms a kind of capital settlement, if I may so speak, of the Muggrebîn Arabs, who extend even to Fezzân and Tripoli. They are dressed in a linen or cotton shirt, over which is wrapped a blanket of fine flannel; all have fire-arms and are good marksmen, and their musquets are their constant companions. Their chief employment lies in breeding horses[*], camels, and sheep. They are very hardy and abstemious, a small cake of bread and leathern bottle of water supplying a man with ample provision for a day.

It is said that several ruins are to be found at *El-wah-el-Ghurbi*. Of the *Oasis Magna*, now El-wah, I shall speak at large in treating of my journey to Dar-Fûr; but must observe that the distance between this Oasis and that styled *Parva* is erroneously laid down in the most recent maps. I was informed by the Muggrebîns at *El-wah*, that *Charjé*, the most northern village of that district, was but two days journey from the nearest part of *El-wah-el-Ghurbi*; that is, about forty miles. *Oasis Magna* seems rightly to correspond with the latitude of

[*] They sell the males, and themselves generally mount mares in their warlike expeditions.

Dendera,

Dendera, and of courſe that of the ſouthern extremity of *Oaſis Parva* ſhould be a little to the South of that of Aſſiût, and not far North of Tinodes Mons, in D'Anville's map; apparently the chain on the Eaſt of both the Oaſes, or الولحات. On the Weſt I obſerved no mountains, nor on the South. The moſt northern Oaſis known near Egypt is that of *Siwa*, already deſcribed.

CHAP. IX.

UPPER EGYPT.

Thebes—Site and antiquities—Painted caverns—Their discovery and plan—Manners of the people at Thebes—Isna—Fugitive Beys—Antiquities—Rain—Assüan or Syene—Obstacles to farther progress—Return to Ghenné.

I found the inhabitants of the Thebaic district had been recently in open rebellion against the Mamlûks, but they were now somewhat more quiet. The Troglodytes of the caverns remained tumultuous, and sometimes opposed the troops of the Bey, by firing from their recesses; at other times they would retreat to the mountains, and leave all pursuit behind.

The massy and magnificent forms of the ruins that remain of antient Thebes, the capital of Egypt, the city of Jove, the city with a hundred gates, must inspire every intelligent spectator with awe and admiration. Diffused on both sides of the Nile, their extent confirms the classical observations, and Homer's animated description rushes into the memory:

" Egyptian Thebes, in whose palaces vast wealth is stored; from
" each of whose hundred gates issue two hundred warriors, with their
" horses and chariots."

These

These venerable ruins, probably the moſt antient in the world, extend for about three leagues in length along the Nile. Eaſt and Weſt they reach to the mountains, a breadth of about two leagues and a half. The river is here about three hundred yards broad. The circumference of the antient city muſt therefore have been about twenty-ſeven miles.

In ſailing up the Nile, the firſt village you come to within the precincts is *Kourna,* on the Weſt, where there are few houſes, the people living moſtly in the caverns. Next is *Abubadjadj,* a village, and *Karnak,* a ſmall diſtrict, both on the Eaſt. Far the largeſt portion of the city ſtood on the Eaſtern ſide of the river. On the South-weſt *Medinet-Abu* marks the extremity of the ruins; for Arment, which is about two leagues to the South, cannot be conſidered as a part.

Modern authors have ſtyled the ſite of Thebes *Luxor,* a name which is not in my journal taken on the ſpot, nor does my memory retain a trace of ſuch an appellation, not to mention that the word is not Arabic. Some write *Akſor,* which convinces me that both are corruptions of *El Kuſſür,* the real term, which is ſtill applied to the ruins by the Arabs. Norden is very imperfect in his Arabic names, as well as his topography.

In deſcribing the ruins, we ſhall begin with the moſt conſiderable, which are on the Eaſt of the Nile. The chief is the Great Temple, an oblong ſquare building of vaſt extent, with a double colonnade, one at each extremity. The maſſy columns and

and walls are covered with hieroglyphics, a labour truly stupendous.   1. The Great Temple stands in the district called *Karnac*.

2. Next in importance is the temple at *Abu-Hadjadj*.

3. Numerous ruins, avenues marked with remains of Sphinxes, &c.   On the West side of the Nile appear,

1. Two colossal figures, apparently of a man and woman, formed of a calcareous stone like the rest of the ruins.

2. Remains of a large temple, with caverns excavated in the rock.

3. The magnificent edifice styled the *palace of Memnon*. Some of the columns are about forty feet high, and about nine and a half in diameter. The columns and walls are covered with hieroglyphics. This stands at *Kourna*.

4. Behind the palace is the passage styled Bibân-el-Molûk, leading up the mountain. At the extremity of this passage, in the sides of the rock, are the celebrated caverns known as the sepulchres of the antient kings.

Several of these sepulchres have been described by Pococke with sufficient minuteness; he has even given plans of them. But in conversation with persons at Assiût and in other parts of Egypt,

Egypt, I was always informed that they had not been discovered till within the last thirty years, when a son of Shech *Hamám*, a very powerful chief of the Arabs, who governed all the South of Egypt from Achmim to Nubia, caused four of them to be opened, in expectation of finding treasure.

They had probably been rifled in very antient times; but how the memory of them should have been lost remains to be explained. One of those which I visited exactly answers Dr. Pococke's description; but the other three appear materially different from any of his plans. It is therefore possible that some of those which he saw have been gradually closed up by the sand, and that the son of *Hamám* had discovered others.

They are cut into the free-stone rock, in appearance upon one general plan, though differing in parts. First, a passage of some length; then a chamber; a continuation of the first passage turns abruptly to the right, where is the large sepulchral chamber, with a sarcophagus of red granite in the midst.

In the second part of the passage of the largest are several cells or recesses on both sides. In these appear the chief paintings, representing the mysteries, which, as well as the hieroglyphics covering all the walls, are very fresh. I particularly observed the two harpers described by Bruce; but his engraved figures seem to be from memory. The French merchants at Kahira informed me that he brought with him two Italian artists;

artists; one was Luigi Balugani, a Bolognese, the other Zucci, a Florentine.

On landing with my Greek servant at *Kourna*, no male inhabitants appeared, but two or three women were standing at the entrance of one of their dens. As we passed in quest of the Shech-el-belad, to request a guide, one of the women said in Arabic, " Are not you afraid of crocodiles?" I replied in the negative. She said emphatically, " We are crocodiles ;" and proceeded to depict her own people as thieves and murderers. They are indeed a ferocious clan, differing in person from other Egyptians. Spears twelve or fourteen feet in length are sudden and deadly weapons in their hands. At Kahira, Mohammed Bey Elfi had told me I should here need a guard of twenty men, but I found two guides assigned me by the Shech-el-belad sufficient.

In the temple at *Medinet Abu* we observed a large quantity of blood, and were told by the peasants of Beirât that the Kournese had there murdered a Muggrebîn and a Greek, travellers passing from Assuân to Kahira, who had strayed thither from mere curiosity, or perhaps with a view of finding treasure, in which the Muggrebîns pretend to superior skill.

At the village called *Beirât* is a native spring; and some others, I was told, are found in the neighbourhood, the water of which is different from that of the Nile, yet sweet.

Walled

Walled towns, it has been observed by Pococke, were not common in Egypt, and therefore, he adds, it is probable that Thebes was never surrounded by a wall.—That the passage in Homer refers not to the gates of the city, must readily be admitted. But it appears to me likely that Thebes was walled, from some feint remains, which are even to this day visible. In the precincts of the vast temple at Aksor, or El-Kussûr, is discoverable a small chamber, lined either with red granite or with porphyry, on ascending to the roof of which from without, and directing the eye to the Southward in a straight line, as far as it can reach, an insulated mass is seen, which has the appearance of having been a gate. With a telescope, from the same spot, are visible other still more imperfect remains, under the same circumstances, in the directions West and North. From their situation, precisely opposed to each other, and at the three cardinal points, at so great a distance, rather than from any stronger circumstance, I was inclined to believe that these may have been three gates.—That to the West is very near the mountains on that side.

After passing three days in and about antient Thebes, we advanced on the 26th Oct. 1792 on our voyage up the Nile.

27th Oct. Came to Isna, a large town, the residence of the fugitive Beys. Here is also found a temple of the same kind as those of Thebes, inferior in size, but tolerably well preserved.

The Beys now resident here, are, *Haſſan el Giddawi, Achmet el Uali, Oſman Bey Haſſan*, and another, whoſe name I did not learn. They are very poor and dejected, in conſequence of their long excluſion from the government. Haſſan Bey has about thirty Mamluks with him; the reſt only eight or ten each. Their whole revenues are drawn from the country near Iſna and Aſſuân, which is but unproductive. Paſſed one night at Iſna, and thence proceeded towards *Edfû*.

The people here have a ſuperſtition concerning crocodiles ſimilar to that entertained in the Weſt Indies; they ſay there is a king of them, who reſides near Iſna, and who has ears, but no tail; and he poſſeſſes an uncommon regal quality, that of doing no harm ("the king can do no wrong"). Some are bold enough to aſſert that they have ſeen him.

28th Oct. Near a village called Hillal, obſerved reliques of an antient town; part of two ſmall Egyptian temples, and a ſtatue of leſs than the human ſize, in a kneeling poſture, but broken off above the knees; the feet and legs remaining entire. The place has been ſurrounded by a thick wall of unburned brick, but of what date it is now impoſſible to determine.

The following day, a little ſhower fell in the morning; the only inſtance I met with of rain in Upper Egypt. Arrived at Edfû, and inſpected a gate or portico, and a ſmall Egyptian temple adjoining.

30th.

30th. Paſſed by *Gebel-el-Silſili*, the chained mountain, where, in antient times, a chain was paſſed acroſs the Nile. Here are ſome ſculptures in the rock, which is of hard free-ſtone, not of granite, as Norden mentions by miſtake.

Same day ſailed by *Kûm-Ombû*, literally the heap or ruins of Ombos. Saw there the temple deſcribed by the traveller juſt mentioned.

On the following day arrived at *Aſſuân*, the antient Syene. The remains of antiquity are here few, and ſome ſeem rather of Roman than Egyptian fabric. Even the modern town is almoſt in ruins, and contains very few houſes and inhabitants; it is chiefly ſupported by a ſmall duty upon dates, paſſing from Ibrîm to Kahira. Near Aſſûan may be ſtill ſeen the tombs of the Mamlûks who fled from Selim on his invaſion of Egypt. They are now very ruinous.

Some remains of antiquity are yet viſible in the iſle oppoſite Syene, antiently called Elephantine*. The Arabs uſe one as an incloſure for cattle. A ſtatue of granite alſo appears, holding a *lituus* in each hand. It is remarkable that many of the preſent inhabitants of this iſland have the negro countenance, hair, and perſon.

About three hours walk from Aſſûan is the *cataract*, in Ar. *Shelal*, more properly *rapides*, being merely an eaſy deſcent

* Now *Gezirtt-er-Sag*, Clauſtra Imperii Romani. TAC.

of

of the river among numerous isles and rocks of granite, which obstruct the current. Far from deafening the spectator, the noise is hardly audible.

Near the cataract I observed some black rocks; but whether of basaltes, or any other substance, the distance prevented me from distinguishing. It is well known that many of the antient statues and engraved stones found in Egypt are of that material, but it is believed to have been drawn from Abyssinia. I observed no quarries of basaltes either in Egypt or the other parts of Africa which I visited.

At Assûan I remained three days, contriving, if possible, to pursue my route up the Nile. But a war having arisen between the Mamlûks of Upper Egypt and the Cashef of Ibrîm, no one was suffered to pass from Egypt to Nubia. The caravans had all been stopped for many months, and not even a camel could be procured. At Kahira I could attain no previous knowlege of this war having originated with the fugitive Beys.

With deep regret for the disappointment in my earnest wish of proceeding to Abyssinia by this route, I was constrained to abandon all hope for that season, and to think of returning.

Left Assûan the 4th of November 1792, and proceeding rapidly down the Nile, arrived at Ghenné on the 7th.

CHAP. X.

JOURNEY TO COSSIR ON THE RED SEA.

Inducements and danger—Route—Account of Cofsir—Commerce—Return by another route—Granite rocks and antient road—Marble quarries—Pretended canal—Earthen ware of Ghenné—Murder of two Greeks, and fubfequent report of the writer's death.

ARRIVING on my return at Ghenné (سنة), I could not refift the impulfe of curiofity excited by the late defcriptions of curious marbles, &c. which had been found in that route. It was not difficult to find the means of paffing, though the Bedouins then infefted the road; but I determined to take nothing that could be of importance to lofe, not intending to ftay long at Cofsir. For which indeed there was another motive—An Englifh veffel, commanded, as was faid, by a Captain Mitchell, having three or four years before moored there, a quarrel had arifen between them and the natives about a fupply of water, which is a commodity furnifhed at Cofsir not without extreme difficulty. From a violent contention blows enfued, and the Captain thought himfelf juftified in firing on the town: in confequence feveral individuals were killed, it is faid there that they amounted to fourteen, and much damage done. The natives were exceedingly exafperated, and fwore to facrifice the

firft

first Englishman that should fall into their hands. I however conceived it possible to pass undiscovered; and so in fact it happened. Having agreed with an Arab for two dromedaries and a man, also mounted on a dromedary, for all which I was to pay fifteen mahbûbs, I left Ghenné at one in the morning of 8th November 1792, and travelling diligently, arrived at Cosîr on the 11th before sun-rise. We took the most northern route, which is not that apparently which Bruce travelled, (and which seems to be the longest by two or three hours,) as being the least frequented by robbers. Our course on the first day occupied twelve hours, the second fifteen, and the third thirteen hours; in all about forty hours. The principal inhabitants of Cosîr came successively to compliment us on our arrival. They all scanned me with an eye of suspicion, and the more so as I could not yet speak the Arabic fluently. But none so much as an old Sherîf, a considerable man in the place, who having travelled to Mecca, Constantinople, Bakdad, and other parts of the Turkish empire, had become acquainted with the various orders of men, and acquired an intuitive discrimination of character which very few in that country possess. After the common salutations had passed, "Are you not a Frank?" said he.—"No," replied I.—"But of Frank origin?"—"No," said I, "I am a Georgian by birth, but have passed so short a time in Constantinople, that I believe I cannot speak Turkish much better than I do Arabic;" (for I knew he spoke a little, and was beginning to address me in that language.) My servant then joined the conversation, and I escaped discovery. The dress, and apparently the language of the people of Cosîr, approach more to those of the Eastern shore of the Arabian gulph, than

to

to those of the Egyptians. They are armed with the *Jembia*, a crooked knife, often not less than a yard long, and commonly a lance. Indeed they altogether appear rather settlers from the opposite shore than native Egyptians. The commerce in coffee here is not inconsiderable. Formerly all Upper Egypt was supplied with coffee by way of Suez and Kahira, but the Beys having laid a very heavy duty on that commodity, the inhabitants began to import from Cosfîr for themselves, whence they are now supplied with the best coffee, and at a cheaper rate than from Suez. The town is provided with excellent fish, and pepper and other spices are brought there free of duty. Some Abyssinian slaves, transported from Jidda, are landed there and carried to Kahira, but in very small number. While I was there, a beautiful girl, of about fifteen, was sold for an hundred mahbûbs, or about 30l. sterling. There is no plenty of provisions at Cosfîr, there being no cultivable land near the town. Even the butter they use there is brought from Arabia. The only good water they have is supplied by the Bedouins from Terfowi, which is at the distance of three hours. If any quarrel ensue with them about the price, the town is compelled to use brackish water. We paid twenty-five medines for the *ghirbé* of fresh water. I observed but two vessels lying in the road, and these were lately arrived from Jidda. The houses in Cosfîr are built of clay, and the number of inhabitants settled there is very small, though the strangers, who are continually passing and repassing, augment them prodigiously. I could observe no remain of antiquity within the limits of Cosfîr, and it was not then possible to stray to a distance from it. Finding the resentment of the people as strong as ever against the Franks,

Franks; in consequence of what had happened between them and the English vessel in 1786, I thought it most advisable to hasten my departure, though otherwise inclined to have made some excursions by sea, as to the emerald mine, *maadden ezzummerud*, &c.

13th Nov. at 7½ hours A. M. we left Cofsir, and proceeding by the strait road, apparently that which Bruce travelled, on the 15th, about five P. M. arrived at the village called Bîr-Ambar, having met a caravan coming from Ghenné the second day on the road. The morning of the 16th at sun-rise we proceeded to Ghenné, which is distant about three hours, having slept at Bîr-Ambar in the house of a villager, who was very civil and hospitable. There was an officer at Cofsir, who belonged to the Cashef of Kenné, but he seemed to have very little authority with the people, being there only to collect the customs.

The road we travelled in going to Cofsir, as well as that we took in returning, have both something in them very remarkable. The rough and lofty rocks of granite and porphyry with which it is on all sides environed have a magnificent and terrific appearance; and the road between them, which is almost level throughout, gives the idea of immense labour in cutting it. All these circumstances concur in testifying the importance Cofsir must once have had as a port. In the route we took in going, at certain distances on the highest rocks is observable a succession of small structures, formed with uncemented stones, and which, by the marks of fire within them, seem to have
served

served as signals. These are numerous, but they are too rude to enable one to fix any time for their erection. They appear to me to be pretty antient. The red granite is in vast quantities, and the chain of rocks consisting of that substance appears to extend itself in a North and South direction. Huge rocks of porphyry, both red and green, are distinguishable, and, as appears, more of it in the road we pursued in going, than in that by which we returned. I observed veins of alabaster in both, but particularly in returning. The *verde antico* it was long before I could discover; at length I found it, in returning, by the signs Bruce had described. In short, this route unfolds a treasure of marbles that astonishes the beholder, and demonstrates, that on any future occasion the quarries may be again wrought, and modern architecture equal that of the best ages of Greece or Rome as to richness and durability of ornament, if ever it shall in justness of proportion, simplicity of taste, or unity of parts in one sublime whole, which indeed seems sufficiently problematical.

The immense excavations in these rocks, which greatly contribute in many places to facilitate the road, are abundantly sufficient to supply any quantity of these marbles that is any where known to exist. And it was more convenient to bring them thence, than from any other part of Egypt, to the Southward, or by a long land carriage from Arabia Petræa and the neighbourhood of Mount Sinai: yet, as the stones were to be carried some way by land, perhaps a day's journey at least, it was necessary to have a road more level and easy, than could have been required for the passage of less ponderous and cumbrous materials.

materials. Whether observation of the fact, without reflecting enough on the probable cause, might have given rise to the report respecting a canal communicating in this quarter between the Nile and the Arabian gulf, or whether it was the effect of misunderstanding the antient writers on the subject, is unimportant; such an idea has prevailed, and it is countenanced by some intelligent authors. In frequenting the places, and not wholly unimpressed by this thought, I have never yet been able to persuade myself that such a canal had existed, or could have been formed. There are no marks, in either of the roads I passed, of water having ever flowed there, and the level of the road, after leaving the river, is much higher than that of the river itself. But the level of the river is certainly not lower than in former ages, and the water, if ever it flowed there, must have flowed from the Nile to the sea, and not from the sea to the Nile.—The conclusion is obvious.

The coloquintida, cœlocynth, abounds near *Birambar*, and between it and Ghenné. The natives scarcely think it worth gathering, so low is the price in Kahira. At Ghenné is a manufactory of the best *bardaks, kullé*, earthen bottles, and jugs for water. They are made of a fine blue or bluish white clay; very thin and light, not too much baked, of a pretty shape and convenient size. Something of the same kind is made in other places, but none so much esteemed as those of Ghenné. The fabric is in few hands, but great numbers are made. They sell for double the price at Kahira which they fetch here. Large jars are also constructed, which are called *hamám*, or bath. These too are very elegantly formed, and both by filtration

purify

purify and cool the water, in a greater degree than might be imagined. The people of the country however drink the water that remains within, not that which has passed through the jar or bottle.

On going to Cofsîr, I had sent my baggage forward to Assiût. Nothing remained therefore but to find a small boat, on my return to Ghenné, in which to be conveyed to Assiût. This offered itself on the second day, and two Derwishes were my companions in that journey, one of them a very intelligent man. We stopped at all the principal towns, but without any new occurrence, and reached Assiût on the 21st.

I remained in that city till the 30th, when we set sail for Kahira, or rather trusted ourselves to the current, the wind blowing constantly from North-west. I stopped a night at Benefoef, intending to have passed thence to Feiume: but finding it not easy to meet with a conveyance, declined that journey, and arrived in Kahira on the 8th of December.

The wind, which was high during our excursion to Cofsîr, and afterwards on the Nile, contained such penetrating cold, that, on coming to Assiût, I found myself affected strongly with a fever. A large dose of James's powder however removed it.

A short time before my arrival at Ghenné, two Greeks, who were going to seek their fortune, as they reported, in Habbesh, came to Kous. The one had a small supply of money, of which the other was destitute—Words arose between them, and

some

some good friend advised them to have recourse to the Cashef of the place to settle their difference. This officer, who was a young man, and noted for the violence of his character, heard their respective narratives, and then, finding that money was the cause of their disagreement, terminated the hopes of the one, and the fears of the other, by an order for the instant death of both.

The report, in reaching Kahira, was charged with various circumstances of aggravation, and even the persons of the sufferers were changed. It was there said, that the Frank who was in Saïd was one of the two massacred, and the Cashef's master was among the number of those who had been deceived. *Keid Aga*, in whose department Kous was situated, sent word of this event, accompanied with a suitable comment, and, as was said, an offer of any reasonable reparation, to the Austrian Consul, the only one resident in Kahira. The latter had forwarded it to the British Consul at Alexandria, when I arrived at Kahira in time personally to contradict it. The death of the two Greeks, it was said, remained unnoticed.

CHAP. XI.

OCCURRENCES AT KAHIRA.

Arrival of the Pasha—Death of Hassan Bey—Decline of the French factory in Kahira—Expulsion of the Maronite Christians from the Custom-house—Riot among the Galiongis—Obstruction of the canal of Menuf—Supply of fish in the pools of Kahira—Expedition of Achmet Aga, &c.

On the 13th October 1796, the newly-appointed Pasha made his entrance into the city, in a manner more public than has been usual for some years. His name is Bekir: he is a Pasha of three *tók* or tails, and was formerly Grand Wizîr. The procession consisted of, first, the great officers of the city, and among them the Janizary aga, then some bostangîs, two and two. Several of the Beys, superbly mounted, two and two, preceded and followed by a body of Mamlûks. Twelve fine led horses, richly caparisoned. The band of music belonging to the Pasha. The tails, the officers and servants of his household; and lastly, the Pasha himself.

Neither Ibrahim nor Murad Bey was present. They both afterwards made their visit of ceremony, when, as usual, nothing remarkable passed. After a convenient interval, Bekir

Pasha sent to the *Shech-el-Belad* and *Defterdâr*, desiring them to meet him to consider of providing the usual Chasné for Constantinople, which he said for some time had been greatly in arrear. The former replied, that all which related to the public revenue was under the management of his brother Murad; and that he (Ibrahim) only concerned himself with the city, and its internal government. The latter gave for answer, that he had long since turned his attention from public affairs to his personal ease and security; that he was now poor, and become a farmer, cultivating wheat and beans. He contented himself with referring the Pasha to the younger Beys, who, he said, shared between them all the public authority. The next message was directed to Mohammed Bey Elfi, Ibrahim Bey el Sogheir, and other of the younger Senjiaks. They replied, that if the Pasha sought for money, all their treasures were buried in *Kara-meidân**, and he had nothing more to do than to meet them there, to become possessed of a part of them.

The Mamlûks commonly exercise on Monday and Friday in each week, at a place called Muftabé, between Kahira and Misr-el-attiké. Here they shoot at a mark, and throw the *jerid*. The Beys are often spectators, and sometimes actors. It was on one of these occasions that Hassan Bey, who had been formerly a slave of Ibrahim *Shech-el-Belad*, and in whom the latter placed much confidence, being present, a mamlûk of his train, having attempted to discharge his fusil, which missed

---

* A place where the troops are exercised, and rencontres between opposing parties frequently have had place.

fire,

fire, threw it on his shoulder, and rode off, to make way for others. In passing the Bey, the powder, which was damp, having taken fire, the piece went off, and lodged the contents in the breast of the Bey. He fell, and immediately expired. The slave fled, but it was not supposed any notice would be taken of what was merely accidental, however unfortunate. To fill up the number, Murzûk, son of Ibrahim Bey, was promoted by his father's interest.

Even as far back as the period of my arrival in Egypt, the French nation complained loudly of the treatment it received from the Beys. Forty or fifty days scarcely elapsed without some new demand for money, which it was understood was never likely to be repaid. Add to this, their commerce was daily decreasing, and no fixed tarif had they been able to establish with the farmer of the customs, for the reception of their goods.

When the war commenced, a consul was newly arrived at Alexandria, and he came to Kahira; but it was to little purpose that he fixed himself there for the protection of trade, when the thoughts of the French government were engrossed by other objects, and they could neither support nor supply their factories.

Affairs continued nearly in the same state till this time, Nov. 1796, when the Consul, *Magallon*, has obtained leave from his government to quit Kahira, and to reside entirely at Alexandria, which is obviously a place of greater security, and more prompt escape, if they have any shipping in the port. The merchants must indeed divide their profits with their agents in Kahira, but in all other respects have ameliorated their condition. At this time there remain only three French commercial houses in Kahira, and a physician. The remainder of the nation is at Alexandria, to the amount perhaps of ten or twelve families.

Nov. 1796. A change has lately taken place in the custom-house here, and at Alexandria and Damiatt, with which the Christians are much displeased. The duties for many years had been farmed to Jews, whose gains and sufferings were both in the extreme. During the last twenty years they have been in the hands of Damascene or other Syrian Christians, whose numbers and wealth have in that period increased. Their mutual jealousies and incessant quarrels were of great benefit to the ruling Beys, who took care to fleece each party alternately, and teach them a wisdom by dear-bought experience, which, however, they were not always able to learn.

Their most solemn asseverations would have led any person uninformed on the subject to imagine, that their whole nation was continually a loser by its bargain with the Beys. But their gains were in reality so vast, that certain secrets, developed by their infidelity to each other, led Murad Bey, in whose jurisdiction the customs were, to imagine that the having the collection

lection of them in his own hands would be a material addition to his revenue. For once his determination accorded with the public good: the plurality of the Kahirine merchants being better contented with the new mode than the old one. The Christians were removed, and spared the sufferings of which they had long so loudly complained. But how vain are human wishes! This novel regulation was scarcely put in force, and the collection of the import and export duties thrown into the hands of Mohammedans, who were immediately responsible for the receipts of their office to the Bey, than the Syrian Christians came forward with very lucrative proposals, if they might be allowed to hope, that the right of farming the customs would be a second time transferred to them. Murad, whose intellect is clear, though constitution, past sufferings, and indifference as to the future, have rendered him absolutely sensual, whose profuseness had left him no option as to the means of gain, but who had yet spirit to scorn the baseness of these parasites, on the offer of some conditional presents of great value, contumeliously dismissed the deputation from his presence. The customs therefore continued in the hands of Mohammedans, and the Christians were reduced to despair.

The Christian merchants of Syria, established here, make such a prodigal and ostentatious display of wealth, that it lessens our wonder at the extortions of the Beys. At one of their weddings, five hundred chickens were served up every day, and other articles in proportion. This fête lasted ten successive days.

The presents to the singers were said to have amounted to fourteen hundred mahbûbs.

A riot happened between the *Galiongis*, or sailors, (mostly Christians,) belonging to Murad Bey, and the Mamlûks. Murad had dismissed a naval officer, beloved by the Galiongis, and their discontent joined with the constant jealousy of the Mamlûks to create a disturbance, in which about seventy lives were lost, and the city was shut up for several days.

Nov. 1796. The waters of the Nile having almost abandoned the Eastern branch, which leads to Damiatt, pursuing the more direct course of the canal of Menûf, after a neglect of many years, it became necessary to apply a remedy. Accordingly, Murad Bey commanded his engineer, Achmed, to undertake this duty. After encountering some difficulties, the purpose was at length effected by driving piles, and the river resumed its former course.

A circumstance is related concerning the propagation of fish in Kahira. As soon as the Nile begins to fill the several pools, *birkets*, in the neighbourhood, the fishermen go to the river, and collecting several sorts of spawn, distribute it into the pools, where in the space of three or four days, it produces fish in abundance.

Nov. 1796. Achmet Aga, a Zanthiote, who has been already mentioned, about this time left Kahira on his way to Dar-

Dar-Fûr, by the return of the caravan with which I came. The Sultan Abd-el-rachmân, desirous of gaining a name among the neighbouring princes, but injudicious and governed by caprice in the choice of the means, and stung with the rage of conquest, though regardless of the means of security, sought for some person to exhibit to him the European invention of artillery; and though he had not yet been witness to its effects, conceived that the possession of some of the gold mines under *Sennaar* would soon be realized on his obtaining these powerful engines. He wrote to the Beys to request they would send him some one from among their servants, who might make him master of this important discovery. He also sought for a medical practitioner.

The person abovementioned had embraced Islamism, and possessed some ingenuity in mechanical operations, particularly the construction of artillery. He was not extremely at ease in Kahira; and Murad Bey, unable to improve his situation from the multitude of prior claimants, consented to his request for permission to depart. He gave him strong recommendations to the monarch, and a horse, camels, and other requisites for the journey. Achmed commenced his route with eclat, having with him fifty or sixty artificers, who had enterprize enough to encounter the difficulties of so long a passage, or who thought no change could render their situation worse. He had also four pieces of brass cannon, six pounders.

Thus an opening seemed offered to furnish the people of Soudân with one more, at least, of the equivocal blessings

of

of civilized fociety.—What may have been the termination of Achmet's voyage I have not heard; but his perfeverance was fcarcely equal to the undertaking, and it feems likely, that when his golden hopes fhould have vanifhed, he would return to Egypt in defpondency, or perifh in Dar-Fûr.

CHAP. XII.

ANTIENT EGYPTIANS.

Their perfons, complexion, &c.

In the hiftory of nations, fome facts may gradually become obfcure, by having appeared to the hiftoriographer of the time, and even to thofe of fome ages after, too notorious to require being particularly recorded. Amid the various information refpecting the manners of the Athenians and Romans to be drawn from their refpective hiftorians, poets, and orators, we are not furnifhed with the means of afcertaining the appropriate enunciation of their own languages. A few cafual hints, from Dionyfius of Halicarnaffus and Cicero, afford all the light that antiquarian labour has been able to throw on this fubject.

The colour of the antient Egyptians has of late become a matter of doubtful inveftigation from the fame caufes; but is in its nature more interefting, and therefore merits a fhort difcuffion. By one of the moft recent and intelligent travellers in that country, a conjecture, apparently novel, has been offered to the public, viz. that the original inhabitants of Egypt were *negroes*, and that, accordingly, the world is indebted for all thofe branches of fcience which had their origin in Egypt, and were

afterwards

afterwards perfected by the Greeks, and for all those monuments of art, the feint remains of which still excite admiration, to a people of that description.

The philanthropy of Volney has induced him to rely more on the arguments he adduces in support of his hypothesis, than the nature of those arguments seems to admit: and the authority of an author who justly holds so high a place in the public estimation, is sufficient to give currency to error.

If plausible arguments were brought to establish the doctrine here mentioned, it would be unreasonable to refuse assent to it solely as militating against a commonly received opinion. But to fix beyond controversy an historical fact, more surely is required than ingenious conjecture, fancied resemblances, and quotations of but dubious meaning.

The subject in question ought not to be clouded by any prejudicated opinion relative to the physical differences between the white and black race of men. The evidence should be patiently weighed, and the whole left to stand on a solid basis, or fall by its own infirmity.

The Coptic language bears a manifest relationship to the Arabic and Syriac, as Volney allows. But are the languages allied, and the nations who speak them strangers to each other? It would seem, on the contrary, the subject of proof, that if the languages be indeed cognate, the nations who speak them must have proceeded from one parent stock; for what resemblance

between

between the sonorous copiousness of the Arabic, and the ineffable mendicancy of the native African tongues * ?

The Ethiopians, or in a more confined sense, the Abyssinians, though so much farther removed from Asia, the source of migration, are far from partaking what is properly called the negro character, as the narratives of the Portuguese writers, who first knew them, with those of Poncet, and in our times of Bruce, abundantly testify. The *Fungni*, or people of Sennaar, with those of Dongola, Mahas, &c. in *Barabra*, or *Nubia*, are, as all the Europeans who have seen them in Kahira can affirm, not negroes. And if all these be colonies from Syria or Arabia Felix, how are we constrained to acknowlege that the Egyptians must have been of the African race?

It has been urged that the Colossal figure of the *Sphinx*, near the pyramids, gave additional countenance to the opinion that the Egyptians were black, the face of that statue having been said to resemble the negro. But, not to mention that the form of the visage is now become entirely dubious, in forming statues of mere ornament, or as representations of the human figure, the artist endeavours to give the features most habitual to him, or what are most admired among his countrymen; but as to a merely emblematical figure, the same reasoning is not conclusive. Would it be imagined that a dog-headed nation once existed from the figure of *Latrator Anubis?* Unfortunately, of the Sphinxes at Thebes, innumerable fragments of which are

---

* Populorum Africæ vocabula plerumque ineffabilia, præterquam ipsorum linguis. PLINY.

yet remaining, scarcely one is entire enough to give any idea of the form of the visage which the sculptor designed to attach to it.

The statues of the Nile, it is said, were made of black marble, in allusion to his coming from Ethiopia. If this symbol, hitherto so unsatisfactorily explained, (the Sphinx,) had any relation to the same subject, might not the negro face be given to it for a similar reason *? It would hardly have been thought necessary to explain why the figure of the Nile was black, if the complexion of the natives of Egypt had been generally acknowleged of the same tinge.

The complete silence of the antient writers, concerning so singular a circumstance as that of the negro character of the Egyptians, if all other arguments were equally balanced, would be sufficient to decide this point in the negative. In defect, however, of historical and positive testimony, strong circumstantial evidence is drawn from the monuments of undoubted antiquity yet remaining. Among these are the small statues of Isis, &c. daily found among the ruins in various parts of Egypt. These are adorned with a profusion of long hair, peculiarly contorted, and the nose, lips, and other features, are far from resembling those of the negro. The same may be observed of the figures in alto relievo and basso relievo, on the walls at Thebes, in the caverns of Gebel-el-Silsili, &c. Of the Colossal

* The best idea of the Sphinx seems to be that of Maillet, who supposes it an emblem of the increase of the Nile under the signs of *Leo* and *Virgo*.

statues at Thebes, the features are too much damaged to be adduced in proof.

The two harpers, and several other human figures in the caverns of Thebes, called *Biban-el-molúk*, (tombs of the kings,) and in which the colours are perfectly well preserved, have the features and complexion exactly resembling the Egyptians of the present day.

The apparent testimony of Herodotus, the earliest historian whose works have reached our days, is not so strong as might at first appear. The terms μελάγχροες και ουλότριχες are merely relative, and apply to the greater or less degree of blackness and crispature of the Egyptians, as compared with the Greeks, to whom the writer was addressing himself; and certainly cannot be confined to positive blackness or woolly hair. To corroborate this interpretation of the passage from Herodotus, may be adduced a similar one from Ammianus Marcellinus, lib. xxii. That author says, that the Egyptians are *Atrati*, a term of equally strong import with the μελάγχροες of Herodotus, but, like it, evidently applied in a comparative sense; for, in the very next sentence, he says, *erubescunt*, they blush, or grow red. It is true, indeed, negroes suffer a certain change of countenance when affected with the sentiment of shame, but it would be rather a bold assertion that the word *erubescere* can ever be applied to characterise the effect of that feeling on a negro. Even in the vernacular idioms of modern Europe, by the term a *black man*, is daily designated one of visibly a darker complexion than ourselves.

ourselves. Besides, what antient writer has described the inhabitants of Colchis? Was Medea, the Love of the Grecian heroes, a negress?

Volney has offered as a general remark on the Mamlûks of Egypt, that they are easily distinguishable from the natives by having light hair. It is certain that dark hair, eyes, and complexion, do not obtain so universally among them as among the native Egyptians or Arabs; yet in fact, their eyes and hair may be observed much more commonly of a dark than light hue. If then the fondness for generalizing his remarks have operated to deprive this author of the knowlege which hourly experience, continued for several months, could not fail to have given him, what may not be credited as to the effect of his prejudices in matters of remote and doubtful history, where truth is to be drawn out only by patient inquiry, and the frequency of error is exactly proportioned to that of conjecture?

But if all the arguments to confute this new theory should fail, one fact remains which is invincible. The persons of the antient Egyptians, preserved as it were entire by the prescience of that people concerning the errors into which posterity might fall, exhibit an irrefragable proof of their features and of the colour of their skin, which is now, by the quantity of mummies that have been imported into Europe, subject to the inspection of the curious almost throughout that quarter of the globe. This resurrection of witnesses also evinces, that the Copts are their genuine descendants, and preserve the family likeness

in

in their complexion of dusky brown, dark hair and eyes, lips sometimes thick, but the nose as often aquiline, and other marks of a total dissimilitude between them and the negro race.

The black complexion of the Africans seems to extend much farther North in the Western, than in the Eastern part of the continent they inhabit. The people of Fezzân, whose capital is in latitude 27° 48″ or about 2° 10″ to the South of Kahira, are black, while the Egyptians, in the same latitude, are only of brown or olive colour. The Fezzâners, however, have not entirely the negro feature. They have frequently children by their negro slaves, the Egyptians but seldom. The island, near Assûan, consists chiefly of blacks; but the townsmen of Assûan are of a red colour, and have the features of the Nubians, *Barabra*, whose language they also willingly speak. The people of El-wah are quite of Egyptian or Arab complexion and feature, none of them black: so that I scarcely conceived myself to have arrived at the confines of the blacks, till we reached the first inhabited part of Dar-Fûr. The first I saw are called *Zeghawa*; they are not negroes, but a distinct race. The Arabs of this empire remain always very distinguishable in colour and feature. The people of *Harráza* are of a reddish complexion. Perhaps this being a very mountainous district may

may occasion some peculiarity. The Fûrians are perfectly black. I have seen some of the natives of Kulla, whence slaves are brought, and which is farther South than Dar-Fûr, that were red. On the whole, one might be inclined to go as far fifteen degrees of north latitude in this part of Africa, to find the line between the Arabs and the Blacks.

CHAP. XIII.

JOURNEY TO FEIUM.

Tamieh—Canals—Feiûm—Roses—Lake Mæris—Oasis Parva— PYRAMIDS—*of Hawara—of Dashûr—of Sakarra—of Jizé, or the great Pyramids—Antient Memphis—Egyptian Capitals.*

On the 28th of December 1792 left Kahira to visit Feiûm, a city distant about sixty miles to the South-west. At Moknân procured from the Shech a letter to one of his officers, residing at Bedis, another village further on to the Southward, commanding him to accompany me to Feiûm. Proceeded through a grove of large date trees, which are watered from several cisterns, all of them supplied from the Nile, during its increase.

Between Bedis and Tamieh passed a natural opening, in the chain which constitutes the Western wall of Egypt. A small canal runs through Tamieh*, and here the country again

---

* Pococke, vol. i. p. 56. conceives this place to have received its name from the Greek word Ταμίεια, there having been a kind of lock there to restrain or let loose the water in the canal which passes by it.

assumes

assumes the aspect of cultivation. This little town is remarkable for a manufacture of mats, though the situation be so insecure, that the Arabs in the preceding night had plundered their whole stock, to the value, as they said, of five or six thousand patackes. The Arabs still haunted the neighbourhood, and we were forced to discharge a few musket shot to keep off a small party that assailed us in the morning.

Passed another canal at Senûris, the seat of an hospitable Shech of the Bedouins. These canals reach from the Nile to the lake called Mœris. Left Senûris at half past seven on the 1st January 1793 and in two hours arrived at Feiûm.

At a small distance to the North are the ruins of an antient town, called by the Arabs *Medinet Faris*, city of the Persians, probably antient Arsinoe. Some mutilated busts and statues found here were offered for sale. I also observed some jars, resembling those used to contain the dead Ibis, and some vitrifications that seemed to indicate an Arab glass-work.

Feiûm stands on the principal canal leading from the Nile to the lake, and is surrounded with cultivated ground, a great part gardens, producing that profusion of roses for which this place was celebrated, and which were distilled into rose-water. The mode of propagating them was by continued layers; the young twigs thence arising being found to produce the largest and most fragrant flowers. The rose-water was excellent, and sent to all quarters; but the cultivation is now running gradually to decay. Wheat and other grain abound in the vicinity.

This

This city is not walled, but is populous, though on the decline; it contains several mosques and okals. There are few Copts, the inhabitants being chiefly Mohammedans. The houses are partly stone, partly unburned bricks. It is governed by a Cashef. The fish from the lake cannot be praised. Provisions tolerably plentiful; water good.

After passing three days at Feiûm, proceeded towards the lake, of which I wished to make the circuit. This is the Mœris of Strabo and Ptolemy; and the testimony of the latter, living in Egypt, seems unquestionable. However this be, the lake, now called *Birket-el-kerun*, probably from its extremities bearing some resemblance to horns, bears no mark of being, as some suppose, the product of human art. The shape, as far as was distinguishable, seems not inaccurately laid down in D'Anville's map, unless it be that the end nearest the Nile should run more in a North-west and South-east direction. The length may probably be between thirty and forty miles; the breadth, at the widest part I could gain, was 5000 toises, as taken with a sextant, that is, nearly six miles. The utmost possible extent of circuit must of course be thirty leagues. On the North-east and South is a rocky ridge, in every appearance primeval: there are some isles in the extremity nearest Feiûm, where there is a flat sandy shore. In short, nothing can present an appearance more unlike the works of men. Several fishermen, in miserable boats, are constantly employed on the lake. The water is brackish, like most bodies of water under the same circumstances.

The western extremity of this lake is in the dominion of the Muggrebine Arabs, who pass thither from *El-wah el-ghurbi*, and other places, and who being there under no control, suffer no person to travel thither, unless under their immediate protection. This information, which I received not till my arrival at Feiûm, frustrated my expectations of reaching some ruins which are said to exist there. The Arab Shech of *Abu-kiffé* told me it would require four days to go round the lake, and return on the other side. That there are no villages near it, nor any thing to be procured but from the Muggrebines just mentioned. On one of the isles at the Eastern extremity it is said that human bones are sometimes found.

From Feiûm travelled South-east. At Hawâra are two small pyramids of unburned brick, and another passage through the mountain. The plain from Feiûm to the Nile is in excellent cultivation, chiefly wheat, then just rising from the ground. Illahôn is a town or large village, filled with persons whose chief employment is the culture of the soil. Passed the *Bahr-bila-ma*, the channel of a large canal. Farther on is Bathen*, a long deep cut, supposed to be the artificial Mœris of Herodotus and Diodorus Siculus.

Returned to Bedis. On the following day passed the pyramids of Dashûr. Five appear successively, exclusive of those of Sakarra. The third after those of *Hawâra*, already men-

* Parallel to this is a narrow cut, called Bahr Yussuf, which runs into the Birket-Kerûn.

tioned,

EGYPT, AND SYRIA.

tioned, is that of Medûn, which has been very elegant, and built in this singular form,

It is composed of large pieces of the usual soft free-stone, joined together with a little cement; and has been hewn off to a straight surface. It would be extremely difficult to ascend to the top, which is now very broad; but it is probable that there was another square, completing its summit, which has been removed. The north side has been injured by tearing out stones, which open a view of the interior, which is however entirely solid. This pyramid has been supposed to be natural rock at the base, but this mistake must have arisen from a part being concealed. On removing the sand, (which rises chiefly in the middle,) and on examining the corners, the stones and cement may be observed to the very bottom.

The fourth is the most southerly of the four pyramids of Dashûr, where are two large and two small. It is in the form of a cone, terminating in au obtuse triangle, and is now much damaged. There is no appearance of any casing on this or any other of the pyramids. The stones do not point to the center, like those of the great pyramids of Jizé. The faces of all these pyramids are directed to the four cardinal points of the compass. Near them stands one of unburned brick, and a small one of stone, not completed.

At Sakarra a great number exist, among which ten are of a large size. The smaller ones are sometimes almost undistinguishable from the sand-hills, and are dilapidated; the stones being used as materials for building at Kahira, Jizé, &c.

The two largest of the pyramids are at about the distance of two hours and a half from Jizé, and are well known to all who have visited Egypt. The dimensions of that which has been opened I found to be as follow:

	Feet.	Inches.
Great chamber	34	5
Breadth	17	2
Sarcophagus	7	8
Breadth	3	2
Depth within	2	10⅝
Thickness	0	6

The galleries and great chamber are situated due North and South, allowing for the variation of the needle.

	Feet.	Inches.
The first passage descending	105	1
Small chamber, length	18	9
———————— breadth	17	1
Antichamber, length	7	5
Main gallery, upper part	150	0
———————— lower part	148	0
Passage to inferior chamber	109	1

An absurd opinion has recently been stated, that the pyramids are hewn out of the rock on which they stand; but the first ocular inspection would set this aside, the joinings of the stones being everywhere marked with cement. But it is unnecessary to dwell on a conjecture so futile.

In the open pyramid, the chamber is lined with granite, and the sarcophagus also formed of that stone. But the materials used in the general fabrication of these edifices is free-stone, of a soft kind and white hue; it is replete with shells. The rock on which they stand is of the same soft stone. Returned to Kahira.

On another occasion I visited the pleasant site of the antient Memphis, on the left bank of the Nile, about two hours to the South of Kahira, in a plain above three miles broad, between the river and the mountains. The land is now laid down in corn, with date trees toward the mountains. Nothing remains except heaps of rubbish, in which are found pieces of sculptured stone. The spot has been surrounded with a canal, and seems every way a more eligible situation than that of Kahira*. Its extent might be marked by that of the ground where remains are dug up, and which is always overgrown with a kind

---

* Τὸν Μῖνα πρῶτον βασιλεύσαντα Αἰγύπτε, οἱ ἱερέες ἔλεγον τοῦτον μὲν ἀπογεφυρῶσαι καὶ τὴν Μέμφιν. HERODOT.

Of the fact of Memphis having been surrounded by water, some evidences appear even at this day. Parts of the banks of the canal yet are visible toward the mountains, and at the extremities of the ground, where ruins are distinguishable.

of

of thistle that seems to thrive among ruins. It is most conveniently visited from the Coptic convent called *Abu-Nemrús*.

None of the fine marbles that are scattered so profusely at Alexandria are discoverable here; whether it be that they were never used, or carried away to adorn other places.

Of the several capitals of Egypt in successive ages, Thebes, or Diospolis, seems the most antient. Next was Memphis, itself a city of the most remote antiquity. Babylon seems to have been only the capital of a part retained by the Persians, after Cambyses had subdued Egypt, and was, by all accounts, founded by the Persians. Alexandria succeeded Memphis, and remained the chief city, till the Saracens founded *Misr-el-Kahira*.

CHAP. XIV.

JOURNEY TO SINAI.

Route—Suez—Ships and ship-building—Trade—Scarcity of water—Remains of the antient canal—Tûr—Mountains of red granite—Description of Sinai—Eastern gulf of the Red Sea—Return to Kahira.

On the 1st of March 1793 left Kahira to proceed to Suez. I had made an agreement with the Arab Shech, who was charged with the care of the caravan, that he and his servant should accompany me, without waiting for its slow progress. But he broke his engagement, as usual with the Arabs, and I was constrained to wait for the departure of a large body, consisting of an hundred and fifty persons and two hundred camels.

The route to Suez is nearly one uniform plain, generally hard and rocky, though here and there spots of deep sand occur. The journey was very slowly conducted, as the camels were permitted to brouze on the verdure which sprinkles the desert solely after the winter. On the third day, a South-west wind having subsided, rain fell for four hours and a quarter. The mornings and evenings were cold, though hot in the day. Some have ignorantly conceived that no rain falls in Egypt. At Alexandria
showery

showery weather will prevail for a week together; and I have sometimes seen rain at Kahira. In Upper Egypt even showers are very rare, and only one fell while I was in that country.

After a heavy progress of five days reached Suez. The town is small, and built of unburned brick. It contains twelve mosques, of which some are stone, but the most are mean buildings. The sea near the town is very shallow, yet there is a small yard for ship-building. Population, Mohammedans, with a very few Greeks. Suez is very modern, probably built within these last three hundred years; being unknown to travellers of a more antient date.

There are here at present four three-masted vessels, and ten others, some with two, some with one. Two building, one of which is pierced for twelve guns; and ten large boats, without masts. The largest of these ships was intended for the Indian trade, the rest for traffic to Jidda; one or two of them had been built in Yemen.

The Arab mode of ship-building is singular. They have no art to bend the timbers; none of them are crooked except naturally so. They are very slender, and where the upper and lower ribs join, do not pass one over the other, but by the side of each other.

At Suez coffee forms the chief article of trade. It is a place of no strength, and has only eight old cannon, seemingly unfit for service; the others were removed to Jizé by Ismaîl Bey.
The

The sea here produces few fish. Oysters indeed, and a few others of the shell kind, are seen; the best fish not coming higher than Cosîr. Meat is scarce, bread of an inferior quality, sometimes hardly eatable. Butter and milk are brought in small quantities by the Arabs. Water is brought from three several places. *Bir Naba*, to the northward, affords the best; the others are *Aiun Mûsa* and *Bir-es-Suez*. It is always bought by the skin at a considerable price, and if a war were to arise with the Arabs, none could be found.

I was very desirous to inspect the Eastern portion of the canal cut by Adrian, according to D'Anville, which extends from *Birket-es-Sheib* to Suez, but my Arab guides would not accompany me, in spite of a previous agreement made for that purpose. All consented that marks of the canal existed, and some of them arose to my own observation.

The ruins of Arsinoe may yet be recognized in a mount of rubbish in the neighbourhood of Suez. The spot is now called *Kolsûm*, and remains exist of a stone pipe for conveying water thither from Bir Naba. A rock, on the African side of the gulf, furnishes *petroleum*, which is brought to Suez, and esteemed a cure for bruises, &c. In crossing the gulf just before Suez, boats are used at high water, which comes in rapidly to the height of four feet; at other times camels, horses, and men ford it with safety.

At Suez I observed in the shallow parts of the adjacent sea, a species of weed, which in the sunshine appeared to be red coral,

coral, being of a hue between scarlet and crimson, and of a spungy feel and quality. I know not if any use be made of it, nor am I acquainted with its Arabic name; but it strikes me, that, if found in great quantities at any former period, it may have given the recent name to this sea; for this was the Arabian gulf of the Antients, whose *Mare Erythræum*, or Red Sea, was the Indian Ocean. This weed may perhaps be the סוף *suph* of the Hebrews, whence ים סוף *Yam Suph*, their name for this sea.

The shores here abound in beautiful shells of various kinds; a circumstance which might also have been remarked in speaking of Maadié near Abukîr.

On the 8th of March 1793, passed the ford at Suez, and on the 14th arrived at Tûr. So many journies to Mount Sinai have been published, that I shall not dwell much on the particulars. The route from Suez to Tûr at first lies along a barren coast, but afterwards some pleasant vales of verdure are found, particularly *Wadi Corondel*, where grow some date trees and shrubs. Mountains of red granite are seen, perhaps too intersperfed with porphyry.

A spot is pointed out by the Greek priests of a small convent near Tûr, where a church is said to have been buried, and miraculous noises still heard, but on visiting it, in the mere expectation of some natural phenomenon, found nothing.

On

On the 18th left Tûr, and on the 22d, at 3½ hours A. M. reached the monaftery of Sinai. Shot a red-legged partridge. The convent is large, with a good garden, to which there is a fubterraneous paffage. Within the walls is a fmall mofque for the convenience of the Arabs. The mountain now called Sinai is high and abrupt. On the North fide of it fome fnow was vifible. The whole is a very remarkable rock of red granite, interfperfed with fpots, to which foil has been brought by human toil, or wafhed down by rain, and in which grow almond trees, (now in bloom,) figs, and vines. Numerous rills of excellent water gufh from various apertures in the precipice, and wander among the little gardens. Sinai has two fummits fomewhat refembling Parnaffus, another fcene of infpiration; and the one termed St. Catherine, being, it is believed, the higheft, may be the Sinai of Mofes.

The weather being very clear, I obferved, from Mount Sinai, the Eaftern gulph of the Red Sea, which appears very fmall, and more round and fhort than is laid down in the lateft maps.

Returned to Suez and Kahira, meeting with nothing memorable on the route.

CHAP. XV.

JOURNEY TO DAR-FÚR,

A KINGDOM IN THE INTERIOR OF AFRICA.

Design to penetrate into the interior of Africa—Difficulties—Caravan from Soudan or Dar-Fúr—Preparations—Departure from Aſſiút—Journey to El-wah—Mountains—Deſert—Charjé in El-wah—Bulak—Beirís—Mughes—Deſert of Sheb—Deſert of Selimé—Leghéa—Natrón ſpring—Difficulties—Enter the kingdom of Fúr—Sweini—Detention—Repreſentations to the Melek—Reſidence—New difficulties—Villany of agent—Sultan's letter—Enmity of the people againſt Franks—El Faſher—Illneſs—Converſations with the Melek Miſellim—Relapſe—Robbery—Cobbé—Manners—Return to El Faſher—The Melek Ibrahim—Amuſements—Incidents—Audience of the Sultan Abd-el-rachman-el-raſhid—His perſonal character—Ceremonies of the Court.

My views to the South of Egypt having been fruſtrated during the laſt year, I was reduced to the alternative of abandoning any further projects in that quarter, or of waiting for a more ſeaſonable opportunity. As it was reported that ſuch an one would ſoon offer, I did not heſitate to prefer the latter, though ſtrongly diſſuaded from it, as generally happens to thoſe whoſe

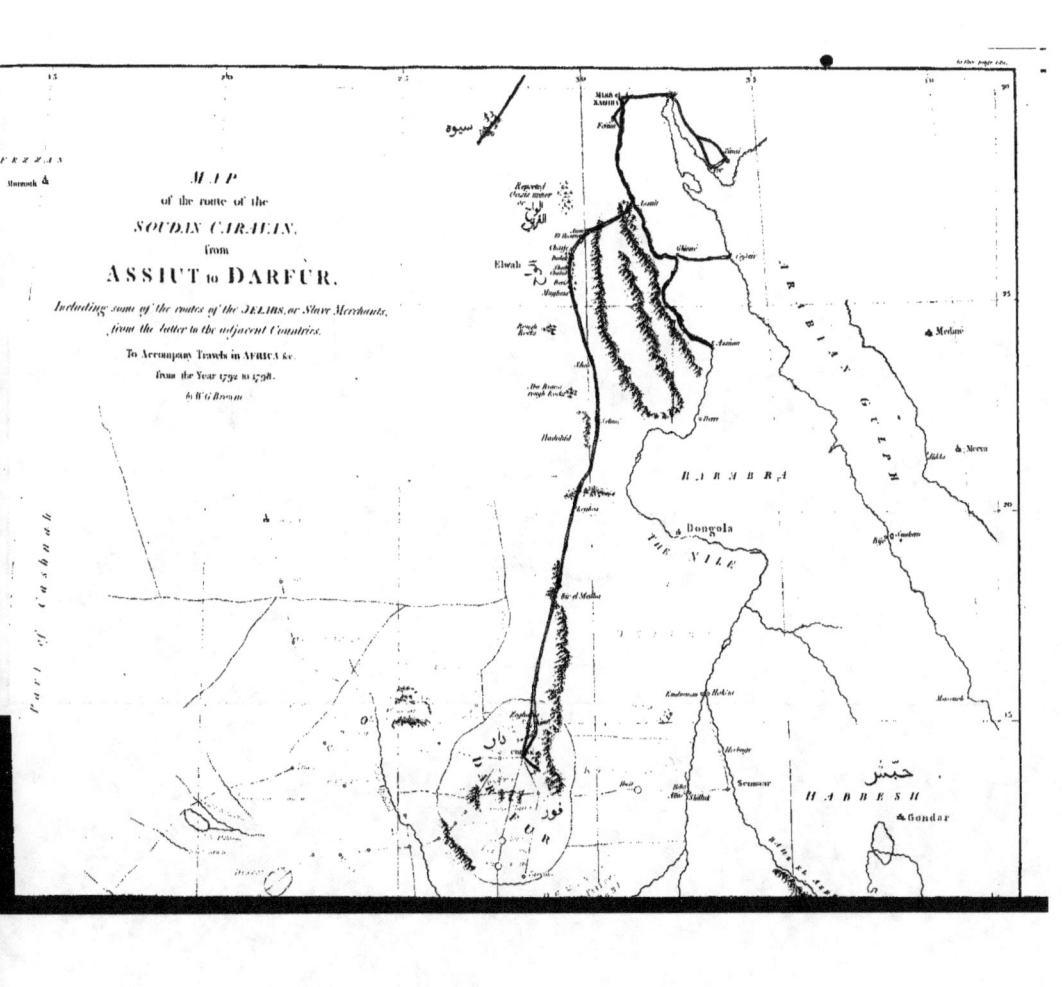

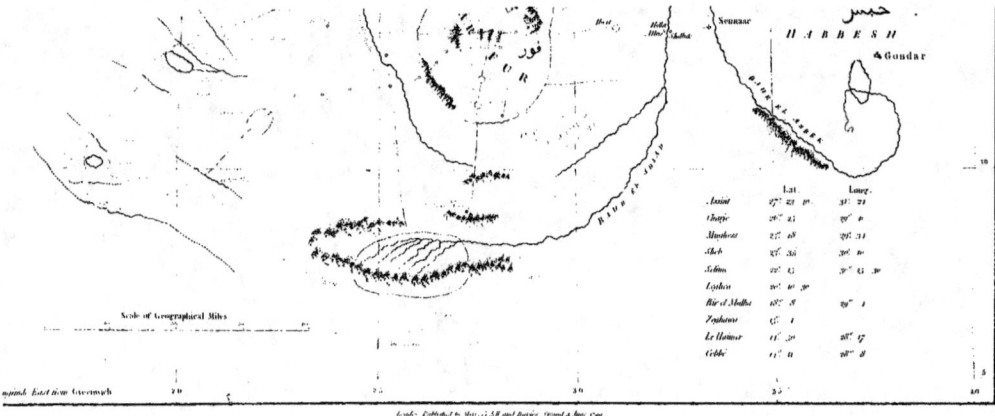

whose designs are any way analogous to mine. The Europeans in this quarter, as well as the natives, being immersed in commerce from their early years, are unable to conceive the advantages promised by voyages of discovery, to which no immediate profit is attached; and accordingly as they know the hazard great, and imagine the atchievement frivolous and useless, even from the best motives they are rather inclined to discourage, than to animate, any one who undertakes them.

From conviction sufficiently clear, arising both from reading and the sentiments of those who were best informed on the subject, that the river whose source Mr. Bruce describes is not the true Nile, I thought it an object of still greater importance, that the source of the more Western river should be investigated. But what might have been a matter of choice, was with me only the result of necessity. The idea of reaching the sources of this river, (the Bahr-el-abiad,) laid down in the maps apparently at about two hundred leagues farther South than Sennaar, seemed to me so hopeless, that this object alone would hardly have induced me to undertake such a voyage. I should rather have been inclined to attempt Abyssinia, and endeavour to certify, as well as circumstances might permit, how far authentic former narratives had been, and what might offer that was new to European observation. For this purpose the obvious and most easy route was by the Red Sea to Masouah. But all accounts concurred in magnifying the difficulty, and almost impossibility, of an European passing there undiscovered; and, being discovered, of his penetrating any farther.

The road from Kahira to Sennaar was the one I should have preferred; but the desolation and anarchy then prevailing in Nubia, which had prevented me from passing the former year, would not probably have allowed me better success in this. Besides, the city of Sennaar was then occupied by the slaves of the last *Mecque,* or king, who had deposed and put to death their master, and still continued to usurp the government. By taking the route of Dar-Fûr, I was taught to believe that I might hope for the advantages of a regular government; and with proper management might expect every favour from the monarch. The local inconvenience of being so much farther removed from Abyssinia was indeed obvious; but on the other hand the choice of more than one route was, it seemed likely, thereby offered; which, in a place where progress is so uncertain, and contingencies so numerous, would be a matter of no inconsiderable importance.

At the moment of my return from Assûan to Assiût, the caravan of jelabs from Dar-Fûr, called *Cafflet-es-Soudân**, the Soudân caravan, arrived at El-wah. It was then reported that the sale of their merchandize and slaves, of which they had no great quantity, would be completed in about two months, and that then they would return home. Their stay, however, was protracted during the whole of that winter; and in the month of March 1793 they commenced their departure from Kahira for the Upper Egypt. They were slow in collecting all that was

---

* Soudân in Arabic corresponds to our Nigritia, merely general words for the country of the blacks.

necessary

neceffary for the journey, and I made ufe of the time fo allowed to draw information from various quarters concerning what was requifite for the voyage. From what caufe I know not, but at that time the perfons of whom I made enquiry gave no intimation that the treatment of Chriftians in their country was marked by any afperity. The late Sultan of Fûr, indeed, as I afterwards learned, had been remarkable for his mildnefs and liberality to all defcriptions of perfons. But this was not all— a native of Soudân is, in Kahira, the moft obfequious and fervile of the human race. He behaves towards a Chriftian whom he meets there nearly as to one of the true believers. In his own country he repays with intereft the contempt that has been fhewn him by the Egyptians.

On the 21ft April 1793, I fet out from Bulak, having embarked on the Nile; and on the eighth day, the wind having been often unfavourable, arrived at Affiût. The firft care was to provide camels for the route, and thefe were unfortunately at that time fcarce. Five however I at length obtained, at about 13l. fterling each. We had alfo made our provifion of food, &c. required for the journey; and the caravan having at length affembled, after about fifty days the expected moment of departure arrived. It was the hotteft feafon of the year, and confequently unfavourable to travelling. Thefe merchants however, difpofed as they are to indolence, and governed by prefent fenfations, when their profit is concerned, efteem the variations of climate unworthy of a thought: and long habit has familiarized them with fuch degrees of heat, that what is infupportable

able to northern nations is with them no serious motive for the remission of labour.

The route taken by the Soudân caravan is in part the same as that traversed by Poncet, in the beginning of the present century, on his way to Abyssinia. He passed by Sheb and Selimé, and thence striking across the desart South-east, crossed the Nile at Moscho. We continued our march from Selimé, almost due South, or with a small variation to the West. Our party having left Assiût on the 25th May, encamped on the mountain above it till the 28th, when it proceeded by short stages towards El-wah. The jelabs commonly pay the Muggrebines for their protection, or rather for forbearing to plunder them, at the rate of about a patacke for each camel. I refused them this tribute, alleging that I was not of the number of merchants who usually trade to Soudân, but a stranger who was employed on business to the Sultan; and though my refusal occasioned a slight dispute, the Arabs thought proper to relinquish their claim. The camels were heavily laden, and the jelabs travelled slowly, and in detached parties, each consulting his own convenience, till the 31st of the same month, when we came to Gebel Rumlie, an high rocky mountain, which we were to descend. It forms the Western side of the ridge, which constitutes, as it were, the wall of Egypt, and the Eastern boundary of the low desert, in which lie the *Oases*. It consists of a coarse *tufa*, and is of rugged and difficult descent. The road seems in many places to have been opened by art. We were a full hour in reaching the bottom. The camels not without great pain carrying their loads on the steep declivity, and being often in danger of falling.

From

From the summit of this rock the view lost itself in an extensive valley, consisting chiefly of rocks and sand, but diversified by small bushes of the date tree, and other marks of vegetation, near the spring where we designed to repose. Nothing could exceed the sterility of the mountain we had passed. Having reached the plain, it became necessary to unload the camels, and allow them some rest. We were employed four hours and a half, the following morning, in passing from the foot of the mountain to Ainé Dizé, the first place where water is found, and the Northern extremity of the great Oasis. An hot wind blowing during the meridian hours, the thermometer here stood during that time under the shade of the tent at 116 degrees.

In marching from Ainé Dizé to Charjé, eight hours were employed. Excepting a small space near the spring, all is waste. The Chabir, or leader, chose to notify his approach to the town by beating drums, (two of which he had borne before him as marks of his office, and as occasion might require, to collect the travellers when dispersed,) and by other tokens of joy, as firing small arms, shouting, &c. One of my camels, in descending the mountain, had fallen and injured his right shoulder, which, as a cure could not suddenly have place, obliged me to change him for another.

There is a *Gindi* or officer at Charjé, and another at Beirîs, both belonging to Ibrahim-bey-el-kebir, to whom those villages appertain; and to them is entrusted the management of what relates to the caravan during the time of its stay there. We left

Charjé

Charjé on Friday the 7th of June, and having passed another desert space, after six hours reached another village, called Bulak. This is a wretchedly poor place, the houses being only small square pieces of ground inclosed with a wall of clay, or unburned bricks, and generally without a roof. It furnishes good water, and the people live by the sale of their dates. The caravan remained a day at Bulak, and having left it on Sunday the 9th, arrived at Beirîs on Monday the 10th, after nearly fourteen hours march through a barren tract. Here the Chabir thought proper to go through the same ceremony as at Charjé.

On the 13th we employed two hours in passing from Beirîs to Mughess, the last village of the Oasis toward the Southern desert. We left Mughess on the morning of the 15th, and on Thursday the 20th, in the morning, arrived at Sheb. At this place, by digging to the depth of a few feet in the sand, is found a supply of indifferent water. A tribe of the wandering Arabs, called *Ababde*, who come from the neighbourhood of the Nile, sometimes infests it. Sheb is marked by the production of a great quantity of native alum, as the name imports. The surface, near which the alum is found, abounds with a reddish stone; and in many places is seen argillaceous earth. Having left Sheb on the 21st, we arrived at Selimé on the 23d. This is a small verdant spot, at the foot of a ridge of rocks of no great height, nor apparently extending very far. It affords the best water of any place on the route; but though there be verdure enough to relieve the eye from the dry sterility of the surrounding surface, it affords no vegetable fit for the support either of man or beast. At Selime is a small building, which has apparently

apparently been raised by some of the tribes resting there, that place being much frequented by the roving parties passing the desert in different directions. The building consists only of loose stones, but the jelabs related many fables concerning it; as that it had of old been inhabited by a princess who, like the Amazons, drew the bow, and wielded the battle-axe, with her own hand; that she was attended by a large number of followers, who spread terror all over Nubia, &c.; and that her name was Selimé*.

On the 24th we rested, and having proceeded the following morning, employed five days more in reaching Leghea. Water there is scarce, and far inferior in quality to that of Selimé, having a brackish taste. The camels throughout the caravan began now to be excessively weak and jaded, and the Chabir was at a loss for the true road: for though several persons in the caravan had traversed this desert ten or twelve times, they were not unfrequently unable to determine which was the right course. One of the party was sent forward to discover some known object that might be our guide, and after having been absent thirty-six hours he returned. While we remained here we felt much inconvenience from a suffocating wind that blew from the South, and raised the sand in clouds. On the 2d of July the caravan left Leghea; and on the eighth, after a severe and fatiguing march, reached the Bir-el-Malha or salt spring. The

* In passing the desert, partly from want of water, partly from being overloaded, (these animals being then scarce and dear in Egypt,) so many camels died, that several merchants of the caravan were obliged to bury their goods in the sand near Selimé, whither they afterwards sent for them.

B B 2   vicinity

vicinity of this spring is remarkable for the production of *natron*, which substance appears under different circumstances, and is of different quality from that of Terané. It is very white and solid; and on immersion in water becomes hot, and discharges a great portion of its air.

Small quantities of it are carried by the jelabs to Egypt, where it is sold at a high price, and is used principally in making snuff. The water found at this place is very unpalatable, being brackish.

A troop of the natives of Zeghawa met us at this well. It is their practice to station a small party there, when caravans are expected, who remunerate themselves for the fatigue of a ten days journey by supplying provisions, and what else may be wanted by travellers, at an exorbitant rate. Many of our companions at this time had great need of their assistance, as their supply had been originally insufficient, and many camels had perished on the road. The vicinity of the Bir-el-Malha is occasionally infested by the Cubba-Beesh, a wandering tribe, who, mounted on the swiftest dromedaries, rapidly traverse the desert, and live by plundering the defenceless. As they are, however, unfurnished with fire-arms, so numerous a body as ours was not in much danger from their attack.

We remained at the Bir-el-Malha till the 12th; on which day we left that place, and travelled with little interruption till the 20th, and then encamped at a spot called Medwa, where however is no supply of water. One of my camels having fallen,

fallen, we were obliged to purchase water of the *Mahría* Arabs* whom we met, or to take up what had lodged in cavities on the earth, in consequence of the rains which were then beginning to fall.

On the 23d we came to the first springs within the limits of Fûr, which are in this place called Wadi Mafrûk. The white ant, *Termis*, was here exceedingly vexatious, building his covered way to every thing within the tent, and destroying all within his reach. This together with the rains, which were now increasing, and began to pour in a torrent through the valley, obliged us to abandon the tents, and take shelter in the next village, (Sweini,) where I obtained an apartment in the house of Ali-el-Chatîb, one of the principal merchants established in the country. In it I passed eight or ten days, not having arrived at Cobbé, one of the towns whither the jelabs chiefly resort, till the seventh of August.

At Sweini resides generally a Melek or governor on the part of the Sultan of Dar-Fûr; and there all strangers, as well as merchants of the country, coming with the caravan, are obliged to wait, till the pleasure of the monarch in disposing of them be known.

Coming as I did under considerable exceptions from the general rule of merchants trading to that country, and, in the

* The *Mahría* Arabs have the art of making wicker baskets, of so close a texture, that they carry in them milk, water, bouza. Much of the earthen ware made by the people of Dar-Fûr is glazed, I know not with what composition.

Arabic

Arabic language, rather as *Daif-es-Sultan*, the king's stranger, in which light the people of the country had hitherto viewed me, I expected to obtain, without delay, permission to continue my journey to the royal residence. I observed to the Melek of Sweini and other public officers, in one among many conversations I had with them, that " intending to visit the Sultan, I should hardly have expected to be put back with frivolous excuses, as the nonpayment of duties which you dare not explicitly demand of me, and tributes under the name of presents, which have never yet been exacted of a stranger. If any duties be payable, beyond what have already been discharged, you are perfectly at liberty to detain all, or such part, of the articles I bring with me, as you judge sufficient to answer your claim; but not to refuse me permission to go to the Sultan, with whom I have business. Or if other reasons operate to prevent my request being complied with, and any suspicions prevail relative to my views in coming here, I desire, without further delay, to be furnished with the means of returning to Egypt, before I suffer, as commonly happens to strangers, from the effects of the climate, while I am yet in the habit of travelling, and while the funds are yet unexhausted which should support me in my progress farther."

The misrepresentations which had been made concerning me, and which had by this time reached the Sultan, manacled the hands of the Melek, and prevented my remonstrance from having any effect. But candour and ingenuousness have no part in the character of slaves; and the antient observation is most just, that " when a man becomes a slave he loses half his virtue."

virtue." I therefore remained in perfect ignorance of the reasons of my detention. Perhaps indeed, without implicating himself, the Melek could not have declared them; or perhaps he was not thoroughly informed as to their nature. The plot that had been laid against me might indeed have deceived much abler heads than theirs, on whose caprices my fate depended.

Finding no mode of advancing, till the rest of the caravan had obtained the same permission, I resolved to follow the example of the other jelabs, and wait patiently the event. The house I was in consisted of a multitude of distinct apartments, built with clay, and covered with a slanting thatched roof, but not closed by doors. The hospitality of the owner allowed all who could find place in it to lodge themselves without distinction. At length, after the expiration of about ten days, an order from the Sultan arrived, directing that all the jelabs should be allowed to proceed to their houses on paying the duties assessed on them.

The circumstances attending myself were peculiar; and many of the disadvantages I had to contend with could not be well foreseen: it is therefore necessary to mark them, that if any occasion should offer they may be serviceable to others, and for this reason they shall be detailed at considerable length.

Before leaving Kahira I was apprised, that all commerce in Dar-Fûr was conducted by means of simple exchange. To carry on this in such a way as not to be grossly defrauded,

especially

especially having my attention engrossed by other objects, and in utter ignorance of the articles fit for bargain and sale in this country, seemed wholly impossible; I therefore sought for a person who might go through this business for me, at least with some share of probity. Such a one arose to the notice of my friends there; and knowing nothing more of the man, as indeed I could not know any thing more, than the character they gave of him, I took him on the general recommendation of being honest, and understanding the business in which he was likely to be employed. The person recommended had been a slave-broker in the market of Kahira; a circumstance which, had it been known to me earlier, would probably have prevented my employing him. Till the moment of departure I had observed in him keenness but no fraud, and in general that submissive acquiescence and absolute devotion to the will of the superior, for which the lower class of Kahirines are externally, at least, remarkable. The hour for commencing our march, however, seemed with him the signal for disobedience and insulting behaviour; and we were not yet far removed from the confines of Egypt, when this misconduct was carried to such an excess that I once levelled my gun at him with a view of inspiring terror. The merchants around us interfered, and for the time this passed off; but the man only sought an opportunity of revenge, which the prejudices of the people of Soudan, in direct opposition to my former information, too soon afforded him means to gratify.

The letters with which I was provided for different merchants in this district, under whose roof I might have had a safe lodging,

lodging, could be of no use to me till I had seen the Sultan; for till then no person knew in what character to receive me. The object of this man therefore was to prevent my introduction to the Sultan, and to preclude me from any opportunity of representing my case. We were no sooner arrived at Sweini, than he found means to employ one of his associates, who had been some years established in the place, to go to the monarch, and infuse into his mind suspicions of me as a Frank and an infidel, who came to his country for no good purpose, and whose designs it behoved him to guard against; and to suggest to him that it would not be proper I should remain at large, nor yet immediately come to his presence, but that some person should be commissioned to watch over and report my actions, and thus frustrate my supposed evil intentions. He added, as I afterwards found, many anecdotes, falsified or exaggerated, of the inquiries I had made, the way I had been employed, and my general behaviour on the road.

Nor was the villain himself idle during the time his coadjutor was thus laudably engaged. I have already mentioned that there were no doors to the apartments of the house we were in. He took advantage of this circumstance and my momentary absence, to take out of a box which had been broken on the road a quantity of red coral, the most valuable article in my package. As the box remained locked, it was not till long after that I discovered this loss. By the help of this commodity he expected to make his way with the great. At the end of a few days this agent returned, bearing a specious letter impressed with the Sultan's seal, ordering that no officer on the road should presume to detain me, or to take any thing from me, till I came to the house of *Ibrahim-el-Wohaishi*, (the name of this very agent,) in Cobbé, where I was to rest myself, till further orders should be given for my admission to his presence. I was not indeed at that time privy to the plot, yet if I could have obtained a knowlege of it, it might not have been easy immediately to counteract its influence; nevertheless I suspected something might have been practised against me.

An order from the despot, which while it was to protect me from his officers on the road, obliged me to confine myself to a particular spot, was a matter of surprise to me; but submission was unavoidable, as I was at that time unprovided even with the means of remonstrance. Had the machinations of my adversaries, which went much farther than my confinement, having been actually employed against my life, been at that time known to me, this severity would not have caused any astonishment, and the means of redress might have been less doubtful. But suspense filled the void of positive suffering—a suspense to which no apparent remedy suggested itself. Those who had known me in Egypt or on the road were dispersed to the East and West, and the people of the place were ill disposed to form any communication with me, being filled with religious horror of one supposed an infidel, but of yet undefined impiety, and whose colour, variously regarded as the sign of disease, the mark of divine displeasure, or at least, the unequivocal proof of inferiority of species, had averted their wonted hospitality, closed their compassion, and inflamed their personal pride and religious fury.

It

It was in this situation that, seeing no means of immediate relief, I began to feel impatience; which, as I continued in a state of perfect inactivity, communicated the more rapidly its pernicious influence to my state of health. On the fourteenth day after my arrival, I was attacked with a violent fever, attended with extreme pain in the head. How long it lasted I cannot precisely say, having on the second day lost my recollection. It was afterwards recalled by the effect of a dysentery, which lasted for two days, and left me too weak to assist myself. I had reflection enough to know, that of the aliments there to be procured, scarcely any could be found that would not be pernicious. After the first attack therefore, I confined myself to the use of bark and water, which last I drank in great quantities.

A little more than a month had elapsed, when the symptoms appearing to diminish, I again pressed to be permitted to visit the residence of the Sultan. But I had reason to regret my impatience; for having at length obtained leave, I proceeded to El Fasher, only to repeat my suffering. The rainy season was almost at an end, but the air, which still continued insalubrious, fatigue, and anxiety renewed the malady, which, after extreme abstinence, and having gone through the short catalogue of remedies which I had had the precaution to take with me, I found unabated. Excessive headachs, lassitude, thirst, occasional constipation, succeeded by extreme irritation of the viscera, continued for several months to shew the inefficacy of my precautions, and to incapacitate me from all personal exertion. At length the heat of the ensuing summer gradually increasing, and producing regular and continued tranfpiration, and the ftate of the air then meliorated, having removed the caufe of indifpofition, it was not long before I gained a certain degree of ftrength.

Arrived at El Fafher, I was firft introduced to the Melek *Mifellim*, one of the principal minifters. This man, when young, had been a flave, and engaged in domeftic offices of the palace, but having been detected ufing fome familiarities with one of the women, the monarch had ordered him to be deprived of the enfigns of manhood. Ignorant and uneducated, he appeared to have a certain quicknefs of apprehenfion, which, together with uncommon gaiety of humour, had rendered him acceptable at court, where he appeared more as a buffoon than a minifter of ftate. He received me with a rude ftare as an object he was unufed to, which was followed by a mingled fmile of contempt and averfion. He was feated with fome other of the royal attendants, under a kind of awning of cotton cloth, on a mat fpred upon the fand. After the common falutations, the Melek and his company entered into converfation on the nature of my vifit to the country; and each made his remarks on my perfon, and offered his conjectures as to my character and intentions.

Their converfation was partly carried on in their vernacular idiom, partly in Arabic. At length a wooden bowl of *polenta*, and another of dried meat, were fet before them. My illnefs deprived me of all inclination to eat; and obferving the company not much inclined to invite me to join them, and yet embarraffed how to avoid that ceremony, I relieved them by declining

declining it, and defiring them to begin. When they were fatiated, and they lofe no time in eating, a great number of foolifh queſtions were aſked me about Europe, fome of which I waved, and fatisfied them as to others in the beſt manner I was able.

One of the principal queſtions was, whether the Englifh paid the Jizié to the Othman Emperor? This, as is well known, is a capitation tax, paid by the Greeks and others, for liberty to worſhip after their own manner. I replied, that England was fo remote from the Imperial dominions, that no war between the two countries could well have place, till all the reſt of Europe ſhould have fubmitted to the Mohammedan arms, which had not hitherto come to pafs: but that, for the purpofes of trade, the inhabitants of the one country frequented the other, and by mutual agreement were confidered as perfonally fecure; that prefents were occafionally made by the Britifh King to the Emperor, in token of amity, but not as a mark of fubjection; and that the latter, on his part, as it did not appear that the decrees of the Almighty had fixed this as the moment of general converfion to the true faith, in virtue of his difpenfing power, and fwayed by the general law of hofpitality to ſtrangers, fanctioned by the authority of the Prophet, judged it lawful, and even a matter of political expediency, to tolerate fuch Europeans as conducted themfelves inoffenfively in his dominions, though they did not pay the Jizié. I thought it neceſſary to enter into this explanation of the terms on which I conceived myfelf to ſtand in relation to them, having by this time learned how rigidly they were difpofed to adhere to the letter of the

Prophet's

Prophet's *dictum*, viz. that no infidels are to be spared but such as pay the capitation tax. When I observed they grew tired of asking questions, I seized the opportunity of explaining why I came there, and what favour I expected would be shewn me.

"Melek," said I, "having come from a far distant country to Misr, (Kahira,) I was there made acquainted with the magnificence, the extended empire, and, above all, the justice and hospitality of the King Abd-el-rachmân, whose dominion be eternal! Having been used to wander over various countries as a *derwish*, to learn wisdom from the aged, and to collect remedies for diseases from the herbs that spring in various soils, I grew desirous of seeing Dar-Fûr. I was told that my person and property would be secure, and that permission would be given me to go wherever I might think proper. Since my arrival within the confines, I have found that all these assurances were fallacious; my inclinations have been thwarted, my person treated with indignity, and my property plundered, while compliance has been refused even to my most reasonable demands. I ask redress.— What I have already suffered from the officers of the Sultan is passed, and cannot now be remedied, but I desire protection for the future. I desire the punishment of the man who has robbed me, and restitution of what has been taken. Nor is this all, I particularly desire permission to go to Sennaar, in order to proceed to Habbesh. I was prevented from going there last year by the straight road. Habbesh is a Christian country, abounding in slaves and gold. There are also many herbs valuable in medicine. Being there, I may easily join my countrymen, merchants who come to Moccha, in the Bahr Yemeni. I desire the Sultan will allow me to proceed thither; and, if it be necessary, grant me his protection, and three or four persons, deserving confidence, to attend me to the frontiers of Kordofân. I have a small present to offer him, consisting of such things as my circumstances permitted me to bring—I hope he may not refuse to receive it, and to grant me the favour I ask." He answered—" Merchant, you are welcome to the *Dar*—The King is kind to strangers, and he will favour you in all you wish. Whatever you want you have only to demand. He has ordered a sack of wheat and four sheep to be sent you.—At this time it is not possible to pass through Kordofân—The Sultan has a great army there, and when the country shall be in subjection to him you may pass unmolested. When you are admitted to his presence, you will tell him who has robbed you, and what you have lost, and he will cause it to be restored." It was now the hour of prayer, and when the company commenced their ablutions I retired.

During three or four days ensuing I suffered so violent a relapse as to be unable to perform the common offices of life, and even to suppose that it was nearly at an end. The moment any symptom of amelioration appeared, I sent word to the Melek that it was my wish to be introduced to the Sultan, and then as soon as possible to be dismissed. No reply was made to this message; but the following day he came to the tent with some of his attendants, and desired to see the merchandize that I had brought with me. As to part of the articles, consisting of wearing apparel suited to the great, &c. I very readily complied.

plied. But this was not sufficient—The Melek insisted also on seeing the contents of a small chest, which chiefly held articles useful to myself, but not designed for sale. There were also in it some English pistols, of which I intended to avail myself as presents at Sennaar, or wherever else I might be able to penetrate. I therefore positively refused to open the chest. He then threatened to have it broke open—I remained unmoved—At length his attendants proceeding to break it open, *Ali Hamad*, the man who was with me, with his usual villany, took the key from its concealment and opened the box. Every thing was taken out, and examined minutely—many small articles appeared no more. The pistols were reserved to be taken by the Sultan, (after a violent but fruitless altercation,) at the valuation made by his own servants; and my telescopes, books, of which they knew not the use, wearing apparel, &c. were graciously left me.

The valuation was to be made the following day, which was done quite against my consent, and in contempt of my warmest remonstrances. Some part of the articles were stated at their full value, and others far below it. The whole was estimated at thirty-eight head of slaves, being at the market-price worth about eighty, exclusively of a present of value for the Sultan. A pair of double-barrelled pistols, silver-mounted, which had cost twenty guineas in London, were valued at one slave, which is commonly purchasable, by those who are experienced in that traffic, for the value of fifteen piastres in Egyptian commodities. On this I exclaimed, that if they meant to plunder, and bargain and sale were not conducted in this country by

consent

consent of the parties, but by force, it would be better to take the whole gratis.—No answer was made, but the day following two camels were brought me as a present.

The violent manner in which my property had been seized, and the general ill-treatment I had received, much augmented the disorder, already severe. I had now been fifteen days in the tent, exposed to great variations of temperature, it being at the close of the rainy season, and so entirely disregarded, that though tormented with thirst, I could rarely obtain water to drink. I judged that the only means of restoration which remained were, to return to Cobbé, and avail myself of the shelter of a clay-house, and that privacy and quiet, the want of which I had so sensibly felt. Being in possession of the greater part of my property, and having left me only so much as would supply the wants of a few months, the Melek did not seem very anxious about my stay. I hired two Arabs, and with the camels that had been given me, and the property that remained, made my way on the third day to the place whence I came.

In the intervals of my illness, I visited the chief persons of the place; and as the eyes of the people became habituated to me, I found my situation growing somewhat more tolerable. Idle, as I certainly was, during this winter, with respect to the immediate objects of my voyage, I grew of course more familiar with the manners and particular dialect of the country; for the Arabic, which is spoken here, differs materially

rially from the vernacular idiom of Egypt. I seldom, indeed, joined in the parties where *Merifi** was introduced, because it was important not to hazard becoming concerned in the riots, which are the frequent consequence of their inebriation. But I was often diverted by the mode of conducting a bargain, which sometimes lasts for several hours; and I listened, perhaps not wholly without instruction, to their legal arguments, and the cool discussions of right, which are the consequence of often submitting disputes to arbitration. I could smile at the quibbling distinctions, by which the niceties of external observance are settled; but I had generally reason to be satisfied with their theory of morals.

It is usual for the graver men, during the heat of the day, to sit and converse under a shed erected for the purpose. When convalescent, I seldom failed to be of this party; for though the conversation contained few sallies of wit, much less profundity of observation, yet it was carried on without ill-humour, with mutual forbearance, and on the whole in an equable course. Perhaps indeed the society appeared less dull, as dissipating reflections which my situation rendered unpleasant.

The following summer (1794) having in some degree recovered my strength, I determined to go and reside for a time near the Sultan, as well to have an opportunity of supplicating for redress of what I had already suffered, as to seize any mo-

---

* A fermented liquor, called *Búza* or *Merifi*.

ment that might offer of pressing my request for permission to advance. On leaving the house which I had inhabited at Cobbé, a dispute had arisen with the owner of it, who wanted me to sign a declaration that nothing had been lost during my residence in his house. This, which was directly the reverse of the truth, I refused to do; and in consequence he called an assembly of *Fukkara* or sacred judges. The result, after much contest, served to skreen him from the responsibility legally attached to his conduct, without averting the charge, and determined me never to return to his roof.

On my arrival at El Fasher, my good friend the Melek Misellim being employed by his master in the South, I went under the protection of the Melek *Ibrahim*, one of the oldest persons in authority there, and lodged myself (as all strangers are obliged to lodge in the inclosure of some of the natives) in the house of a man named *Musa*, now only an inconsiderable officer, though one of the sons of Sultan *Bokar*. This Musa was one of the most upright and disinterested men I have known in that country, and indeed among the Mohammedans of any country. Calm and dignified in his demeanour, though poor and destitute of power, he never insulted, though his religion taught him to hate. No motive could have been strong enough to induce him to eat out of the same plate with a Caffre, but he was punctiliously observant of the rights of hospitality which that religion also dictated, and daily provided me with a portion of food from his kitchen. He often said that, as it was a precept of my faith to hate the Prophet, he was bound to encourage the same sentiment towards me; but that he was neither obliged to injure me, nor excused in doing so.

The Melek Ibrahim is a man of about sixty years of age, tall but not athletic, and characterised by the roughness rather than the expression of his features. He has no beard, and the little hair which remains either on his head or face is grey. His manners and even the motions of his body are ungraceful, and without the ease of superior rank, or the majesty of superior intellect. Yet his understanding seems clear and comprehensive, and his sagacity not unworthy the station assigned him—one of the first in the empire. He is indeed a bigot in matters of faith, but in all that concerns not the prevailing superstition, his judgment is cool, and little liable to error. He once held the reputation of integrity above the rest of his order, but his present riches render this character ambiguous. Generosity, however, holds no place among his virtues. The uniform tenor of his life is governed by mean avarice; and though the most opulent man in the empire, except the Sultan, so little does he possess of Arabian hospitality, that the man used to be regarded as unhappy who went supperless to his evening councils. He had never yet seen a Frank, and regarded me nearly as the British or French commonalty view the dwarfish Goîtres of the Alps. I could collect from his conversation that he looked on Europeans as a small tribe, cut off by the singularity of colour and features, and still more by their impiety, from the rest of mankind.

When

When I entered the court where he was sitting, he bad me welcome, and received with complacency a present which, in compliance with custom, I brought on the occasion. He even thanked me for it; but expressed strong surprise at my journey to Dar-Fûr. I complained of the injuries done me, and he assured me of redress for the past, and protection for the future. At the same time it was clear that he esteemed the present a tribute, and conceived that personal safety was more than I could reasonably expect. His conduct afterwards was a further proof of his sentiments; for though I remained at El Fasher three entire months, I saw him only when I forced myself on his notice, and experienced no return of civility, much less any compensation for what I had already suffered.

During this time I was solicitous to attend regularly the levees of the Sultan, which are from six in the morning till ten; but could very rarely obtain admittance, and when I did had no opportunity of speaking. Whether the general prejudice against me, or the machinations of my enemies, produced this pointed disregard, which, as was said, a stranger scarcely ever experienced before, circumstances afforded no sufficient ground to decide. I suspected the former; but probably both had their share.

On returning to my temporary habitation, a shed, as was usual with me on the sun's approach to the meridian, fatigued with heat, oppressed with thirst, and not without inclination for food, my repast was commonly a kind of bread gently acid, moistened with water. I grew acquainted with a few of the

people

people who attend the court, as well as with many strangers who were suitors there. Their conversation sometimes amused me, but more often I found their continued and unmeaning questions harassing and importunate, and their remarks either absurd or offensive. The tædium of solitude, unfurnished with the means to render it agreeable, was however removed. I occasionally frequented the markets, which are usually held from four o'clock in the afternoon till sunset. But my person being there still strange, the crowd that assembled inclined me to a precipitate retreat.

The Fûrians here seemed unacquainted with the sports of the field. I occasionally went out with a gun after the commencement of the rainy season, when the face of the country became green; but little offered itself worthy attention, either in the animal or vegetable kingdoms. During the early part of the summer the earth had been parched, and destitute of all vegetation.

After waiting in fruitless expectation at El Fasher, as the time of my departure was drawing near, an accident happened, which, though not of the most pleasing kind, contributed to make me noticed, and obtained for me at length an interview with the Sultan.—The slaves of the house used frequently to collect round me, as if to examine a strange object—I joked occasionally with them, without any other view than that of momentary relaxation. One day as I was reading in the hut, one of them, a girl about fifteen, came to the door of it, when, from a whim of the moment, I seized the cloth that was round her waist, waift, which dropped and left her naked. Chance fo determined that the owner of the flave paffed at the moment and faw her. The publicity of the place precluded any view of farther familiarity, but the tumult which fucceeded appeared to mark the moft heinous of crimes, and to threaten the moft exemplary vengeance. The man threw his turban on the earth, and exclaimed, " Ye believers in the Prophet, hear me! Ye faithful, avenge me!" with other fimilar expreffions.—" A Caffre has violated the property of a defcendant of Mohammed;" (meaning himfelf, which was utterly falfe.) When a number of people was collected around him, he related the fuppofed injury he had received in the ftrongeft terms, and exhorted them to take their arms and facrifice the Caffre. He had charged a carbine, and affected to come forward to execute his threats, when fome one of the company who had advanced fartheft, and faw me, called out to the reft that I was armed, and prepared to refift.

It was then agreed among the affembly that fome method of punifhment might be found, that promifed more fecurity and profit to the complainant, and would be more formidable to the guilty. The man whom I have already mentioned as my broker was to take the flave, as if fhe had really been violated*, and agreed to pay whatever her mafter fhould charge as the

---

* By the law of the Prophet, any illicit connection with the female flave of another makes the perfon guilty refponfible for her value to the owner. Thus the perfonal injury is expiated. The public offence of *Zinna*, whoredom, incurs a punifhment varying according to the character and circumftances of the offender; but the pofitive teftimony of four witneffes is neceffary to eftablifh this fact.

price.

price. The latter had the modesty to ask ten head of slaves. He was then to make his demand on me for the value of ten slaves, and if I carried the matter before the Cadi, which he supposed I should hardly venture to do, he had suborned witnesses to prove that I had received of him property to that amount.

On my removal from Cobbé to El Fasher, I had caused my small remaining property, among which were few articles of value, but many of much use to me, to be lodged in the house of *Hossein*, (the owner of the slave,) and his companion. On my return thither, which happened within a few days after the accident, I claimed it: they resisted, as they alleged, at the suit of my broker, and would not deliver it till the value of ten slaves should be paid to him. I had from the first considered their conduct as so violent, that if it reached the ears of the government, the claim must unquestionably be abandoned: and indeed my adversaries had only rested their expectations on the timidity which they had been accustomed to observe in Christians of the country, whose accusation and condemnation are in fact the same. I had not neglected to give the transaction all the notoriety I could, without having recourse to public authority, and those to whom I had applied were decidedly in my favour: I therefore now went to my adversaries, Hossein and his companion, and in their presence offered to Ali Hamad a promissory note for the value of ten slaves, at the market price on my arrival in Kahira. It was refused; and my chest, in which were some German dollars and other articles, was still detained by them; the rest was given up.

In

In the mean time much had been said on the subject, both among the natives and foreigners; and the flagrant injustice I was likely to suffer forcibly struck all that were not in a state to profit by it, but none more than the Egyptian merchants: they were indignant to see that so enormous a penalty should be forfeited to those who had no claim but effrontery to demand it; and that they had no share, and were too numerous to expect to be all rewarded for connivance; accordingly some of them were diligent in carrying the news to the monarch.

It is not to be imagined that he would have moved in the business, from any love of justice, or commiseration with the sufferings of a person to whom himself had shewn such pointed disregard, not to say manifest injustice. But he was told that the Franks enjoyed great favour with the Senjiaks, and that whatever one of their number suffered in Fûr, might be retaliated on the jelabs on their arrival at Kahira, with very little effort, by getting their property there seized by the magistrate, either as an indemnification for what should have been lost, or a security for what might happen. Add to this, he thought his own dignity compromised, should a foreigner thus be permitted to vindicate himself by force in his country. I had indeed been told that the Sultan was apprised of the transaction previously to my departure from El Fasher, and that he intended to grant me redress; but after waiting about fifteen days without hearing any thing farther of his intentions, weary of suffering, I determined to return. I had been there but a short time when a *fulganawy* (messenger) arrived express from the court, with orders for me to repair to El Fasher immediately. The object of the message was kept in profound secrecy, nor could I discover whether it portended good or evil. I left Cobbé the same evening, and arrived at the end of my journey the following day about noon.

I repaired as before to the Melek Ibrahim, who on the following day introduced me at the public audience. The Sultan, as he retired to the palace after it was over, ordered all the parties to appear. Being come within the inner court, he stopped the white mule on which he was mounted, and began a short harangue, addressing himself to Hossein and Ali Hamad, my servant, in which he censured, in a rapid and energetic style, their conduct towards me.—" One," said he, turning to Ali, " calls himself Wakîl of the Frank; if he were a Sherîf and a Mûslim, as he pretends, he would know that the law of the Prophet permits not a Mûslim to be Wakîl to a Caffre: another calls himself his friend—but both are agreed in robbing him of his property, and usurping the authority of the laws.—Henceforth I am his Wakîl, and will protect him." He then ordered all the parties to repair to the house of Musa Wullad Jelfûn, Melek of the jelabs, under whose appropriate jurisdiction are all foreign merchants. Here it may not be improper to relate briefly how I had been before received by the Sultan.

On my first audience I was too ill to make much observation: I was seated at a distance from him; the visit was short, and I had no opportunity of opening a conversation. He was placed on his seat (*cûrsi*) at the door of his tent. Some person had mentioned to him my watch, and a copy of Erpenius's Grammar,

which

which I had with me. He asked to see both; but after casting his eyes on each he returned them. The present I had brought was shewn him, for which he thanked me, and rose to retire.

During the following summer, the first time I got admission to him, he was holding a diwan in the outer court. He was then mounted on a white mule, clothed with a scarlet *Banish*, and had on his head a white turban; which however, together with part of his face, was covered with a thick muslin. On his feet were yellow boots, and the saddle on which he was seated was of crimson velvet, without any ornament of gold or silver. His sword, which was broad and straight, and adorned with an hilt of massy gold, was held horizontally in his right hand. A small canopy of muslin was supported over his head. Amid the noise and hurry of above a thousand persons who were there assembled, I was unable to make myself heard, which the nature of my situation obliged me to attempt, though not exactly conformable to the etiquette of the court, that, almost to the exclusion of strangers, had appropriated the diwan to the troops, the Arabs, and others connected with the government.

On another occasion I contrived to gain admittance to the interior court by a bribe. The Sultan was hearing a cause of a private nature, the proceedings on which were only in the Fûrian language. He was seated on a kind of chair, كرسي, which was covered with a Turkey carpet, and wore a red silk turban; his face was then uncovered: the Imperial sword was placed across his knees, and his hands were engaged with a chaplet of red coral. Being near him I fixed my eyes on him, in order to have a perfect idea of his countenance, which, being short-sighted, and not thinking it very decent to use a glass in his presence, I had hitherto scarcely found an opportunity of acquiring. He seemed evidently discomposed at my having observed him thus, and the moment the cause was at an end, he retired very abruptly. Some persons to whom I afterwards remarked the circumstance seemed to think that his attendants had taught him to fear the magic of the Franks, to the operation of which their habit of taking likenesses is imagined by some of the Orientals to conduce. He is a man rather under the middle size, of a complexion adust or dry, with eyes full of fire, and features abounding in expression. His beard is short but full, and his countenance, though perfectly black, materially differing from the negro; though fifty or fifty-five years of age, he possesses much alertness and activity.

At another of my visits I found him in the interior court, standing, with a long staff tipped with silver in his right hand, on which he leaned, and the sword in his left. He then had chosen to adorn his head with the folds of a red silk turban, composed of the same material as the western Arabs use for a cincture. The Melek Ibrahim presented him, in my name, with a small piece of silk and cotton, of the manufacture of Damascus. He returned answer, *Barak ulla fi!*—May the blessing of God be on him!—a phrase in general use on receiving any favour, and instantly retired, without giving me time to urge the request of which I intended the offering should be the precursor. It is expected of all persons that, on coming to El Fasher, they should

should bring with them a present of greater or less value, according to the nature of the business in hand. It is no less usual before leaving the royal residence, to ask permission of the Sultan for that purpose. With this latter form, which was to me unpleasant, I sometimes complied, but more frequently omitted it. But on this occasion, having been long resident there, I thought fit to make a last effort to promote my design. The day preceding that which I had fixed for my return happened to be a great public audience. I found the monarch seated on his throne (*cûrsi*), under a lofty canopy, composed not of one material, but of various stuffs of Syrian and even of Indian fabric, hung loosely on a light frame of wood, no two pieces of the same pattern. The place he sat in was spread with small Turkey carpets. The Meleks were seated at some distance on the right and left, and behind them a line of guards, with caps, ornamented in front with a small piece of copper and a black ostrich feather. Each bore a spear in his hand, and a target of the hide of the hippopotamus on the opposite arm. Their dress consisted only of a cotton shirt, of the manufacture of the country. Behind the throne were fourteen or fifteen eunuchs, clothed indeed splendidly in habiliments of cloth or silk, but clumsily adjusted, without any regard to size or colour. The space in front was filled with suitors and spectators, to the number of more than fifteen hundred. A kind of hired encomiast stood on the monarch's left hand, crying out, *a plein gorge*, during the whole ceremony, " See the buffaloe (جاموس), the offspring of a buffaloe, a bull of bulls, the elephant of superior strength, the powerful Sultan Abd-el-rachmân-el-rashîd !

May

May God prolong thy life!—O Master—May God assist thee, and render thee victorious!"

From this audience, as from those which had preceded it, I was obliged to retire as I had come, without effecting any purpose. I was told there were occasions when the Sultan wears a kind of crown, as is common with other African monarchs; but of this practice I had no opportunity to bear testimony. When he appeared in public, a number of troops armed with light spears usually attended him, and several of his slaves were employed to bear a kind of umbrella over his head, which concealed his face from the multitude. When he passes, all the spectators are obliged to appear barefooted, and commonly to kneel—His subjects bow to the earth, but this compliance is not expected from foreigners. Even the Meleks, when they approach the throne, creep on their hands and knees, which gave occasion to an Egyptian to remark, that the *Jarea** in Fûr was a Melek, and the Melek a *Jarea*—alluding to the servile behaviour of the ministers, and the publicity of women in the domestic offices of the palace.

The Sultan Abd-el-rachmân, soon after he became possessed of sovereign authority, with the ostensible motive of testifying his attachment to the religion of the Prophet, but more perhaps with a view of obtaining greater weight among his subjects, by some mark of the consideration of the first of Mohammedan princes, thought proper to send a present to Constantinople.

---

* A female slave.

tinople. It confisted of three of the choicest eunuchs, and three of the most beautiful female slaves that could be procured. The Othman emperor, when they were presented, had, it is said, never heard of the Sultan of Dar-Fûr, but he returned an highly-ornamented sabre, a rich pelisse, and a ring set with a single diamond of no inconsiderable value.

CHAP. XVI.

DAR-FÛR.

Residence with the Melek Musa—Dissimulation of the Arabs—Incidents—Return to Cobbé—Endeavours to proceed farther into Africa—Necessity of exercising Medicine—Festival—Punishment of Conspirators—Art of the Sultan—Atrocious Conduct of my Kahirine servant—At length find an opportunity of departure, after a constrained residence in Dar-Fûr of nearly three years.

My reception with Musa Wullad Jelfûn was very different from that which I had experienced in the house of Misellim, or Ibrahim. All the principal people saluted me, and sought my conversation. The Melek, by those who knew him, was esteemed a man of consummate dissimulation, and boundless ambition; quick of apprehension, decisive, and energetic. I found him easy and dignified in his manner; and, by his communication with foreigners perhaps, more polished, and better informed, than the rest of his order. His behaviour toward myself was complacent; and he affected to seek opportunities of hearing my sentiments on such subjects as occurred. During three days we were generally seated with him, and partook of his table, which was remarkable for the abundant supply, if not

for

for the delicacy of the food. On these occasions I was indeed frequently harassed with questions, the simplicity of which disgusted me, and was even in some instances indirectly reviled for my supposed attachment to a sect, whose tenets among Mohammedans are thought absurd and even impious. However, when they were led to imagine that the favour of the Sultan was beginning to brighten my prospects, their disposition on that head appeared much more easy and tolerant. But I was also frequently impressed with the clear intelligence, and penetrating sagacity, with which the claims of the respective suitors were investigated, and the equity and firmness with which they were terminated by this officer. Oftener than once even, during my short abode with him, the best constructed plans to disguise the truth, and elude the purposes of justice, were laid open and rendered abortive; for it is remarkable with how much artifice the Arabs, however ignorant in other respects, defend themselves, whether right or wrong, as long as they have any profit to hope, or loss to dread. So clear is their discernment, so retentive their memory, and so firm their resolution on these occasions, that no word, no look, not even an involuntary movement escapes them, which can in the smallest degree betray their cause; and the longest cross-examination, or questions put at the greatest distance of time, will bring to light no fact unfavourable to the interest which they are to defend.

In obedience to the Sultan's command, I gave in an exact statement of the property I had lost, and substantiated the proof by the strongest circumstantial evidence. With regard to the slave, the most complete redress was accorded me. The charge brought against me was judged absolutely futile, and she was restored to her master; while he, on the other hand, was compelled to give up the chest, &c. which had been violently withheld. The plunder which had fallen into the hands of my servant and his accomplice was not so easily restored. The Melek, tired of gratuitous justice, began to think that a lucrative composition was more eligible. The offenders, who had been obstinate in the first instance, seeing how the cause relative to the *jarea* (female slave) had been decided, thought proper to offer to the Melek marks of their gratitude for the lenity they expected from him; and the Sultan was unwilling to imagine that the sufferings of a Caffre could fall heavy on himself at the day of final retribution. In fact, his disgust at the complaints continually preferred, and jealousy and resentment against some of the Egyptians, who in this and other instances appeared to have usurped his authority, certainly influenced him in the first part of the proceedings, rather than any love of justice.

At length the Melek, who in reality was supreme arbiter of the contest, contented himself with giving me in intrinsic value about four head of slaves, instead of twenty-four or twenty-five, which at first he had unequivocally declared due to me, and promised I should receive. And thus the matter was terminated.

I a second time retired to Cobbé, with little expectation of ever leaving the country. Of the property which the king's agents had on my arrival purchased, no part of the price had yet

yet been discharged. I had been insulted with the mockery of justice, yet obliged to thank my oppressors for the compensation with their corruption and malignity alone had rendered incomplete.

I had not indeed omitted to renew to the Melek Musa, the request which had been previously made to Misellim and Ibrahim. I explained to him in the manner least exceptionable, my intention in coming thither, completely did away all the suspicions, which my enemies had at first been assiduous to excite, and too successful in establishing; and concluded with desiring permission to go to Sennaar, or to accompany the first *Selatea* (an armed expedition for the purpose of acquiring slaves) to the South or South-west; or finally to have a safe-conduct, and one of the Sultan's slaves, acknowleged as such, to accompany me to *Bergoo* (the first Mohammedan kingdom to the West). By the *first* route I hoped to have reached Abyssinia; or, if that had been impracticable, to have gone through Nubia to Egypt, or by Suakem to the Red Sea, and thence to Mocha or Jidda. By the *second* I was almost certain of settling some important points relative to the White River, possibly of tracing it to its source. And by the *third*, either of passing directly West, and tracing the course of the Niger, or of penetrating through Bornou and Fezzan to Tripoli.

To the first proposal, he answered in a manner which gave me no reason to doubt his sincerity, that the road to Sennaar was at present impassable, the Sultan being as yet master of but one half of Kordofan; that the natives of all that part of it which remained unsubdued, were his implacable foes, and would infallibly destroy any person who came from Dar-Fûr; that he thought however, if I waited another year, that route might possibly be more secure; and in case it should be so, that he would use all his efforts to obtain the Sultan's permission for my departure. Of the *Selatea* he said, that I should only encounter certain death by attempting it, as between the jealousy of those who accompanied me, and the actual hostility of the country attacked, there would be no hope of escaping. I hinted that the Sultan might give me a few attendants, whom I was very ready to pay, and an order to enable me to pass unmolested, as his physician in search of herbs. He replied that he would propose such a measure, but did not expect it would receive the Sultan's approbation, whom he represented as very adverse to strangers, and still suspicious of me individually, in consequence of the reports that had been spread on my arrival. To the third proposal, he answered, that he had no hope of my succeeding; and if I should attempt it, would by no means be answerable for what might happen, since the utmost distrust subsisted between the monarchs of Fûr and Bergoo, and the most implacable enmity to Christians in the latter country. He concluded with strongly recommending it to me to seize the first opportunity of returning to Egypt; but assured me, that if he could accomplish either of the measures I so much wished, he would not fail to inform me, and afford me the necessary aid. I left matters thus when I retired to Cobbé, dejected, and little expecting to realize even my least sanguine hopes. Not more than six weeks after this conversation had taken place, I was sent for in haste to attend the Melek, who was confined by an

old

old disorder in his lungs. I found him yet sensible, but his eyes were fixed, and the extremities incapable of motion. In five hours afterwards he expired. Thus were blasted my returning hopes of success; for no mediator now remained between myself and the monarch, and no longer was there near the court a man, even of seeming liberality and good sense, to whom my projects might safely be opened.

The transactions I had been engaged in, and my frequent appearance in public, had given me a degree of notoriety, which I shunned rather than sought. Having learned by accident that I was in possession of a few medicines, which indeed were rather studiously concealed, all the town grew indisposed, and sought for remedies. Under various pretences, I as often as possible declined administering any; but one or two of the sick having recovered, spread the news of their supposed cure, with such additions as they thought proper. It then became necessary for me to attend at El Fasher, whither I was sent for on several occasions, in the course of the subsequent year. Soon after Musa's death, a messenger arrived requiring my presence, but, as is usual with them, without specifying the object. Judging it might possibly be something favourable to my interests, I used all possible dispatch. On my arrival I was directed to attend the *Faqui Seradge*, the principal Imam, who was ill of a fistula. It appeared that palliatives could afford him no relief, and I declined the responsibility attached to more violent remedies. On this occasion however the Sultan had seen me, and addressed me personally, telling me that he should give orders for the payment of what was due to me, and that he should

consult

consult my inclination in all things. I began to press my request for permission to travel; but to this he turned a deaf ear, and soon left the place of audience. Another time I was called to a Melek, a man of advanced age, who had been blind of one eye for nine years, but was much displeased at being told his disorder was incurable. Many instances of the same kind occurred.

The same winter I was sent for by Misellim, to receive a part of what was due to me. He was at Gidîd, a town about forty miles from Cobbé. I was not long detained, having been permitted to return in a few hours after my arrival. But the payment was made in oxen, a commodity to me of very little value. They however afforded me subsistence for some months, which otherwise probably I should have wanted.

The first week of the month *Rabía-el-achir*, this year, was distinguished by a festival which I conceive peculiar to this country—the *Geled-el-Nahâs*, the leathering of the kettle-drum. It lasts eight or ten days successively; during which time the Meleks and great men offer to the monarch considerable presents. I have known the Melek of jelabs take with him in his visit of congratulation presents, of various kinds, worth sixty head of slaves. Almost all, except absolute mendicants, are obliged to come forward with some offering, proportioned to their rank. In recompence of this involuntary generosity on the part of the people, a kindness almost as involuntary, but somewhat cheaper, is exhibited on the part of the Sultan—his kitchen during the time is devoted to the public service. But as too great a number of of animals is frequently slaughtered on the first day, the meat often remains to be devoured in a corrupt state; which gave occasion to some one to remark, that the festivals of Fûr resembled those of the Leopard *. The celebrity is also marked by a review of the troops. But as their equestrian exercises are no more than a clumsy imitation of those of the Mamlûks, a more particular description of them would afford nothing new. They serve however to characterise the mode of warfare, where victory is always the effect of personal exertion. The monarch and his chief officers have fine horses of Dongola, which they mount without skill, carrying in one hand five or six javelins, in the use of which they are adequately expert.

During the summer of 1794, five men, who had exercised considerable authority in some of the provinces, were brought to El Fasher as prisoners. It was said that they had been detected in treasonable correspondence with the hostile leader (Hashem) in Kordofân. They did not undergo any form of trial, but as the Sultan chose to give credit to the depositions that were made against them, his command issued for their execution. Three of them were very young men, the youngest not appearing to be more than seventeen years of age. Two of them were eunuchs. A little after noon they were brought, chained and fettered, into the market-place before one of the entrances of the palace, escorted by a few of the royal slaves, armed with spears. Several of the Meleks, by the monarch's express order,

---

* It is not usual with Mohammedans to eat meat in such a state. It is reported in Soudan, I know not how truly, that the Leopard, after he has seized his prey, leaves it till it become putrid before he eats of it.

were present, to witness, as he termed it, what they might expect to suffer if they failed in their fidelity. The executioner allowed them time only to utter some short prayer, when he plunged the knife in the neck of the oldest of them, exactly in the same manner as they kill a sheep. The operation too is marked by the same term (*dhebbah*). He fell and struggled for some time: the rest suffered in their turn. The three last were much agitated, and the youngest wept. The two first had borne their fate with becoming firmness. The crowd, that had assembled, had scarcely satiated itself with the spectacle of their convulsive motions, while prostrate in the dust, when the slaves of the executioner coolly brought a small block of wood, and began mangling their feet with an axe. I was surprized at this among Mohammedans, whose decency in all that concerns the dead is generally worthy of applause. Nor did it diminish my astonishment, that having at length cut off their feet, they took away the fetters, which had been worn by the criminals, in themselves of very inconsiderable value, and left the bodies where they were. Private humanity, and not public order, afterwards afforded them sepulture.

It happened this year that some excesses had been committed by persons in a state of inebriation, and the Sultan having had cognizance of the fact, could find a remedy only in force. He ordered search to be made in all houses throughout the country for the utensils for making *merisé*; directed that those who should be found in a state of intoxication should be capitally punished; and the women who made it should have their heads shaved, be fined severely, and exposed to all possible ignominy. The

The Furians had however been habituated to Merísé before they had known their monarch, or the Iſlam. The ſeverity of the order, therefore, and the numbers treſpaſſing againſt it, defeated the Sultan's purpoſe. It was indeed put in execution, and a few miſerable women ſuffered unrelenting tonſure, and innumerable earthen jars were indignantly ſtrewed piecemeal in the paths of the faithful; but the opulent, as is uſual, eſcaped with impunity, and ſome were bold enough to ſay, that the eyes even of the Sultan's women were ſtill reddened with the voluptuous beverage, while prieſts and magiſtrates were bearing the fulminating edict from one extremity of the empire to the other. It is certain that, ſubſequent to this new law, the minds of the troops were much alienated from the monarch, and it is thought that no other cauſe than this was to be ſought. The monarch who admits of no licence will never reign in the hearts of the ſoldiery; and he muſt give up the hope of their affections, who is diſpoſed to become an impartial cenſor of the public morals.

Innumerable reports had been propagated at different times, that the Jelabs would be allowed to depart. But none was well authenticated; nay, as afterwards appeared, all were falſe. It is probable they were artfully circulated by order of the Sultan, with a view to cajole the foreign merchants, who, having now collected the intended number of ſlaves, were at a heavy expenſe for their daily ſuſtenance, and of courſe ill bore the unexplained delay, while his own merchandize was ſold at a prodigious advance in Egypt. In effect, two ſmall caravans found their way thither, between the time of my arrival at

Fûr, and that of my departure; but they confifted only of the Sultan's property, and that of one or two individuals, whom he particularly favoured. For a great quantity of merchandize having accumulated in his hands, he was determined to difpofe of it to advantage, before the other merchants fhould be permitted to produce theirs for fale.

They were therefore reftrained by the ftrong arm of power, to favour the monarch's pernicious monopoly; while the latter, with fingular effrontery, gave out, that he had fent to negociate with the Beys the reception of the commodities of Soudân, on more advantageous terms than they had been before admitted.

The man whom I had brought with me from Kahira as fervant, had availed himfelf of the property he had plundered to purchafe feveral flaves. He ftill continued to live in an apartment within the fame inclofure with myfelf, and I occafionally employed one of his flaves to prepare my food.

He knew too much of me to imagine that I fhould lofe any opportunity that might offer of punifhing him, and accordingly was defirous of anticipating my defign. I had received warning of his views, and was cautious, fleeping little at night, and going always armed; not that I much expected any thing would be attempted by open force, though in effect two men had been employed by him, under promife of a reward, to ftrangle me. Finding that meafure unfuccefsful, he obtained fome *corrofive fublimate*, and put it into a difh that one of the flaves was dreffing. She was honeft and generous enough to

inform

inform me of it, or the scheme would probably have taken effect, as I had certainly then no suspicion. The villain on returning, after a few hours, and finding that the poison had not produced its effect, vented his rage on the slave, and had nearly strangled her with a cord, when I interfered and forced him to leave her. The next scheme was an accusation of debauching his slaves, which after a tedious investigation before the civil judge, and then the Melek of Jelabs, I was able to refute. Other attempts, planned with sufficient art, were made against my life, which, however, I had equal good fortune in escaping.

In the summer of 1795, I received the second payment for the property in the Sultan's hands, which consisted of female camels (*naka*). The same injustice operated on this occasion as before. After all the other creditors of the monarch had been satisfied, I was directed to choose from what remained: two of which, as usual, were allotted as equivalent to a slave, though of so inferior a kind, that three would not have been sufficient to purchase one.

After having received these, I was preparing to return to Cobbé, when a message came to require my attendance on a sick person. The patient was brother of the Melek of the Jelabs. He was in the last stage of a peripneumony, and I immediately saw the case was desperate; but was forced to remain there with the sick man, administering such remedies as his situation permitted the application of, till he expired. Two guides were sent to accompany me home, but coming to a torrent that

crossed

crossed the road, (it was the middle of the *Harif*, or wet season,) they were fearful of passing it, and returned, after endeavouring in vain to persuade me to do the same. I was obliged to abandon the camel, which belonged to the Melek, and pursue my journey on foot.

The time I was constrained to devote to this patient afforded me an opportunity of remarking the *True believer's practice of physic*. No mummery, that ever was invented by human imbecility to banish the puny fears of mortality, was forgotten to be put in practice. The disease was sometimes exorcised as a malignant spirit, at others deprecated as the just visitation of the Deity: two or three thousand *fathas* were to be uttered, and numbered at the same moment on a chaplet; and sentences of the Koran were then written on a board, which being washed off, the inky water was offered to the sick man to drink, when he was no longer able to open his mouth. But though this puerile anxiety prevailed so long as the man remained alive, the moment he was dead, all sunk into undisturbed composure, except a few of the women, who officiously disquieted the living, with vociferations of affected sorrow for the dead.

Near the end of the year 1795, a body of troops was mustered and reviewed, who were to replace those that had died of the small-pox in Kordofân, which it was said amounted to more than half the army. The spoils which had been taken from Hashem, were also on this occasion ostentatiously displayed. They consisted of eighty slaves, male and female, but the greater proportion of the latter, many of them were very beautiful,

beautiful, nor the less interesting, that though the change in their situation could not be very important, their countenances were marked with despondency. To these succeeded five hundred oxen and two hundred large camels; the whole procession concluded with eighty horses, and many articles of less value borne by slaves. Shouts rent the air, of " Long live el Sultan Abd-el-rachmân el rashîd! May God render him always victorious!"

A short time after I caused a petition to be drawn up, which was presented by Ali-el-Chatîb to the Sultan, in which I stated my sufferings, requested payment of what yet remained due to me, and permission to proceed on my journey to Kordofân. Though the person who presented it was a man of considerable weight, no answer was given. I therefore followed it up by a visit in person, which I had resolved should be my last. My arrival was no sooner known, than I was directed as before to attend some sick person. This I positively refused to do; and it was many days before I could be admitted at court, for Fowaz, the Melek of Jelabs, was grown tired of his office. I therefore accompanied (11th December 1795) the Chatîb to the monarch's presence, and shortly stated what I came to request, which the former seconded, though not with the zeal that I might have wished. To my demand of permission to travel no answer was returned. But the generous and hospitable monarch, who had received from me the value of about 750 piasters in goods, and notwithstanding that my claim was well supported, condescended to give me twenty meagre oxen, in value about 120 piasters! The state of my purse would not per-

mit

mit me to refuse even this mean supply, and I bad adieu to El Fasher, as I hoped for ever.

Another accident happened at this time, which awaked my attention to personal security. Being retired at night to a small distance from my apartment, a spear was thrown over the fence, grazed my shoulder, and stuck in the ground near me. I ran to the place whence it came, but saw no one, and in vain endeavoured to discover the owner of it.

Having applied the value of the oxen to preparatives for the journey to Egypt, the report of the caravan's departure growing daily stronger, I lost no time in joining the Chabîr, who was then encamped at *Le Haimer*, (3d March 1796,) a small village about three days' journey North of Cobbé, where was a tolerable supply of water, but no other requisite for living.

Two nights previously to leaving Cobbé I received a letter, impressed with the seal of Fowas, Melek of Jelabs, importing that he (Fowas) had obtained from the Sultan for me the permission I had so often earnestly sought, *viz.* of passing through Kordofan to Sennaar, and that nothing remained but to repair to El Fasher, and set out from that place. My astonishment was great at finding that what had so constantly and contumeliously been refused, should now be spontaneously offered. I therefore immediately went to some of the merchants, in whom I had the greatest confidence, to inquire their opinion. All of them strongly dissuaded me from paying any attention

to

to the Melek's letter, hinting at the same time that they understood what it meant. I acquiesced, notwithstanding my earnest desire of going eastward; and it afterwards was proved to me in a way sufficiently clear, that this letter was the result of a scheme concerted between the Melek and my servant Ali, by which it was contrived that I should reach the eastern confine, and there perish by the hands of my attendants.

During my residence at El Fasher and Cobbé, I had been repeatedly assured, and that from those persons who were best informed, that the Sultan never meant to permit my departure; and the imperfect compensation he had directed for what had been brought him confirmed that opinion. But as I knew much is done among persons of that description by whispers, I took care to spread them thickly in his way. To the Chabîr I promised an ample recompence for his assistance, and set before him the consequences of his appearing in Kahira without me. I also offered proofs that I had been able to dispatch letters to Egypt, unknown to the government here. The Chabîr did not neglect to use his interest with the Sultan; and whether the latter was really intimidated by these vain insinuations, whether he had begun to hold a more favourable opinion of me from my having been so long in the country without attempting any thing improper, or whether he was not in reality much more tranquil and indifferent on the subject than we at that time imagined, I cannot even now with certainty affirm.

We arrived at Le Haimer about a month before Ramadan, and it was not till the sixth day of El Hedge, the second month after

after that faſt, that we actually commenced our journey to Egypt. In the mean time having pitched the tent under a great tree, where we were ſheltered from the rays of the ſun, and in tolerable ſecurity, I fed on polenta (*as-cidé*) and water with the camel-drivers. I had collected eight camels for the journey, but the beſt of them was ſtolen while grazing. Another died; and to ſupply his place I was obliged to ſeek one on credit, for my whole exchangeable property at that time amounted only to about eight piaſters.

While the caravan was aſſembling, an incident happened which may deſerve mention. The Muggrebîns of Elwah, having paſſed by Selimé, croſſed the deſert (a route of three or four days) to Dongola, where they carried off goods and captives. Among theſe was a Dongoleſe girl, of fourteen years of age, who was ſold in Upper Egypt, and carried to Kahira, where ſhe was bought by an Arab, who had afterwards returned to Dar Fûr with his property. The girl being recognized by ſome Dongoleſe, of her own tribe, reſident in Fûr, the queſtion came before the Melek of the diſtrict, and was referred to the monarch. Her maſter pleaded the purchaſe at a valuable conſideration; but it was decided that having been free, ſhe was not a ſubject of ſale, and ſhe was reſtored to her friends.

This pretext of an accuſation for purchaſing free perſons is often uſed to extort money from rich merchants, and an inſtance happened, within my knowlege, in which the purchaſer was condemned, not only to forfeit two females, but to pay a fine of ſeven ſlaves for each. Such is the ſole attention which the government pays to the freedom of the ſubject.

Our

Our voyage, once commenced, was continued with little remarkable, except the violent heat. We returned by the only caravan route, *Bir el malah*, *Leghea*, *Selime*, *Sheb*, and *Elwah*. Our provisions were indifferent, and in small quantity. The camel-drivers regaled themselves with the flesh of those animals, when they chanced to be disabled on the road. When we came to *Beiris* we were met by a Cashef, who welcomed the Jelabs with an exhibition of fire works; on this occasion he treats the chief merchants with coffee, and presents to each a *benish* of coarse cloth, worth about a guinea, expecting, however, in return, a slave from each, worth at least ten guineas. When I arrived at Assiût it was four months since I had eaten of animal food. The hard living, heat, and fatigue, occasioned a diarrhea which much weakened me; but before leaving Assiût, where I passed about twenty days, it was considerably abated.

CHAP. XVII.

DAR-FÛR.

Topography of Fûr, with some account of its various inhabitants.

THE town called Cobbé, as being the principal residence of the merchants, and placed almost in the direct road from the North to the South extremity of the country, shall, for the sake of perspicuity, though not centrally situated, be considered as the capital of Dar-Fûr.

I found it to be in lat. 14° 11′ long. E. G. 28° 8′. This town is more than two miles in length, but very narrow, and the houses, each of which occupies within its inclosure a large portion of ground, are divided by considerable waste. The principal, or possibly the only view of convenience by which the natives appear to have been governed in their choice of situation and mode of building, must have been that of having the residence near the spot rented or inherited by them for the purpose of cultivation. The town is full of trees of several kinds, among which are the palm, *deleib*, &c. but chiefly the *beglig* and the *nebbek*, which give it an agreeable appearance at a small distance, for being situated in a plain, it is not distinctly visible more than four or five miles in any direction.

During

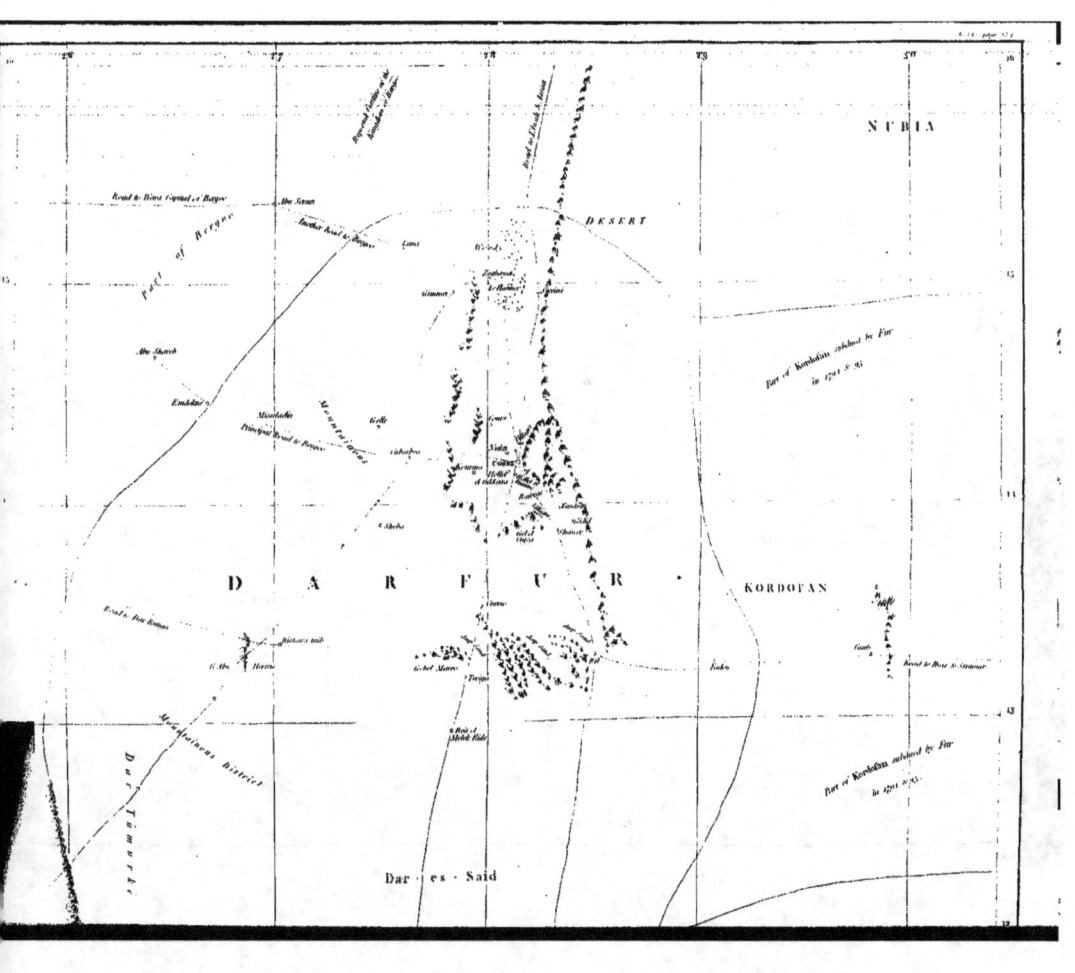

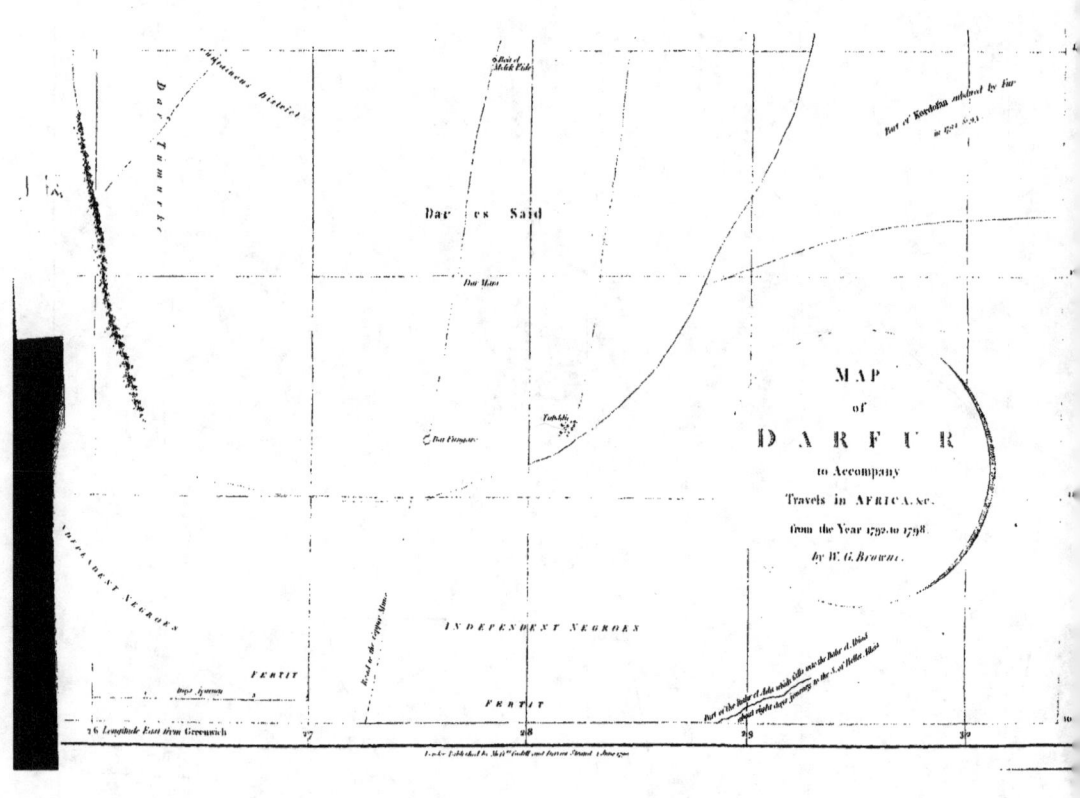

During the rainy season, the ground on which it stands is surrounded by a *wadi* or torrent. Fronting it to the East, (for the town extends from North to South,) is a mountain or rock, distinguished by the same appellation. It is not memorable for its height, nor indeed for any thing but as being the resort of hyenas and jackals; yet it forms part of a ridge of hills, or rocks, for there is little earth on them, which runs from North to South for many leagues.

The inhabitants are supplied with water from wells, of small depth, which are dug within the inclosure of many of the houses; but the best of them are those which are in or near the bed of the torrent. The water is generally turbid, and though not apparently possessing any injurious quality, has often an ungrateful flavour. The quantity too is not always equal to the public consumption, which sometimes throws the people into difficulties before the periodical return of the rains. Their manner of digging is so unskilful, that the soil often collapses; and the same well is seldom useful for more than three or four months successively.

There are some villages, at small distances, in various directions from Cobbé, which are dependent on it, and increase its apparent population. To the N. E. by N. *Hellet Hassan*, inhabited altogether by the people of *Dongola*. It has been *governed many years by the *Chabir Hassan wullad Nasr*, one of the oldest

* Here is one among many instances of tacit submission to the authority of the head of a tribe, though unfurnished with any express deputation from the government.

of them, who had been formerly once, or more than once, *Chabir* (leader) of the jelabs on their journey to Kahira, and a man, as I have generally understood, respectable for his talents and his virtues. North and North-west, *Nūkti* and *Hellet-hummār*. South, *Hellet-el-Atamné* and *Hellet Jemin-Ullah*. South-west and West, *Hellet-el-Fukkara* and *Bweri*. There are some other smaller ones, the names of which I have either never learned or have forgotten.

On all sides Cobbé is surrounded by a plain. To the West and South-west it extends to the foot of *Kerda* and *Malba*, two rough mountains or rocks, at about twenty-miles distance in that direction. South it is bounded by *Gebel Cusa*, at near twelve miles distance, near which are seen some villages. South-east it extends to *Barbogé*, and is there bounded, on the North-east, by *Gebel Wanna*, and on the East South-east by a wadi or torrent, which bears its name, and the sands (*goze*) beyond it. But to the East there is no extent of level ground; the whole road from *Sweini* North, to *Gidid* South, being bounded in that direction by a mountain, first under the name of *Téga*, and then under that of *Wanna*. Gebel Cobbé stands almost insulated, and is placed West of the latter. In Cobbé there are very few houses, perhaps none, inhabited by natives of Fûr. The people are all merchants and foreigners. The other more noted towns of the empire are, *Sweini, Kúrma, Cubcabia, Ril, Cours, Shoba, Gidid, Gellé*. Sweini is situated almost North of Cobbé, at the distance of more than two days diligent travelling. Koûrma, a small town, West by South, at the distance of four and a half or five hours—twelve or thirteen miles. Cubcabia, cabîa, a more confiderable one, it was not in my power to vifit, but it is defcribed as nearly due Weft, at the diftance of two days and a half. The road is rocky and mountainous, and of courfe may be fuppofed fomewhat circuitous. Cours, a place of little note, North-weft by Weft, at five hours and a half travelling from Cobbé. Ril is fomething more than three days removed from it, in the direction South-fouth-eaft; and as the road is good and lies through a plain, this cannot be eftimated at much lefs than fixty miles. Shoba is two days and a half from Cobbé.

Gidîd is nearly South-eaft, and about one day and a half from Cobbé. Gellé is not far from Cubcabîa, but fome hours further removed to the South. Sweini is the general refort of the merchants trading to Egypt, both in going and returning, and thence derives its chief importance. Provifions, of moft kinds which the country affords, are found there in plenty, and and while the jelabs remain there, a daily market is held. The Chatîb, and fome other of the principal merchants have houfes there, for the convenience of lodging their property, as the caravans pafs and repafs. A Melek, with a fmall number of troops, is always ftationed there to receive them. The town therefore may be confidered as in fome meafure the key of that road, though not entirely fo, as there are two others which lead from the center of Dar-Fûr towards Egypt, without going to Sweini.

The poorer people who conftantly live there, are either of the province called Zeghawa, or Arabs.

In

In Kourma, the merchants who occupy almoſt the whole of the place, are called the *Jciára*, moſt of them born in the Upper Egypt. Excluſively of them and their dependents, the number of people in that town is inconſiderable. Twice in the week a market is held there for meat and other proviſions, as at Cobbé.

Cubcabîa is a conſiderable town, and its inhabitants various and numerous. It forms the key of the Weſtern roads, as Sweini of the Northern; and is the depôt of all the merchandize that is brought from that quarter. A market is held there twice a week, in which the chief medium of exchange for articles of ſmall value is ſalt, which the inhabitants make by collecting and boiling the earth of thoſe places where horſes, aſſes, or other animals have been long ſtationary. This market is celebrated for the quantity of *tokeas*, and for the manufacture, if ſo it may be called, of leather, which they are very dextrous in ſtripping of the hair, tanning, and then forming into large and durable ſacks for corn, (*geraubs*,) water, (*ray*,) and other purpoſes. The tokeas are cotton cloths, of five, ſix, or eight yards long, and eighteen to twenty-two inches wide: they are ſtrong but coarſe, and form the covering of all the lower claſs of both ſexes. The inhabitants are partly Fûrians, who ſpeak their own language, in part Arabs, and partly from ſome of the Weſtern countries, as Bergoo, &c. There are alſo ſome of the race called *Felatîa*, and other deſcriptions.

In Cours are found ſome merchants from the river; the remainder are *fukkara*, who affect extraordinary ſanctity, and are diſtinguiſhed

guished for their intolerance and brutality to strangers. Rîl is inhabited partly by Fûrians; but there are also some foreign merchants. During the reign of Sultan Teraub there appear to have been many more there; for he had built a house, and made the town his usual residence in time of peace. But Abdel-rachmân has abandoned it, probably from the fear attendant on usurpation. Rîl* is the key of the South and East roads, as Cubcabìa of the West, and Sweini of the North; and therefore a Melek with a body of troops commonly resides there, as a guard to the frontier, and to keep the Arabs, who abound in that neighbourhood, in subjection. It is a place eminently fitted for the Imperial residence, being abundantly supplied with fresh water from a large pool, which is never completely dry, with bread from *Saïd* †, with meat, milk, and butter from the Arabs, who breed cattle, and with vegetables from a soil well adapted to horticulture; nor are they without a kind of tenacious clay, which, with little preparation, becomes a durable material for building. In Shoba, another town of some note, was an house of Sultan Teraub. The place is said to be well supplied with water, and there are some chalk pits near it, from which that material was drawn at the time I was in the country. These pits were then almost exhausted, for the purpose of

---

* Sultan Teraub used always to reside at Rîl, but the present monarch, or usurper, is induced by his fears to wander from place to place. The first place I saw him at was *Heglig*; the next was *Tini*; the third was *Tendelti*, where he passed about a year.

† The Fûrians, it may be remarked, distinguish the South part of their empire by this term, as well as the Egyptians.

adorning

adorning the royal residence, and some others, with a kind of white-wash. In Shoba reside some jelabs; the rest of the people are Fûrians, and occupied in other pursuits.

Gidid has also a competent supply of water, and is near the road from Cobbé to Rîl. Its bearing from the former is South-east. It is a town of *Fukkara*, who are reported to be so little famous for hospitality, that they will hardly furnish to a traveller water to allay his thirst. In this town are many houses, and some of them belong to merchants who derive their origin from the Eastward.

Gellé was esteemed less flourishing than most other towns of Dar-Fûr, being under the galling tyranny of a priest. The *Faqui Seradge*, one of the two principal *Imams* of the Sultan, a man of intrigue and consummate hypocrisy, had gained an ascendancy over his master, and distanced all competitors at court. Gellé was his native place, and the people of the town were become his dependents. His unsated avarice left them neither apparel nor a mat to lie on; and his immortal malice persecuted them for having no more to plunder. The greater part of the people are either *Corobáti* or *Felatia* (two tribes); of the latter sort is the *faqui*.

The greater part of the people inhabiting Cobbé consists, as hath been already observed, of merchants. The generality of them are employed in trading to Egypt, and some of them are natives of that country; but the greater number come from the river. The latter class, if from circumstances a conjecture

may

may be hazarded, seem first to have opened the direct communication between Egypt and Fûr. For many years their native countries, Dongola, Mahas, and all the borders of the Nile as far as Sennaar, which, according to report, are in all the gifts of nature much superior to Dar-Fûr, have been the scene of devastation and bloodshed, having no settled government, but being continually torn by internal divisions, and harassed by the inroads of the *Shaikie* and other tribes of Arabs, who inhabit the region between the river and the Red Sea. Such of the natives as were in a condition to support themselves by traffic, or by manual labour, in consequence emigrated, and many of them retired to the West. These people, accustomed in their native country to a short and easy communication with Egypt, and impelled by the prospect of immense profit, which a farther attempt of the same kind promised them, opened the route which the Jelabs now pursue. But to return to *Cobbé*.—

Some Egyptians, chiefly from Saïd, a few Tunisines, natives of Tripoli, and others, come and go with the caravans, only remaining long enough to sell their goods. Others have married in Dar-Fûr, and are now perfectly naturalized, and recognized as subject to the Sultan. The fathers being no more, the children are in many instances established in their room, and are engaged in the same occupations.

The remainder of them consists of foreigners, coming from Dongola, Mahas, Sennaar, and Kordofân, who are generally remarked as indefatigable in commerce, but daring, restless, and seditious, (which consideration has induced the present Sultan

tan to use some efforts to banish them from his dominions,) and the offspring of those whose parents have emigrated, and who are themselves born in Dar-Fûr. The latter are often people of debauched manners, and not remarkable for the same spirit of enterprise as the actual emigrates. Gradually formed to the despotism which coerces their external deportment, and seeks to crush and sterilize even the seeds of energy, somewhat of the spirit of their progenitors yet remains: the affections indeed are turned askance, but not eradicated. The pushes that should have been made *ad auras æthereas*, opposed revert to *Tartarus*. The luxuriancy of mental vigour, though repulsed and forcibly inverted, still extends its ramifications. Its pallescent shoots pierce the dunghill, when not permitted to open themselves to the influence of the sun. The active mind may descend to brutal sensuality, when it can no longer expand itself in a more sane exercise.

The people first mentioned commonly among themselves use the language of *Barabra*, though they also speak Arabic. The latter are generally unacquainted with any language but the Arabic. They usually intermarry with each other, or with the Arabs. Some of them avoid marrying, and cohabit only with their slaves, seldom taking to wife a Fûrian woman. Both these descriptions of men are easily distinguishable from the natives of the country *, being usually of a more olive com-

* On the East of Fûr there is a particular tribe of Arabs, who curl their hair, as it were, in a bushy wig, resembling that of the antient figures in the ruins of Persepolis. It is probable that many fragments of antient nations may be found in the interior of Africa. Carthaginians expelled by the Romans, Vandals by Belisarius, &c. &c.

plexion,

plexion, and having a form of visage more nearly resembling the European, with short curly black hair, but not wool. They are a well-sized and well-formed people, and have often an agreeable and expressive countenance, though sometimes indicating (if so much faith may be given to physiognomy) violent passions and a mutable temper. Such are the inhabitants of Cobbé. South-east of the town, in a large open space adapted to the purpose, a market* is held twice in the week, (Monday and Friday,) in which are sold provisions of every kind, and, in short, all the commodities which the country produces, or which are derived from Egypt and other quarters. Slaves however, though sometimes brought to the market, are now commonly sold privately, which is not unfrequently complained of as an evil, inasmuch as it facilitates the sale of such as have been stolen from other quarters. The people of Barabra and Kordofân cannot relinquish their favorite liquor, and as all who drink persist in drinking till they are completely inebriated, the natural violence of their temper is increased, and gives occasion to continual disputes, which frequently are not decided without blows, and occasionally terminate in bloodshed.

* In the market held at Cobbé, there are slaughtered ordinarily from ten to fifteen oxen, and from forty to sixty sheep; but all the villages, six or eight miles round, are thence supplied.

It is usual for the people of the town to lay in their annual stock of grain when cheapest, which is commonly about the month of December. At that time two, sometimes three *mids* (pecks) of millet (*Dokn*) may be had for a string of beads, worth about one penny sterling in Kahira.

There are in the town four or five *Mectebs*, where boys are taught to read, and, if they wish it, to write. Such of the *Fukkara* as fill the office of lecturer, instruct gratuitously the children of the indigent; but from those who are in easy circumstances they are accustomed to receive a small remuneration. Two or three lecture in the Korân, and two others in what they call *Elm*, theology.

There was, at the time of my arrival, only one small mosque, a little square room, formed by walls of clay, where the *Fukkara* were accustomed to meet thrice in the week. The *Cadi* of the place was a certain *Faqui Abd-el-rachmân*, a man much in the decline of life, originally of *Sennaar*. He had studied at the *Jama-el-azher* in Kahira, and was much reputed in the place for the justice and impartiality of his decisions, and the uniform sanctity of his life. He sunk under the weight of years and infirmity, during the second year after my arrival, and the charge of Cadi was committed by the monarch to another, who was almost incapacitated from executing the duties of it, as well by a painful disorder as by his great age. The more active part of the office, therefore, was discharged by his son, who was as remarkable for corruption as the *Faqui Abd-el-rachmân* had been for integrity. Whether from indignation at this man's unworthiness, or envy of his pre-eminence, is uncertain, a division ensued among the *Fukkara*, and part of them united under *Haffan*, part under *Bellilu*, a man said to be learned in the laws, but of a forbidding and ungracious deportment. The former, with the countenance and assistance

of

of the Sultan, had commenced building a mosque more spacious than that above mentioned; but I observed it went on slowly, though the material for building was nothing better or more costly than clay. The area inclosed was about sixty-four feet square, and the walls were to be three feet thick.

CHAP. XVIII.

DAR-FÛR.

On the mode of travelling in Africa—Seasons in Dar-Fûr—Animals—Quadrupeds—Birds—Reptiles and Insects—Metals and Minerals—Plants.

ONE mode of travelling, with small variations, obtains through all the north of Africa. I mean by *caravans* (from كرو *Karu*, to wander from place to place). When the inhabitants have occasion to pass the boundaries of their respective states, they form themselves into a larger or smaller body, united under one head. Their association is produced by considerations of mutual convenience and security, as even the most easy and safest of the roads they are to pass, would yet be difficult and dangerous for a single traveller.

Three distinct caravans are employed in bringing slaves, and other commodities, from the interior of Africa to Kahira. One of them comes straight from Murzûk, the capital of Fezzân, another from Sennaar, and the third from Fûr. They do not arrive at fixed periods, but after a greater or less interval, according to the success they may have had in procuring slaves, and such other articles as are fitted to the market, the orders of their respective rulers, and various other accidental circumstances.

The Fezzân caravan is under the best regulations. The merchants from that place employ about fifty days in their passage from Murzûk to Kahira; which city they as often as possible contrive to reach a little before the commencement of Ramadan, that such as find themselves inclined to perform the pilgrimage, may be prepared to accompany the Emîr of Misr. The sale of their goods seldom employs them in the city much more than two months; after the expiration of which, those who have no design of visiting Mecca return to their native country. The arrival of this caravan is generally annual.

The other two are extremely various in their motions; sometimes not appearing in Egypt for the space of two or even three years, sometimes two or more distinct caravans arriving in the same year. The perpetual changes in their several governments, and the caprices of their despots, are in a great degree the occasion of this irregularity. The road also between these two places and Kahira, is often infested by bodies of independent Arabs, as that of Sennaar, by the Ababdé and Shaikié, and that of Fûr by the Cubba-Beesh and Bedeiât: the latter is however for the most part much safer than the former. The departure of a caravan from Dar-Fûr forms an important event. It engages the attention of the whole country for a time, and even serves as a kind of chronological epocha.

The

The period of their arrival in Kahira is as uncertain as that of their departure; for they travel indifferently either in winter or summer. The journey from Aſſûan to Sennaar requires much leſs time than that from Aſſiût to Dar-Fûr.

Many obſtacles exiſt to the erection of any permanent marks by which the roads of the deſert might be diſtinguiſhed. Yet I have obſerved that the people of our caravan, in ſuch places as afforded ſtones for the purpoſe, uſed to collect four or five large ones, thus raiſing ſmall heaps at proper diſtances from each other. This affords them ſome ſatisfaction at their return; but in many places, where the ſand is looſe and deep, it becomes impracticable. They are then obliged to rely on the facility acquired by habit, of diſtinguiſhing the outline and characteriſtic features of certain rocks, as they are perfectly ignorant of the compaſs, and very little informed as to the fixed ſtars. Though the names of the conſtellations be little known to them, yet they diſtinguiſh ſuch as may guide them in their courſe during the night. With all theſe aids however their deviations from the true line are not infrequent. Three times, in the courſe of our journey, the whole caravan was quite at a loſs for the road, though ſome of the members of it had made ten or twelve different journies to and from Dar-Fûr. During the whole of my route I had reaſon to ſuſpect that the accounts in books of travels, which have generated ſuch terrific notions of the moving ſands of Africa, are greatly exaggerated. While we remained at Leghea, indeed, a violent gale ſprang from the North-weſt, and raiſed a cloud of ſand. At that time I placed

a wooden

a wooden bowl, capable of containing about two gallons, in the open air. Thirty minutes had elapsed when it appeared completely filled with sand. Our companions indeed affected to relate various stories of caravans that had been overwhelmed. But as neither time nor place were adduced, it would seem not unreasonable to doubt the truth of the assertion.

If caravans have been thus buried on their road, it may be presumed that accident can only have happened after they have been deprived of the power of moving, by the influence of a hot wind, want of water, and other causes. A number of men, and other animals, found dead, and covered with sand, would be sufficient ground for succeeding native travellers to believe, as they are strangers to ratiocination, or, though not entirely persuaded, to relate, as they delight in the marvellous, that the persons they had found had been overwhelmed on their march; when in fact this accumulation had not happened till they were already dead. But perhaps the matter scarcely merits this discussion.

Our company consisted of nearly five hundred camels. This exceeds the number usually employed by the Jelabs on their return from Egypt, which is often not more than two hundred. In passing from Dar-Fûr to Egypt, they esteem two thousand camels, and a thousand head of slaves, a large caravan. Of persons of other countries, but particularly Egyptians, trading for themselves, there were not more than fifty, including five or six Coptic Christians, whose admittance in Dar-Fûr the monarch of that country has since forbidden. Several of this number were Muggrebines, or Occidental Arabs; the remainder, amounting to one hundred and fifty or two hundred, including the chabîr, or leader, were subjects of Fûr. Few particulars of other caravans are known to me but by report.

The Arabs and Jelabs find the camel too indispensable to their long and fatiguing voyages, not to employ much care in nourishing him. This *ship of the land*, (مركب البر,) as he is called, is exclusively the bearer of their fortunes, and the companion of their toils. Much care is observed in rearing him, and not unfrequently the merchant pays nearly as much for the camels to carry his merchandize, as he did for the commodities themselves; what then must be the profit that covers his expenses, his fatigue, indemnifies him for accidental losses, and yet leaves him a gainer? But if this patient and enduring animal be thus rendered subservient to their wants, or their avarice, he is not at least tortured for their caprice.

Horses are very little used by the Jelabs. They generally furnish themselves with Egyptian asses, which alleviate the fatigue of the way, and are afterwards sold in Soudân at an advanced price. The strength and spirits of this animal are recruited with a small quantity of straw and water; the horse has not the same recommendation; and these people, though not averse from parade in cities, find the labour and hazard of these voyages too enormous, not to augment their profits by all possible economy.

The

The provisions they use are scanty and indifferent, and by no means testify any foresight for the necessities of the sick, or for the procrastination of the voyage by those innumerable accidents that may befal them.

I did not observe that any of them were furnished with dried meat, as is common with the Fezzanners. But few used coffee and tobacco, and the rest contented themselves with a leathern bag of flour, another of bread baked hard, a leathern vessel of honey or treacle, and another of butter. The quantity of each was regulated by the number of persons, and seldom exceeded what is absolutely necessary. In travelling from Dar-Fûr to Egypt another article is much in use, especially for the slaves, which Egypt itself does not afford, or produces in no quantity. The grain chiefly in use among the Fûrians is the small *kassob*, called among them *dokn* (millet). Of this, after it has been coarsely ground, they take a quantity, and having caused it to undergo a slight fermentation, make a kind of paste. This will keep a long time, and when about to be used, water is added to it; if properly made, it becomes a tolerably palatable food. But the natives are not very delicate. From its acidity they esteem it a preventive of thirst. The fermentation gives it also a slight power of inebriating, and it has a narcotic tendency. The substance so prepared is called *ginseia*. The want of materials for fire on the road prevents the use of rice, and other articles that would require cookery.

Experienced travellers, among every ten camels laden with merchandize, charge one with beans, and straw chopped small, which, sparingly given, serves them during the greater part of the voyage. Those with whom I travelled were not so provided, these articles being then very dear in Egypt; and in consequence numbers of camels perished. In coming from Dar-Fûr, they use for the same purpose the *dokn*, and coarse hay of the country, but not altogether with the same salutary effect.

The water, in leaving Egypt, is commonly conveyed in goat skins artificially prepared; but no skill can entirely prevent evaporation. On their march from Soudân to Egypt, the Jelabs oftener use ox-hides, formed into capacious sacks and properly seasoned with tar or oil. A pair of these is a camel's load. They keep the water in a better state for drinking than the smaller; and these sacks are sold to great advantage throughout Egypt, a pair of the best kind being sometimes worth thirty piasters. They are the common instruments for conveying water from the river to different parts of each town. The camels are not allowed to partake of this store, which, after all the care that can be taken of it, is often very nauseous, from the tar, the mud which accompanies the water in drawing, heat, &c. Six of the smaller skins, or two of the larger, are generally esteemed sufficient for four persons for as many days.

The *Cubba-Beesh*, and the *Bedeiât*, the latter of whom seem to me not of Arab origin, when they make any attempt on the caravans, commonly shew themselves between Leghea and the Bîr-el-Malha. But this road is so ill provided with any thing that is necessary for the sustenance of man or beast, that neither

the

the wandering tribes, nor the ferocious animals, which infest other parts of the continent, are commonly found there. The Egyptians and other whites therefore, though they commonly carry fire-arms with them from the North, generally take advantage of the market of Fûr, and return without any. The natives of Soudân are furnished with a light spear, or spears, the head of which is made of unhardened iron of their country. They have also a shield of about three feet long, and one foot and a half or three-quarters broad, composed of the hide of the elephant or hippopotamus, very simple in its construction.

Intercourse with Mecca.

No regular caravan of Hadgîs leaves Dar-Fûr, but a number of the natives make their way to Mecca, either with the caravan of merchants trading to Egypt, or by way of Suakem and Jidda. The present king was about to establish his attorney (*waquîl*) at Mecca, but some obstacles had prevented his reaching that place, when I came away. Fear of the sea, or I know not what other cause, prevents them from choosing the route by Suakem, though it be so much shorter and less expensive than that by the way of Egypt; but the territory between Fûr and Suakem is not subject to any settled government, and those who have travelled with property have frequently been plundered there. The *Tocrúri* however, who come from various parts, and somewhat resemble the Derwishes of the North, travelling as paupers, with a bowl to drink out of, and a

leathern

leathern bag of bread, frequently take that route and pass in safety.

Seasons, &c.

The perennial rains, which fall in Dar-Fûr, from the middle of June till the middle of September, in greater or less quantity, but generally both frequent and violent, suddenly invest the face of the country, till then dry and steril, with a delightful verdure. Except where the rocky nature of the soil absolutely impedes vegetation, wood is found in great quantity, nor are the natives assiduous completely to clear the ground, even where it is designed for the cultivation of grain.

As soon as the rains begin, the proprietor, and all the assistants that he can collect, go out to the field, and having made holes at about two feet distance from each other, with a kind of hoe, over all the ground he occupies, the *dokn* is thrown into them, and covered with the foot, for their husbandry requires not many instruments. The time for sowing the wheat is nearly the same. The *dokn* remains scarcely two months before it is ripe; the wheat about three. Wheat is cultivated only in small quantities; and the present Sultan having forbidden the sale of it, till the portion wanted for his domestic use be supplied, it is with difficulty to be procured by purchase. The *Mahrick*, or greater *kassob*, which is a larger grain than the *dokn*, is also common, and a small supply of sesamum, (*Simsim* in Arabic,) is sown. What they term beans is a species of legumen different from

from our bean. In what are called gardens are *Bamea, Meluchîa,* lentils, (*adis,*) kidney beans, (*lubi,*) and some others. The water melon, and that called in Kahira *Abd-el-awi,* together with some other kinds, abound during the wet season; and indeed before, if they be watered. Sultan Teraub was solicitous to procure every thing the gardens of Egypt produce, and caused much care to be taken of the culture of each article brought: but the present prince does not turn his thoughts to that kind of improvement, and little of the effect of his predecessor's laudable anxiety is at this moment distinguishable. There are several species of trees, but none that produces fruit worth gathering, unless it be the Tamarind (*Tummara *Hindi*). The date trees are in very small number, and their fruit diminutive, dry, and destitute of flavour. That tree seems not indigenous in the country, but to have been transported from the neighbourhood of the Nile, Dongola, Sennaar, &c. The inhabitants appear not well to understand the management of this useful production; and perhaps the great drought will never admit of its flourishing, whatever diligence or care may be used to increase the number or improve the kind.

ANIMALS.

Quadrupeds.

Of animals the list found in Dar-Fûr with which my own knowlege furnishes me, is not very extensive; nor will it be interesting so much as containing any thing new, but as it will shew the peculiar circumstances of the country, as distinguished from

* Fruit of India.

other neighbouring regions, and somewhat indicate the present state of the people.

The horse is used, but not in great number, nor are the natives very solicitous as to the breed. The only good horses they possess are bred in the country of Dongola, and by the Arabs to the East of the Nile. These are generally larger than we are accustomed to find the Egyptian horses. They are perfectly well formed, and full of fire, yet tractable. Their action is grand beyond what I have observed in any other species; but it is said they are not remarkable for bearing fatigue. The Arabs, who breed them, are in the habit of feeding them with milk. They rarely, if ever, castrate them. Horses and mares are indiscriminately used for the saddle. The horses of Soudân are none of them shod.

Two or three distinct breeds of sheep, *Ovis aries*, exist in Soudân, not however very materially differing from each other. The large-tailed sheep, which are found elsewhere, I believe are here unknown. The meat is inferior to that of the Egyptian sheep. They are covered with coarse wool, resembling hair, and apparently wholly unfit for any manufacture. The goats, *capræ cervicapræ*, are much more numerous than the sheep, and the flesh of the former is somewhat cheaper than that of the latter. The goats grow perhaps rather larger, but otherwise differ not from those of Egypt. It is not uncommon to castrate both these animals, but neither is it a very general practice.

The

The afs here is of the fame appearance, and the fame indocile nature, with that of Great Britain. The only good ones are what the Jelabs bring with them from Egypt: yet the animal is much ufed for riding; indeed few perfons mount an horfe but the military, and thofe who are in immediate attendance at court. An Egyptian afs fetches from the value of one to that of three flaves, according to the weight he is able to bear. A flave will purchafe three or four of the ordinary breed; yet they are not anxious to improve them. Perhaps the animal degenerates: but it is certain that his external appearance undergoes a great change.

The bull is fometimes caftrated. Yet of the animals flaughtered in the market I have generally obferved that the emafculated are feweft in number; nor is any preference given to the one over the other for food. Indeed, the character of animals in the entire ftate appears materially to differ from what is remarked of the fame animals with us. The horned cattle, fed by the tribes in the vicinity of the rivers, amounts to a very confiderable number, and the tribute paid out of them to the monarch forms a valuable part of his revenue. Thence they are brought to the feveral towns for flaughter. The beef is good: the Egyptians diflike it, but with the natives it is a conftant article of food. Cows are alfo in abundance, but their milk is not very palatable: fome of the fettlers make it into a kind of cheefe, but the inhabitants are not generally acquainted with that procefs; they have, however, a mode of giving it an acefcent tafte, and in that ftate it may be kept a few days, and is neither difagreeable nor infalubrious.

The camels of Fûr are of a mixed breed, and they are found of all colours and sizes. Those which come directly from the West or South are large, smooth-haired, and most frequently of a colour approaching to white, or light brown. Those which are brought from Kordofân are many of them black, and are remarked to be less docile than the others. There are few countries where the animal abounds more than in Dar-Fûr. They are remarkable for enduring thirst, but not for bearing great burthens. The camels in this country are particularly subject to the mange, (*Gerab,*) which attacks them chiefly in winter, and in some pastures much more than in others. This malady is very contagious. It is cured by the application of a kind of tar, procured by distillation per deliquium, from the seeds of the water-melon. When the male camel is found unruly, they sometimes deprive him of one or both testicles. It is a cruel operation, as immediately after having incided with an ordinary knife, they sear the wound with an hot iron till the hemorrhage be stopped. It may be doubted whether this practice be permitted by the law of the Prophet; but, however bigoted their minds, where advantage is hoped for, their faith is ductile. The flesh of the camel, particularly of the female, (*naka,*) which is fattened for the purpose, is here much used for food. It is insipid, but easily digested, and no way unpleasant. The milk also is much in esteem. The camels bred in Fezzân, and other countries to the West, as well as those of Arabia, are for labour reckoned superior to those of Fûr, and fetch an higher price. The former are larger and able to carry an heavier burthen, but not so capable of enduring thirst. In Soudân they seldom carry above five hundred weight, and oftener three or three

three and a half: while in Egypt they are frequently obliged to toil under eight, ten, or even more. From these are selected the camels which bear the sacred treasure to the tomb of the Prophet. Soudân affords many fine dromedaries, but those of Sennaar are most celebrated. Incredible stories are told of the long and rapid journies performed by them; as that they will hold out for four-and-twenty hours, travelling constantly at the rate of ten miles per hour: however this be, they are indisputably swift, and perform long journeys almost without refreshment.

The dogs of Dar-Fûr are of the same kind as those of Egypt, and live on the public like the latter. I have understood that there is in some parts of the country a species of dog, used in hunting the antelope, (*ghazâl*, Ar.) and another sort to guard the sheep; of the sagacity of the latter wonderful tales are told, as well as of the courage and fidelity of both. Experience has not enabled me to confirm the report. The common house-cat is scarce; and if I am rightly informed, there are none but what have been originally brought from Egypt. They are of the same kind as with us.

The wild or ferocious animals are, principally, the lion, the leopard, the hyena, (Fûr. *murfain*, *dubba*, Ar.) the wolf, the jackal, *canis aureus*, the wild buffaloe: but they are not commonly seen within the more cultivated part of the empire, at least that which I have visited, excepting the hyena and the jackal; the former come in herds of six, eight, and often more, into all the villages at night, and carry off with them whatever they are able to master. They will kill dogs, and asses, even within the inclosure of the houses, and fail not to assemble wherever a dead camel or other animal is thrown, which, acting in concert, they sometimes drag to a prodigious distance; nor are they greatly alarmed at the sight of a man, or the report of fire-arms, which I have often discharged at them, and occasionally with effect. It is related, that upon one of them being wounded, his companions instantly tear him to pieces and devour him; but I have had no opportunity of ascertaining this fact. The people of the country dig pits for them, and lying in ambuscade, when one is entrapped, stun him with clubs, or pierce him with their spears. The jackal is harmless, but his uncouth cry is heard far off, and wherever there are rocks to shelter them, their howling community dwells undisturbed.

In the countries bordering on the empire of Fûr, where water is in greater abundance, the other animals mentioned are very numerous, and much dreaded by travellers, particularly on the banks of the *Bahr-el-Ada*. To those already enumerated, may be added, the elephant, the rhinoceros, the camelopardalis, the hippopotamus, and the crocodile.

The elephant is seen, in the places he frequents, in large herds of four or five hundred, according to report. It is even said that two thousand are sometimes found together; but I do not suspect the Arabs of extreme accuracy in counting. These people hunt him on horseback, having singled out a straggler from the herd; or aim at him with spears from the trees; or make

pits

pits into which he falls. His hide is applied to many useful purposes. The African elephant is smaller than the Asiatic, and probably of a different species. The meat is an article of food in great esteem with them. The fat forms a valuable unguent, and the teeth, as is well known, supply the merchants with immense profits.

The buffaloe is not found tame in Soudân. The wild one is hunted by the Arabs, and serves them for food. The hippopotamus is killed for his skin, (which being remarkably tough, makes excellent shields, and whips not wholly unlike our horse-whips); and for his teeth, which are much superior to ivory. The horn of the rhinoceros, to which animal the Arabs have applied a term somewhat less appropriate than the Greek, but still characteristic, (*Abu-kurn*, father of the one horn,) makes a valuable article of trade, and is carried to Egypt, where it is sold at an high price, being used for sabre-hilts, and various other purposes. The more credulous attribute to it some efficacy as an antidote against poison.

The antelope and the ostrich are extremely common throughout the empire. The civet-cat is not seen wild in the quarter which I visited, but is frequent enough farther to the South. Many are preserved in cages in the houses of the rich. The women apply the odour extracted from them to add to their personal allurements; and what is not thus disposed of becomes an article of trade.

The

The lion and leopard, though common in a certain district, are not found near the seat of government. The Arabs hunt them, strip off the skin, which they sell, and often eat the flesh, which they conceive generates courage and a warlike disposition. They occasionally take them young, and bring them for sale to the Jelabs, who sometimes carry them as presents to the great men in Egypt. I purchased two lions: the one was only four months old when I bought him. By degrees, having little else to employ me, I had rendered him so tame, that he had acquired most of the habits of a dog. He satiated himself twice a week with the offal of the butchers, and then commonly slept for several hours successively. When food was given them they both grew ferocious towards each other, and towards any one who approached them. Except at that time, though both were males, I never saw them disagree, nor shew any sign of ferocity towards the human race. Even lambs passed them unmolested. The largest had grown to the height of thirty inches and a half over the shoulders.

The *ennui* of a painful detention, devoid of books and rational society, was softened by the company of these animals; and the satisfaction was not small, even from this species of diversion. At length, towards the end of my stay, after they had been with me more than two years, finding it impossible, under the circumstances I then was, to carry them with me, I shot the one; and the other, either from disease or the loss of his companion, died a few days afterwards. The Sultan had also two tame lions, which, with their attendant, came into the market to feed.

The

The remaining quadrupeds may be classed more briefly; for being all known, they will require no particular description.

Ar.
Mus Jaculus—Jerboa.
Simia Æthiops—Abelang.
Histria ciestria— Porcupine.
Simia cynamolgos—kurd Ar.

BIRDS.

1. *Charadrius Kerwan*—Oriental dotterel.
2. *Numida Meleagris*—Guinea fowl.
3. *Tetrao Coturnix*—Egyptian quail.
4. *Vultur Percnopterus*—White-headed vulture.
5. *Psittacus Alexandri*—Green peroquet.
6. *Columba domestica*—Common pigeon.
7. *Tetrao rufus*—Red partridge.
8. Owls (not common).
9. *Columba Turtur*, very common.

No. 4. This bird is of surprising strength, and is said by the natives to be very long-lived, *sed fides penes auctores*. I have lodged a complete charge of large shot, at about fifty yards distance, in the body of this bird: it seemed to have no effect on him, as he flew to a considerable distance, and continued walking afterwards. I then discharged the second barrel, which was loaded with ball: this broke his wing, but on my advancing to seize him, he fought with great fury with the other. There are many thousands of them in the inhabited district. They divide the field with the hyena: what carrion the latter leaves at night, the former come in crowds to feed on in the day. Near the extremity of each wing is a horny substance, not unlike the spur of an old cock. It is strong and sharp; and a formidable instrument of attack. Some fluid exsudes from this bird that smells likes musk, but from what part of him I am uncertain.

No. 2. This beautiful bird is found in great numbers in Fûr, of which the common fowl, though it now abounds, is not a native. The voice of the Guinea fowl, when apparently elated, is very peculiar. No external difference, even in this their native climate, is to be observed between the male and female of this bird. They are carried as a profitable commodity to Kahira, where however, in a domestic state, it is said they seldom or never breed.

5. These birds, in the beginning of summer, fill the trees in the vicinity of the town I lived in. They are caught unfledged, and brought up in the houses, till they become quite domestic; are then carried to Egypt, and taught a kind of speech, which being acquired, they are sold at a high price.

Of fish I saw none but what were too much disguised by drying to be recognised.

The

The fish in the river *Ada*, I am told, confift of nearly the fame fpecies as thofe of the Nile in Upper Egypt. They are caught in wicker bafkets, and ufed for food.—The natives have alfo a way of drying them, but it does not prevent their being fo offenfive to the fmell, as to be ufelefs to any but themfelves. Numerous huts built of reeds are found on the bank of the river, as well for the ufe of the fifhermen, as of thofe who enfnare the ferocious animals that come to drink its waters.

The Chameleon abounds in Dar-Fûr; the *viverra Ichneumon*, *nims*, and almoft all the fpecies of lizard are alfo feen there.

Of Serpents, the *Coluber Hayé* of Egypt, the *Coluber vipera*, and the *anguis Colubrina*, were the only ones I faw: and no more than one or two of each; though it was reprefented to me that in fome places they are numerous. The Fûrians have not the art of charming them, like the Egyptians and Indians. I expofed myfelf to much ridicule by collecting a number of chameleons in my apartment, to obferve their character and changes; the people there think them impure, and relate many foolifh ftories concerning them.

A great number of infects and reptiles, which I had taken care to conferve, accident has deprived me of, and I cannot now furnifh a catalogue. The fcorpion is fmall, of a brown hue, and his venom not extremely violent. The natives cure the sting by immediately applying to the part a bruised onion, which is renewed till the pain subsides.

The white ant, or *Termites*, is found in vast numbers, and is exceedingly destructive, eating through every thing within its reach, whether vegetables, cloth, leather, paper, provisions, &c. A bull's hide, if not newly covered with tar, is no defence against it. The *Apis mellifera* (common bee) abounds; but they have no hives, and the wild honey is commonly of a dark colour, and unpleasant taste. I have observed a beetle, not very large, which is characterized by burying its eggs in a small ball of horse's or other dung, and then rolling the ball from place to place in the sand or clay, till it attains a size greatly exceeding that of the animal itself. Great quantities of cochineal are visible; which, if the natives, or the Egyptians who visit them, had any reflection or spirit, it might be thought would be applied to some useful purpose.

The locust of Arabia, *Gryllus*, is very common, and is frequently roasted and eaten, particularly by the slaves. The *Scarabeus Ceratoniæ*; the *Culex Egypti*, *namús* in Ar. (mosquito), is particularly vexatious in the rainy season.

METALS AND MINERALS.

Of metals, the number found in the district known to me, is small. But in its neighbourhood, to the South and West, if
I have

I have been rightly informed, almoſt all deſcriptions are to be met with. The copper brought by the merchants from the territories of certain idolatrous tribes bordering on Fûr, is of the fineſt quality, in colour reſembling that of China, and appears to contain a portion of zink, being of the ſame pale hue. The large rings into which it is formed (of ten or twelve pounds weight each) are very malleable: of the ore I never was able to procure a ſpecimen. Iron is to be found in abundance, and the Pagan negroes, on whom the Mohammedans look with contempt, are the artiſts that extract it from the ore; an art of which the former, as far as I have ſeen, are ignorant. Though their iron, through the ſtupidity of the inhabitants, never acquire the more uſeful character of ſteel, its effects in the form of knives and javelins are yet commenſurate with the malign diſpoſitions of mankind. And though ſoft and periſhable, with increaſed trouble in renewing the edge, the tools formed of it anſwer all the purpoſes of their rude workmanſhip.

The method by which I obſerved a workman ſupply the defect of a furnace for fuſing metals appeared worth noticing. He had a leathern bag, which, on compreſſion, forced the air through a wooden pipe for bellows, and placed over the fire, made in a ſmall hole in the earth, the remains of a water jar, with which ſimple apparatus the effect was rapid and not inconſiderable.

Silver, lead, and tin, I have never heard mentioned here, but as coming from Egypt. Of gold, in the countries to the East and West, the supply is abundant. Little comes to Dar-Fûr, except by accident. What is produced in the West reaches the northern markets by means of other caravans. The monarch occasionally obtains a small quantity for his own use from the East.

Alabaster, and various kinds of marble, exist within the limits of Fûr. The rocks chiefly consist of grey granite. But of stone adapted to building, or convertible into lime, either there is none, or the quantity must be extremely small. The granite serves for hand-mills without being cut, for the metal of which their tools are composed is too soft to be employed for that purpose.

Fossile salt is common within a certain district: and there is a sufficient supply of nitre, of which however no use is made. A quantity of sulphur is brought by the Arabs, who feed oxen (*Bukkara*) from the South and West. But of the place where it is found I have heard no description. It must also exist on the mountain called Gebel Marra; as it is related there are hot springs there; which animals, particularly birds, are observed not to approach; this, if true, may be the effect of sulphureous vapours.

PLANTS.

Though my residence in Dar-Fûr was so much protracted, I feel myself able to furnish only a very imperfect catalogue of its vegetable productions. These are to be sought chiefly in the districts to the South, where water abounds, and where the extreme restraint under which I found myself prevented me from seeking them.

During seven or eight months in the year the whole surface of the earth to the North is dried up by the sun, and the minute plants which spring and flourish during the *Harif**, are mingled in the general marcescence, as soon as that season is passed. Even the trees, whose fibres pierce more deeply into the substance of their parent soil, lose the distinctive marks of their proper foliage, and exhibit to the distant observer only the sharp outline of their grosser ramifications.

Of the trees which shade our forests or adorn our gardens in Europe, very few exist in Dar-Fûr. The characteristic marks of those species which most abound there, are their sharp thorns, and the solid and unperishable quality of their substance. 1. The Tamarind is not very common in the quarter I frequented; but those which were visible to me were of great height and bulk, and bore a copious supply of fruit.

* Season of the rains.

2. The Plane, platanus Orientalis, *Deleib*, is found, but seems rather to have been brought from Egypt, than indigenous.

3. Sycamore of Egypt, *Ficus Sycomorus*, *Gimmeiz*, a few near Cobbé; said to be much more common to the southward. I did not observe that it produced any fruit.

4. *Nebbek* Ar. *Paliurus Athenæi*. Of this there are two species in Dar-Fûr. They term the largest *Nebbek-el-arab*. There is a difference in their fruit, as well as in their external appearance. The one is a bush, with leaves of dark green, not very different from those of the ivy, but much thinner. It appeared to be the same I had seen in the gardens of Alexandria. The other a tree, growing to considerable size, but having both the leaves and fruit smaller, and the fruit of darker colour, and somewhat different flavour. Both of them equally thorny. The natives eat the fruit fresh or dry; for it dries on the tree, and so remains great part of the winter months. In that state it is formed into a paste of not unpleasant flavour, and is a portable provision on journies.

5. *Heglig* or *Hejlij*, Ar. This tree is about the same size as the one last mentioned, and is said to be a native of Arabia, though I have seen it only in Fûr.—The leaf is small, and the fruit it bears is of an oblong form, about the size of a date. Colour brown, tinctured with orange; dry, and of a viscous quality. The nucleus is large in proportion to the fruit, which adheres to it with great tenacity. This is also formed into a paste, but of no agreeable flavour. It is however eaten by the

Arabs,

Arabs, and by some esteemed efficacious as a remedy for certain diseases. It seems a slight diuretic. The wood is hard, and of a yellowish colour; it grows in great abundance, and is very thorny. This, together with the *Nebbek*, chiefly furnish thorns for the fences.

6. *Enneb*, a small tree, to the fruit of which they have given the name of grapes. It bears leaves of light green hue, and the fruit, which is of a purple colour, is attached, not in bunches, but singly to the smaller branches, and interspersed among the leaves. The internal structure of the fruit is not very unlike the grape, which it also resembles in size. But the pulp is of a red hue, and the taste is strongly astringent.

7. *Shaw*, Ar. a shrub about the size of the Arbutus, having, like it, a leaf of strong texture, of oval form, pale green, wider at the lower, and narrower at the upper extremity than the arbutus.—The leaf has the pungency and very much the taste of mustard. This shrub I saw chiefly in *Wadi Shaw*, a place we passed in going and returning, between Sweini and Bîr-el-malha. The natives cut off the smaller branches, which they use to rub their teeth, alleging that the acrid juice of this plant has the property of whitening them.

From an exact correspondence as to the place of its growth, viz. near the salt springs, the camels not eating it, and some other circumstances, I take this to be the *Rack* of Bruce, vol. v. p. 44. though unable to recognize it in the figure there given.

8. Ce-

8. Ceratonia Siliqua, *Charôb*.

9. Solanum sanctum, nightshade, *Beidinjan*, or *Melingán*, brought originally from Egypt, and used for food.

10. *El Henne*, from Egypt, growing into use.

11. *Sophar*, Ar. Cassia sophera, wild senna, native, and grows in plenty after the rains.

12. *Súnt*, Mimosa Nilotica, in great quantity.—It is from this tree, which is also called *Seiál*, that the gum, brought to Egypt by the caravans, is chiefly gathered. There are also found the trees called by Bruce *Ergett Dimmo*, and *Ergett-el-Kurún*, and the *Farek*, Bauhinia Acuminata of the same writer.

13. A kind of legumen called *Fúl*, bean. It is not much used for food, but as an ornament by the women, being strung in the form of beads, when quite dry, at which time it is very hard. It is also used as a weight of four or five grains.

14. A beautiful legumen, of a scarlet colour, with a black spot at the point of attachment to its cyst. It is called in Dar-Fûr *Shtúsh*; is about the size of a small pea, hard and polished; grows on a plant resembling tares; is strung and used as an ornament by the women.

15. The common onion, Allium cepe, *Baſſal*, Ar. is abundantly supplied in Dar-Fûr, but inferior in size, taste, and colour, to that of Egypt.

16. Gar-

16. Garlick, Allium sativum, *Tûm* Ar. cultivated and used for food.

17. Water-melon, Cucurbita citrullus, *Butteik* Ar. This grows wild over almost all the cultivable lands, and ripens as the corn is removed. In this state it does not attain a large size. The inside is of a pale hue, and has little flavour. As it ripens, the camels, asses, &c. are turned to feed on it, and it is said to fatten them. The seeds, as they grow blackish, are collected to make a kind of tar, *Kutrân*. Those plants of the melon which receive artificial culture grow to a large size, and are of exquisite flavour.

18. Common melon, Cucumis melo, *Kawûn* Ar. is occasionally cultivated, but rarely brought to perfection.

19. Cucumbers, Cucumis sativus, *Cheiar* Ar. of which the Jelabs have introduced the culture, as well as of the preceding.

20. Gourd, Cucurbita Lagenaria, *Karra* Ar. This serves for drinking-vessels and other purposes. It is found in abundance. When fresh, it is used for food, and being properly dressed with meat, is very palatable. Grows to a large size.

21. Cœlocynthis, *Handal* Ar. very common.

22. Momordica Elaterium, *Adjûr* Ar. also very common.

23. *Ushar*. This plant abounds so much as to cover whole plains. No other use is made of it than to spread its branches and leaves under mats and goods, which it is said guards them from the *Termis* or white ant.

24. Nightshade, Solanum foliis hirsutis, *Enneb-el-dib*.

25. Hemp, Cannabis vulgaris, *Hashish*, Ar. is now become an article of regular culture, being used in various ways as an aphrodisiac, and in different proportion as a narcotic. *Hashish* is a general name for green herbs, but chiefly appropriated to this: it is chewed in its crude state, inhaled by means of a pipe, or formed, with other ingredients, into an electuary, *maijun*. In Egypt the consumption of this article is much greater than in Dar-Fûr, but the best is that of Antioch in Syria.

26. Rice, Oryza, *Oruzz* Ar. is brought in small quantities by the wandering Arabs, who find it growing wild in the places they frequent. It is little used or esteemed, and indeed has no quality to recommend it.

27. Cayenne pepper, *chetti* or *Tchetti*, in the language of the country, is extremely common in one district, whence it is dispersed over the country and used with food.

28. Kidney-bean, *Lubi* Ar.

29. *Meluchia*.

30. *Baméa*.

30. *Baméa*, in great abundance.

31. A plant of the same size with the *Meluchia*, of very dark green, strong smell and taste. It grows in great quantity, and with the natives forms a principal article of food. They call it *Cowel*.

32. Sesamum, *Simsim*, Ar. From this an oil is extracted. It is also bruised in a mortar, and mixed with the food. It is even used by the great to fatten their horses.

33. *Mahreik*, and *Dokn*, the holcus dochna, of *Forskal*, as has been already mentioned, are the basis of their provision, but chiefly the latter.

34. Tobacco is produced in abundance in Fertît and Dar Fungaro. It seems to be unquestionably of native growth.

CHAP. XIX.

DAR-FÛR.

Government—History—Agriculture, &c.—Population—Building—Manners and customs—Revenue—Articles of commerce, &c.

Government.

THE magistracy of one, which seems tacitly, if it be not expressly favoured by the dispensation of Mohammed, as in most other countries professing that religion, prevails in Dar-Fûr. The monarch indeed can do nothing contrary to the Korân, but he may do more than the laws established thereon will authorise: and as there is no council to control or even to assist him, his power may well be termed despotic. He speaks in public of the soil and its productions as his personal property, and of the people as little else than his slaves.

When manifest injustice appears in his decisions, the *Fukkara*, or ecclesiastics, express their sentiments with some boldness, but their opposition is without any appropriate object, and consequently its effects are inconsiderable. All the monarch fears is a general alienation of the minds of the troops, who may at their

will

will raife another, as enterprifing and unprincipled as himfelf, to the fame envied fuperiority.

His power in the provinces is delegated to officers who poffefs an authority equally arbitrary. In thofe diftricts, which have always or for a long time formed an integral part of the empire, thefe officers are generally called *Meleks*. In fuch as have been lately conquered, or perhaps, more properly, have been annexed to the dominion of the Sultan, under certain ftipulations, the chief is fuffered to retain the title of Sultan, yet is tributary to and receives his appointment from the Sultan of Fûr.

In this country, on the death of the monarch, the title defcends of right to the oldeft of his fons; and in default of heirs male, as well as during the minority of thofe heirs, to his brother. But under various pretences this received rule of fucceffion is frequently infringed. The fon is faid to be too young, or the late monarch to have obtained the government by unjuft means; and, at length, the pretenfions of thofe who have any apparent claim to the regal authority are to be decided by war, and become the prize of the ftrongeft.

It was in this manner that the prefent Sultan gained poffeffion of the Imperial dignity. A preceding monarch, named *Bokar*, had three fons, *Mohammed*, furnamed *Teraub*, *el-Chalife*, and *Abd-el-rachmân*. Teraub the eldeft (which cognomen was acquired by the habit of rolling in the duft when a child) firft

obtained

obtained the government. He is said to have ruled thirty-two lunar years, one of the longest reigns remembered in the history of the country. The sons he left at his death being all young, the second brother, under pretence that none of them was old enough to reign, which was far from being the fact, and in some degree favoured by the troops for the generosity by which he was eminently distinguished, under the title of *Chalife*, vicegerent of the realm, assumed the reins of government. His reign was of short duration, and characterised by nothing but violence and rapine. He had been only a short time seated on the throne, when a discontented party joining with the people of Kordofân, in a war with whom his brother Teraub had perished, found employment for him in that quarter. Abd-el-rachmân, who, during the life of his brother, had assumed the title of *Faquir*, and apparently devoted himself to religion, was then in Kordofân. He took advantage of the situation of the Chalife, and the increasing discontent of the soldiery, to get himself appointed their leader. Returning towards Fûr, he met his brother in the field, and they came to an engagement, which, whether by the prowess of Abd-el-rachmân, or the perfidy of the other's adherents, is unknown, was decided in favour of the former. The Chalife was wounded; and while one of his sons parried the blows that were aimed at his life, they perished together covered with wounds. The children of Teraub, the rightful heirs, were in the mean time forgotten, and are now wandering about, scraping a miserable subsistence from the parsimonious alms of their usurping uncle. Abd-el-rachmân thought fit to sacrifice but one of them, who being of mature age,

age, and, according to general report, endowed with talents greater than the rest, was the chief object of his suspicion and his fears.

The usurper, after the victory, found himself in peaceable possession of the throne; yet judging it right to maintain for a time the shew of moderation and self-denial, he employed that dissimulation for which his countrymen are famous, in persuading them that his affections were fixed on the blessings of futurity, and that he was indifferent to the splendour of empire. He refused even to see the treasures of his deceased brother, in gold, slaves, &c. and as he entered the interior of the palace drew the folds of his turban over his eyes, saying the temptation was too great for him, and invoking the Supreme Being to preserve him from its effects. For a certain time too he confined himself to the possession of four wives (free women) allowed by the law of the Prophet. At length, finding his claim unquestioned, and his authority firmly established, the veil of sanctity, now no longer necessary, was thrown aside, and ambition and avarice appeared without disguise. He now wastes whole days in misanthropic solitude, gazing in stupid admiration on heaps of costly apparel, and an endless train of slaves and camels, and revels in the submissive charms of near two hundred free women. Abd-el-rachmân assumed the Imperial dignity in the year of the Hejira 1202, of the Christian æra 1787. The discontent of the people however, and particularly of the soldiery in consequence of the severity of his regulations, and his personal avarice, were (1795) very much increasing,

increasing, which made me imagine his reign would not be long.

History.

Mohammed Teraub, already mentioned, was preceded by a king named Abd-el-Casim; Abd-el-Casim by Bokar; Bokar by Omar. Some of the earlier kings are yet spoken of under the names of Solyman, Mohammed, &c. But as the people of the country possess no written documents, I found those of whom I inquired often at variance both with regard to the genealogy and the succession of their monarchs. In all countries these are points of small import; but especially in one of which so few particulars are known to us. It may yet be remarked, that they commonly mention the reign of Solyman, as the epocha when Islamism began to prevail in the country. Describing this Sultan, at the same time, as of the *Dageou* race, which swayed the sceptre long before that of Fûr became powerful. Circumstances have inclined me to believe, that the reign of this prince must have been from one hundred and thirty to one hundred and fifty years ago.

On what the natives relate of their early history, little dependence can be placed: but it seems that the *Dageou* race came originally from the North, having been expelled from that part of Africa now, nominally at least, under the dominion of Tunis *.

Harvest,

* I remember to have borrowed, while at Damascus, a small quarto volume, written in easy Arabic, without either title or conclusion, which contained a kind of

Harvest, food, &c.

In that part of the country where I resided are found neither lakes, rivers, marshes, nor any other appearance of water but the wells which are dug for domestic consumption, except during the rainy season. At that period torrents, of greater or less dimensions, intersect the country in all directions. The rainy season lasts from before the middle of June to the middle or end of September. This season is called Harif*.

I have observed that the rain, which is generally very heavy and accompanied with lightning, falls most frequently from 3 P. M. till midnight.

The changes of the wind are not periodical but instantaneous. It is with a southerly wind that the greatest heat prevails; and with a South-East that the greatest quantity of rain falls. When the breeze is from the North or North-west it is most refresh-

---

of history of the progress of the (*ashab*) early propagators of Mohammedism, and which enumerated, if I mistake not, a tribe under the denomination of Fûr فور among their adversaries, after the taking of *Bahnese* in Middle Egypt, and their consequent invasion of the more Southern provinces.

* If but a small quantity of rain fall, the agricultors are reduced to great distress; and it happened, about seven years before my arrival, that many people were obliged to eat the young branches of trees pounded in a mortar.

ing, but does not generally continue long in that quarter. The hot and oppressive winds which fill the air with thick dust blow constantly from the South.

One day, while I was sitting in the market-place at Cobbé, I observed a singular appearance in the air, which soon discovered itself to be a column of sand, raised from the desert by a whirlwind. It was apparently about a mile and a half distant, and continued about eight minutes; this phenomenon had nothing of the tremendous appearance of the columns of sand described by Bruce as rising between Assuân and Chendi, being merely a light cloud of sand.

The harvest is conducted in a very simple manner. The women and slaves of the proprietor are employed to break off the ears with their hands, leaving the straw standing, which is afterwards applied to buildings and various other useful purposes. They then accumulate them in baskets, and carry them away on their heads. When threshed, which is awkwardly and incompletely performed, they expose the grain to the sun till it become quite dry; after this an hole in the earth is prepared, the bottom and sides of which are covered with chaff to exclude the vermin. This cavity or magazine is filled with grain, which is then covered with chaff, and afterwards with earth. In this way the maize is preserved tolerably well. In using it for food, they grind it, and boil it in the form of polenta, which is eaten either with fresh or sour milk, or still more frequently with a sauce made of dried meat pounded in a mortar,

mortar, and boiled with onions, &c. The Furians use little butter; with the Egyptians and Arabs it is an article in great request. There is also another sauce which the poorer people use and highly relish, it is composed of an herb called *Cowel* or *Cawel*, of a taste in part acescent and in part bitter, and generally disagreeable to strangers.

As a substitute for bread, cakes of the same material are also baked on a smooth substance prepared for the purpose, which are extremely thin, and if dexterously prepared not unpalatable. These are called *kissery* (fragments or sections); they are also eaten with the sauce above mentioned, or with milk, or simply water; and in whatever form the grain be used, the rich cause it to be fermented before it be reduced to flour, which gives it a very agreeable taste. They also make no hesitation in eating the dokn raw, but moistened with water, without either grinding or the operation of fire.

The Sultan here does not seem wholly inattentive to that important object, agriculture. Nevertheless, it may be esteemed rather a blind compliance with antient custom, than individual public spirit, in which has originated a practice adopted by him, in itself sufficiently laudable, since other of his regulations by no means conduce to the same end.

At the beginning of the *Harif*, or wet season, which is also the moment for sowing the corn, the King goes out with his Meleks and the rest of his train, and while the people are employed in turning up the ground and sowing the seed, he also

makes

makes several holes with his own hand. The same custom, it is said, obtains in Bornou, and other countries in this part of Africa. It calls to the mind a practice of the Egyptian kings, mentioned by Herodotus. Whether this usage be antecedent to the introduction of Mohammedism into the country, I know not; but as it is attended with no superstitious observance, it would rather seem to belong to that creed.

Population.

The number of inhabitants in a country in so rude a state as this is at present, it must necessarily be extremely difficult to compute with precision. Possibly the levies for war may furnish some criterion. The Sultan, for about two years, had been engaged in a very serious war with the usurper of Kordofân. The original levies for this war I have understood consisted of about two thousand men. Continual reinforcements have been sent, which may be supposed to amount to more than half that number. At present the army does not contain more than two thousand, great numbers of them having been taken off by the small-pox, and other causes. Even this number is very much missed, and the army is still spoken of as a very large one. It seems to me from this and other considerations, that the number of souls within the empire cannot much exceed two hundred thousand. Cobbé is one of their most populous towns; yet from the best computation I have been able to make, knowing the number of inhabitants in the greater part of the houses, I cannot persuade myself that the total

total amount of both sexes, including slaves, much exceeds six thousand. Of these the greater proportion are slaves.

The houses are separated from each other by wide intervals, as each man chooses for building the spot nearest to the ground he cultivates; so that in an extent of about two miles on a line, not much more than one hundred distinct inclosures properly to be termed houses are visible. The number of villages is considerable; but a few hundred souls form the sum of the largest. There are only eight or ten towns of great population.

The people of Dar-Fûr are divided into those from the river, of whom I have already spoken, some few from the West, who are either Fukkara, or come for the purposes of trade. Arabs, who are very numerous, and some of whom are established in the country, and cannot quit it; they are of many different tribes, but the greater number are those who lead a wandering kind of life on the frontiers, and breed camels, oxen, and horses. Yet they are not, for the most part, in such a state of dependence as always to contribute effectually to the strength of the monarch in war, or to his supplies in peace. These are *Mahmíd*, the *Mahría*, the *beni-Fesâra*, the *beni-Gerâr*, and several others whose names I do not recollect. After the Arabs come the people of Zeghawa, which once formed a distinct kingdom, whose chief went to the field with a thousand horsemen, as it is said, from among his own subjects. The Zeghawa speak a different dialect from the people of Fûr. We must then enumerate the people of Bégo or Dageou, who are now subject

to

to the crown of Fûr, but are a diſtinct tribe, which formerly ruled the country. Kordofân, which is now ſubject to Fûr, and a number of other ſmaller kingdoms, as *Dar Bérti*, &c. *Dar Rugna* has a king, who is however dependent, but more on Bergoo than on Fûr. What are the numbers of each is very difficult to ſay, as there are few or no data whence any thing ſatisfactory can be deduced.

Building.

This art, in which more refined nations diſplay ſo much ingenuity, and conſume ſo much of their property, is here limited by the neceſſity that produced it. A light roof ſhelters the Fûrian from the ſun and rain, and he fears not to be cruſhed by the maſs which he has raiſed for his ſecurity. The conflagration may deſolate his abode, but his ſoul is not appalled, for he has raiſed no monument of vanity to become its prey. The walls, wherever that material is to be procured, are built of clay; and the people of higher rank cover them with a kind of plaſter, and colour them white, red, and black. The apartments are of three kinds, one is called a *Donga*, which is a cube commonly formed in the proportion of twenty feet by twelve. The four walls are covered with a flat roof conſiſting of light beams laid horizontally from ſide to ſide; over this is ſpread a ſtratum of uſhar, or ſome other light wood, or, by thoſe who can afford the expenſe, courſe mats; a quantity of dried horſe's or camel's dung is laid over this; and the whole is finiſhed with a ſtrong and ſmooth coating of clay. They contrive

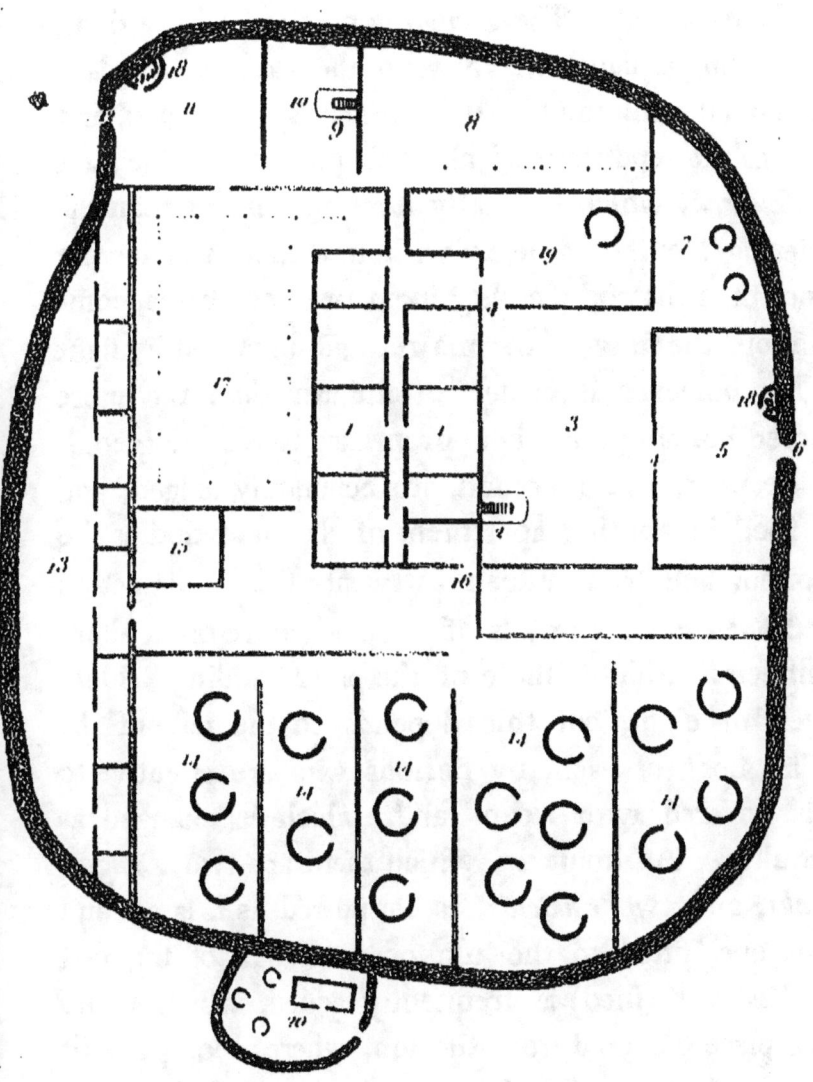

Sketch of a Plan of the Residence of the Sultan of Fur.

Scale of 5 Inches to 100 Feet.

For the Description of this Plate, to which the References are made, see the End of the Appendix.

trive to give the roof a slight obliquity, making spouts to carry off the water. The roof thus constructed is a tolerable protection from the rain, and the whole building is in a certain degree secure from robbers, and the other inconveniences which are there to be expected. The *Donga* is provided with a door, consisting of a single plank, hewn with the axe, as the plane and saw are equally unknown. It is secured by a padlock, and thus constitutes the repository of all their property. The next is called a *Kournak*, which is usually somewhat larger than the *Donga*, differing from it in being without a door, and having no other roof than thatch, shelving like that of our barns, composed of Kassob, the straw of the maize, and supported by light rafters. This however is cooler in summer than the more closely covered buildings, and is appropriated to receiving company, and sleeping. The women are commonly lodged, and dress their food in another apartment of the same kind as the last, but round, and from fifteen to twenty feet in diameter: this is called *Sukteia*. The walls of the *Donga* are often about twelve or fifteen feet high; those of the other buildings seldom exceed seven or eight, but this depends on the taste of the owner. The floor of each, by persons who are attentive to neatness, is covered with clean sand, which is changed as occasion requires. An house in which there are two *Dongas*, two *Kournaks*, and two *Sukteias*, is considered as a large and commodious one, fitted to the use of merchants of the first order. A *Rukkúba* (shed) is frequently added, which is no more than a place sheltered from the sun, where a company sit and converse in the open air. The interior fence of the house is commonly a wall of clay. The exterior universally a thick

hedge,

hedge, confisting of dried branches of acacia and other thorny trees, which secures the cattle, and prevents the slaves from escaping; but which, as it takes no root, is never green, and has rather a gloomy aspect. The materials of the village houses require no particular description; they are commonly of the form of the *Sukteia*, when they rise above the appellation of hut, but the substance is the straw of the maize, or some other equally coarse and insecure. Tents are not used, except by the Meleks and great men, and these are ill-constructed. In time of war materials to construct huts are found by the soldiers, and applied without great difficulty; and the *Sarcina belli* of each man is a light mat adapted to the size of his body.

Manners.

The troops of the country are not famed for skill, courage, or perseverance. In their campaigns much reliance is placed on the Arabs who accompany them, and who are properly tributaries rather than subjects of the Sultan. One energy of barbarism they indeed possess, in common with other savages, that of being able to endure hunger and thirst; but in this particular they have no advantage over their neighbours. On the journey, a man whom I had observed travelling on foot with the caravan, but unconnected with any person, asked me for bread—"How long have you been without it?" said I.—"Two days," was the reply.—" And how long without water?"—" I drank water last night."—This was at sun-set, after we had been marching all day in the heat of the sun, and we had yet six hours to reach

reach the well. In their persons the Fûrians are not remarkable for cleanliness. Though observing as Mohammedans all the superstitious formalities of prayer, their hair is rarely combed, or their bodies completely washed. The hair of the pubes and axillæ it is usual to exterminate; but they know not the use of soap; so that with them polishing the skin with unguents holds the place of perfect ablutions and real purity. A kind of farinaceous paste is however prepared, which being applied with butter to the skin, and rubbed continually till it become dry, not only improves its appearance, but removes from it accidental sordes, and still more the effect of continued perspiration, which, as there are no baths in the country, is a consideration of some importance. The female slaves are dexterous in the application of it, and to undergo this operation is one of the refinements of African sensuality. Their intervals of labour and rest are fixed by no established rule, but governed by inclination or personal convenience. Their fatigues are often renewed under the oppressive influence of the meridian sun, and in some districts their nightly slumbers are interrupted by the dread of robbers, in others by the musquitoes and other inconveniences of the climate.

An inveterate animosity seems to exist between the natives of Fûr and those of Kordofân. From conversations with both parties I have understood that there have been almost continual wars between the two countries as far as the memory of individuals extends. One of the causes of this hostility appears to be their relative position; the latter lying in the road between Dar-Fûr and Sennaar, which is considered as the most practicable, though not the direct communication between the the former and Mekka. Nor can caravans pass from Suakem to Fûr, as appears, but by the permission of the governors of Kordofân. The jealousy of trade therefore is in part the origin of their unvaried and implacable animosity.

Nothing resembling current coin is found in Soudân, unless it be certain small tin rings, the value of which is in some degree arbitrary, and which alone obtains at El Fasher. In that place they serve as the medium of exchange for small articles, for which in others are received beads, salt, &c. These rings are made of so many various sizes, that I have known sometimes twelve, sometimes one hundred and forty of them, pass for a given quantity and quality of cotton cloth. The Austrian dollars, and other silver coins, brought from Egypt, are all sold for ornaments for the women, and some little profit attends the sale of them, but the use of them in dress is far from general.

Gold not being found within the limits of Fûr, is seldom seen in the market; when it appears there, it is in the form of rings of about one-fourth of an ounce weight each, in which state it comes from Sennaar. The Egyptian *mahbûb*, or other stamped money, none will receive but the people of that country. The other articles chiefly current, are such as belong to their dress, as cotton cloths, beads, amber, kohhel, rhéa, and on the other hand, oxen, camels, and slaves.

The

The disposition of the people of Fûr has appeared to me more cheerful than that of the Egyptians; and that gravity and reserve which the precepts of Mohammedism inspire, and the practice of the greater number of its professors countenances and even requires, seems by no means as yet to sit easy on them. A government perfectly despotic, and at this time not ill administered, as far as relates to the manners of the people, yet forms no adequate restraint to their violent passions *. Prone to inebriation, but unprovided with materials or ingenuity to prepare any other fermented liquor than *bûza*, with this alone their convivial excesses are committed. But though the Sultan hath just published an ordinance (March 1795) forbidding the use of that liquor under pain of death, the plurality, though less publicly than before, still indulge themselves in it. A company often sits from sun-rise to sun-set drinking and conversing, till a single man sometimes carries off near two gallons of that liquor. The bûza has however a diuretic and diaphoretic tendency, which precludes any danger from these excesses.

In this country dancing is practised by the men as well as the women, and they often dance promiscuously. Each tribe seems to have its appropriate dance: that of Fûr is called *Secondari*, that of Bukkara *Bendala*. Some are grave, others lascivious, but consisting rather of violent efforts than of graceful

* The inhabitants of a village called *Bernoo*, having quarrelled with those of another hamlet, and some having been killed on both sides, all the property of both villages was forfeited to the king, the inhabitants being abandoned to poverty.

motions.

motions. Such is their fondness for this amusement, that the slaves dance in fetters to the music of a little drum; and, what I have rarely seen in Africa or the East, the time is marked by means of a long stick held by two, while others beat the cadence with short batons.

They use the games of *Tab-u-duk* and *Dris-wa-talaité*, described by Niebuhr, which however appear not indigenous, but to have been borrowed of the Arabs.

The vices of thieving, lying, and cheating in bargains, with all others nearly or remotely allied to them, as often happen among a people under the same circumstances, are here almost universal. No property, whether considerable or trifling, is safe out of the sight of the owner, nor indeed scarcely in it, unless he be stronger than the thief. In buying and selling the parent glories in deceiving the son, and the son the parent; and God and the Prophet are hourly invocated, to give colour to the most palpable frauds and falsehoods.

The privilege of polygamy, which, as is well known, belongs to their religion, the people of Soudân push to the extreme. At this circumstance the Musselmans of Egypt, with whom I have conversed on the subject, affect to be much scandalized: for whereas, by their law they are allowed four free women, and as many slaves as they can conveniently maintain, the Fûrians take both free women and slaves without any limitation. The Sultan has more than an hundred free women, and many of the Meleks have from twenty to thirty. Teraub, a

late

late king, contented himself with about five hundred females as a light travelling equipage in his wars in Kordofân, and left as many more in his palace. This may seem ridiculous, but when it is recollected that they had corn to grind, water to fetch, food to dress, and all menial offices to perform for several hundred individuals, and that these females (excepting those who are reputed *Serrari,* concubines of the monarch) travel on foot, and even carry utensils, &c. on their heads, employment for this immense retinue may be imagined, without attributing to the Sultan more libidinous propensities than belong to others of the same rank and station.

This people exceeds in indulgences with women, and pays little regard to restraint or decency. The form of the houses already described secures no great secrecy to what is carried on within them, yet even the concealment which is thus offered, is not always sought. The shade of a tree, or long grass, is the sole temple required for the sacrifices to the primæval deity. In the course of licentious indulgence father and daughter, son and mother are sometimes mingled. The relations of brother and sister are exchanged for closer intercourse; and in the adjoining state, (Bergoo,) the example of the monarch countenances the infraction of a positive precept, as well of Islamism, as of the other rules of faith, which have taken their tincture from the Mosaic dispensation.

But however unbridled their appetites in other respects may be, pæderasty, so common in Asia and the North of Africa, is in Soudân little known or practised. The situation, character, and
treatment

treatment of women is not exactly similar, either to that which marks the manners of Asia, and other parts of Africa, or to that which is established in Europe. In contradistinction to the women of Egypt, in Soudân, when a stranger enters the house, one of the more modest indeed retires, but she is contented to retire to a small distance, and passes and repasses executing the business of the house in the presence of the men. In Egypt, a veil is invariably the guardian of real or affected modesty. In Dar-Fûr none attempt to conceal their faces but the wives of the great, whose rank demands some affectation of decency— who from satiety of indulgence become coquets, or whose vanity induces them to expect that concealment will ensnare the inexperienced with the hope of youth which has ceased to recommend them, or beauty by which they could never boast to be adorned. The middle and inferior rank are always contented with the slight covering of a cotton cloth, wrapped round the waist, and occasionally another of the same form, materials, and size, and equally loose, artlessly thrown over the shoulders. They never eat with the men, but shew no hesitation at being present when the men eat and drink. The most modest of them will enter the house, not only of a man and a stranger, but of the traders of Egypt, and make their bargains at leisure. On such occasions, any indelicate freedom on the part of the merchant is treated with peculiar indulgence. The husband is by no means remarkable for jealousy, and provided he have reason to suppose that his complaisance will be attended with any solid advantage, will readily yield his place to a stranger. Nothing can shock the feelings of an Egyptian more than to see his wife in conversation with another man in public. For similar conduct,

individuals

individuals of that nation have been known to inflict the last punishment. A liberty of this kind has no such effect on a Fûrian.

Defendit numerus, junctæque in umbone phalanges.

The universality of the practice prevents its being esteemed either criminal or shameful.

Some of the most laborious domestic offices in this country are executed by women. They not only prepare the soil and sow the corn, but assist in gathering it. They alone too are engaged in the business of grinding and converting it into bread. They not only prepare the food, in which (contrary to the practice of the Arabs) it is esteemed disgraceful for a man to occupy himself, but fetch water, wash the apparel, and cleanse the apartments. Even the clay buildings, which have been mentioned, are constructed chiefly by women. It is not uncommon to see a man on a journey, mounted idly on an ass, while his wife is pacing many a weary step on foot behind him, and moreover, perhaps, carrying a supply of provisions or culinary utensils. Yet it is not to be supposed that the man is despotic in his house: the voice of the female has its full weight. No question of domestic œconomy is decided without her concurrence, and, far from being wearied with the corporeal exertions of the day, by the time the sun declines, her memory of real or imaginary injuries affords matter for querulous upbraiding and aculeate sarcasms.

Whoever, impelled by vanity, (for no profit attends it,) receives to his bed the daughter of a King or powerful Melek, (women of this rank are called *Miram*,) finds her sole moderatrix of his family, and himself reduced to a cipher. Of his real or reputed offspring he has no voice in the disposal, government, or instruction. The princess, who has honoured him with the limited right over her person, becomes not the partner, but the sole proprietor, of all that he possessed; and her most extravagant caprices must not be thwarted, least her displeasure should be succeeded by that of the monarch.

The man cannot take another wife with the same ceremonies or dowry; and if any dispute arise concerning inheritance, the right is always decided in favour of the *Miram*. Finally, he is almost a prisoner in the country, which he cannot leave, however distressed, and however he may be inclined to retrieve his fortune by trade, without special permission from the Sultan, and the immediate and unqualified forfeiture not only of the dowry he gave, but of all the valuables he received in consequence of the honourable alliance.

Previously to the establishment of Islamism* and kingship, the people of Fûr seem to have formed wandering tribes, in which state many of the neighbouring nations to this day remain. In their persons they differ from the negroes of the coast of Guinea. Their hair is generally short and woolly, though some are

* About a century and a half ago.

seen with it of the length of eight or ten inches, which they esteem a beauty. Their complexion is for the most part perfectly black. The Arabs, who are numerous within the empire, retain their distinction of feature, colour, and language. They most commonly intermarry with each other. The slaves, which are brought from the country they call *Fertit*, (land of idolaters,) perfectly resemble those of Guinea, and their language is peculiar to themselves.

In most of the towns, except Cobbé, which is the chief residence of foreign merchants, and even at court, the vernacular idiom is in more frequent use than the Arabic; yet the latter is pretty generally understood. The judicial proceedings, which are held in the monarch's presence, are conducted in both languages, all that is spoken in the one being immediately translated into the other by an interpreter (*Tergimân*).

After those who fill the offices of government, the *Faqui*, or learned man, i. e. priest, holds the highest rank. Some few of these *Faquis* have been educated at Kahira, but the majority of them in schools of the country. They are ignorant of every thing except the Korân. The nation, like most of the North of Africa, except Egypt, is of the sect of the Imâm Malck, which however differs not materially from that of Shafei.

Revenues of Dar-Fûr.

1. On all merchandize imported the king has a duty, which in many instances amounts to near a tenth; as for instance, on every camel's load of cotton goods brought from Egypt, and which commonly consists of two hundred pieces, the duty paid to the king by the merchants of Egypt is twenty pieces: the Arabs who are under his government and the natives pay more; some articles however do not pay so much.

2. In addition to this, when they are about to leave Dar-Fûr on their return to Egypt, another tax is demanded on the slaves exported, under pretence of a voluntary douceur, to be exempt from having their slaves scrutinised. This, on our caravan, which comprised about five thousand slaves, amounted to 3000 mahbubs, between 6 and 700l. to be paid to the Chabîr on their arrival in Egypt.

3. All forfeitures for misdemeanors are due to the king; and this is a considerable article; for in case of a dispute in which blood is shed, as often happens, he makes a demand of just what proportion he thinks right of the property of the village in which the offence was committed, of the whole, of an half, of a third, of every species of possession, and this most rigorously estimated.

4. In

4. In addition to this, every one who is concerned in a judicial proceeding before him, must bring a present according to his rank and property: this is another considerable source of revenue.

5. Of all the merchandise, but especially slaves, which are brought *from the roads*, as they call it, that is, from all quarters except Egypt, the king is entitled to a tenth; and in case of a *Selatéa*, that is, an expedition to procure slaves by force, the tenth he is entitled to becomes a fifth, for the merchants are obliged to wait six weeks or two months before they can sell any of their slaves, and then are obliged to pay in kind one tenth of the number originally taken, one half of which is by that time generally dead.

6. At the time of *leathering the kettle-drum*, which happens every year on the 27th of the month Rabia-el-awil, all the principal people of every town and village, nay, as I have understood, every housekeeper, is obliged to appear at El Fasher, with a present in his hands, according to his rank and ability. This is another considerable source of revenue. The present of the Melek of the Jelabs on one of these occasions, I have known to be valued at 900 mahbûbs, or about 200l. sterling. At this solemn festival, all the troops, not in actual service, are obliged to be present, and as it may be called, reviewed; that is, every man who has or can procure an horse, mounts and shews him in the public meeting.

7. A number of presents are daily and hourly received from all the great people of the country, as well as from the merchants who come on business, and those who solicit offices. The merchants generally present some kind of manufacture for clothing, such as light woollen cloth, carpets, arms, &c. and the people of the country, camels, slaves male and female, *tokéas*, oxen, sheep, &c.

8. But one of the most considerable articles of revenue is the tribute of the Arabs who breed oxen, horses, camels, sheep. Those who breed horses should bring to the monarch all the males which are yearly produced by their mares; but this I am told they often contrive to avoid. The customary tribute of the Arabs who breed oxen, or *Bukkara*, as they are called, is one tenth *. But when I was there, they having neglected paying it for two years, the Sultan sent a body of troops, who seized all they could lay hands on, to the number of twelve thousand oxen. If the tribute were regularly paid, it might amount to four thousand oxen per annum: but these Arabs live in tents, and consequently change their habitations frequently, and when they feel themselves united, are not much inclined to pay tribute. Those who breed camels should also pay a tenth of their property yearly; and I have understood that they acquit themselves of the obligation with more regularity than the former. These also however are sometimes rebellious, and then nothing is received from them. Two tribes, *Mahria* and *Mahmid*, were at war

* A great tribute is also paid in butter.

during

during my refidence in Fûr, and a battle took place between them, in which many fell on both fides; the monarch, to punifh them for their contumacious behaviour, fent a Melek with a detachment of about fixty horfemen, who feized on one half of the camels of every Arab, and where they found five took three, as the fifth could not be divided. The owners of fheep and goats pay a tenth.

9. Every village is obliged to pay annually a certain fum in corn, *Dokn*, which is collected by the king's flaves. The monarch has alfo lands of his own, which are cultivated by his flaves, and which ferve to fupply his houfhold; for, though a merchant, he does not fell corn. The whole of the diftrict of Gebel Marra, to the Weft, is entirely appropriated to his ufe, and the wheat, wild honey, &c. which are abundantly produced there are all referved for his table.

10. The king is chief merchant in the country, and not only difpatches with every caravan to Egypt a great quantity of his own merchandife, but alfo employs his flaves and dependents to trade with the goods of Egypt, on his own account, in the countries adjacent to Soudan.

Articles

Articles of Commerce.

Gold rings are sometimes worn in the nose by women of distinction. Sea-shells (*Cowries*) are among other female ornaments, but not very current. The red legumen, called *Shûsh*, is much worn in the hair.

Commodities brought by the Jelabs from Egypt are:

1. Amber beads.
2. Tin, in small bars.
3. Coral beads.
4. Cornelian ditto.
5. False Cornelian ditto.
6. Beads of Venice.
7. Agate.
8. Rings, silver and brass, for the ancles and wrists.
9. Carpets, small.
10. Blue cotton cloths of Egyptian fabric.
11. White cotton ditto.
12. Indian muslins and cottons.
13. Blue and white cloths of Egypt called *Melayés*.
14. Sword blades, strait, (German,) from Kahira.
15. Small looking-glasses.
16. Copper face-pieces, or defensive armour for the horses' heads.
17. Fire arms.
18. Kohhel

EGYPT, AND SYRIA.

18. Kohhel for the eyes.
19. *Rhéa*, a kind of moss from European Turkey, for food, and a scent.
20. *Shé*, a species of absynthium, for its odour, and as a remedy: both the last sell to advantage.
21. Coffee.
22. *Mahleb, Krumphille, Symbille, Sandal*, Nutmegs.
23. *Dufr*, the shell of a kind of fish in the Red Sea, used for a perfume.
24. Silk unwrought.
25. Wire, brass and iron.
26. Coarse glass beads, made at Jerusalem, called *Hersh* and *Munjûr*.
27. Copper culinary utensils, for which the demand is small.
28. Old copper for melting and re-working.
29. Small red caps of Barbary.
30. Thread linens of Egypt—small consumption.
31. Light French cloths, made into Benîshes.
32. Silks of Scio, made up.
33. Silk and cotton pieces of Aleppo, Damascus, &c.
34. Shoes of red leather.
35. Black pepper.
36. Writing paper, (*papier des trois lunes*,) a considerable article.
37. Soap of Syria.

Transported

Transported to Egypt:

1. Slaves, male and female.
2. Camels.
3. Ivory.
4. Horns of the rhinoceros.
5. Teeth of the hippopotamus.
6. Ostrich feathers.
7. Whips of the hippopotamus's hide.
8. Gum.
9. Pimento.
10. Tamarinds, made into round cakes.
11. Leather sacks for water (*ray*) and dry articles (*geraub*).
12. Peroquets in abundance, and some monkeys and Guinea fowl.
13. Copper, white, in small quantity.

CHAP. XX.

Miscellaneous observations on Dar-Fûr, and some of the adjacent countries.

THE preceding chapters concerning Dar-Fûr, contain mostly facts of which I was an eye-witness, or received from undoubted authority. But as every information, however minute, may either conduce to facilitate farther progress in this part of Africa, or may perhaps interest the curious reader, as relating to regions little known, I shall now proceed to some matters, related to me on the spot, but the accuracy of which I cannot pretend to vouch.

The people of Fûr are represented as using many superstitious ceremonies at the *leathering of the kettle-drum,* a ceremony before mentioned. Among others, it is said, they put to death, in the form of a sacrifice, a young boy and girl. Even to this day, many idols are worshipped by the women of the Sultan's *Harem.* The mountaineers offer a kind of sacrifice to the deity of the mountains, when they are in want of rain.

Several superstitious notions prevail among the slaves. One of them having died suddenly, it was imagined that he had been possessed by the devil, and none of them would wash the body.

body. It was with difficulty that they could be prevailed on even to carry it to the place of interment.

The people of Dageou, a country on the West, represented as not far from Bergoo, it is said, conquered the country now called Fûr, and retained it till they were exhausted by mutual contentions; upon which the present race of kings succeeded, but from what origin I have not been able to discover. Probably, Moors driven from the North by the Arabs. The race of Dageou is said to have come from the vicinity of Tunis. It is reported, that they had a custom of lighting a fire on the inauguration of their king, which was carefully kept burning till his death. At present there is a custom in Fûr, of spreading the carpets on which the several deceased Sultans used to sit, before the new prince, and from the one he prefers, it is judged his character will be analogous to that of its former possessor.

The Sultan Omar, one of the predecessors of Teraub, carried on a long and destructive war with the neighbouring country of Bergoo, in which he exhausted his treasures and people, and at the same time greatly weakened the adverse country.

The families between which the pretensions to authority now lie, are those of Abd-el-Casim, Teraub, and Chalifé, his brother. Each of them has a number of warm partizans among the soldiery, who would never be faithful to any of the other families. The competitors are so numerous that much confusion

sion is expected to follow the death of the present Sultan; and it is inferred that the kingdom will be divided.

I shall now proceed to state some relations that were made to me concerning Kordofân and other adjacent countries.

A king, of the name of *Abli-calik*, is the idol of the people of Kordofân, where he reigned about fourteen years ago, and is renowned for probity and justice. The kings of Kordofân had been deputed by the Mecque of Sennaar, till after the death of the son of *Abli-Calik*, when it was usurped by Fûr, in consequence of the weakness and dissensions of the government at Sennaar.

The people of Kordofân are reported to be not only indifferent to the amours of their daughters and sisters, but even attached to their seducers. The father or brother will even draw the sword against him who offends the *Refik*, or companion of his daughter or sister. Very different is the mode of thinking in Sennaar, where immodesty is only permitted among the female slaves. The chief merchants have companies of these slaves, and derive great profit from their prostitution.

Afnou, a country beyond Bornou to the Westward, is said to produce such abundance of silver, that the natives construct defensive armour of that metal. The coats of mail are jointed, and represented as very beautiful. Of the same material, it is reported, are made pieces to protect the head and breast of their horses, the former having the chaffron, or horn, known in our days of chivalry.

Among the Southern countries, whither the Jelabs of Bergoo and Fûr sometimes journey to procure slaves, is *Dar Kulla*. The chief article they carry to Kulla is salt, twelve pounds of which are estimated as the price of a male slave, *sedasé*, about twelve or fourteen years of age. A female brings three pounds more, whimsically computed by the natives, as, a pound for the girl's eyes, another for her nose, and a third for her ears. If copper be the medium, two rotals are esteemed equal to four of salt. *Hoddûr*, a large sort of Venetian glass beads, and tin, are in great esteem. Of the latter they make rings and other ornaments.

The natives of Kulla are represented as partly negroes, partly of a red or copper colour. Their language is nasal, but very simple and easy. It is said they worship idols. They are very cleanly, to which the abundance of water in their country contributes: and they are remarkable for honesty, and even punctilious in their transactions with the Jelabs.

They have ferry-boats on the river, which are impelled partly by poles, partly by a double oar, like our canoes. Slaves are obtained in Dar Kulla either by violence, *Selatéa*, or by the following method. In that country the smallest trespass on the property of another, is punished by enslaving the children or young relations of the trespasser. If even a man's footstep be observed among the corn of another, the circumstance is

attended

attended by calling witnesses, and application to a magistrate, and the certain consequence of proof is the forfeiture of his son, daughter, nephew, or niece, to the person trespassed on. These accidents are continually happening, and produce a great number of slaves. A commission to purchase any thing in a distant market, not exactly fulfilled, is attended with a like forfeiture. But above all, if a person of note die, the family have no idea of death as a necessary event, but say that it is effected by witchcraft. To discover the perpetrator, the poorer natives, far and near, are obliged to undergo expurgation by drinking a liquor which is called in Dar-Fûr *Kilingi*, or something that resembles it; and the person on whom the supposed signs of guilt appear, may either be put to death, or sold as a slave.

The people of Kulla are strangers to venereal complaints, but are subject to the small-pox. In that part of the country which is visited by the Jelabs there is a king; the rest is occupied by small tribes, each of which is ruled by the chief who happens to have most influence at the time. The *Kumba*, or Pimento tree, is found there in such plenty, that a *rotal* or pound of salt will purchase four or five *mid*, each *mid* about a peck.

The trees are so large, from the quantity of water and deep clay, that canoes are hollowed out of them sufficiently capacious to contain ten persons.

It was related to me by Jelabs who have visited that country, that the inhabitants of Dar Bergoo make war by sudden incursions,

sions, traversing and laying waste a large space in a short time. They leave their women behind, and are thus better adapted to military operations than the Fûrians, who follow an opposite practice, never marching without a host of attendant females. The people of Bergoo seldom make *Selatéa*.

Some of the idolatrous nations, dependent on Bergoo, are represented as making war in a very formidable manner. The combatants never retreat; and the women behind light a fire, in which they heat the heads of the spears, and exchange them for such as are cooled in the combat. They also use poisoned weapons.

There is a remote part of the pagan country, from which slaves are brought, which the Arabs distinguish by the term *Gnum Gnum*, (a sobriquet,) whose inhabitants eat the flesh of the prisoners they take in war. I have conversed with slaves who came thence, and they admit the fact. These people are also in the habit of stripping off the skin of the hands and faces of their slaughtered foes, which afterwards undergo some preparation, and are worn as a mark of triumph. Their arms, a spear or javelin, are of iron, wrought by themselves. After having heated them to redness, they stick the point into the trunk of a particular tree, and there leave the weapon till the juice has dried on. In this manner it acquires, as is reported, a most deadly poison.

A few

EGYPT, AND SYRIA.

A few of the more common vocabula in the language of *Dar-Runga*.

Water	Tta.
As eide (a pudding)	Gnung.
Come and eat	Gagra.
Quickly	Undelak nonnerâ.
Bring the bowl	Kiddeki, Kiddeki.
A mat	Kubbenâng.
Cloths	Lemba.
Shoes	Bŏrŏ.
Sun	Agñing.
It is hot	Agñing betrân.
Moon	Medding.
A wooden mortar	Bedding.
Aſs	Guſſendĕ.
Horſe	Filah.
Dog	Ming.
Houſe	Ttong.
Kingdom	Kuſſé.
Wood of any kind	Unjŭm.
Fire	Niſſiek.
Woman	Mmi.
Man	Kameré.
Is it I?	Ammẽ?
Reprimanding	Ggó!
Grain	Aſſé.

Maize

Maize	Dimbiti.
Millet	Gurwendi.
Fowl	Kidi.
Winged ant	Agñemâ.
Spear	Sûbbûk.
Knife	Dangala.
Foot	Itar.
Eye	Khaſſo.
Ear	Neſſo.
Hand	Tuſſo.
Light blue	Endréng.
Dung	Abûrr.
Urine	Niſſich.
Copper	Simméri.
Tin	Fueddah.
Beads	Arrû.
Loins (of the human body) *alſo*	Arrû.
One	Kadenda.
Two	Embirr.
Three	Attik.
Four	Mendih.
Six	Subotîkeda.
Seven	Ow.
Eight	Sebatéis.
Nine	Atih.
Ten	Bûff.
Rain	Kiñga.
God, *alſo*	Kiñga.

By

By God, *an adjuration*	Kiñga go!
Honey	Tuggi.
Fish	Kogñong.
Meat	Missich.
Gruel	Ba-birré.
Stone	Diffi.
A star	Beité.
The stars collectively	Beité-jûk.
Slave of either sex	Guiah.
Male slave	Guiah méré.
Female slave	Guiah Mmi.
Mountain	Ddéta.
Wind	Wwi.
Cinders	Firgi.

CHAP. XXI.

MEDICAL REMARKS.

Psorophthalmia—Plague—Small-pox—Guinea worm—Scrophula—Syphilis—Bile—Tenia—Hernia—Hydrocele—Hemorrhoides and Fistula—Apoplexy—Umbilical ruptures—Accouchemens—Hydrophobia—Phlebotomy—Remedies—Remarks—Circumcision—Excision.

From the following detached remarks, the result chiefly of personal observation, if the physiologist can derive any amusement, or the traveller the smallest mitigation of his personal sufferings, the purpose of committing them to paper is answered.

If any medical professor should chance to advert to them, the writer is too conscious of the superficiality of his own knowlege not to perceive, that little satisfaction will be derived. But persuaded, that the art of healing, even at this day, abounds little less in experiments than in the age of one of its brightest ornaments, who makes the confession, he is induced to believe, scarcely any fact relative to it, or any experiment, faithfully narrated, can be wholly destitute of its use.

Psoroph-

Pforophthalmia.

It is remarked that in Egypt, but particularly in Kahira, the blind, and those who have defective vision, bear a large proportion to the number of the inhabitants. The fact observed, which cannot be disputed, has been explained in various ways. It has by some been considered as proceeding from the habitual use of rice. By others, as the effect of the subtle dust which floats in the air. Even the water of the Nile has been supposed to co-operate at least, if not to be the sole agent, in producing this remarkable disease.

To explore the origin of this or any other malady, all its appearances must first be accurately noted. The ophthalmia of Egypt leads us through a diversity of symptoms, from slight inflammation and defluxion, to the total and irrecoverable blindness occasioned by opacity of the Cornea. To enumerate them all correctly, and compare them in a variety of cases, must be the task of an oculist long resident on the spot, and accustomed to numerous patients. A transient observer, however diligent in his inquiries, may more easily prove the falsehood of the assigned causes, than trace the real one.

The Nile water, it may be supposed, when taken into the stomach, can have no effect on the eyes, but by first altering the state of the fluids, into which it, as well as other aliments, is gradually converted. Whether from mineral or vegetable impregnations, it could never operate solely on the eyes, without affecting any other part of the animal economy. The effect of opium is seen on the blood and muscular fibres; of mercury on the glands and lymphatics; of cantharides on the nerves: and too great a portion of these, taken into the body, may have a pernicious effect on the eyes, but always through the medium of other parts. The whole *materia medica*, perhaps, furnishes no drug or mineral that is known, when taken into the stomach, to have a local and partial effect on the eyes. Such an effect is even irreconcileable with the general and constantly observed operation of all remedies applied to the human body.

Besides, if the injury were solely or even in part to arise from the use of the Nile water, all those who drink it must be equally affected, allowing for the different degree of firmness in the stamina of each. But certain orders of men are rarely attacked by this disease, and they too who are continually using the river water both internally and externally.

Rice is one of the most nutritive and salubrious of the farinaceous aliments, and certainly does not operate to render the humours acrid, and thereby to inflame the eyes. It is used as a main article of food by the natives of a large portion of Asia, and forms no inconsiderable part of the consumption in other countries, without being observed to produce any such effect as is here attributed to it; and may therefore fairly be denied to have any such power.

Something

Something more plaufible indeed offers itfelf as to the injurious operation of an external caufe. Nothing can be more fubtle than the duft into which the vegetable foil of Egypt refolves itfelf when it becomes dry. This, during a certain portion of the year, is in a manner fufpended in the air, from a caufe which exifts in few other countries, I mean the want of rain. It alfo contains a large portion of nitre, which is copioufly produced in Egypt. This circumftance, however, is common to many other places. This light duft, doubtlefs of a very irritating quality, not only floats in the ftreets, but pervades the apartments of every dwelling, infinuating itfelf into the moft artfully conftructed inclofures: by it therefore the eyes may and muft be in fome degree affected. But Nature has not ordained that a part fo much expofed fhould be deftitute of its appropriate protection. The fecretions of the lachrymal glands are, in general, abundantly fufficient to counteract the injury fuftained by the action of corrofive or irritating fubftances on the external fabric of the eye, being always produced exactly in proportion to the circumftances that demand them, as daily experience confirms: yet it cannot be denied, that the continually repeated operation of an offending caufe, when no remedy is applied, may be more than commenfurate with the efforts of Nature to reftore herfelf.

Such is precifely the condition of the Kahirines. The accommodating the quality of diet to the fymptoms of derangement in the economy is a precaution unknown to them: and of their remedies, many are fo prepared, or fo adminiftered, as to augment rather than to annihilate difeafe. No idea offers itself to them, but of topical applications to remove a local complaint. If any thing be applied in these *flussioni* (dysophthalmia) it is generally *kôhhel* (calx of tin mixed with sheep's fat) or *tûtti*, a still more powerful astringent, applied in coarse powder, and naturally tending to increase rather than to allay the irritation.

When thus incommoded, the Egyptians of the lower class esteem water pernicious, and therefore rarely wash their eyes; but as the collected dust begins to cause an uneasy sensation, apply their fingers or a coarse cotton cloth to remove it. The higher orders, who are neat in their persons, and regular in their ablutions, are rarely observed to be greatly harassed by this complaint. And the progress of the disorder, when in its nascent state, has several times been stopped, under my observation, by the use of rose-water, solution of sacchar. saturn. &c. as in other places.

But as no single one of these causes, nor even all of them together, appear sufficient to account for all the phenomena, another, more powerful, is to be sought; and none suggests itself more opportunely than that alleged by Savary, who imagines that the defect of vision is principally brought about by the habit of being exposed to the nocturnal air during the summer, at which season a heavy dew falls, and a great transition happens from the heats of the day. In fact, if the face of those who sleep exposed be not completely covered, an itching and unpleasant sensation is always felt in the eyes at rising.

It is ordinarily experienced in the city, where, from being confined in the day, people feel most disposed to seek for coolness and refreshment on their terraces at night.

The Mamlûks, and higher order of Arabs, that is, Mohammedan merchants, and the superior rank of Copts and Franks, are least affected, as being cleanly, not exposing themselves to the night air without necessity, and being well covered. The Arabs of the desert are as free from blindness as any people. They never sleep with the face exposed, and have moreover the advantage of being devoid of the dust and other supposed causes of psorophthalmia in the city. The disorder appears no where so much as in Kahira, because no where are all the causes so much combined: yet it is seen in Alexandria, Damiatt, and in Upper Egypt, which shews that the cause is not confined to Kahira. Among the poorer class of all countries prevails a kind of *insouciance*. That of Kahira is particularly exposed to the changes of temperature and the nocturnal dew, and is ill clothed. Hence the disorder is mostly found among the populace. A disposition to inflammation often appears in the eyes of children, but yields to proper remedies. Hence it may be imagined, that with attention the Egyptians would not suffer more than other nations.

Some travellers have thought that the ophthalmic disease in Kahira was occasioned by the fetid exhalations of the Chalige, and the drains; and have even observed, that those who are most severely affected in winter, recover as soon as the water has filled the Chalige and the pools. This is also a common idea
with

with the natives. "The ſtink blinds me," is a frequent expreſſion on coming into a place of fetid odour; and it may be remarked, that the ordinary maxims of *indigenæ* are rarely to be entirely diſregarded. Whatever miaſms however may iſſue from the canal, they cannot be equally diſperſed over the city, as blindneſs is; and the Franks, Greeks, and other ſtrangers who reſide neareſt this depôt of impurity, would be moſt affected if that were the cauſe. It may yet be one cauſe. Another I take to be the ſubtile duſt above mentioned; but the moſt powerful, indiſcreet expoſure to the nocturnal air and dews. The collective influence of theſe is ſtrengthened by the cloudleſs ſplendour of a vertical ſun, reflected from the ſterile expanſe of ſand, which offers no ſombrous object on which the eye may repoſe itſelf.

Theſe conſiderations, it may be acknowleged, do not carry conviction; but too many local diſeaſes are yet unexplained, to leave any wonder if the cauſe of this ſhould yet remain problematical.

Plague.

All the improvements in the art of healing which modern Europe can boaſt as its own, are the reſult of more frequent experiment, and more patient and minute inveſtigation, than exiſted in the antient.

To conjecture ingeniouſly is a matter of ſmall effort, and in treating of what is properly the object of experiment, it is not

only

only of no value, but often of dangerous result. But it is suited to the indolence of the human mind, and flattering to personal vanity, which delights to perform much by a single energy. Hence, an hypothesis supported by some insulated fact, perhaps only by specious error, is often advanced with warmth, and the most important considerations militating against it, are forgotten, or warped to serve the purpose of the inventor. Thus the increase of the Nile was once confidently attributed to the Etesian winds; and the malady which has so often almost depopulated Kahira, is still by some imagined to proceed from the putrid deposition of its waters.

We have at length disposed ourselves to the habit of tracing the cause of disease, by combining a number of minute, and often varying, symptoms. A practice which, if correct in its detail, can never but be accurate in its deductions. Relative to the Plague, however, whose very name distracts the timid, and appals even the courageous, our reasonings and our deductions are quite of a different description. Respecting its cause, all is conjecture. No experienced or well-informed practitioner has watched the bed of the sick; none has accurately examined the different appearances which the disease assumes in different persons, nor even in its different stages, in the same person. Scarcely any, it is believed, has been tranquil enough to hear patiently from the mouth of the sufferer an account of his sensations, which, recounted by a third person, never fail to vary.

Where this malady appears, the physician and the priest, the pride of science and the security of faith, confident and

boastful

boastful when the patient alone is threatened, are both equally alert in their efforts to escape. The ignorant and unreflecting Muslim, indeed, awe-struck, and resigned to the unalterable decree of Fate, hangs over the couch of his expiring relative. But the report, guided by prejudice, is likely to mislead, and the observation can be of little value when the sole sentiment is stupor.

Thus the Plague remains almost destitute of a local habitation, though it have a name in nosology.

Who can at this day determine, whether the pestilence mentioned by Thucydides be the same as that of Modern Egypt and Turkey? Or whether the epidemical diseases, which have for several centuries, at intervals ravaged different parts of the Turkish empire, have been all specifically the same? The Europeans frequenting the Levant, have written profound treatises on the plague, simply from having seen a quantity of dead bodies carried past the doors of their houses, which the double optics of fear have occasionally magnified from 500 to 10,000.

The facts that appear chiefly to be ascertained relative to the plague, are, 1st, That the infection is not received but by actual contact. In this particular, it would seem less formidable than several other disorders. 2. That it is communicated by certain substances, by others not, as by a woollen cloth, or rope of hemp, but not by a piece of ivory, wood, or a rope made of the date tree; nor by any thing that has been completely immersed in water. It would appear from the report of the

the Kahirines, that no animal but man is affected with this disorder; though, it is said, a cat passing from an infected house, has carried the contagion. 3. That persons have often remained together in the same house, and entirely under the same circumstances, of whom one has been attacked, and died; and the others never felt the smallest inconvenience. 4. That a person may be affected any number of times. 5. That it is more fatal to the young than the old. 6. That no climate appears to be exempt from it; yet, 7. that the extremes of heat and cold both appear to be adverse to it. In Constantinople it is often, but far from being always terminated by the cold of winter, and in Kahira by the heat of summer; both circumstances being, as may be conjectured, the effect of indisposition for absorption in the skin, unless it be supposed that in the latter case, it may be attributed to the change the air undergoes from the increase of the Nile.

The first symptoms are said to be thirst; 2. cephalalgia; 3. a stiff and uneasy sensation, with redness and tumour about the eyes; 4. watering of the eyes; 5. white pustules on the tongue. The more advanced symptoms of buboes, fœtor of the breath, &c. &c. are well known; and I have nothing authentic to add to them. Not uncommonly, all these have successively shewn themselves, yet the patient has recovered; in which case, where suppuration has had place, the skin always remains discoloured, commonly of a purple hue.—Many who have been bleeded in an early stage of the disorder, have recovered without any fatal symptoms; but whether from that or any other cause, does not appear certain. The same operation is reported to have been

commonly

commonly fatal in a late stage. It is said that embrocating the buboes continually with oil has sometimes wrought a cure; but this remedy is so difficult and dangerous for the operator, that it would appear experiments must yet be very defective. The natives of Kahira are too supine to seek for any remedy, and too bigoted to avoid the danger.

The plague which happened in Egypt so early as the year 1348, when Constantinople was yet subject to the Greek emperor, and Egypt in possession of Mohammedans, may be supposed to have originated in the latter. But not to mention that there were many other places from which it might be brought, this single instance, not given in detail, is insufficient to overthrow the testimony of the modern inhabitants, who with one consent affirm, whether Mohammedans or Christians, that the plague is not endemial in Egypt, but that all the instances of it which they are able to trace are proved to have been derived from abroad.

The learned Dr. Mead has brought the plague from Ethiopia, where famine and the small-pox indeed carry off numbers; but where the plague was never known to exist. It is not remembered to have penetrated far into the Upper Egypt, except in some few instances, when it was known to have been carried thither by the boats from Kahira. No more is required to account for its introduction into Egypt at this day, than the admission, that it is never completely extinct at Constantinople, which, it seems, has scarcely been denied.

The

The imagination of one of our poets has drawn the pestilence from the filth of Kahira, and the mud of the Nile. But, not to mention that there is less disposition to fermentation and putrefaction in the atmosphere of Egypt, than in almost any other that I have heard described, Kahira is very far from being impure. No offensive substance remains in the streets twenty-four hours; and even what is left to annoy passengers in London and Paris for months, is there carried away and preserved for burning.

The mud of the Nile becomes dry in a very short space of time after the water has left it, except in the canal (Chalige) which is indeed not very odoriferous; but so far from emitting pestilential exhalations, that the Franks who especially dwell close to it, are never infected with the plague, and are in general among the most healthy of the inhabitants of that metropolis.

Small-pox.

The small-pox is a disease much dreaded by the people of Soudân, whether Moors or Negroes, and little less by the Bedouins of Egypt. The Christians of Kahira are many of them in the habit of inoculating. A few of the Mohammedans use the same practice. It is however almost impossible to persuade them to adopt our mode of treatment.

Inde-

Independently of the general ill confequence of improper management of the patient, the chief reafon of the extraordinary fatality of this complaint among the negroes, appears to be the thicknefs of the fkin, which refifting the effort of nature to protrude the morbid matter to the furface, tends to throw it back into the circulation. A proprietor of flaves, who was rather anxious for the confervation of his property, than fcrupulous in his attachment to religious prejudice, defired me to inoculate five of them. A ftrong dofe of fenna was adminiftered as preparative, and they were afterwards reftrained as to diet. Three of them had not in the whole forty puftules, and foon recovered. The other two fuffered much; and the eruption, though not confluent, proved fatal to one of them. Whether he had caught it before, been improperly treated, or whether it was the effect of habit of body, was not clear. Thefe were of the true negro caft, called, *Fertit*. They were all under twelve years of age.

Guinea Worm.

The Mohammedans of Fûr, and the Arabs, call the idolaters in their neighbourhood *Fertit*, (فرتيت à فرت *improbus fuit*). The difeafe called the Guinea Worm is known among them by the fame name. It is extremely common, and very troublefome to the flaves, and fometimes to free perfons. It is by fome efteemed contagious, which however is rather furmifed than certified. It confifts of a whitifh tumour, at firft hard and painful. Often fhews itfelf about the knee, in the flefhy part

of

of the thigh, and in the foot, just below the instep. As it is matured, a small white worm appears, which is to be wound off by degrees, and in coming out is followed by the discharge of purulent matter. If broken in the extraction, it is sometimes very inconvenient, and often lasts four or even six months. There is no certain cure for this disease, which most frequently shews itself in the beginning of winter, after the rains; but generally disappears at the commencement of the hot season. It seems to originate in the water, which is replete with animalcules, and which no care is used to purify.

They find by the termination of the tumour the extremity of the worm, which they call *wullad-el-Fertit*, and in that spot, puncture the skin with a red-hot iron, which they conceive forces it out; but which always appeared to me a painful operation, without any kind of effect. There is observed in some individuals a greater disposition to this disease than in others, but it is not confined to age, sex, or colour.

Scrophula. ✳

The scurvy is very uncommon in Egypt and Syria. In the former I saw no instance of it. In Dar-Fûr I have observed it in the gums, but never any general dissemination of scrophulous humour appearing in the blood. As the transpiration is seldom interrupted, and generally copious, it must doubtless carry off much of the acrid humours, and prevent their accretion. Salt provisions, which generate the scurvy in the North of Europe,

✳ Scorbutieus is not the same as the kings evil.

Europe, are almost unknown; and much of the diet of the people consists of vegetables. All these circumstances have their influence, but none of them perhaps so much as the Nile-water, which is a perfect solvent; and by the change of its component parts during the increase, has a particular tendency to throw off impurities from the blood.

Syphilis.

The disease which attacks the principle of generation, and destroys, in its source, one among the few solaces with which human life is sparingly diversified, which the heroism and the philanthropy, or the ambition and the avarice, of Europeans have propagated wherever the malign destiny of other nations has ordained that their dominion should be established, does not appear in Egypt with all the terrors that mark its course in other countries.

The temperature, the air, the mode of living, perhaps simply the first, which maintains continued transpiration, render it much milder in its effects than with us, or even in the islands of the Archipelago.

The institutes of the Prophet, indeed, have tended to diminish promiscuous concubinage, yet there is no such deficiency as to impede the propagation of the disease, if it were as virulent as in other places.

Ulcers

Ulcers of long duration, noseless faces, and all the disgusting consequences of this malady are indeed occasionally visible. But they are in very small number, and notoriously the result of extreme negligence, and of repeated infection, where no means have been employed to exterminate it.

It may truly be esteemed fortunate that this disease prevails with no violence in Egypt, for its only certain remedy, mercury, is there found much less efficacious than in the more temperate latitudes. Administered even in smaller doses than in Europe, it is said ptyalism is either produced very early, or it passes off with the fæces, without any visible effect.

A Frank practitioner of Kahira, accustomed to the climate, ordered two drams of Mercury in thirty pills, with Gum Arabic and Syrup of Cichory, to be taken one a day. In this case, he declared, that the pills having been administered during the first seven days, and then, with the intermission of three days, two having been given each day for five days more, had produced no visible effect on the disease, but passed off by stool. In other cases he had known much smaller doses, in the space of two days, had caused inflammation of the salivary glands, and he was obliged to abandon the use of it, and have recourse to other means of cure.

The natives, who are unacquainted with the use of mercury, and indeed of minerals in general as employed internally, are yet provided, as they say, with efficacious remedies for the venereal disease. They use flax oil, fresh, as it is expressed, from the feed. A Greek, who was in the service of Murad Bey as a mariner, (*galeongi,*) and who was known to me in Kahira, had been infected, and on applying to a Frank physician, was told that it would be necessary immediately to use mercurials. The man was not inclined to confinement or to regimen, and went to a Copt at Jizé, who professed to relieve the sick. This man ordered him to take two coffee-cups of flax oil every morning fasting, and directed no regimen, but that of keeping himself warm. The Greek observed none, for he continued freely the use of *aqua vitæ*, and even sacrificed to Venus, (for persons who have been once infected and fully cured, are, it is said, in no fear of reinfection,) and was often in the heat of the sun. He had continued this method for two months, when a general eruption took place over his body, but chiefly about the head and glands of the throat. In this condition I saw him. His Esculapius ordered him to cover the pustules of his face with a kind of red earth, found in some parts of Egypt. They gradually became dry, and came off without leaving any mark. At the end of the third month from the time he had applied to the Copt, and one month after the appearance of the eruption, the man was in perfect health, and the skin had completely recovered its tone and polish.

In the cure of the simple gonorrhea, a decoction of mallows is commonly used, and they seem to place their chief confidence in diuretics. I never heard of an injection, but from those who were acquainted with European practice. Certain herbs and roots macerated, are applied locally in case of inflammation and tension (chordee).

Shankers

Shankers, &c. externally, are repeatedly washed with soap and water, and then kept covered with the red earth above mentioned. I never saw the effect, but the cure is said to be rapid.

In Dar-Fûr I have not observed the venereal disease more formidable than in Egypt. I saw a few individuals who were mutilated in the organs of generation by its effects.

The old women, who are physicians in ordinary, use a decoction of certain roots, of which I never came at the knowlege, infused in *bouza*, which appear to operate succesfully. Gleets are frequent; and continued indulgence produces early debility and impotence.

The great advantages of the *étuves*, or warm baths, is evident in very many instances in Kahira. But it is difficult to admit Savary's assertion (vol. i. p. 108) in its full extent, viz. that they operate as a radical cure of the venereal disease. They doubtless assuage many of its graver symptoms.

In no country are pulmonary diseases more rare than in Egypt, which could not happen if the baths had any tendency to cause them.

Leprosy.

The leprosy is more frequent in Syria than in Egypt. It exists however in the latter country, with all its concomitants of swelled and distorted joints, a livid, spotted, parched, and cracked skin, &c.

I have seen it under all its forms of *Borras*, *Jiddâm*, &c. In Kahira there is no provision for the unhappy sufferers, who are allowed to beg about the streets, but forbidden by their religion from the contact of others, and excluded from society by an inefficient police. I have heard of a cure of the leprosy in its worst stage, by the use of corrosive sublimate in small doses. The natives seem not to know any specific.

In Dar-Fûr, the *Borras*, which is not uncommon, gives to the blacks the appearance of being *pyebald*, changing to white both the skin and hair. A case of, what I was convinced was *Jiddâm*, beginning in the hands, was cured under my observation by a slave, a native of the kingdom called *Baghermi*, but the means he had used he could not be prevailed on to disclose.

Bile.

Complaints proceeding from too copious secretion of bile are extremely common both in Egypt and Dar-Fûr. *Murâr*, the bile, or gall, is the generic name for all diseases of this kind, at least in their nascent state; for they are not solicitous in the choice of names, till distinct appearances teach them to seek a more characteristic appellation. There seems to be no efficacious remedy for these maladies, and therefore they take their course;
and

and all the inconveniences consequent upon them are common, and increased by general inattention to diet.

The *tubbâl*, or *tebbâl*, deriving its name from the spleen, *morbus spleneticus*, is very frequent. One of its outward symptoms is a tumor hard to the touch, but subject to increase and diminution, in the neighbourhood of the spleen, and general inflation in the supra-umbilical region.

In Egypt Christians and the less scrupulous Mohammedans use *aqua vitæ* to remove the present sensation. It operates as an anodyne, which is all they seek. In Dar-Fûr the leaves of senna pulverised, and, by admixture with honey, formed into balls, (the common cathartic,) is the only medicine administered with any salutary effect. I found James's powder of great service to those with whom it operated as an emetic. The distention of the spleen prevents the stomach from receiving a proper quantity of food, yet the inclination for food is undiminished.

The liver being rendered incapable of its functions, by repeated extravasations of bile, the blood, which at all times circulates slowly from the spleen through that gland, now much retarded, occasions schirrosities of the spleen, and at length perfectly stagnant in and distending it, it becomes corrupted by the fæces contained in the colon near it, and begins to putrify. In this state the disease frequently terminates in death. But these schirrosities sometimes remain for years, without producing any very dangerous symptoms.

The

The passage of the bile into the intestines being intercepted, having passed from the gall bladder to the liver, it at length returns to the blood, which occasions *the jaundice*, another disease not uncommon among the Fûrians, termed by them *Saffafir*, and, among the blacks, first visible in the eyes.

To alleviate the effects of any unusual increase of the cystic bile, the natrôn of the country is very efficacious.

Tenia.

From the nature of their diet, which consists in a great degree of vegetables and fruits, with a large portion of sugar, honey, &c. the inhabitants of Egypt, of all denominations, are particularly subject to the Tenia or tape-worm (*Dûd* Ar.) I have seen pieces of vast length preserved by the European physicians, who yet appear to have found no specific for it. The natives mistake the symptoms of this disease, ascarides, &c. for distinct maladies, and treat them accordingly. The commonalty, Jews, and devout Christians, who unremittingly use insalubrious food during their *fasts*, are most affected with it, though none are exempt. In those who are thus incommoded, a tumor commonly appears about the navel, and discoloration of the skin next the eyes.

Bruce seems to be of opinion, that the great prevalence of *worms*, with which the Abyssins are much afflicted, proceeds

from

from the common use of raw meat. Not to mention that it is not yet proved that the habitual use of raw meat generates worms in the human intestines, that complaint cannot well be more common than among the people of Egypt, who never use meat but when fully prepared by fire.

Hernia.

Ruptures are common in Egypt, chiefly among the lower orders, particularly the boatmen, few of whom are seen without a greater or less degree of this dangerous accident, and to many of whom it is fatal. Their life is almost amphibious, and it may in some measure be the effect of the pendent situation of the parts; but it seems chiefly to arise from the exertions they are obliged to make in lading and unlading their boats, and propelling them, as frequently happens, by applying their shoulders. In the people of this city, who carry heavy loads on their backs, and raise great weights, it is also common. Clumsy and ineffectual trusses are made in Kahira, which rather distress and embarrass than relieve or secure the patient. The scrotum is sometimes cauterized, and with effect, if the intestines be not incarcerated. In Dar-Fûr this disease is uncommon; yet it is sometimes seen there.

Hydrocele.

The hydrocele is remarkably frequent in Syria, and, above all, in the town of Beirût. It is also frequent in Egypt, but most among

among the Christians of both countries. Some attribute it to the Nile water; others to the air; others to the use, or rather abuse of *aqua vitæ*; others to food of a particular kind: none of which seems to be the real cause. The natives of both countries have a method of inciding securely, which discharges the water, and of course produces temporary relief: but the malady is rapidly regenerated. The only radical cure is the actual cautery, which, though unskilfully, is yet successfully applied to such patients as are bold enough to encounter the danger.

Hæmorrhoides and Fistula in ano.

The hæmorrhoides (*bowasír*) are very common both in Egypt and Dar-Fûr. In the latter, they cure them by the cautery. The *Fistula in ano* is also seen there, and is cured by a topical application, but without incision.

Apoplexy.

I have known two instances in Dar-Fûr of what appeared to me to be apoplexy. The one was of a male slave, about sixteen years of age, the other of a man about forty; both of them of plethoric habit. The boy dropped down senseless, after having been standing near a large fire in cool weather. Pulsation ceased, and a great hæmorrhage took place from the nostrils. After one hour and a half he expired. Bleeding was recommended to the proprietor, but the by-standers would not consent,

saying

saying it was *Sheïtân*, the devil had possessed him. The man was dead before I saw him; much extravasated blood appeared about him. He had been at work in the sun. The *coup-de-soleil*, properly so called, does not often occur. When much exposed in walking or at work, they protect their head from the ill effect of the rays descending perpendicularly, by winding their shirt round it, and leaving the trunk uncovered.

Umbilical ruptures.

Among the slaves, and even free persons in Dar-Fûr, prominencies of the navel, and umbilical ruptures, of greater or less magnitude, are very common. Though the chord be remarked to be larger in the negroes than with us, this circumstance must probably be occasioned by ignorance, carelesness, or some mismanagement at the birth. It does not appear to be attended with positive inconvenience. The chord, when divided, is here cauterized as in Egypt.

Accouchemens.

The accouchemens of the Arabian females are remarkably easy. There are stories of the Bedouïn women sitting down near a water and delivering themselves. Certain it is, that both the Mohammedan and Coptic females in the cities and towns are equally averse from the attendance of a man on these occasions;

and however unskilful the accoucheuses may be imagined, few accidents have place.

The women of Fûr, in like manner, are assisted by their own sex, and are seldom long confined: yet nature seems to render child-bearing more difficult to them than to the Egyptians, and their care after delivery is not always such as to prevent both the mother and the child from suffering. I have known several instances where cold caught after the accident has proved of serious consequences to the mother.

Hydrophobia.

The *rabies canina*, or hydrophobia, is either very unusual or entirely unknown both in Egypt and Fûr. I never heard of an instance of it in either country, which appears not entirely unworthy of remark, not only as multitudes of dogs are found in each, which in many instances can have no access to water, to the want of which was once vulgarly attributed that dreadful malady, but as one fact more in the series which must finally conduct us to its cause.

Idea of Orientals respecting remedies.

Among the inhabitants of Egypt and Africa the classification of remedies is remarkably simple. They have only two *grand divisions*, مبردات refrigerants, and محر heating medicines. They esteem

esteem all the former beneficial, and the latter generally pernicious: so that if the most skilful physician were to prescribe for his patient what the latter supposed to possess an heating quality, it would be impossible to persuade him to use it.

Phlebotomy.

Scarification, or superficial incision of the skin, is commonly recurred to for various diseases, and at all ages, from two years till sixty. The head, breast, loins, legs, are all subjected to this simple and apparently little efficacious treatment. Sometimes, however, violent and obstinate pains in the head, proceeding from extraordinary exertion, and other causes, are removed by superficially inciding the skin, near the coronal suture, which occasions a sufficient discharge of blood.

The other mode of bleeding is by horns, prepared for that purpose, which operate on the same principle as our cupping glasses. These are applied in a very simple manner, and without occasioning any pain, remove such quantity of blood, as the operator judges necessary. Adhesion is produced by applying the mouth to the smaller aperture of the horn, which, when this is accomplished, is stopped. The incision is commonly made with a razor.

Bruises.

The bitumen found in the mummy pits is diffolved with butter by the Egyptians, and not only applied externally, but taken inwardly, in large dofes, for bruifes and wounds; it is faid to have a furprifing effect.

Petroleum.

Petroleum, which is brought from the weftern fhore of the Arabian gulf, near to Suez, is taken inwardly as well as outwardly applied, and is much efteemed.

Bezoar.

The Orientals have ftill great confidence in the *bezoar*, or *benzoar*. For a fmall one they are, not unfrequently, contented to pay a fum equal to feven guineas. Even the European phyficians adminifter it in fome cafes pulverifed, as an alterative, and, as they fay, with fuccefs.

Sal ammoniac.

Perhaps none of the drugs of Egypt is more extenfively ufeful than fal ammoniac. That medicine feems, as it were, a fpecific,

cific, carefully provided, for the prevailing diseases of the country. Acting mildly, both as a carminative and diuretic, nothing is more effectual to remove the cephalalgia and lassitude often experienced during the great heat, which precedes the Nile's augmentation, than a few drops of this spirit taken in water. Pulmonary complaints, occasioned by bad air, the suffocating heat of the southerly winds at certain seasons, and the ill effect of sudden transition from the burning heat of the sun to the chilling nocturnal dew, are often relieved by it. It might even be suggested, that as regular and continued transpiration seems very adverse to pestilential infection, a proper use of sp. sal. ammon. might not be wholly contemptible as an antidote to its infection.

Aphrodisiacs.

No part of the materia medica is so much in requisition as those which stimulate to animal pleasure. The *lacerta scincus*, in powder, and a thousand other articles of the same kind, are in continual demand. For this chiefly fields are sown with *hashish*, the *bang* of the East Indies. It is used in a variety of forms, but in none, it is supposed, more efficaciously than what is in Arabic called *Maijún*, a kind of electuary, in which both men and women indulge to excess. The impotence of age, and the languor of satiety or disease, ponder in vain the oracles of the descendant of Ismaîl, for the invigorating influence of the benign deity of Canopus.

Characteristics

Characteristics of the negroes.

A great and striking difference as to the firmness and density of the skin, between the negro and the white, whether it may or may not be called *specific*, as far as relates to the animal, is the cause of several peculiarities, as well when they are in health as under the power of disease. In all cutaneous maladies, or such as ultimately relieve themselves by suppuration, the sufferings of the blacks are excessive. Blows of the whip, which in a white subject would become encysted tumors, discharge, dry up, heal, and disappear in a few weeks, often remain in a negro more than a year.

The bright red colour of the muscular fibres, an apparently stronger power of contraction, and the whiteness, solidity, and weight of the bones, constitute other peculiarities. The eyes have generally very distinct vision. There are few instances of myopes, and blindness is very uncommon. The teeth are white and firm; they rarely complain of odontalgia, and retain their teeth to old age. Both the Fùrians and neighbouring negroes are attentive to preserve them clean, which is done by rubbing them with the small fibrous branches of the tree called *Shaw*.

Natrôn.

Natrôn is much used as a veterinary medicine.

As

As often as the camels, horses, asses, sheep, &c. drink, a large piece of it is put into the trough of water. The natives conceive that it renders them more eager of their food, and thus tends to fatten them. Some camels refuse it, but in general they acquire a preference for that water which is most strongly impregnated. When they refuse it, the natrôn is pulverized, formed into balls, with the flour of maize, and forced down their throats before they drink.

For the human race natrôn is used to remove the head-achs, intermittent and remittent fevers, &c. which prevail during the rainy season. Two or three ounces of crude natrôn are dissolved in water, and taken fasting. It operates as a drastic purge, and with some as an emetic. With robust and plethoric habits, there seems to be no inconvenience from the use of it, but I experienced from it an unfavourable rather than beneficial effect.

Tamarinds.

The tamarind, *Thummara Hindi** one of the most useful as well as valuable of the productions of the country, supplies the want of many others. In defect of lemons and other acids, this fruit, mixed with water, constitutes an agreeable and refreshing drink. When dried by beating in a mortar, it is formed into cakes, each of 2 or 300 drams in weight. The decoction of it

---

* *Thummara Hindi* means simply *Fruit of India*, not *date*, as insinuated by the learned author of the *Botanical Observations*, in *Asiatic Researches*, vol. iv. p. 250.

is a mild cathartic, and also operates as a diaphoretic; and the natives attribute to it superior virtue as an antidote against certain poisons.

Lactation.

Savary remarks, that in Egypt each mother affords nourishment to her own infant, even in compliance with a command of the Prophet, and that this prevents many diseases. No doubt can exist that the milk of the mother, long secreted and reserved for the child, is the proper nourishment at the birth, and by its acrid quality tends to facilitate the evacuation of the fæces, accumulated during the period of gestation, much better than any thing that can be substituted in its room. But when this effect is once produced, in many cases the milk of any other woman may be better than that of the mother; nay, that of the mother may be insalubrious *à principio*; and it is as yet far from being proved, that the milk of the mother is in all cases the best possible milk for the child.

If the mother abstain not from the male embrace, and become gravid, the milk becomes, as is well known, poison to the offspring.—The Arabic language has even a single word to express, *quæ lactans consuescit viro*, which they conceive extremely injurious.

Opium (Ar. Aphiüm).

The use of opium, as is well known, is carried to excess in Constantinople. Some persons have so long accustomed themselves to that powerful drug, that a dose of two drams, or more, will have no effect in exhilarating them, or producing that agreeable stupor which they seek. In such cases, they will swallow, in a convenient vehicle, several grains, to the amount, it is said, of ten, of corrosive sublimate of mercury, as a stimulus.

This effect of opium, as an antidote to one of the strongest mineral poisons, appears incredible, and would scarcely have been related, but on authority the least questionable. A reflection has in consequence forced itself on me, which I offer as a query. Mithridates, king of Pontus, is said to have so fortified himself with antidotes, that when misfortune obliged him to have recourse to poison to terminate his existence, though repeatedly administered to him, under different forms, it had no effect. Pontus, at that time no less than at present, furnished the best opium. Could Mithridates have used any antidote so powerful? And was not this effect of that drug more likely to be known in its native country than any where else? It may possibly be replied, that mineral poisons were not then in use, and that to the small number of vegetable ones then known, many other antidotes, capable of producing the same effect, might have been found. It is not however enquired, whether single antidotes might not have been found to obviate the influence of distinct poisons, but what could produce so complete a change in the human body, as that no poison should have any effect on it?

Circumcision.

The practice of circumcision may be traced to such remote antiquity, that its origin baffles all research: yet apparently its history has not received all the illustration of which it is capable from a diligent collection of facts. It has been ascribed to the structure of the organs, in certain countries, which it is said impede coition, or facilitate the appearance of morbid symptoms. But what may have been perfectly true of individuals, it may perhaps not be permitted to assume with regard to a whole nation, much less with relation to the inhabitants of an extensive region.

Among the Fûrians circumcision appears to be no other than a religious ceremony, performed in compliance with an express command of the author of their faith; and it is very doubtful whether it was ever practised among them before their conversion to Mohammedism. It is now often neglected till the male have attained the age of eighteen or more years, and this omission seems to be considered by them as a matter of indifference; nor are there persons who habitually and regularly exercise that art, as in Egypt and other Mohammedan countries.

Excision.

Excision.

The excision of females is a peculiarity with which the Northern nations are less familiar: yet it would appear, that this usage is more evidently founded on physical causes, and is more clearly a matter of convenience, than the circumcision of males, as it seems not to have been ordained by the precept of any inspired legislator. A practice so widely diffused, it may be said, was hardly invented but to remedy some inconvenience commensurate in its extent. But, if so, how happens it that one race of idolatrous negroes, near Fûr, has a habit of extracting two or more of the front teeth of children before puberty? That it is customary with another race, in the same quarter, to file the teeth to a point*? that other nations cut open a second mouth? and innumerable other singularities which prevail among savages, and are as little to be reduced to any principle of convenience or utility.

This excision is termed in Arabic *Chafadh* خفض, and the person who performs it خافضة. It consists in cutting off the clitoris a little before the period of puberty, or at about the age of eight or nine years †.

Strabo

---

* This is observable in many of the slaves. They seem to esteem it a beauty. In filing the teeth, they also force the gums from them, to make them appear longer: the teeth in this case suffer discoloration, but do not appear to undergo a consequent decay.

† Qui Africæ aut Asiæ plagis peragratis, primi hunc exsecandi morem Occidentalibus narravere auctores, ab ore incolarum re acceptâ, et novitate ejus perculsi,

Strabo is apparently the first who mentions this custom, which is nevertheless undoubtedly very antient. Lib. xvii.

—— και τα παιδια περιτεμνειν, και τα θηλεα εκ]εμνειν, &c.

By the terms very well marking the distinction between this operation and the circumcision of males.

The Mohammedans of Egypt conceive it to have no connection with their religious creed. Similar are said to be the sentiments of the Christians of Habbesh. In Dar-Fûr many women, particularly among the Arabs, never undergo excision: yet it has not been my fate to see or hear of any of those κλειτοριδες μεγαλαι which are supposed to have brought it into vogue.

Thirteen or fourteen young females underwent ختان in an house where I was. It was performed by a woman, and some of them complained much of the pain, both at and after it. They were prevented from locomotion, but permitted to eat meat. The parts were washed every twelve hours with warm water, which profuse suppuration rendered necessary. At the end of eight days the greater part were in a condition to walk, and liberated from their confinement. Three or four of them remained under restraint till the thirteenth day.

---

culsi, de modo excisionis toto cælo errare solent, nymphas exsecari perhibentes: prorsus ineptè quidem, sed septâ pudicitiâ vitam agentibus, nunquam illis nudam velè longinquo vidisse, multo minùs muliebria attrectavisse, uti manifestum, contigerat.

It

It often happens that another operation accompanies that of excifion, which is not, like the latter, practifed in Egypt, viz. producing an artificial impediment to the vagina, with a view to prevent coition. This happens moft frequently in the cafe of flaves, whofe value would be diminifhed by impregnation, or even by the neceffary refult of coition, though unaccompanied by conception. But it is alfo adopted towards girls who are free; the impulfe being too ftrong to be counteracted by any lefs firm impediment. This operation, like the former, is performed at all ages from eight to fixteen, but commonly from eleven to twelve; nor are they who undergo it always virgins. In fome the parts are more eafily formed to cohere than in others. There are cafes in which the barrier becomes fo firm, that the embrace cannot be received but by the previous application of a fharp inftrument*.

Among fome tribes of blacks, there exifts a practice of piercing the fkin in certain forms by way of ornament.—Each of the punctures leaves an indelible fcar, as diftinctive as colour, which is not ufed. This practice, which is of the fame defcription as that of fome of the South-fea iflands, is ufed on the face, breaft, loins, &c.

The blacks who are caftrated for the ufe of Kahira or Conftantinople, undergo that operation in the Upper Egypt, before

* Quoties autem confibulatio fortior meatûs etiam urinarii aditum claudere minetur, plumâ vel offeâ quâdam tubulâ adhibitâ, illam in ore urethræ inferunt, ibidemque tenent, ufque dum canalis majoris aditui amplius invigilare non fit opus.

their

their arrival at the former; some families, there resident, having the hereditary exercise of this antient practice.

The numbers which undergo it are not very considerable, and it is fatal only to a very small proportion of them.

Those slaves which are emasculated for the exclusive use of the Fûrian monarch suffer within his palace.

CHAP. XXII.

FINAL DEPARTURE FROM KAHIRA, AND JOURNEY TO JERUSALEM.

Voyage down the Nile to Damiatt—Vegetation—Papyrus—Commerce—Cruelty of the Mamlûk government—Voyage to Yaffé—Description of Yaffé—Rama—Jerusalem—Mendicants—Tombs of the kings—Bethlehem—Agriculture—Naplofa—Samaria—Mount Tabor.

HAVING engaged a *canjia*, or small boat, to sail down the Nile from Kahira to Damiatt, I departed on Friday the 2d of December 1796. No occurrences worthy of particular commemoration happened during this little voyage, but we passed several towns of considerable note, among which may be mentioned Manfûra, remarkable for the defeat of St. Louis; a circumstance preserved in the name which denotes, *The place of victory.* Its condition is flourishing, owing to its being a station on the road between Kahira and Damiatt; and it was then governed by a Cashef deputed by Ibrahim Bey. The mosques amount to seven, which is the only circumstance I can offer relative to its population, my stay there having been only for a few hours.

Sifté

Sifté and Miet Ghrammer are on the same route, about half way between Kahira and Mansûra, and situated on opposite banks of the Nile. Both are towns of the second order, and abounding with people, chiefly Mohammedans, very few Copts residing there. The river is here narrow but deep, not exceeding three hundred yards in breadth; and it may not be improper to remark in general concerning that celebrated stream, that its greatest breadth, when free from inundation, may be estimated at seven hundred yards, or something more than one third of a mile. Where narrowest, the distance between the banks may be one hundred yards. The depth from three to twenty-four feet.

That channel of the Nile which extends from Kahira to Damiatt is in general free from windings, and is interspersed with a few small islands.

There are several populous towns in the Delta, of which Mehallé-el-Kebîr is the chief. In point of population it is said to be equal to Damiatt. The next in consideration are probably Semmenûd and Menûf.

To form a general idea of the Delta, the reader may conceive a vast plain, intersected in all directions, by minute channels, (the canal of Menûf being almost the only important stream,) by which and by pumps the interstices are watered, and brought to the utmost fertility. As to real inundation on the rise of the Nile, that must be regarded as confined to a small space bordering on the sea.

On

On the 5th of the same month I arrived at Damiatt. This noted port presents an agreeable aspect on the first approach from the South, the town being built somewhat in the form of a crescent on a gentle bend of the river, and being surrounded with cultivated lands, which extend to the large lake called Manzalé. The distance from the sea is about six miles, and there is a bar across the Nile, so that vessels are obliged to have part of their cargo sent after them in small boats, and put on board after they have past the bar.

Damiatt is blessed with a soil almost unrivalled, and exuberant in orange and lemon trees, and other rich vegetation of the East, which would present an appearance very striking to a traveller accustomed to an English winter. Nor were my emotions unpleasant at here beholding, for the first time, the celebrated *Papyrus*, pushing its green spikes through the mud of the adjacent ditches *.

This plant formerly abounded so much in the vicinity of Damiatt, that it was profaned, so to speak, in the fabrication of sleeping mats, which were transported to different parts of Lower Egypt. But of late years, by the sacred ignorance and supine neglect of the Mamlûks, who regard themselves as merely tenants for life, and delapidate at will this noble domain, the channel of the Nile, which ought to flow to Damiatt, pur-

* In the neighbourhood of Damiatt the Papyrus is termed *el-Berdi*. Another name is also given it, evidently derived from the term in use among us, *El-Babír*.

suing the straiter course offered to it by the canal of Menûf, deserted its bed, and left access to the sea-water. Hence the plants of papyrus, as well as the other vegetables, were deprived of the prolific influence of the Nile, and expired in the noxious effluvia of a marine marsh. I was told by an European there, who had resided between thirty and forty years, that the papyrus used to attain the height of eight, nine, or more feet. The stem was about an inch or more in diameter; and of such substance as to serve my informer and his son for walking-sticks.

The gardens of Damiatt contain some mulberry trees and plantains. The *Tethymalus*, wart-weed, is found there in great quantity. Scammony is not uncommon. The East side of the river, from Damiatt to the North extremity of the coast, consists of sand hills, and most part of the way is lined with reeds.

Among the crops of Lower Egypt in particular must not be forgotten the Lucerne, *Birsîm*, which grows with surprising luxuriance.

Damiatt is vivified by a considerable trade, being the depôt between Egypt and Syria, and the mart of all the productions of the Delta; exporting particularly rice and flax to Syria, and importing cotton in return, which is manufactured there and in other parts of Egypt. Its European commerce is very inconsiderable: some Venetian and Ragusan vessels bring small cargoes of cochineal, and other commodities. Formerly there were

were several French merchants, but their usual misconduct with regard to the sex occasioned their expulsion.

Of an antient round building, called the Tower of St. Louis, which was standing in Niebuhr's time, and which till of late existed at Damiatt, nothing now remains but a piece of brick wall, which was on the outside of the foss, and of which the mortar is no less hard than the brick. The remainder of the materials were applied by Mohammed Bey Abu-dhahab to the structure, which his fear of the Russians induced him to erect at a great expense, at the extremity of the shore. It was not sufficient to build this fort on the firm ground, nearest the mouth of the river; he chose to lay the foundation in the sand and mud, at the extreme point of land on the eastern side; and though now from the strength of the foundation a part remains, much has fallen, and the rest is surrounded by, and under water.

There are two mounts of ruins near the Eastern extremity of the town, on the most Northern of which is a piece of brick wall remarkably strong, which is reported to have been part of an ancient castle. From this elevation is seen the field of battle between the Christians and Saracens, in which St. Louis was, according to the Arabs, taken prisoner. It is called the *field of blood*, as the conflict is represented as having been so obstinate, that the earth and water were stained with blood for a considerable time after.

There is nothing farther worthy of remark in this town, except two mosques. One of them is a rich foundation of the same nature as the *Jama-el-Azher*, which it is said maintains five or six hundred poor shechs, many of whom are blind or paralytic. The other is an old and famous mosque, which has been raised, as is said, on the ruins of a Christian church, part of which is reported to exist under the building. Even the mosque itself is now deserted, and in a great measure fallen to ruin; the door which leads to the passage below is bricked up, so that I could make no observations on that part. The mosque is spacious, and contains a great number of marble columns. I observed, however, only one of porphyry, and one of red granite. The rest are of common blue and white, and yellow and white marble; one of the latter is reported to have the virtue of curing the jaundice; and for this purpose the poor people affected with this disorder scrape it and drink the powder, which is in such repute that a considerable cavity may be observed in the column. Another fine porphyry column I was told was lately carried away by a Mokaddem of the Bey, employed in collecting his rents here, for the purpose of forming a tomb for himself. The population of Damiatt may be partly conceived from the number of its mosques, which are supposed to be fourteen. There is also a Greek convent, in which strangers are lodged, there being no caravanserai in the place.

The lake *Manzalé* is of very considerable extent, being somewhat more than thirty miles in length, and is navigated by a number

number of small vessels employed in fishing, and in carrying the people to and from the islands. The fish called *Bûri*, a kind of mullet, particularly abounds; it is salted and dried at Damiatt, whence it is conveyed through the Lower Egypt and Syria, and even to Cyprus. It affords an insipid and insalubrious meal; yet is much used by the common people, especially by the Christians in their frequent fasts. The desert islands interspersed in the lake are haunted by numbers of aquatic birds, which migrate thither in autumn and winter: they are ensnared in nets, and furnish a livelihood to many of the lower class of the people, who sell them in the markets. The water of this lake is brackish, but not very salt. Where the most easterly branch of the Nile fell into it, still remain some ruins of the antient city of Tanis, which I had not an opportunity of visiting.

A circumstance had recently occurred, tending to paint the character of the people under the Mamlûk government. A Cashef, but not of the highest order, under Murad Bey, who had been disgraced a short time before, retired to Damiatt to avoid his master's anger. He had not long resided there, when, having heard more favourable tidings, he made an inquiry for some person, capable of exchanging for him a sum in Turkish money, for the like in that of Europe current in the country. Accordingly three Jews were found who promised to supply him according to his desire. They went round the city, and borrowed much in addition to what they already possessed, and at length carried to the Cashef to the amount of between five

and

and six thousand patackes. He was no sooner furnished with the money, than he directed the Jews to be murdered, and his boats being ready, caused their bodies to be packed in baskets, and put into a small boat of his train. He then set off for Kahira. On arriving at a village a little way up the river, the baskets were disembarked, and he ordered them to be safely lodged till further directions should be given. It was some time before the villagers took notice of the packages, or dared to open them in the absence of the owner. But at length having observed a quantity of blood near one of them, and entertaining suspicions, they opened the three, and news were immediately carried to Damiatt that the three Jews had been found in this condition. Those under whose cognizance such accidents are, made a memorial of the whole affair to Murad Bey. He replied only by loud laughter, saying, "Are they not three dogs? There is an end of them."

It must not be omitted that at Damiatt there is a considerable manufactory of cotton and linen clothes, for the use of the baths and other domestic purposes.

On the 19th of January 1797, I embarked on board a little merchant vessel, trading to the coast of Syria, and commanded by an Arab. Owing to the stormy weather, and the unskilfulness of the mariners, no small danger was incurred in the voyage, and we were constrained to throw overboard a part of the cargo, which consisted in rice and raw hides. Another vessel, which sailed in company, was lost that same night.

After

After a navigation of five days, I arrived at Yaffé. The first land we had discovered was the mountain of Ghaza.

Yaffé presents an object rather extraordinary in the Levant, a good wharf. The situation of the town is so unequal, that the streets are paved in steps. The air, formerly deemed insalubrious, has, by the draining of some adjacent marshes, been rendered perfectly healthy; but, on the other hand, the extensive groves of orange and lemon trees, which adorned the vicinity, have been destroyed in the sieges undertaken by Ali Bey and his successor Mohammed Abu-dhahab, the latter of which was particularly destructive; the Mamlûks having used these trees for firing. The government is now mild, and the population, gradually increasing, may be estimated at six or seven thousand souls. It is walled, and has two principal gates and a smaller one; the latter and one of the former yet remain; the other is shut up. Yaffé is commanded by an eminence on the North, within musket-shot, where Ali Bey pitched his camp. Though there be a small river in the proximity, water is scarce, being carried by the women: one of the governors engaged to remedy the inconvenience, but was strangled by order of Jezzâr, Pasha of Damascus, before he could accomplish his purpose.

Ships cannot come up to the wharf, and there is no port, nor even secure place of anchorage. The commerce is inconsiderable, being solely with Egypt, and with a few pilgrims who pass to and from Jerusalem. Yaffé is governed by an officer appointed by the Porte.

There

There are three small convents of Christians, Armenian, Greek, and Roman-catholic, and a few Jews. When the French, about 1790, were banished by Jezzâr Pasha from his government, several retired to Jaffé, where their consul died the winter before I arrived.

It shall be only farther remarked, that the houses in Jaffé are neatly built with stone, and that considerable quantities of coral are found in the adjacent sea.

Having hired two mules for myself and a Cypriote servant, I proceeded to Rama, distant about three hours. I had previously taken care to get permission from the agent of the convent at Yaffé to travel to Jerusalem, a precaution here necessary to prevent any disturbance from the Arabs.

At Rama there is a spacious and strongly built convent of the Franciscan order, a commodious edifice, and kept in excellent repair. The town is pleasantly situated, and in a good soil. In its vicinity I observed some antient groves of olive trees. Between Yaffé and Rama seven villages appear in sight.

Having left Rama early in the morning of the ensuing day, we entered the gate of Jerusalem about sun-set. The ground between Rama and Jerusalem is rugged, mountainous, and barren. My servant having loitered behind, was seized by some Arabs, thrown from his mule, and pillaged.

I must

I muſt confeſs the firſt aſpect of Jeruſalem did not gratify my expectation. On aſcending a hill diſtant about three miles, this celebrated city aroſe to view, ſeated on an eminence, but ſurrounded by others of greater height; and its walls, which remain tolerably perfect, form the chief object in the approach. They are conſtructed of a reddiſh ſtone. As the day was extremely cold, and ſnow began to fall, the proſpect was not ſo intereſting as it might have proved at a more favourable ſeaſon.

It is unneceſſary to dwell on the deſcription of a city trivial in innumerable books of travels, but a few miſcellaneous remarks ſhall be made as they happen to ariſe.

Mendicants perfectly ſwarm in the place, allured by the hope of alms from the piety of the pilgrims. The religious of *Terra Santa* retain great power, and there is one manufacture that flouriſhes in the utmoſt vigour, namely that of reliques, crucifixes inlaid with mother of pearl, chaplets, and the like. Yet the church of the holy ſepulchre is ſo much neglected, that the ſnow fell into the middle; the beams, ſaid to be cedar, are falling, and the whole roof is in a ruinous ſtate.

The Armenian convent is elegant, and ſo extenſive as to preſent accommodation for no leſs than a thouſand pilgrims.

During twelve or thirteen days a very deep ſnow lay upon the ground. The catholic convent has a large ſubterraneous ciſtern, into which the ſnow, melting from the roof and other parts, is conveyed, and supplies the monks with water for a great portion of the year.

The best view of Jerusalem is from the Mount of Olives, on the East of the city. In front is the chief mosque, which contains, according to the tradition of the Mohammedans, the body of Solomon. From the same mount may be discovered, in a clear day, the *Dead sea*, nearly South-east, reflecting a whitish gleam. The intervening region appears very rocky.

The *tombs of the kings*, so denominated, are worthy of remark, being of Grecian sculpture on a hard rock. There are several ornaments on the sarcophagi of foliage and flowers, and each apartment is secured with a massive panneled door of stone. Great ravages have been made here in search of treasure. These tombs have probably been constructed in the time of Herod and his successors kings of Judea.

A very considerable part of the inhabitants is Christian, between whom and the Muslims there exists all that infernal hatred which two divinely revealed religions can alone inspire.

At about the distance of two hours, or six miles, stands Bethlehem, in a country happy in soil, air, and water. The latter is conveyed in a low aqueduct or stone channel, which formerly passed to Jerusalem. The *fons signatus* is an exuberant spring: it is received successively by three large cisterns, one of which is well preserved. In coming from the cisterns, and at a small distance is seen what is termed the *deliciæ Solomonis*, a beautiful

rivulet

rivulet which flows murmuring down the valley, and waters in its courſe ſome gardens of excellent ſoil. The brinks of this brook are adorned with a variety of herbage. Olives, vines, and fig trees flouriſh abundantly in the neighbourhood. The olive trees are daily decreaſing in number, as they are ſacrificed to the perſonal enmities of the inhabitants, who meanly ſeek revenge by ſawing down in the night thoſe that belong to their adverſaries. As this tree is of ſlow growth, it is ſeldom replaced. Such is the charity of Chriſtians in the cradle of Chriſtianity. A more pleaſing object ariſes in the convent here, which contains under one roof the different tenets of Latins, Armenians, and Greeks.

About the ſame diſtance from Jeruſalem, towards the wilderneſs, is the convent of St. John, ſituated in the midſt of a romantic country, ſtudded with vines and olive trees. In the village of St. John and its diſtrict the Mohammedans form the greater part of the population.

The mode of agriculture here purſued may be worthy of obſervation. As the country abounds in abrupt inequalities, little walls are erected, which ſupport the ſoil, and form narrow terraces. Small ploughs are uſed drawn by oxen; and it requires no ſlight dexterity in the driver to turn his plough, and avoid damaging the walls. The ſoil thus ſecured is extremely favourable to cultivation. The breed of black cattle is in general diminutive. Horſes are few in number, and aſſes reſembling the European are chiefly uſed for travelling.

We may safely estimate the present population of Jerusalem at from eighteen to twenty thousand. It is governed by an Aga, appointed by the Pasha of Damascus; but he is allowed so few troops, that all Palestine may be regarded as in the power of the Arabs. The Christian women, who abound in Jerusalem, wear white veils, as a distinction from the Mohammedan, who wear other colours. Arabic is the general language, except among the Armenians and Greeks.

I left Jerusalem in the commencement of Ramadan, 2d of March 1797. After an uncommonly severe winter, the spring was now begun. Having rode about three hours, we arrived at Beruth, where we passed the night; and the following day, about three in the afternoon, reached Naplosa or *Nablûs*. This capital of the district called Samaria is populous. The site is remarkable and picturesque, being between two hills, upon one of which is the castle.

The adjacent country in general is fertile in vines and mulberry trees, though rather mountainous. Naplosa has several mosques, and carries on a considerable traffic with Damascus and the coast: there is also a cotton manufacture. Jews abound of the Samaritan heresy; but the inhabitants are very hostile to Christians, who have no establishments here. The town is in fact governed by the chief inhabitants, though a nominal deputy be appointed by the Pasha of Damascus.

On my journey from Naplosa to Nazareth, during the first part of the route, which was rocky and mountainous, I observed

only

only three villages in the space of as many hours; but the vales are full of olives, fig trees, and vines, and even the rocks are shaded with a variety of verdure. Having passed the mountains of Naplosa, (*Ebal* and *Gerizim*,) we came to an extensive plain of excellent land, which however after rain is almost inundated. Near its northern extremity is seated a small fortress, which repulsed Jezzar Pasha at the head of five thousand men, and some pieces of artillery: it displays seven or eight small round towers, and has two gates. The peasants of Samaria are hardy and warlike, and generally go well armed.

Sebasté or Samaria is now a miserable deserted village. Ginæa is a decent town, half way between Naplosa and Nazareth. The latter is a pleasant village, seated on an easy slope, with a respectable convent: most of the inhabitants are Christians. While I was there, the Samaritans had made an inroad, and carried off some cattle: the Nazareens armed themselves, and made reprisals of seventeen oxen. In the neighbourhood is Mount Tabor, whence there is a delightful prospect, and which is noted for the absurd doctrines it gave name to in the ecclesiastical disputes of the Greek empire.

CHAP. XXIII.

GALILEE—ACCA.

Improvements by Jezzar—Trade—Taxes—White promontory, and river Leontes—Tyre—Seide—Earthquake—Kesrawan—Syrian wines—Beirût—Anchorage—Provisions—River Adonis—Antûra—Harrîsê—Tripoli—Ladakia—Journey to Aleppo or Haleb.

GALILEE is here divided from Samaria by a ridge of hills. Six hours were employed in passing from Nazareth to Acré, by the Arabs more properly termed *Acca*. At a village on the route observed a sarcophage, now used for watering cattle, and some scattered fragments of columns. But few villages appear between Nazareth and Acré, though the land is fertile.

Acré is fortified with a wall of very moderate strength, having only one gate. It is a pretty large town, but many of the houses are empty: yet the population may be estimated between fifteen and twenty thousand. There remains part of a double fosse, which extended round the town, but is daily dilapidated for modern erections. There is no castle nor other relique of antiquity.

The

The whole face of the city has been changed, being enlarged and adorned with the improvements of the celebrated Achmet Pasha, who has built an elegant mosque and baths, two markets, a palace, and reservoirs for water. There are three Khans, or places for receiving goods, answering the purpose at once of a warehouse and inn. There are also five or six mosques, a small establishment of the Franciscans, and a Greek and Armenian church. In one of the Khans the Europeans lodge.

A mean tomb has been erected by the Pasha, to the memory of the celebrated Shech Daher, close to the sea, and at a little distance from the northern extremity of the wall.

Acré stands on a promontory, near a small gulph, and has no haven. Vessels anchor in favourable weather near the shore, but the European ships anchor opposite Haifa, a small place at the foot of Mount Carmel, where the water is generally smooth. The trade of Acré is pretty considerable; the Europeans bring broad cloth, lead, tin, and a variety of other articles, and export cotton in return. From Egypt there are large imports of rice. The soil of Egypt is not very proper for cotton, which is a staple commodity of Syria.

The long reign of Achmet Pasha *el Jezzâr**, accompanied with immense influence and great wealth, might naturally lead to conceive, that, blending his interests with those of his subjects, he would have exerted his authority in promoting their happi-

* The butcher.

ness.

"nefs. On the contrary, the large plain near Acré is left almost a marsh, and marks of idle magnificence have been substituted for the useful cares of agriculture. A striking contrast arises between his conduct and that of the Shech Daher, his predecessor, who raised Acré from a village to a large town, and doubled the population of the district.

Jezzâr was the first governor in the empire who laid a tax on articles of consumption, as wine, grain, and the like. Even meat and fish are materials of impost. He has erected granaries, a laudable design, but deficient in the execution; for the grain being ill preserved, and the oldest served out first, it is not only disagreeable as food, but unprolific when distributed for seed to the peasants. These imposts form the peculiar revenue of the Pasha; the other resources arising as usual from the tax on land, which amounts to about a twentieth of the rent, the capitation tax on Christians, and the customs; which last in this government are arbitrary, and neither regulated by the rules of the Porte, nor the capitulations entered into by Europeans. Nevertheless, the chief source of the riches of Jezzâr is the Pashalik of Damascus, which, by means of the usual largesses at the Porte, he contrived to add to his former government, a precedent very unusual in the Othman empire. His military force was once computed at twelve thousand; but, at the time of my visiting Acré, did not exceed four or five thousand.

Till the year 1791 the French had factories at Acré, Seidé, and Beirût. At that period they were all expelled from the territory of Jezzâr by a sudden mandate, which allowed them only

three

three days to abandon their respective habitations, under pain of death.

Passing over the common, but just rule of supposing, that in a quarrel of this magnitude neither party was perfectly free from error, it may be fit to inquire what motives induced this ignominious expulsion, when a simple dismission, to be signified by various other means, would have answered the same purpose.

To this it can only be answered, that the character of Jezzâr is impetuous, and even capricious, on all occasions. Sometimes a warm friend, and then suddenly a bitter enemy, equally, to all appearance, without any adequate reason. As to the conduct of the French, themselves and the other nations in the Levant accord so ill, that I have never obtained a very accurate statement of it. It seems to have originated in the behaviour of a drogueman of the nation, who having in some way offended the Pasha, was by his order summarily strangled or hanged. The French remonstrated, and threatened him with an application to the Porte, which he did not greatly fear, and he punished, *as he termed it, their insolence*, (in asserting their undoubted right, according to the capitulations between them and the Porte,) in this concise manner. Many complaints were made, subsequent to this period, by the ministers of the Republic at the Porte, but to no purpose: that court in fact was otherwise engaged, and it may be doubted whether it could have punished the Pasha. The events that followed suspended the prosecution of those claims, which, as the merchants thus suddenly banished had lost much, it appeared they had a right to prefer: but at length Aubert du Bayet sent a young officer of the name of Bailli to the Pasha to demand redress in a tone perhaps rather too high.

This gentleman, on arriving at Acré, April 1797, wrote a letter in French to the Pasha, which he had the bizarre idea of finding some Levantine drogueman to translate, *verbatim*, in the presence of that personage. The terms, it seems, in which this letter was conceived were so bold, that none could be found to present it, and the Pasha, under one pretence or other, refused to see the agent. On this Bailli retired to Yaffé. The answer Jezzâr sent to the claim of the Republic was, that private merchants were at liberty to settle under his government on the footing of any other nation, but that he would acknowlege no consul, nor consent to offer them any indemnification for the losses of the late factory.

Jezzâr had early conceived an enmity against that nation, which was probably increased by those who rivalled them in commerce.

On the 2d of April 1797 I set out from Acré to Seidé. The road runs near the sea-side, through a track overgrown with thorns and thistles. The shore is abrupt, and, as usual, accompanied with deep water. Some remains of antiquity present themselves, but so much injured, and so scattered, that it is impossible to guess their destination. I slept in the house of the Shech in a small village on the South of the White Promontory. The villages between Acré and Seidé are thinly scattered, and the

the population apparently small. We met several parties of the Pasha's troops, both infantry and cavalry, which seemed in excellent order.

On the following morning we passed the White Promontory, a sublime and picturesque mountain. The road is occasionally cut through the rock of calcareous stone, as white as chalk. On the right the rock is covered with bushes: the left is a perpendicular precipice to the sea, which was calm when I passed; but when it rages the scene must be tremendous. The tradition of the natives ascribes this road to Alexander the Great.

We passed the Leontes, now an inconsiderable stream, and easily fordable: but after rain it swells to a rapid torrent, as is the case with most of the rivers that fall from the Syrian mountains to the sea. After crossing four small clear streams, running over their beds of pure gravel, and the dry courses of some rivulets, we arrived at Tyre, enchanted with the beautiful verdure and varied scenery of the adjacent country.

The magnificent city of Tyre, now corruptly called *Sûr*, is reduced to a few miserable huts inhabited by fishermen, situated in the northern extremity of the isle. The isthmus, which joins it to the continent, is about three quarters of an English mile in length; the isle itself is of an irregular form, at the broadest part not exceeding half a mile, and the circumference of the antient city could not exceed a mile and a half. Except three fragments of granite columns nothing of antiquity appeared. The isle is now desert and rocky, destitute even of shrubs and grass. It appears that the port which is on the North of the isthmus might be restored, though a back water be wanting. The few peasants or fishermen who frequent the spot seemed quite unconscious of the classic ground on which they trod.

On the land-side, a little to the South of the isthmus, observed remains of an aqueduct, which formerly conveyed water to Tyre. Under its low arches was a considerable quantity of stalactites grown to a large size. There is also a cistern, somewhat resembling those of the *fons signatus* above mentioned, but smaller. The fountain rises with such force as to turn a mill a little lower down. Here are a few fruit trees, and a place where coffee is sold.

From the White Promontory to Seidé, antiently Sidon, extends a narrow plain by the sea-shore. North-east by East appear the summits of the mountains of Kesrawân, covered with snow. Arrived at Seidé near sun-set.

Seidé is a larger town than Acré. The situation is good and the air salubrious. There are many Christians and some Jews. The sea here encroaches on the land. The castle, built by the noted Fakr-el-dîn, is surrounded by the water. There was formerly a small, but convenient port, formed by a ridge of rocks, which was filled up by order of that Emîr, to prevent the Turkish vessels from entering, he being at war with that power. The castle, styled of St. Louis, which from an adjacent height on the South commands the city, still remains, as does a part of the

the city walls. There is but one gate of the latter; it fronts North-east. The magnificent palace, built by Fakr-el-dîn, in the Italian manner, is now ruinous.

An earthquake which destroyed Ladakia in 1796 was felt here, but not so violently as that which happened in the year 1785, in which many persons perished, and which was succeeded by a plague which almost depopulated the place.

A large tessellated pavement of variegated marbles, representing a horse, festoons, &c. and in some places tolerably perfect for ten feet in length, remains, close to the sea, on the northern extremity of the city; a proof of marine encroachment. Many antient granite columns are worked into the walls, and some stand as posts on the bridge leading to the fort. Near the gate of the city is a small square building, which contains the tombs of such of the Emîrs of the Druses as died when Seidé was in their possession.

Seidé is surrounded with gardens, in which grow a number of mulberry trees, silk being the chief commodity. The rent of houses and the mode of living are cheaper than at Acré, and the government more mild and regular; so that strangers are not liable to insult. Formerly, there was a considerable commerce carried on with Marseilles, but since Jezzâr banished the French it has ceased.

On the 6th of April 1797 I left Seidé to visit the district of Kesrawân, where we arrived in four hours, on horseback, after

travelling

travelling through a rugged road, continually ascending, till we reached the convent of *Mochaulus*, delightfully situated half way up the mountain, in a romantic country. On passing a bridge over *Nahr-el-aweli*, observed several fine falls of the stream. In Kesrawân is also *Mush-Mushé*, a convent of Maronites, which we reached next morning, after three hours riding. The mountains in the neighbourhood are covered with fir trees, some of them of large growth. The vales, and part of the mountains, are planted with vines, producing excellent wine, white and red. There are also many mulberry trees, which furnish plenty of good silk, but the natives have not the common skill to form it into thread. Corn and lentils also abound.

The botanist and florist may find in this part of the mountain full employment, as it is covered with innumerable herbs and shrubs, many of them odoriferous, and adorned with flowers of various tints. Myrtle and lavender grow wild in great quantities on the mountain, and the rose of Jericho embellishes the vales and banks of the rivulets. From this convent are seen Seidé, the sea and the adjacent coast.

As Kesrawân and Mount Libanus produce the best wines of Syria, it may not be improper to offer a few remarks on that topic. The white wine made at Jerusalem has a sulphureous taste, and is very strong; the red somewhat resembles Tent, and is comparatively mild in its effects. The wines of Syria are most of them prepared by boiling, immediately after they are expressed from the grape, till they be considerably reduced in quantity, when they are put into jars or large glass bottles, (*damesjans,*) and preserved for use.

There

There is reason to believe, that this mode of boiling their wines was in general practice among the antients. It is still retained in some parts of Provence, where it is called *vin cuite*, or cooked wine; but there the method is to lodge the wine in a large room, receiving all the smoke arising from several fires on the ground-floors; an operation more slow, but answering the same purpose. The Spanish Vino Tinto, or Tent, is prepared in the same way.

The wines thus managed, are sometimes thickened so much as to lose their transparency, and acquire a sweetish taste. Numerous are the kinds made in Syria; but the chief is the Vino d'Oro, or *golden wine* of Mount Libanus. This is not boiled, but left to purify itself by keeping; the quantity produced is small. It is, as the name implies, of a bright golden colour, and is highly prized even on the spot.

There is little reason to doubt, that if the wines of Syria were properly managed, they would equal any that France or Spain produces.

In Kesrawân the Christians are so much more indulged than in other places, that they can here enjoy their favourite amusement of deafening each other with bells. The monks of *Mush-Mushé* serve themselves in every thing, and are of course not idle, however fanatically inclined; they are cooks, bakers, butchers, carpenters, taylors, gardeners, husbandmen, each having his distinct province. I met here *Hassan Jumbelati*, who is of one of of the most powerful families among the Druses, and at this time holds an office under the *Emir Beshir*. He is a great drinker, but appears not unintelligent. He was very inquisitive as to the motives and history of the French Revolution, and the present religious creed of that nation; on hearing the detail of which, he however made no interesting remarks.

From Kefrawîn we returned to Seidé. On the 9th of April set out for Beirût, the antient *Berytus*. The route was through a deep sand, and after passing two rivers, the *Nahr el aweli* (before mentioned,) and the *Damer* or antient Tamyras, we arrived at Beirût, the approach to which is, even now, grander than that of any other town on the Syrian coast, though the fine groves have been neglected since the death of Fakr-el-Dîn, Emîr of the Druses, its munificent improver. A grove of pines, planted by his orders, is now reduced to half its former bounds. No trace is found of the statues, which his residence in Italy had enabled him to collect; nor of the gardens and apartments which he had formed on the European taste.

Beirût is a small place, and was not even walled till the Russians bombarded it; and Jezzâr, on getting possession, built the walls to give it a more formidable appearance. There are several towers, but the walls are thin and of no strength; the flatness of the situation is also a disadvantage. There is, however, a commodious wharf.

The suburbs are almost as large as the city itself, consisting of gardens, with a house for the owner in each; and these inter-

interspersed among the numerous fruit-trees, (especially olives and figs,) which this fertile soil supports, give the whole a picturesque and beautiful appearance.

Most of these gardens belonged to Christians, till the Pasha, by his exorbitant demands, obliged them to sell their possessions. Here it may be observed, that Christians may hold land in this place, which is not permitted at Acré. The streets of the city, like the others in this part of the world, are narrow and irregular.

The high tower, which Maundrel mentions as standing North-east of the city, was first destroyed by Jezzâr, as he thought an enemy might use it in offence; but he afterwards rebuilt it, with smaller stones and in a less substantial manner, as a place-d'armes for his own soldiers.

European vessels, in the summer, anchor near a small point of land which runs into the sea before the city, and is called Beirût Point; but in the winter, they cast anchor to the North, in a kind of gulf, which is sheltered from the North and East wind by the mountain, and is said to be very secure. The staple commodity of the country is raw silk, which is carried to Kahira, Damascus, and Aleppo, and part of it to Europe. They also fabricate a kind of jars and jugs in earthen ware, which, from the peculiar nature of the clay in the adjacent country, are highly esteemed, and carried to all parts of the coast.

Provisions are generally dear; the fish is more valued than that of Seidé, as the sea has here a rocky bottom, while at Seidé it is sand or mud. The red wine of Libanus which is brought here, is palatable, but cannot be transported from the mountain without a licence from the custom-house, so that it is dearer than formerly; yet the present price is only forty piasters the *cantar*, or about four pounds sterling the hundred weight.

From Beirût, on the 22d April, I went to *Antûra* on Mount Libanus, distant about four hours. In the way passed the *Nahr Beirût*, and after the *Nahr el Kelb*, the largest stream in this part of the country. The former is the noted river of Adonis, famous for vines, so exquisitely described by Milton.

Antûra is a pleasant village, surrounded with mulberry trees, but presenting nothing remarkable. Not far from this place is a convent of nuns, where Mr. Wortley Montague lodged his wife[*]. The dress of the Christians in this quarter seems

---

[*] He brought her thither during the process, instituted at Rome, relatively to her first marriage, and before that marriage was set aside. A long history attends this part of the life of this remarkable man. Montague having persuaded the first husband, who was captain of a merchant-man in the service of persons at Marseilles, to leave his wife, whom he had brought with him to Egypt, under M.'s protection at Rashid, the latter took advantage of his absence on a voyage home, to persuade the woman that her husband was no more. He then made an offer of himself, which was accepted. On a disclosure of the affair, Montague had interest and address enough to set aside the first marriage, which had been solemnized before either of the parties were of age. The religious were persuaded that Montague was a zealous convert to the Catholic faith.

unre-

unrestrained; they wear turbans adorned with various colours, even green; and they are freely indulged in the exercise of their religion: so natural is despotism to this clime, that those who live under their own Christian shechs or governors, are almost equally oppressed with those subject to Turks. The shechs fleece the poor people, and Jezzâr fleeces the shechs.

I afterwards visited *Harrisé*. Here the Maronite patriarch resides, who exercises an authority almost regal over the Christians of that rite. From *Harrisé* returned to Beirût.

As in consequence of a dispute between Jezzâr and the Pasha of Tripoli it was become unsafe to travel there, I joined a party of disbanded soldiers, and proceeded to Tripoli in their company. Our journey being quick, I had few opportunities for observation on the road.

This part of the country is noted for producing the best tobacco in Syria. That plant is cultivated in several districts, particularly in the neighbourhood of Tripoli, Gebeilé, and Ladakia.

On the third day arrived at Tripoli, about ten o'clock in the morning, having slept as usual in the open air.

Tripoli is a city of some extent, situated about a mile and an half from the sea. Vessels moor near the shore, and are sheltered by a ridge of rocks, but the situation is not very secure.

The

The air is rendered unwholesome by much stagnant water. The town is placed on a slight elevation, the length considerably exceeding the breadth. On the highest ground, to the South, is the castle, formerly possessed by the Earls of Tripoli; it is large and strong. Hence is visible a part of Mount Libanus, the summit of which is covered with snow. The gardens in the vicinity are rich in mulberry and other fruit trees. The city is well built, and most of the streets are paved.

It is the seat of a Pasha, who at present is the son of Abdallah, Pasha of Damascus.

Here is found a number of Mohammedan merchants, some of the richest and most respectable in the empire. Silk is the chief article of commerce. Five or six French merchants escaped hither from Acré *.

Antiquities I observed none. The history of Tripoli during the crusades must be known to every reader. The present population I should be inclined to estimate at about sixteen thousand.

---

* The *Santons*, or Mohammedan saints, are still permitted to continue their excesses. I was informed that one of them, very vigorous in transitory amours, met the wife of a rich Mohammedan merchant, newly married. The female attendant who was with her fled, and he accomplished his purpose in the open street. The merchant, complaining to the Pasha, only received this answer, "You ought to esteem yourself very happy, for your wife will probably be brought to bed of a *welli*," that is, a saint.

The *miri*, or fixed public revenue paid by Tripoli to Conſtantinople, is only about a thouſand pounds ſterling, twenty purſes, a-year. Syria at preſent contains only four Paſhaliks, Damaſcus, Aleppo, Acré, and Tripoli; the laſt of which is the ſmalleſt in territory and power.

On the 30th of April proceeded towards Ladakia, the antient Laodicea, built by Seleucus Nicanor in honour of his mother. We arrived on the third day at night. The firſt appearance of this city was moſt melancholy, as preſenting all the ravages of the earthquake, which in the preceding year (1796) had laid a great part of it in ruins, and deſtroyed numbers of the inhabitants. Ladakia has a convenient but very ſmall port, acroſs the mouth of which is a bar of ſand. The place is ſituated in a plain, extending on the North and South as far as the eye can reach; but bounded by hills towards the Eaſt. It has no walls, and only a part is paved; but the ſtreets are clean, the air is ſalubrious, and refreſhed by the fragrance of ſurrounding gardens. Water is ſcarce. The ſnow-capt ſummits of Libanus now vaniſh from the eye.

In the town are eight moſques. It is governed by a deputy of the Paſha of Tripoli.

On the 5th of May departed for Aleppo, in a ſmall caravan, conſiſting only of Citoyen Chauderlos, the French conſul-general, two Turks, and myſelf. On the ſecond day paſſed through one of the moſt picturesque countries which I had ever ſeen. Lofty rocks and precipices, ſhaded with luxuriant
foliage,

foliage, of various form and character, but of the most lively verdure, and flowers of the most diversified hues and the strongest odours, alleviated the task of climbing by rugged and difficult paths the steep ascent of the mountain, and torrents wandering through the valleys in their stoney channels, or dashed from the rocks in sheets of foam, filled the ear with their soothing murmurs, the eye with their untaught meanders, and the imagination with some of the most agreeable images that delight in the works of the poet.

The third day was occupied in traversing a country romantic like the former, and we passed the night in the open air, at *Shawr*, where the river Orontes winds majestically through the plain. The town of *Shawr* is populous, and has a good caravanserai; but we preferred the open air, to avoid the vermin which lodge in such places. Adjacent is a good stone bridge of seven arches. These conveniences have been originally provided for the caravan, which rests here in its route from Constantinople to Mecca.

On the fifth day arrived at *Keftin*, a village remarkable for its pigeon-houses, which supply the adjacent country, even to Aleppo. The neighbouring lands abound in wheat and barley, sown in ridges; the soil is rich, and requires no farrow. The women here go unveiled, and at *Martrawân*, which is not far removed, are by their friends presented to strangers.

The people are termed *Anfarié* in Arabic, a sect of pretended Mohammedans, who are said to worship the pudendum muliebre.

muliebre. With Christians they affect to be of their faith. The women are fair, have black eyes, and tolerable features. The strange practice above commemorated, seems a relique of the antient dissolute manners of Antioch and Daphne.

Thence to Aleppo is a journey of eight hours; for two hours through corn lands, the rest passes a barren country. That city is visible at the distance of two hours, and as you approach displays a most magnificent appearance.

CHAP. XXIV.

OBSERVATIONS AT ALEPPO.

Sherifs and Janizaries—Manufactures and commerce—Quarries—Price of provisions—New sect—Journey to Antioch—Description of antient Seleucia—Return to Aleppo.

The country adjacent to Aleppo is broken with many inequalities, and even the city stands partly on high and partly on low ground. A small river, called *Coik*, descends from *Aintab*, and, after passing through the city, is lost in a marsh on the West.

So many descriptions of this famous capital having appeared, I shall only offer a few remarks on such objects as struck me during my residence there.

The site is rocky, and the few gardens chiefly produce pistachios. The city is well built, and paved with stone. The tall cyprus trees, contrasted with the white minarets of numerous mosques, give it a most picturesque appearance. The population and buildings seem to be on the increase; but this affords no proof of public felicity; for, in proportion as the capital swells,

the

the adjacent villages are deserted. The houses are clean, airy, substantial, and commodious. The people in general are distinguished by an air of affected polish, hardly to be observed in the other towns of Syria. Their dialect too has its characteristic marks. The Arabic prevails, though many speak the Turkish language.

A new Pasha had been lately appointed at the time I arrived, but was prevented from entering the city, by the feuds which had prevailed between the Sherifs and the Janizaries, and induced the latter to suspect that the Pasha had a design of punishing them. This officer was a young man, the son of the Pasha of Adene; his title El Sherîf Mohammed Pasha; of an unblemished character, but unequal, in point of talents and personal weight, to compose the violence of these factions, which, after he had resided a short time in the city, obliged him to retire. The Sherîfs, or descendants of Mohammed, here form a considerable faction; a circumstance also observable at Bagdad, but not in so remarkable a degree. In Aleppo they form a body of near sixty thousand. The Janizaries do not exceed one-fourth of that number. The Sherîfs consist of all ranks, from the highest Imâm to the lowest peasant, and are far from excelling in courage: the Janizaries are of superior valour, though little acquainted with the use of arms or aspect of battle. Hence the force of the factions is merely balanced, and continual disputes arise for offices of profit or power, which generally terminate in bloodshed. In the course of this summer, 1797, several of these took place; in one of them it is supposed near three hundred perfons perifhed. This imperfect exercife of authority may be eftimated among the fymptoms of decline in the Turkifh empire.

The manufactures are in a flourifhing ftate, being carried on with great fpirit both by Chriftians and Mohammedans: filk and cotton form the chief articles. Large caravans frequently arrive from Bagdad and Baffora, charged with coffee, which is carried round to the Perfian gulf from Moccha, with the tobacco and cherry-tree pipes from Perfia, and muflins, fhawls, and other products of India.

Befides the manufactures of Aleppo, and the productions of the furrounding country, which are fent to Europe by fea, three or four caravans, laden with merchandize, proceed annually through Anatolia to Conftantinople. Piftachio nuts form no mean article of trade, being the chief produce of the adjacent territory, in the foil of which that tree particularly delights. Aleppo alfo maintains a commercial intercourfe with Damafcus, Antioch, Tripoli, Ladakia, and the towns on the Eaft towards the Euphrates.

The laft peftilence is fuppofed to have deftroyed fixty thoufand of the inhabitants.

The women of Aleppo are rather mafculine, of brown complexions, and remarkable for indulging in the Sapphic affection.

The quarries which supplied the stone for the construction of the city, are not far removed from the Antioch gate. They are every way worthy remark. On both sides of a road, cut through the solid rock, are seen the openings of caverns, capable of giving shelter to a vast number of persons. From these again, which are tolerably light, open a number of other passages, in all directions, from the principal apartments. These I had neither time nor instruments to investigate; but the people of the place pretend that one of these passages goes to the castle, another to Antioch, &c. Traditions similar to which abound in every country, which presents any caverns natural or artificial.

The material is a soft stone or tufa, replete with petrified shells. It would appear that the artificers designed those quarries for some useful purpose, as they have not only left rough columns, and cut perpendicular shafts, which admit some portion of light, but the walls are hewn to a much greater degree of smoothness than is usually seen in quarries. It is certain they have afterwards been occupied, as marks of fire, mangers for horses, and even burial places, may be observed. In latter times, disbanded *dellis*, not being admitted into the city, have here fixed their abode, and become dangerous to passengers, whom they have robbed, and sometimes murdered.

There is a large burying-place without the city. Here I observed the tomb of an Englishman, dated 1613.

The dress of the people of Aleppo resembles that of Constantinople more than that of Egypt and southern Syria: both men and women, in rainy weather, wear a kind of wooden patten, which has no agreeable effect either on the eye or the ear.

The hire of a camel from Aleppo to Ladakia or Scanderoon, about sixty miles, was a century ago four piasters, thirty years ago eight piasters, and is at this time nineteen. The price of commodities is much changed in the course of not many years. But since the year 1716 it has increased in a tenfold proportion. I saw an authentic document, that the *ardeb* of rice at that time sold for eleven piasters; it now fetches one hundred and eighteen piasters. They at that time sold 185 rolls of bread, of a particular kind, for a piaster; they now only sell forty of the same kind for that sum. Meat is good and in plenty; it is sold for fifty paras the rotal, 720 drams, or about $4\frac{1}{4}$d. a pound. There are no fish, save a few small eels, found in the *Coik*. Wine is very dear, none being produced in the neighbourhood. On the other articles of provision nothing remarkable occurs.

At Aleppo I first observed the practice of illuminating the mosques on Thursday night, to usher in the Mohammedan Sabbath; this is unknown at Kahira, and other cities of the South.

About this time, the beginning of June 1797, intelligence arrived, that the Pasha of Bagdad had sent a strong detachment
of

of troops, to be joined by the Arabs friendly to the Porte, in repressing the incursions of *Abd-el-aziz ibn Meſſoûd el Wahhâbbé*, a rebel against the government, who by the rapid success of his arms, and his increasing followers, had lately grown formidable. This man, a native of *Nedjed*, respected among the Arabs for his age and wisdom, had two years before first made public his determination to resist the authority of the Porte. He has since collected a considerable body of men, but it is said they are only furnished with spears and swords. He pretends to a divine mission, and gives no quarter to those who oppose him. To invite Christians and Jews to his party, he only requires an annual capitation tax of three piasters and a half. Of the people under his jurisdiction, every owner of a house is obliged to serve in person or find a substitute; and, to encourage them, he divides the spoil into five parts; taking one himself, he gives two to the substitute and two to the principal, or if the latter serve he has four parts. It was supposed his views pointed to Mecca, which he had threatened to attack. His confession of faith is only—" There is no God but God;" inferring, that a prophet, when dead, deserves no homage, and that of course to mention him in a creed, or in prayers, is absurd. He enjoins the absolute necessity of prayer, under the open canopy of heaven, and destroys all the mosques he can seize. Of the five dogmata of Mohammed, he admits alms, fasting, prayer, and ablution, but rejects pilgrimage. He denies the divine origin of the Korân, but prohibits the use of all liquors but water. Being advanced in age, he had taken care to secure the attachment

ment of his followers to his son, who was generally his substitute in the field*.

On the 11th of June set out from Aleppo for Antioch, where I arrived on the 14th. Part of the route is mountainous. We passed the Orontes at a ferry. Country cultivated with Hashîsh, a kind of flax.

Entered Antioch, now called Antáki, by *Bab-Bolús*, the gate of St. Paul. The walls are extensive, but the houses are chiefly confined to one corner. Numerous towers flank the walls, which are strong and lofty, and run from the river Orontes, the southern boundary of the city, up to the summit of the mountain. There is a substantial bridge over the river, which winds through a fertile vale. A large castle on the mountain, now ruinous, commands an extensive prospect.

Antioch is governed by a *Mohassel*, who derives his appointment from Constantinople. He received me with great politeness, and desired me to make what researches I pleased.

---

* This sect, represented to me by the Arabs, and others in Syria, as having only at a late period originated, is precisely mentioned by Niebuhr, Description d'Arabie, ed. Paris, p. 208. with a little variation as to the tenets of its founder. He dates its rise in the year 1760, which is very possible, considering that the later accounts all agree that *Abd-el-aziz el Wahhâbi* is a man of very advanced age.

The

The barley harveft was begun. The length of the plain of Antioch is about three leagues and a half, the width two leagues. The language is here generally Turkifh.

It muft be remarked with regard to Aleppo and Antioch, that the latter has by far the moft convenient fituation. The former has no navigable river, the land is little productive, and it is placed at a great diftance from the fea. Antioch poffeffes every oppofite advantage, except that of a navigable river, which however far exceeds the diminutive Coik; the air is fuperior to that of Aleppo, and it is within five hours of the fea. The mountain produces wine, which is fold cheap, and there is plenty of fea-fifh. The mouth of the river forms a haven for fmall veffels, with very deep water.

Between Antioch and the fea, the ridge abounds in mulberry trees, which furnifh a copious fupply of filk, though not of the beft kind.

From Antioch I fet out for *Suadéa*, the antient *Seleucia*, and port of Antioch, and only about four hours removed from it. It prefents to the mind the idea of the immenfe labour ufed by its former poffeffors to render it convenient for traffic, which is now rendered ufelefs, by the negligence of its prefent mafters. The road from Antioch is pleafingly diverfified by mountain and plain; yet to appearance the country is but thinly inhabited, though filled with all kinds of flowering and odoriferous plants, particularly myrtles, oleanders, and cyclamens. Having croffed four rapid and tranflucid ftreams, which defcend into

the

the Orontes, I passed the night with a hospitable native, in a garden of mulberries, which afforded support to his numerous family.

A large gate of Seleucia yet remains entire; it approaches to the Doric order. The rock near it has been excavated into various apartments. A part exists of the thick and substantial wall which defended Seleucia toward the sea. The port must have been commodious and secure, though but small, being formed by a mole of very large stones. Though the port be at present dry, the sand in the bottom appears not higher than the surface of the sea. A little to the North is a remarkable passage, cut in the rock, leading by a gentle descent, from the summit of the mountain towards the water. It is above six hundred common paces long, from thirty to fifty feet high, and about twenty broad. In the middle of it is a covered way, arched through the rock, but both the ends are open. A channel for water runs along the side, conveying the pure element down from the mountain to Seleucia. The whole rock above is full of artificial cavities, for what purpose does not appear. There is a Greek inscription on the South side of the cavern, comprising, I believe, five lines. Having no glass, and the inscription being lofty, I could only discover the letters TETAP, which form a part of the last line but one.

Returning towards the sea, I observed some catacombs. One of the chambers contains thirty niches for the dead, another fourteen. These catacombs are ornamented with pilasters, cornices, and mouldings.

Returned

Returned to Antioch, and on the following day set off for Aleppo. The Kûrds occasionally attack the caravans going between these two cities. The Turcomâns form another tribe of rovers; they generally pass the winter in the plains near Antioch, returning in the summer to Anatolia.

CHAP. XXV.

JOURNEY TO DAMASCUS.

Entrance of the Hadjis—Topography of Damascus—Trade and manufactures—Population—Observations on the depopulation of the East—Government and manners of Damascus—Charitable foundations—Anecdotes of recent history—Taxes—Price of provisions—Sacred caravan.

After waiting some time in Aleppo for the departure of the caravan, I at length left that city on the 23d of July for Damascus. The heat was great, but nothing equal to that of Africa. The beasts of burden, employed in this caravan, were only mules and geldings.

The route from Aleppo to Damascus has been often described. On Wednesday the 8th of August entered Damascus at daybreak. The approach is remarkable, being ornamented for many miles with numerous gardens, and then by a paved way, extending for a great length.

On the day after my arrival, was entertained with the entrance of the grand caravan from Mecca. The street was lined for some miles, for such is its length, with innumerable spectators, all impressed with curiosity, some with anxiety to see their friends

friends and relations, many with reverence for the sacred procession. Some of the more opulent Hadjis, or pilgrims, were carried in litters, (*tattarawân*,) but the greater number in a kind of panniers, two and two, placed on the back of camels. They did not appear much fatigued, though it was said they had suffered from the want of water.

On the Saturday following, was the entrance of the Pasha of Damascus, who is constantly the *Emír-el-Hadje*, or chief of the caravan by office. First appeared three hundred dellis, or cavalry, mounted on Arabian horses, variously armed and clothed, but on the whole forming no mean display. These were succeeded by fifteen men on dromedaries, with musquetoons, or large carbines, placed before them, and turning on a swivel in every direction. This destructive instrument of war is said to have passed from the Persians to the Syrians. Some of the great officers of the city followed, well mounted, and decently attired. Then came part of the Pasha of Tripoli's Janizaries, well clothed and armed; that Pasha himself, with his officers, and the remainder of his guard. Next was the tattarawân belonging to the Pasha of Damascus, another body of four hundred dellis, a company of thirty musquetooners, a hundred and fifty Albanians, in uniform, and marching two and two, like our troops. Before the latter was borne the standard of the Prophet, *Senjiak Sherifi*, of green silk, with sentences of the Korân embroidered in gold, and the magnificent canopy brought from Mecca, guarded by a strong body of Muggrebíns, or western Arabs, on foot. Then passed the Pasha's three tails, (generally of white horses,) borne by three men on horseback; twelve horses, (a Pasha of two tails has only six,) richly caparisoned, and each bearing a silver target and a sabre; six led dromedaries, in beautiful housings; numbers of the chief persons of the city followed, among whom were the Aga of the Janizaries, the governor of the castle, and the Mohassel. Last came the Pasha himself, in a habit of green cloth adorned with fur of the black fox, preceded by his two sons, the oldest about fourteen, all mounted on the most spirited steeds of Arabia, and followed by his household troops, to the number of four hundred, well armed and mounted. More than a hundred camels had preceded the rest, bearing the tents and baggage of the Pasha. The whole was conducted without any noise or tumult, to the great credit of the Damascene mob, who had been waiting several hours without their usual repast.

Damascus has been often described; but a residence of about two months may enable me to suggest some particulars worthy of notice. The walls are of a circular form, suburbs large and irregular. The situation is in an extensive plain, filled with gardens, to the length of more than three leagues, and the breadth of more than a league and a half. At no great distance to the East, rises a ridge of Anti-Libanus. The river Baradé is above the city divided into many streams, which are distributed through the gardens; so that there is a supply for all. The air is excellent, the soil exuberant in fertility. Fruits more abundant than I have ever seen, particularly the grapes and apricots, which are of excellent flavour.

Near

Near the mountain are some Saracenic remains of a mosque and palace, with many inscriptions in Cuphic characters. These are vestiges of the destructive warfare conducted by Timûr Leng, the hero, the robber, the warrior, the scourge. The walls are antient, not very lofty, but strong. Gates nine. The city is divided into twenty-three districts, each under its distinct magistrate.

That beautiful tree, the Lombardy poplar, abounds all over the plain. It is a native of Syria. When old it becomes ragged and uncouth, as usual in other regions, a monument of fugitive beauty.

Damascus is the seat of a considerable trade; and its manufactures afford a support to a great number of Mohammedans and Christians: they consist of silk and cotton, mixed or separate, but chiefly mingled together, in the form of what they call *Cottoni* or *Alléja* *. Much soap is also fabricated †, which

---

* The machine used in the manufacture is very simple, but the fabric is very complete, and executed with tolerable expedition. To make a *cottoni* requires one hundred and twenty-five drams of silk. Half that quantity is sufficient for a light *alléja*. The wages of a manufacturer for making the former are sixty paras. The fabric of white silk is technically called in Arabic *craishi*; the *alléja*, *darekli*; the *cottoni*, *dadâr*. The ordinary length of each of these is about ten pikes (draa). The width about a pike.

† The manner of making soap here deserves mention. They use oil of olives, putting to an hundred weight twenty-five pounds of kali, and five pounds of pulverized chalk. The latter articles are boiled till the water be sufficiently impregnated; the oil is then poured in, and the whole boils for three days over a fire composed of stones of olives.

is

is carried to different parts of Syria and to Egypt. Such of the European articles as are used by the Orientals, are drawn from Scidé, Beirût, and Tripoli, to and from all which places, there are regular caravans, iron, lead, tin, cochineal, broadcloth. From Persia and the East the caravans of Bagdad convey shawls, muslins, and the rich fabrics of Surat, a part of which is consumed in the city, and a part passes on to other places in Syria and to European Turkey. To maritime commerce the Damascenes were formerly very adverse, and it is only within these few years that they could be prevailed on to send goods by sea to Constantinople.

Timûr Leng, on his conquest of Syria, about the beginning of the fourteenth century, conveyed all the celebrated manufactures of steel from Damascus into Persia. Since that period, its works in steel have been little memorable. They were formerly of the highest reputation in Europe and the East. The famous sabres appear to have been constructed, by a method now lost, of alternate layers, about two or three lines thick, of iron and steel: they never broke, though bent in the most violent manner, and yet retained the utmost power of edge; so that common iron, or even steel, would divide under their force.

So far as my researches have enabled me to ascertain the population of Damascus, I should not be inclined to compute it at less than two hundred thousand souls. That of Aleppo may be estimated at two hundred and eighty thousand.

Some

Some modern travellers appear to me to have miftaken the nature of the gradual depopulation of the Eaft. The villages in general are fo much deferted, that, in the neighbourhood of Aleppo for inftance, where within the prefent century ftood three hundred villages, there now remain no more than ten or twelve. Yet, this depopulation of the villages fwells the cities and towns, not indeed in the fame proportion, but ftill with a rifing tide. The caufes feem to be, 1. In the cities the modes of gaining a livelihood are more multifarious, and fmall or no capital is required, whereas in agriculture it is indifpenfable. 2. In the cities the property is not tangible, fo to fpeak; it is veiled from the eye of government, fo as to be fafe from the exceffive exactions impofed on the peafants, whofe property is of the moft unweildy and felf-apparent defcription. The peafantry, both in Syria and Egypt, are not *Villani*, but as free as any clafs of men; and it happens unfortunately, that even a good governor cannot fufficiently protect them, for he muft either refign, or pay the ufual tributes at the Porte. Money he muft have, and the modern minifterial arts, of diving into the moft fecret receffes of property, being there unknown, he of courfe taxes that which is moft apparent, and the moft difficult to remove.

Yet the diftinction between a good and a bad governor is, even here, fufficiently felt; the population and commerce of Damafcus being on the increafe, by the juftice and equity of the prefent Pafha; whereas, both had been materially injured by the violence of Jezzar.

At

At this moment the shops in the extensive bazars, much larger than those of Aleppo, are all opened, and furnished with every species of commodity, and each caravan brings a supply of persons who, shunning oppression elsewhere, come here for temporary profit or fixed residence. The rent of houses, though still low, is sensibly increasing, and the suburbs spreading by new buildings.

The Pashalik is the first in Asia. The present Pasha is Abdallah, a man of about fifty years of age, tall and personable, and of noble extract, his ancestors having been invested with Pashaliks in the last century. It is hardly necessary to mention, that every Pasha has absolute power of life or death, there being no appeal from his jurisdiction.

The inhabitants of Damascus were formerly noted for their maltreatment of the Franks, but at present I found the pride of their ignorance somewhat abated, and observed no difference between them and other Oriental citizens. It is deeply to be regretted, that religion, intended to conciliate mankind, should be the chief cause of their ferocity against each other, and should, in an equal proportion, have mingled poisons and antidotes. The Mohammedan himself a god, all the rest of mankind dogs! can any benefit recompense the pride, the fury, the eternal enmity, destruction, and slaughter, inwoven into the very soul by such misanthropic dogmata?

A striking contrast exists between the inhabitants of Damascus and those of Aleppo. The Aleppins are vain and seditious;
the

the Damascenes, on the contrary, sober, industrious, and unostentatious. The females and children have commonly regular features and a fair complexion: the dress of the women nearly the same as at Constantinople; white muslin veils, except the prostitutes, who, as usual all over the East, expose their faces. To paint the face is an improvement unknown among the Oriental fair, save the Greeks alone.

The charitable establishments in Damascus are numerous, among which may be noted that constructed by Sultan Selim, for the reception of strangers; though his munificence have been since diverted into other channels. The building consists of a vast quadrangle, lined with a colonade. It is entirely roofed in small domes, covered with lead. The mosque is grand. The entrance supported by four large columns of red granite. It is covered with a cupola, and has two minarets. A handsome garden lies adjacent. The apartments are numerous, and the kitchen or *mutbach*, on the side opposite to the mosque, is suited to the grandeur of the establishment.

The celebrated Asad Pasha, mentioned by Niebuhr and Volney, left an only daughter, of whom, on her marriage with Mohammed Pasha Adm, sprang the present Pasha Abdallah. Mohammed Pasha Adm was preceded by Osmân, and succeeded by two of his own brothers successively, the last of whom, named Derwîsh, was expelled by the intrigues of Jezzâr, who gained his office, and married the daughter of Mohammed Pasha Adm. This marriage of ambition, not of affection, terminated in a divorce a year after. Among other instances of his bad treatment of this lady, it is recorded that Jezzâr, meeting her one day in the house, where she happened to have *cab-cab*, or Arabian pattens on her feet, pulled a pistol from his cincture, and fired it at her, saying, " Art thou the wife of an Arabian peasant? dost thou forget that thou art the wife of a Pasha?"

Jezzâr retained his ill-won pashalik of Damascus only a few years; his government was a continual scene of oppression and cruelty, and he is supposed to have extorted from the people not less than twenty-five thousand purses, or about a million and two hundred thousand pounds sterling; and to have put to death near four hundred individuals, most of them innocent. His own misconduct and suspicious designs, when leading the caravan to Mecca, conspired with the machinations of his enemies at the Porte to deprive him of his office: but living monuments of his cruelty remain, in the noseless faces and earless heads of many of the Damascenes. Thus driven from Damascus, he returned to his former pashalik of Acré and Seidé, where he remains. This government, which he held along with that of Damascus, he has retained upwards of twenty-seven years.

Jezzâr was succeeded by the present Pasha Abdallah, whose administration, though eminent as before observed for equity, is yet liable to the charge of mismanagement of the public revenue, and of an indecorous timidity. Under the energetic sway of Jezzâr, the sacred caravan had met with no obstructions on its route; but that of the present year, not only found the reservoirs

reservoirs for water destroyed or damaged, so that many camels perished for want of that indispensable article, but even the pilgrims were insulted by the Arabs, probably incited by the arts and malicious revenge of Jezzâr. By dint of bribes, however, at the Porte, Abdallah prevented his expected deprivation.

In the province of Damascus there are no taxes upon commodities of any kind, so far as I could discover. The land-tax, and the capitation-tax on Christians, constitute the only resource, except contingencies; as fines, and *avanias*, or arbitrary exactions. The *miri*, or public revenue, may amount to ten thousand purses, or half a million sterling.

Meat is at present sold for thirty-six paras the rotal, or fourpence sterling the pound Avoirdupois. A quantity of bread, sufficient for a meal for four persons, might be purchased for a para. It is very white and good, and remarked to be best when the Janizary Aga, who has a censorial power over the bakers, is not in the city. Grapes, of the finest flavour, the rotal three or four paras. Fish, from the river, is to be had at a moderate price, but not remarkably good. Milk, cheese, and butter, very cheap. Wild-fowl abounds on Mount Libanus, and partridges, in the season, are sold for five paras the brace. Tame fowls for four or five paras each, pigeons, a pair for the same sum.

The air or water of Damascus, or both, are supposed to operate powerfully against that loathsome disease the leprosy

(*borras*).

(*borras*). The inquiries I had occasion to make tended to prove, that if the disease were not too far advanced, it was always stopped in its progress, while the patient remained there.

The whole expense of the sacred caravan from Damascus to Mecca used formerly to amount to four thousand five hundred purses, and an increase has since taken place. The Pasha carries with him, exclusively of this, one thousand purses for his own use. Jezzâr was accustomed to take two thousand for the purpose of buying coffee, which he resold to vast advantage. The 4500 purses are deducted from the imperial treasury (*chosné*), and the Pasha is rendered accountable for the safety of the caravan. He receives the Senjiak Sherifi, or Ensign of the Prophet, from the governor of the castle, giving an acknowlegement in writing, before witnesses, in which he solemnly pledges himself to bring it back. Similar forms are observed on restoring it to its place. As soon as the Pasha arrives near the city on his return, a messenger is dispatched to Constantinople, who is obliged to perform the journey in twenty-five days. He carries water from the famous well Zem-zem, near Mecca, and some dates from Mediné, which are presented to the Emperor on his visit to the mosque. After this, the Wizîr presents a list of the Pashas for the ensuing year; the Sultan reads it, and if he object to any name, affixes to it a mark, after which the firmâns are made out in due form.

CHAP. XXVI.

Journey from Damascus to Balbec—Syriac language—Balbec—Recent discoveries—Zahhlé—Printing-office—Houses of Damascus—Return to Aleppo.

On Thursday the sixteenth of August 1797, set out from Damascus for Balbec or Heliopolis, attended only by the owner of the mule I rode on. Arrived at the convent of *Seidnaia*, which commands a fair view of the city of Damascus, and the plain. Vines and fig-trees adorn the country through which I travelled. The wine has less flavour and body than that of Kasrawân, but is esteemed more grateful to the stomach.

From *Seidnaia* I proceeded to *Maltila*, a village situated in the mountain, where is a convent, said to be of the time of Justinian. Thence went to *Yebrûd*, the antient *Jabruda*, a place higher up the mountain, in a romantic situation; the inhabitants are chiefly Mohammedans. I met there a Greek bishop, who was going to a place near Balbec, an intelligent and curious man. We proceeded in company till we came to Balbec.

Soon after arrived at *Mara*, a small town on the North of the road. It is remarked that at this town and at *Maltila* alone
the

the Syriac still continues to be a living language; descending from father to son, without the use of books. Two of the muleteers I observed to converse together more willingly in that language, than in the Arabic, which in found it nearly resembles.

On the 19th passed under *Dahr-el-chúr*, supposed to be the highest summit of the Anti-Libanian chain of mountains. The following day having set out four and a half hours before day-break, the muleteers lost the road, and we were obliged to wait for sunrise, chilled with the intense cold of these high mountains, which we felt severely in our hands and feet. Arrived at Balbec about noon the same day, after descending for nearly three hours through a ravine, or deep glen in the mountain, a rugged and, in some places, a steep road.

From the high grounds we had a perfect view of Balbec, and went to seek our lodging under some walnut-trees, on the North of the castle. Some precaution was necessary against the *Metaweli*, Mohammedans of the sect of Ali, who once formed a powerful and ferocious tribe; even now, though crushed in a great degree by the exertions of Jezzâr, they continue to persecute strangers, who have often suffered from their predatory disposition.

The antiquities of Balbec have been often described, and I did not observe any thing particular to add on that topic. Proceeded to *Zahblé*, a pleasant town among the mountains. Observed the Lombardy poplar in abundance. At *Zahblé* met

with

with a young man, a Druse, who informed me, that near Balbec, two or three years ago, in digging, the body of a man was found, interred in a kind of vault, having a piece of unstamped gold in his mouth; near him was a number of leaden plates, marked with characters to them unknown; they were fold and melted. In another place was discovered a small statue, very perfect, but I could not learn where it had been deposited. *Zahblé* is a large town, chiefly, if not solely inhabited by Christians; it sends forth seven hundred men fit for war. The town is divided into five districts, each having its separate Shech, who pays tribute to the Emîr of the Druses; they complain of oppression; and the state of the place, and the adjacent country, shews that their complaints are not void of foundation. The town is sheltered by mountains, but the locusts are very destructive. Tobacco is one of the chief articles of cultivation. A rivulet rolling from the rocks turns the mills and waters the grounds; air salubrious and never tainted with excessive heat.

Near *Zahblé* saw what is called the *tomb of Noah*, a long structure, seemingly part of an aqueduct. It extends about sixty feet, the stature of Noah according to Oriental tradition. The pilgrims who came formerly to worship in the mosque near it were very numerous; and the religious revenue is said to amount to three hundred purses annually.

Among the mountains the people have an air of health not observable in the cities. Magic is still credited, and several are accused before the bishop for incantations, producing love or enmity.

enmity. The pious antipathy between the Greeks and Catholics reigns here in all its fury.

After a journey of two days, through a rugged route along the ridge of the mountain, arrived at the convent of St. John, where the printing-office is. Paper being dear, and no demand for books, the press is stopped. Arabic books alone were edited.

On my return by *Zibdané* observed there a gate of Grecian architecture. Passed through a rich vale, watered by the *Baradé*, formerly the Chrysorrhoas, to Damascus.

So numerous are the fruit-trees in the vicinity of this city, that those which die and are cut down, supply it with abundant fire-wood. They are also used for building, together with the the walnut-tree and Lombardy poplar. The houses in Damascus are remarkably large and commodious, and well supplied with water; of many the furniture is worth from one to five hundred purses, or from five thousand to twenty-five thousand pounds, in divans or large sophas, of the richest silk, embroidered with pearl, Persian carpets, mirrors, &c.

The *melingana*, a species of the solanum, is consumed here in such quantities as a common vegetable, that fifty hundred weight is estimated the daily supply of the city.

Returned from Damascus to Aleppo, 7th October 1797, a journey of twelve days. Almost every town or village on the
route

route has its market, so that there is no occasion to prepare provisions; the caravanserais are in a ruinous situation.

On visiting the castle of Aleppo, observed a remarkable fact considering the populousness of the city. There were only eighteen prisoners, eight of whom were confined for debt, and the remainder on account of the riot between the Janizaries and Sherîfs. The debtor is not permitted, in the whole Turkish empire, to be confined above one month; during which term, according to the Mohammedan doctors, his property must appear, if he have any, and if none, they consider it unjust to detain him. But this mild regulation is sometimes frustrated; for if a claim lie for four thousand piasters, for example, the creditor may first proceed against him for five hundred, and bring a fresh charge at the end of every month till the whole be paid, or till the debtor have remained in prison one month on every distinct process.

CHAP. XXVII.

Journey from Aleppo towards Constantinople—Route—Aintâb—Mount Taurus—Bostan—Inhabitants, their manners and dress—Kaisaria—Angora—Walls and antiquities—Angora goats—Manufactures—Topography—Journey to Ismit—Topography—General remarks concerning Anatolia or Asia Minor.

ON the 21st of October 1797, set out from Aleppo on my journey through Anatolia to Constantinople. I had a horse for myself, and another for an Armenian servant; seventy mules carried the merchandize of the caravan.

The direct road lies by Beilan and Adene, Konia, Kutahia, and Bursa, but *Kutchuk Ali*, the Pasha of Beilan, being in a state of rebellion, we were constrained to turn to the North-east by an unusual route, through the cities of Aintab, Kaisarîa, and Angora.

Between Aleppo and Aintab the country is well watered, and, though somewhat stony, capable of being cultivated in a threefold degree.

On the 30th arrived at Aintab, a large town or city, inhabited by Mohammedans and Christians, both Armenian and Greek.

Greek. It has a fortrefs and a garrifon of Janizaries. Here the Turkifh language firft becomes general. The chief commerce is leather and raw hides; fkins of goats are dyed red and yellow, into what is called Turkey leather. The houfes are built of ftone, which is very cheap; there are five principal mofques; through fome of the ftreets devolve ftreams of water, and the air is falubrious. On the South fide is a large burying ground, which at a diftance feems an extenfive fuburb. On the North is the caftle, apparently coëval with that of Aleppo, built on an artificial elevation. The city however is entirely commanded from the adjacent hills. It is governed by a *Mitfellim*, appointed by the executive power at Conftantinople. The Janizaries and Sherifs are here as riotous as at Aleppo. Staple commodities are, the leather above mentioned, cottons for their own ufe, and various-coloured woollens, of which jackets are made, and fent to other parts. It alfo produces *dips*, a confection made of the grounds of wine and almonds.

After travelling for feveral days, afcended Mount Taurus, now called *Kurfin*. The afcent and defcent occupied three days. This is a chain of high rocky mountains, running from Eaft to Weft, the inhabitants are chiefly Kûrds; and the Turcomans retire here in the fummer from the plain of Antioch, as before mentioned. Many thoufand acres abound with cedars of great fize and age; favines and junipers cover fome of the brows. The cedars throw around a delicious odour. Some of our company, when they wifhed to warm themfelves, the air being cold to excefs, would fet fire to the dead trees by kindling a little

little dry grafs, which would inftantly feize the branches, and foon confumed the whole tree. The bafes of the mountains generally confift of tufa. Moft of the hills are divided by rapid rivulets of the pureft water.

On commencing the afcent of Mount Taurus, obferved feveral roads leading to the right; one of them conducts to the copper mines of Tokat, which are very rich, and yield a confiderable revenue to the emperor.

After defcending Mount Taurus, arrived in the extenfive plain of Boftân, which confifts of fertile foil, is watered by the river formerly called *Sarus*, and furrounded with mountains.

Boftân is a town rather of fmall fize, and prefenting nothing memorable. Here I firft obferved little two-wheeled carts, drawn by two oxen. The wheels are folid, and the axle turns with them, fo that their progrefs is fufficiently vociferous. Market poor. The inhabitants, like thofe of Anatolia in general, form a ftriking contraft to the more polifhed natives of Syria. They infpected us with ftupid curiofity, and without the ufual tokens of falutation practifed by the Arabs. The common drefs a fhort jacket and fringed turban. The women here are of fair florid complexion, and wear on their heads broad flat pieces of metal, to fhelter their faces from the fun and rain. Thefe refemble common eating plates, and are faftened with ftrings under the chin; the rich have them of filver, others are copper. Their perfons and motions are uncouth and deftitute

of

lascivious mincing, the *motus Ionici*, of the Egyptian and women.

n Boſtân to Kaiſarîa the country is plain, but ill culti-
nd thinly inhabited. Near the city there are however
productive fields, and watered by the river *Yermok*.
ver we had paſſed a day's journey from Kaiſarîa, run-
 the South. Near that city the Lombardy poplar again
 in abundance.

arîa is diſtinguiſhed at a diſtance by two remarkable hills,
them lofty, and at this time covered with ſnow. This is
f the town. The other, which is to the South, is round
plated, but not ſo high. The town is on the ſouth ſide
ertile plain, well watered by the *Yermok* and ſome rills,
ntains a good number of inhabitants. They are now
ing. In entering the town I obſerved numbers of the
, ſtrong, and large camels, which are bred by the Turco-
The black buffaloe, like that of Egypt, is very com-
ere. Kaiſarîa is governed by a *Mitſellim*, who is ap-
l from Conſtantinople. The city belongs to the Reis
. It is ſurrounded by walls, now in bad repair. Great
ies of timber are brought here from the mountains, and
rted to various quarters.

ora is eight days' journey nearly North-weſt from Kaiſa-
On the fourth day paſſed a plain, watered or rather
ted by the river *Tumm*. On the eighth day paſſed a
bridge,

bridge, over a rapid but apparently shallow river, one of the branches of the Halys, at a spot where it makes its appearance from betwixt abrupt rocks. Route variegated with hills, but on the whole rather plain.

Reached Angora on the 22d of November, two hours before sun-set. This city is visible at some distance, being in a lofty situation. It has a striking and agreeable appearance. It is situated on a small river. The castle is very antient, and in former times may have appeared impregnable, being raised on a high perpendicular rock. There is a chain of outworks to a considerable extent, occupying all the high ground.

The city has been surrounded by a substantial wall, in some places apparently double. Marks of a ditch also are visible. I passed three gates, and was told there were three or four more. Fragments of Greek inscriptions may be observed on two of the gates. On the North-west are said to be remains of an amphitheatre, which circumstances prevented me from visiting.

In the city are the ruins of a magnificent *Curia*, erected in the time of Augustus. The architecture is Corinthian, and parts of the inscriptions are well preserved, complimentary to that emperor.

The stones which form the walls are durable, and of an excellent quality. The city must have been strong, being commanded by no adjacent height. Market well supplied, especially

with

with honey and excellent bread. The people are the most polished I have yet seen in Anatolia.

The trade is chiefly in yarn, of which our shalloons are made, and their own manufacture of Angora stuffs. Of the latter I am told they make yearly from fifteen to twenty thousand pieces, of thirty Stambûl pikes each, or nearly twenty-two yards. The breed of goats they say is on the decline. There is however a great extent of country which is capable of supplying food to their flocks; so that the number might be easily augmented. Each goat produces on an average from two to three hundred drams annually. The hair is taken from the whole body, and not the belly alone. They are shorn once a year, the sheep twice. The wool of the latter is particularly fine and long. Of the goats' hair they have, it is reported, made shawls here, equal in quality to the Kashmirian, and as wide. They cost the maker one hundred piasters a-piece; but the manufacturers were unable to work flowers in them. They have also made good cloth; but the fabric was abandoned for want of encouragement. A special regulation constrains them to work the shalloons with double thread, otherwise they might be made much finer. The best of the Angora stuffs, worked by the piece, stands the manufacturer in about seventy *paras* the pike, or two thousand (= 3l. 10s. or 3l. 15s.) the piece. I should observe that in the manufacture of camlets no wool is used. Wax is exported, and in this part of Anatolia are cultivated large quantities of *opium*.

The

The Angora cats are confined to the same district with the goats. The soil is a fine red marl; but there is no peculiarity so striking in the site, soil, or air, as to offer any probable induction concerning the origin of those two remarkable breeds of animals, so dissimilar from those of other regions of the East.

Angora is one of the neatest cities I have yet visited. The streets are paved with large granite, but without foot-paths. Wax is produced in the neighbourhood, to the value of two thousand piasters a year; one fourth of which quantity is generally consumed in the city itself. It is surrounded by mountains, but there are numerous gardens near it, producing much fruit, especially excellent pears, which are sent for presents to Constantinople. The esculent plants barely suffice for the city, and the corn is brought from other places, the land being employed most profitably in the pasturage of the goats.

On the 16th of November 1797 proceeded towards Ismit or Nikmid, the antient Nicomedia, a maritime town, distant ten days. On the first day of our route saw the river of Angora running north through the plain. Two days after met fifty camels laden with fuller's earth for the manufacturers of Angora. The 30th of November observed in the side of a hill a most beautiful appearance of strata, to the number of nine or ten in the breadth of eight feet, the widest of them grey chalky stone, then a wide one of red earth, or marl, then narrow ones of red earth and chalk alternately, each about four inches wide; surface gravel.

December

December 7th, set out from Koſtabec three hours before sun-riſe, and did not reach Tourbali till about one in the afternoon. The general face of the country is a rocky foreſt of pines and oaks. We kept moſtly in the valley, till half paſt nine in the evening, when we aſcended a very high mountain, which we alſo in part deſcended before we reached Tourbali. Several ſmall ſtreams deſcend both to the North and the South; one in particular, forming the river that runs by Angora. This part of Mount Olympus muſt in courſe be very high.

I found grapes in almoſt all the towns, after leaving Angora, but thoſe of Teracli were the beſt I had ſeen ſince leaving Damaſcus; they are white, and of a fine flavour, and ſome of them of very large ſize.

December 5th, after paſſing Yeywa, came to a long well-built bridge over the conſiderable and rapid river, which diſembogues into the Black ſea, called *Sakaria:* a long bridge leads over the marſhy lands to *Iſmît*, a large town, extended in length, built on the ſide of a hill to the eaſt of the plain. The mountains near it are lofty, and become viſible long before one arrives there. Iſmît is paved, but dirty, and built of wood. Moſt of the houſes have a garden attached to them. The khan is neat, but not very large—Few remains of antiquity. A great number of Greeks reſides here.

On the 7th left Iſmît, and after paſſing along the ſhore to Scutari, where we arrived in the morning of the 9th, proceeded immediately to Conſtantinople.

Some general remarks arife concerning Anatolia, formerly Afia Minor. The parts through which we paffed have more of the wild and romantic* than of the cultivated afpect; foil very various, but a deep clay is the moft prevailing. Wheat and barley, and the yellow durra, *Holcus Arundinaceus*, form the chief, if not only products of agriculture. The whole is pervaded by hordes of Kurds and Turcomans. Numerous mendicants. The little fecurity there is arifes from the fuperior ferocity of a few Pafhas, which allows of no robbery fave their own. The depopulation is gradual, conftant, and infallible, and indubitably arifes from the extreme badnefs of the government, than which nothing more wretched can well be conceived.

* Throughout Syria and Anatolia is eftablifhed a kind of tolls called *ghafar*, demanded under pretence of keeping up the roads, and freeing them from robbers. A fixed fum is exacted from all Chriftians; and even an European, though furnifhed with a travelling firman, often finds it difficult to avoid paying them. Mohammedans pay what they pleafe, or even nothing.

In Syria thefe tolls are of no apparent ufe; the demand is fomewhat confiderable, the roads are not repaired, and there is no defence but immemorial cuftom. In Anatolia, where there are woods, fome refponfibility is attached to the office of toll-gatherer, in cafe a traveller is robbed; and the fum paid is more reafonable.

CHAP. XXVIII.

Observations at Constantinople—Paswân Oglo—Character of the present Sultan—State of learning—Public libraries—Turkish taste—Coals—Greek printing-house—Navy—Return to England.

When I arrived at Constantinople there was a considerable alarm raised by the progress of the arms of *Paswân Oglo*, Pasha of Widdin. Originally Aga of that city, that is, chief of the Janizaries and commandant, he formed a powerful opposition to the Pasha, consisting of many rich and eminent inhabitants, who were dissatisfied with the Pasha's conduct. By numerous intrigues and disputes the latter was gradually deprived of his authority, and Paswân Oglo usurped his place. After the last Russian war, the Porte being much in want of money, had recourse to new and unpopular measures of finance. Taxes were for the first time imposed on articles of consumption, as grain and wine. Paswân availed himself of the discontents occasioned by these impositions, and as his power increased boasted that he would correct such abuses.

The Porte, following its usual policy of rewarding where it cannot punish, of decorating the head which it wishes to strike off,

off, confirmed Paſwân in the Paſhalik. His military force at first did not exceed four or five thouſand, but, by the influx of the diſcontented, was now ſwelled to fifteen thouſand or more, of enthuſiaſtic and determined followers. Moſt of them conſiſted of the Janizaries on that ſide of Romélia, who were extremely diſſatisfied at having paſſed unrewarded after the brilliant actions they had performed againſt the Auſtrian arms, and at the encouragement given to the recently eſtabliſhed corps of Fuſileers, an innovation which ſtung their ancient prejudices.

The Aga of the Janizaries at Conſtantinople, being conſulted on the ſuppreſſion of the rebellion, gave his opinion, that there was danger left the Janizaries ſhould go over to their brethren. The Diwân aſſembled in great perplexity, all were irreſolute, till the Capitan-paſha, Huſſein, ſaid, " Nothing can be more eaſy than to cruſh this rebel." The members inſtantly retorted, that if it were ſo eaſy, why not undertake that duty himſelf. Huſſein exclaimed, " Only give me the means, and I pledge myſelf to conduct them!" He was in conſequence appointed, and abundant ſupplies of men and money were aſſigned. Inſtead of Janizaries, the Timariots or feudal troops of Aſia were ſummoned. Before I left Turkey a ſlight ſkirmiſh had taken place. The troops which marched againſt Widdîn were computed at one hundred and fifty thouſand. Paſwân Oglo, unable to meet ſuch a multitude in the field, was contented to defend Widdîn. His ſucceſs and further progreſs are ſufficiently known.

A new inſtitution had been recently ordained by the reigning Sultan. Perceiving that his troops had been unable to oppoſe

those

those of Russia, he had, with the assistance of the French, who supplied non-commissioned officers to instruct them, founded a regular corps of infantry, consisting of about one thousand. They were clothed in a tighter dress, and their arms* supplied by government. The French have also assisted the Turks in casting a great number of brass field-pieces and battering cannon; nor are they without some flying artillery.

The present Sultan is not deficient in discernment, or warm wishes to promote the happiness of his people; but through the usual imperfection of his education, he is the slave of his own impetuosity, and a stranger to the recesses of the human heart. His motives are generally right, but the means, opposed by popular prejudices, are often ineffectual.

Sultan Selim, after correcting the police of the capital, turned his beneficent views to the encouragement of learning among his subjects. He has revived the mathematical school, in which, however, small progress had been made; his ignorance of the world leading him to think that his orders can form minds, and that a pension confers capacity. He has restored the printing office, and a new Arabic type was casting by an ingenious Armenian. But whether the improvement of the type may contribute to the diffusion of solid knowlege among the Turks, may fairly be questioned. The first book ordered to be printed was a Persian dictionary. An engraver on copper is also settled here, the subjects are the armillary sphere, some plans of fortification, the box-compass, and the like.

* Musket and bayonet.

The Turks are remarkable for half-measures. In the mathematical and marine school, a substantial and commodious building, they are furnished with every thing—except instruments and books; the class small or none; but the end of the institution is considered as completely answered, as there are professors who meet and smoke their pipes together.

There are several *Kuttub-chans*, or public libraries, among which the principal are those of St. Sophia and the Solimanié Jamafy; but none so elegant as that built by Raghib Pasha, formerly Grand Wizîr. The magnificent institutions of this great man being envied by the Sultan of the day, his head was the forfeit of his virtues. This library is an insulated building, in the middle of a square court, consisting entirely of marble, and very neat and convenient. A large tomb, decorated with gilt brass, in which Rashib Pasha is buried, forms the centre of the library. Around are numerous books, on all subjects, chiefly as usual theology; convenient seats and elegant carpets and cushions for the readers. A librarian constantly attends. The light is well disposed, and the place perfectly quiet; so that I have no where seen a building or institution more complete of the kind. The apartment is raised above the ground by seven or eight easy steps. Fronting the street there is a school, founded by the same Pasha. It is a convenient room, of thirty-five feet long and proportionate width, where about an hundred boys are taught to read and write, and the more simple part of their theology. There is only one class, which attends every day for two hours in the morning and two in the afternoon.

I met

I met with a Mohammedan, a native of *Balk*, who understood the first six books of Euclid. A young Englishman, who has embraced Islamism, and is lately established at Constantinople, had translated Euclid into Turkish, and published an astronomical ephemeris. Having received some encouragement, he was proceeding to read lectures on mathematical subjects. Many scribes are found here who write elegantly and correctly.

The national taste does not seem rapidly to improve. One of the Sultanas, sisters of the monarch, has not long since built a villa on the Bosphorus, half in the European style, half in the Chinese.

There is a considerable market for books, containing many shops, well supplied.

Strata of coals are found at about four hours distance on the European side. An officer in the service of the Porte informed me that he had at first obtained the exclusive right of working them. He sent them to the Crimea. Since that time better coals having been found in that country, and the right of working them having been soon afterwards taken from him, the mine was neglected, and then discontinued. It was difficult to work on account of the sandy soil which fell in. He said he could sell them at Constantinople for a para the oke.

Went to a Greek printing-house conducted by an Armenian. They were printing a small exhortation in the Greek language,
written

written by Anthimus, Patriarch of Jerusalem, against the prevailing tenets of Deism and Atheism. They throw off about a thousand sheets a day.

The navy has of late been greatly improved by Le Brun and other French ship-builders. On the 2d of April 1798 there were eight ships of war at anchor in the Bosphorus; three seventy-fours, four fifties, one forty. The whole navy amounts to fifteen ships, fit for service, and of considerable force.

The Turkish women, in fine weather, ape the European custom of taking the air in their carriages, in a great square; but they are concealed in small latticed waggons, and veiled. They thus lose the best part of the display, " the mighty pleasure of being seen."

I shall close my remarks on Constantinople with observing, that the country between it and Adrianople is completely plain, and that the capital is, on the land side, incapable of any defence against a victorious army. The uncertainty of the winds and channels join with the forts to defend the other side from any sudden assault.

Proceeding through Wallachia to Vienna, Prague, Dresden, Leipsic, Potsdam, Berlin, and Hamburg, I arrived in London on the 16th of September, 1798, after an absence of nearly seven years.

CHAP. XXIX.

Comparative view of life and happiness in the East and in Europe.

———— *Et qui plus est, il me semble que je n'ay rencontré guere de manieres, qui ne vaillent les nostres.* MONTAIGNE.

THE great contrast which is observable between the manners and personal character of the Orientals and Europeans, insensibly leads to a comparison of its result in society. The character of every nation merits the attention of the philosopher; and the less that nation resembles ourselves, the more its distinguishing features require our investigation.

While vanity instigates us to claim an undisputed superiority, experience often compels us to doubt the validity of the sentence on which we insist. We are fearful of being reduced to acknowlege, that the labour, the thought, the agitation which have place among us, often augment not the happiness of the individual, and are of doubtful utility to the collective body. It is not however designed to insist on any such concession;

and only a few confiderations fhall be offered in the order that they arife.

> ——Animo fatis hæc veftigia parva fagaci
> Sunt, per quæ poffis cognofcere cætera tutè.
>
> LUCRETIUS.

Impatience, activity, and fanguine hope, are habits of an European. By education his imagination is exalted and his ideas are multiplied. By reading, and frequent intercourfe with foreigners, he is enabled to prefent to himfelf the ftate of diftant times and remote nations. Their knowlege, their arts, their pleafures become familiar to him; and, from a fixed principle of the human mind, the lively idea of all thefe advantages generates the hope of appropriating them. His firft attempt is haply crowned with fuccefs, and he is thus ftimulated to farther effort: but as the bounds fixed to his attainments are removed the farther he advances, and improvement is infinite, his ultimate difappointment is inevitable, and it is felt with a poignancy proportioned to the confidence of his firft hopes.

The habits of the Oriental, on the contrary, are indolence, gravity, patience. His ideas are few in number; and his fentiments in courfe equally rare. They are, however, generally correct, fpringing from the objects around him, and for the moft part limited to thofe objects.

A chief caufe of this contraft, muft be the mode of education in each community. Education fhould be the art of forming man on the principles of nature; by due attention to her unerring progress, no advantage of life can remain unimproved, and no duty can be misunderstood. But in no nation with whose history we are acquainted, has such a system been established. Almost every one forms its disciples on the narrow views of that community, and nature is distorted and paralised by authority.

The leading fault of education in the various parts of the Turkish empire, originates in the prevailing superstition. Wherever this does not operate, the practice is sufficiently rational.

The children of the Arabs early attain the character of manhood. A grave demeanour, fortitude in suffering, respect for age, filial affection, contempt for frivolous amusements, frugality, temperance, hospitality, are taught in the easiest and most effectual manner—by example; and where there is least probability of counter-instruction—in the house of the father.

They are early taken out of the hands of women, and sent to study the Korân; an employment which indeed has only the negative advantage of saving a portion of their time from positive idleness. As they advance towards maturity, little coercion is employed, but no incitement is administered to error. The father gradually accustoms himself to treat his son on the footing of an equal; who, on the other hand, seldom forgets the respect which is not imperiously exacted.

The dress of children is free from ligatures, their diet simple, and they are accustomed to variations of season, and enured to fatigue. These are a part of the advantages of Oriental education. Among its more serious inconveniences may be enumerated, an excessive credulity, the offspring of profound ignorance, and a keenness bordering on dishonesty and falsehood. It is not easy to gain knowlege which is not sought. The boy respects his father, and the summit of his ambition is to imitate his sire. The parent is guided chiefly by the reflection, how far he may extend his pursuit of gain with impunity; of course a very refined morality is not to be expected from the son. Happiness once confined to the small circle of a family, little anxiety remains for the world at large. Hence the faintness of the conception of a community, and the duties arising from it.

In Europe, education is the art of moulding the soul to the times; and the preceptor is commonly successful in conveying the instruction, of which experience has taught him the advantage, and which he is no stranger to the mode of applying. Advancement is the object; and to obtain it activity is required. This end is gained; but in the art of directing the powers of his mind to the attainment of his own happiness, or to the public utility, or of preserving his body sane and vigorous, the man remains still a child; and thus the true object of education is frustrated. We have on this head then, it would seem, no great reason to boast our superiority.

The

The distinctive character of a nation is not to be sought in great cities. The manners of these reciprocally approximate. In that part of Egypt where the character of women is unsophisticated by mixture, however strong their passions, they are not unchaste. This perhaps proceeds more from the influence of public opinion, than the sanctions of municipal law.

Among the people, as they are to take part in domestic duties, their education is bounded by the useful. Among the opulent it extends to the ornamental, and many females in Kahira are taught to read and write. Instead of complaining of their seclusion as an injury, they may sometimes be observed tenacious of it as a mark of respect. That seclusion, though originating in the real or supposed licentiousness of the sex, is, at this time, far from being the effect of individual jealousy, but by long adoption, become a part of bien-séance. "I consented to become your wife," said a woman to her husband, in my hearing, "that I might be veiled or private, *masturé*, and remain tranquil in my family; not to be sent to the market, to meet the eyes of *chalk-illah*, all the world."

This seclusion of women has an important effect in society; and the Orientals are accordingly, as has often been remarked, in a great degree strangers to the passion of *love*. It is thought indecent in company to speak much of women, and no man would venture to declare, that he had a preference for a particular woman, or intended to marry her.

Social intercourse is thus rendered less vivacious and amusing, but numberless inquietudes are avoided. They who affirm, however, that nothing is sought from women, among the people of the East, but sensual gratification, seem to err. Why should a man, by having several women, necessarily become insensible to what is amiable or estimable in any individual among them? Or is individual character rendered absolutely indistinct by their being associated together?

They are equally in error who assert, that women in the East are slaves. Perhaps it might correctly be said that they are treated as children; but, supposing this to be true, do not tenderness and affection operate towards children?

They hold not the same rank as in Europe; and if they did, the intrigues carried on in the *harem*, would render their husbands and themselves miserable. In their present state, accidents of this kind are not without ill effects, but, in general, serve rather to minister a cause of diversion, than to produce any very serious evil. Of course they give much less disturbance than in Europe.

The spirit of Chivalry, fostered by the Crusades, changed, in the heated imagination of the youthful hero, the lovely object of his desires, into a deity that was to be adored. The visible nature of the divinity fanned the flame of devotion. Whether the fair benignly smiled, or scornfully averted her countenance from the humble votary, her perfections were equally the subject of his eulogies, and her will of his propitiation.

tion. But all his services were sublimely disinterested, and were to remain without hope of remuneration, till giants should be immolated to her perfections, and widows and orphans chaunt forth in her presence the praises of their generous deliverer.

These chaste amours, in which all was elevated, and all exquisitely unnatural, according to modern ideas, were yet the foundation of the rank women hold in modern Europe. This system, forced and contrary to nature, could not long have place, and perhaps the sex itself grew satiated with the frigid adulation of distant votaries, however flattering to its vanity. A more licentious gallantry then took place, and the charm was quickly dissolved. The intercourse between the sexes being at length reduced to the simple gratification of the sensual desire, society was almost in the same state in the West, as in the East, at the period when the seclusion of females first took place.

But the Europeans adopted a different plan. They either despised the security of bolts and bars as ineffectual, or too much of their former respect yet remained to allow the attempt. The sex at length wearied, but not satiated with simple sensuality, was governed in the choice of its indulgences by caprice; and the men were studiously employed to attract the œillades of their mistresses, and to chain this fickle sentiment, by varied foppery and grimace. Hence the romantic tales of our novels, hence the inconsequential conduct of their heroes, and hence the agitations of our societies, at which the Orientals would smile.

It

It is not said, that the miseries and violent dissensions which exist in families, result from the rank females hold in European society. Eternal litigations, and all the confusion of severe laws and loose morals are not attributed to that cause. It is only hinted that these evils are coëtaneous with that state of society, and that the pure institution of matrimony may be enforced by the commanding voice of religion, and sanctioned by municipal law, yet those evils may remain without a remedy.

The young of each sex are, in Europe, brought together, and taught to attach themselves to each other: but interdicted from uniting, unless equal in rank, fortune, &c. Passion however is strongest at an early age, when the reason which should guide it is weakest. But the public institutions eternize the punishment of a momentary folly. Parental authority, at other times, interferes, and pretending only solicitude for the child's happiness, renders both the parent and the offspring miserable.

The husband is vain of exhibiting in public his admired bride. From familiarities with a variety of men which, by being public, are authorized, she is induced to try them in private. The man becomes unhappy and ridiculous, the wife disgraced, and the lover impoverished. Little or nothing of this is known in the East.

Another striking dissimilitude between the Europeans and Orientals is observable in the number and quality of their

respective

respective laws, and the administration of public justice. Though a multitude of commentaries has been written on the simple maxims contained in the Korân, applying them to the particular cases which occur in society, the whole falls far short, in point of extent, of the most simple systems of jurisprudence with which we are acquainted. The single circumstance of each man being advocate in his own cause, contracts all judicial proceedings to a small compass, and, whether justly or unjustly, all legal disputes are speedily terminated. So that no man can bequeath to his family the inheritance of judicial ruin.

It will no doubt be thought, that the corrupt character of judges, and the sale of their decrees, are evils for which no advantages can compensate; and here, at least, it may be urged, that in Europe the administration of justice is more equal, and the right is not generally to be shaken by a bribe.

On the other hand, whatever may be the integrity of the judges in their decisions, the length and delay of the proceedings is sufficient to re-produce all the evils which are thought to be obviated by the absence of judicial corruption. If one of the parties be poor and the other rich, the latter commonly has the option of ruining the former by throwing impediments in the way of a decision; and it is of little importance to a man to know that he is ultimately victorious, when his property is already consumed, ere the cause draw near its termination.

But independently of the immense expense of a process in most countries of Europe, the anxiety and suspense while it is depending, tend to lessen the happiness of society, and are, by their frequency, serious evils.

Domestic manners furnish a more minute, but not unimportant contrast. In receiving strangers at his house and when they leave it, the Oriental testifies no great emotion. The visitor is welcomed rather by actions than words. An Arab or Turk having once accorded protection, which he does with a kind of distance and hauteur, never afterwards withdraws it, and his word may be relied on. In visiting, as is well known, the common but absurd practice, which obtains among ourselves, of urging those to stay longer, of whose company one is already tired, is obviated by the simple use of a little scented wood in a censer.

In their communications every thing tends rather to tranquillize the mind, than to excite the passions. The quarrels of the mere mob, indeed, evaporate in idle vociferation; but among persons of any breeding, the voice is scarcely ever raised above its ordinary tone.

The greatest number of menials in a family (and in the East they are very numerous) occasions no confusion. All is conducted in silence and order. All such directions as are in the common routine of affairs, are given by signs, and are instantly understood; not from pride, or as implying the vast distance

between

between master and servant, but principally to avoid all *equivoque*, when persons of various descriptions are present, and, by making secrecy a uniform habit, to avoid all suspicion from the adoption of mystery in giving orders before company, when any thing is to be said which it is not intended that company should hear.

The ingenuity of man in contriving his own unhappiness, is in no part of the world more conspicuous than in Europe. Our mutual intercourse is so beset with forms, that it becomes doubtful whether it be a good or an evil; and the individual, not unfrequently, leaves a company dissatisfied that he ever entered into it. Hence a continued desire of changing place and forming new acquaintance.

Whenever a number of persons meet together, eating and drinking seem to be a necessary bond of union; and they often do not separate without that kind of festivity which impairs the health of each, and creates dissensions, as it were, by its mechanical operation. The sole benefit which results from the social meals of the Arabs, is to us entirely unknown.—No man thinks himself incapacitated from injuring his neighbour, in consequence of having divided with him a loaf of bread, and a little salt, at the convivial board.

In the East social intercourse is less artificial, and less hampered with rules. It is maintained with more complacency, and relinquished, not without hope of renewal. We too have now indeed abandoned a part of its more inconvenient formalities;

ties; but some of its oppressive and despotic laws continue unaltered. The exterior may be changed; but the substance is identical.

In the East, they who are guilty of excess in drinking bury their inebriation in the gloom of their closet. By this, present disturbance, and future ill example are equally obviated, whatever may be the ill consequence to the wretched victim of intemperance. Of excess in eating there are few examples; for their longest meals, even when a series of dishes is presented, as at the tables of a Pasha or a Bey, are terminated in a few minutes. The moderation and temperance of diet indeed throughout the East are matters of high praise; and, whether virtues of climate, habit, or reflection, merit imitation among ourselves. The reward is present, uninterrupted health and tranquillity of mind.

If the multitude of wants constitute human inquietude, it must be remembered how much of what to us is indispensable is, to them, as if it had never been.

With them society is rendered tranquil and easy by mutual forbearance; with us it is vexed with the necessity of mutual adulation.—In the one region each man sets a fashion to himself, in the other all the constituent parts are wearied with serving an idol that the collective body alone has set up. Each stands bareheaded from respect to the other, when both might remain covered without inconvenience to either.

Politeness

Politeness is, with the one, an easy compliance, with which all are satisfied; with the other, it is a difficult effort, from the practice and the experience of which the parties mutually retire discontented.

The fashions to which we are slaves, are indeed many of them so little founded in reason, that one is sometimes disposed to consider them as imagined by the indolent and restless, to occupy the thoughts and time of those who have no better employment; or invented, like certain dogmas, to shew the merit of implicit credence. A certain dress is to be worn, a certain establishment kept up, under pain of indelible ignominy; and the man whose circumstances disable him from complying with this terrific mandate, with timid irresolution hides his head.

See the European in conversation, even among his equals, he is not so solicitous to express such thoughts as rise in his mind, as to find some employment for his tongue. It is not to give utterance to what naturally occurs, but that conversation may be *kept up*, that all are anxious. Garrulities, and misconceptions are civilly uttered for arguments; and the abortions of fancy and caprice, hold the place of the sane offspring of judgment and reflection. Yet we laugh at them for using short and few phrases, (*phrases courtes et rares*, as Volney describes them,) when they have nothing to say!

It is with them however neither ridiculous nor irksome to be silent. They go into company to be diverted, not to labour,

and

and they esteem effort in conversation a vain toil. The raillery and repartee of the Occidentals is, among them, supplied (it must be allowed very inadequately) by the *Meddahs*, storytellers, and professed jokers.

Human life in the East is exposed to a variety of casualties. Pestilence, famine, tyranny, all conspire to diminish its security. It is natural to set a smaller value on any advantage, in proportion to the facility of privation. Hence the Orientals are not much disturbed at the thoughts of death, but resign life without a sigh. The mind is tortured when the blossoms of hope are suddenly torn from it; but their gradual decay is not incompatible with a kind of tranquillity.

The European, more dissatisfied with the present, and only supported by the hope of what is to come, attached beyond measure to the advantages which his anxieties have been prolonged to acquire, has already, even at an early age, fixed to himself a period, short of which he thinks it *hard and unjust* to be deprived of life.

Concerning past events the fatalist is consoled by reflecting, that nothing he could have done would have altered the immutable order of things, and that his efforts before would have been as vain as his regret now is. This idea, indeed, is perhaps not destitute of ill effects, but it surely produces some good. If, by persuading them that the evils which they suffer are unavoidable, it prevent them from endeavouring to avoid them,

it

it also prevents their repining at what must at all events be endured as the immutable law of the universe.

The European attributing more power to volition, ascribes to his own want of judgment or energy the result of whatever terminates unfavourably. Thus a part of his life is occupied by self-accusation, which, however, ensures no amelioration for the future.

In the East, if age be respected, it is respected, in part at least, from the decorous behaviour of the aged. In Europe, if it be rendered ridiculous, it is so too often, by a vain effort to perpetuate the character and manners of youth.

The commanding influence of a system so flattering to the pride of its professors, and operating so powerfully on their hopes and fears as Mohammedism, aided by the dread of present suffering, has so far counteracted the strong impulse of avarice, that *gaming* is in a great degree banished from society in the East. All the evils and inconveniences therefore of that practice, so severely felt thoughout Europe, are almost unknown in the Turkish empire.

If activity and a careful provision for the future, and that each should contribute his efforts to the good of the whole, be necessary to constitute the happiness of a people, how happens it that the Orientals, among whom these requisites are wanting, should yet be happy?

The

The fyftem of morals contained in the writings of the Orientals, is at once fublime without being impracticable, and levelled to the ufe of mankind, without being loofe or low. Yet it is ufual with us to talk of their brutal ftupidity! But this fyftem is not practifed among them—and is the Chriftian fyftem of morals practifed among Chriftian nations?

The Arabian and Perfian hiftories and romances abound with traits of magnanimity, of generofity, juftice, and courage, no way inferior to, but in fome inftances exceeding thofe of other nations. The Greeks and ourfelves have indeed ftigmatifed them with the name of barbarians; but impartial inquiry proves that they are fufceptible of all that is admired in a polifhed people; that crimes are treated among them as among other nations, and that though their paffions may be expreffed in a different way, they have always the fame fource and the fame object.

No man who reflects on his paft enjoyments and fufferings can doubt but that the latter, by their intenfenefs, duration, and frequency, have been decidedly predominant.

To render them more equal, that is, to be lefs miferable, or to make life tolerable, either the number of pleafures muft be augmented, according to the fyftem of the Epicureans, or that of pains muft be diminifhed, according to that of the Stoics. The Orientals ftrive to attain the one object like ourfelves, by fenfuality; and here it is not to be conceived that they are happier than we are; but the other they gain in a much more

complete

complete degree than ourselves, and are much more exercised in the stoical system, which seems the most effectual to the purpose.

The passions, indeed, it is said, are to the mind what motion is to the body; and the absence of either causes and marks, in each respectively, symptoms that may be termed morbid.

A perfect absence of passion is certainly preternatural, if it may not be called impossible; but as our passions are more likely to be called into action by painful than by pleasurable sensations, it seems little doubtful, that the mind, on which they operate most feebly, will remain in the most tranquil state. This tranquillity, this absence of pain, (for joy, however poignant, is but a transient gleam, a coruscation, which passing, renders the obscurity which succeeds it more sensible,) is the single species of happiness of which mankind is allowed to partake.

A man of great sensibility has his feelings hourly wounded by minute accidents, at which one of less lively sensations would smile.

Such a one is transported with love, and, if that love be successful, his gratification is exquisite. He is suddenly moved by compassion,—how refined his feeling in offering relief to distress! He ardently desires fame,—how is he elated with the slightest praises! But how often is his warm affection requited with neglect, or its gratification found impossible? How often will his compassion be excited, without the means of affording relief? And how much more is mankind disposed to obloquy than to eulogy?

But this is not all; the same mind which is strongly acted on by these passions will also have its peace disturbed by pride, ambition, anger, jealousy, and resentment. The subjects of all these tormenting emotions crowd on it too closely to allow its complacency to be permanent. The sunshine of the morning will inevitably, ere night, be succeeded by a tempest.

Some slight omission of ceremonial will offend its pride, some *sordid repulse* will check its ambition; it will flame with anger at the breaking of a jar, or pine with jealousy at the like frailty in a mistress.

Something of the same kind has place with regard to taste. A man of delicate taste feels refined enjoyment from the contemplation of a beautiful landscape or a fine picture, or the perusal of an elegant poem; and is equally disgusted at the sight of any thing deformed, disproportioned, or unnatural in either. But, it may be said, he has the option of contemplating a disagreeable object, but not of feeling an unpleasing sensation. And is it indeed so easy, in being perpetually conversant among mankind, to avoid observing their works? or does not the man who reads unavoidably fall on absurdities which disgust him? Social man has been too long employed in counteracting nature, not to have moulded all to his dwarfish intellect; and the abortive efforts of imagination are numberless both in the arts and in letters.

Then

Then it will be said, human happiness is reduced to apathy; and the lively taste and ardent passions, which have established the superiority of Europeans, only serve to diminish their sum of felicity! This would be pushing the argument too far; but each will draw his own conclusions.

The chief points of contrast between the Europeans and Orientals being thus marked, it will be seen how far it may be doubted on which side lies the greater degree of happiness.

APPENDIX.

No. I.

Illustrations of the Maps.

In compiling the two maps which accompany this work, the writer has made use of his own observations in that part of it to which those observations had extended. For the remainder of the information exhibited in each, he has trusted to the report of the more intelligent natives, who having frequently traversed the neighbouring countries, might be supposed in some measure qualified to describe what they had seen. Yet he has not ventured to lay down a single position which had not previously been confirmed by the distinct and concordant testimony of at least three or four individuals. Even with this castigation, it is unnecessary to remark how impracticable is the task of approximating the bearings, from the oral testimony of those who have no clear idea of bearings, and scarcely know how to distinguish the eight principal points. Almost equally difficult is it to give the face of a country, or an account of its productions, which the informant perhaps traversed between sleep and waking, or when too much occupied

pied with the sufferings of the road, or the end he had in view, to be at leisure to attend to its detail.

The names of places so obtained and positions so adjusted, it has been thought proper to distinguish by dotted letters, with a view to denote hesitation and uncertainty. The part with which he was himself more particularly acquainted, or which was sufficiently supported by the authority of former maps, is marked with ordinary letters. The writer's own route is pointed out by a green line, the reported routes by a single engraved line, without colour.

The loss already mentioned of a large portion of his detached papers, has effectually deprived him of the power of presenting the chart of the route with all that exactness and minute detail which ought invariably to accompany all geographical researches. But if he have been compelled to use the *result* of his celestial observations, which alone his journal furnished, without the recapitulation of particulars, he has been careful to compare them with the bearings which fortunately were most of them preserved, without venturing to force the latter to the former: *e. g.* the result of his observation, as he found it briefly noted, would have brought *Charjé* and *Mughes* several miles farther East; but having found the distance and bearings exactly accord with this position with respect to *Assiút*, he has preferred it to the attempt of fixing the position of those places, by observation of which he was unable to give adequate proof of the accuracy.

The

The position of *Assiut* is fixed, both in latitude and longitude, by observation. That of *Charjé* in latitude by observation; in longitude, as above described. While at *Sheb*, the Writer had an opportunity of observing his position at leisure, both in latitude and longitude. At *Selimé* he enjoyed the same satisfaction. The mountains, to the East of the road, are laid down according to their appearance to the eye of the observer from the villages of *Elwah*, and the route of the caravan beyond them. Their S. E. extremity, as here marked, rests solely on the report of a native of *Mahas*. The distance from *Selimé* to the river, has been judged fully established by the uniform and unvarying testimony of a number of Jelabs of *Dongola*, &c. who travel that route.

The latitude of *Leghéa* was variously observed, both in going and returning. Its longitude is only determined by the bearing of the road, relatively to *Bír-el-Malha* S. and *Selimé* N. Several days consumed at *Bír-el-Malha*, afforded the means of determining its position both in latitude and longitude.

Sweini and *Zeghawa* have been placed only according to the bearing and distance computed from *Cobbé* and *Le Haimer*. But the two latter places are fixed without much doubt by frequent lunar observations, the occultations of Jupiter's satellites, &c.

With regard to *Cubeabéa* and *Ril*, no more could be done than to place them according to the uniform and constant report of the natives. They are both places much frequented, and

in

in so small a distance no mistake of importance can have arisen.

The bearings of the road from *Cubeabéa* to *Wara*, and thence to the capital of *Bornou*, are not laid down but from numerous inquiries, and some labour employed in adjusting them. That road occupies sixty days. The position of the capital of Bornou varies from that which is allotted to it in the latest maps, but scrupulously adheres to the bearings and distance given. *Abu-Shareb* is from *Cobbé* nearly W. by N. *Abu-Shareb* to *Wara*, N. W. by N. From *Wara* to the capital of *Baghermi*, between W. N. W. and N. W. by W. Road winding S. From *Baghermi* to *Kottocomb*, N. by W. ¼ W. From *Kottocomb* to *Bornou* nearly in the same direction.

Sennaar, as well as the course of the Nile, the coast of the Arabian gulf, *Mafouah*, *Gondar*, *Swakem*, &c. have the same position as in M. Rennell's map. *Sennaar* is in longitude 33° 30′ 30″. *Cobbé* being in 28° 8′, the difference between them will be 5° 2′ 30″.—*Ril* cannot be more than twelve or thirteen miles E. of *Cobbé*, but *Ril* is only twenty-three days journey from *Sennaar*. There remain therefore on a direct line 4° 50′ which is about twelve and a half geometrical miles *per* day; and admitting the smallest possible deviation, will give fourteen miles by the road. This on so long a journey is much more than might be expected, and by no means accords with the route to *Bornou*, which allows only about nine miles for each day's march.—D'Anville's position of *Sennaar* (29° 39′) would bring it too near to *Ril*, leaving only eighty miles between

between them, or three miles and quarter *per* day. Whether the truth lie between the obfervation of Mr. Bruce and the conjecture of D'Anville, or whether the former be well eftablifhed, and the length of each day's march may be accounted for from the ftraitnefs and facility of the road, fome future occafion muft determine. One circumftance would feem clear, viz. the diftance between the *city Sennaar*, and the *Bahr-el-abiad*, which the repeated and unvaried teftimonies of the natives relatively to the interval of three, or three and half days, leave no room to doubt, have hitherto been placed much too far apart.

The road from *Wara* to *Dar Kulla* exhibits a remarkable coincidence as to the number of rivers and lakes which it paffes, with that part of Major Rennell's laft general map of Northern Africa, which forms what he confiders as the alluvies of that portion of the continent, though it be neither in the fame latitude nor longitude.

Of thefe various ftreams little defcription was obtained. The country they flow through is faid to be great part of the year wet and marfhy; the heat is exceffive, and the people remark that there is no winter. The courfe of the rivers, if rightly given, is for the moft part from E. to W.

The river called *Bahr Miffelad* is faid to be a confiderable one. It's fource is not defcribed, but appears to be not far diftant from the fuppofed fite of the copper mines. Thofe who frequent this road, ordinarily pafs two years from the time of leaving *Wara* till their return to that place, or *Cobbé*. Of the time actually employed in the route they differ in their report, but it may be estimated at from 150 to 180 days; at a medium 165. *Wangara* I have never heard mentioned. Whether it may be the same country with some one of those described is uncertain; but its production being gold, does not accord with any of them; that commodity not being, as far as was related to me, found in any quantity to the W. *Zamphara* is yet known to several of my informers, as a country near to *Bornou;* but no particular description was given.

The dotted lines which are seen in the general map, and seem to mark with too much precision the extent of the empires *Bergoo, Baghermi,* and *Kordofân,* are chiefly designed to shew the relative situation of those districts, and how they border on each other, or on Fûr. The authority recurred to was only that of the inhabitants of each country, who affirmed that their native empire extended so many days from E. to W. and so many from N. to S. For the general form of *Dar-Fûr* the authority is somewhat stronger; the precise termination of that empire being accurately known to the several reporters in each principal direction.

The writer, during his stay in Dar-Fûr, could never find the variation of the needle greater than sixteen degrees W. In what relates to that country, therefore, he has been guided by that quantity of variation.

No. II.

ITINERARIES.

From Cobbé to Sennaar.

	Bearing.	Days.
From Cobbé to Shawer		1¼
From Shawer to Ril	S. S. E.	2

At Ril is a large pool of water, never completely dry, and a little to the E. of it a spacious house built by Sultan Teraub, eldest brother of the present Monarch.

| From Ril to Fadow | E. | 3 |
| From Fadow to Cawb | | 3 |

Near Cawb commences a ridge of hills, running N. and S. or nearly so.

From Cawb to Dar Hummâr		2
From Dar Hummâr to Emdì } Mean bearing	E.	3
From Emdì to Kreiga		0¾

In each of these towns are Fukkara, who administer justice.

| From Kreiga to Ibeit* | E. | 1 |

* Ibeit is one of the principal towns of Kordofân: it is also the name of a small district.

Between Kreiga and Ibeit is Abu-Harrâs, a place distant from the former three hours. Its neighbourhood is laid out in gardens belonging to the people of Dongola established there, in which they cultivate onions, &c. The situation of Abu-Harrâs is in length N. and S. and the wells which supply it with water are to the S. of the town.

	Bearing.	Days.
From Ibeit to Miteina	.	0¾
From Miteina to Autosh	. .	2
From Autosh to Yafsîn	. .	0¾

Yafsîn is a town of Fukkara.

| From Yafsîn to Breiffa, *deep sand* | . | 0¾ |
| From Breiffa to Cone | . | 1 |

Cone is at the foot of a mountain of the same name, which lies S. of the road. Near Cone, a little S. of the road, is a pool of water, and this is a place where travellers commonly repose themselves.

From Cone to Kinnana	. .	1
From Kinnana to Deggîn	. .	1
From Deggîn to Hellet Allais*, on the Bahr-el-abiad, the place which the ferry-boats frequent . .		1

Hellet Allais is situated on the W. of the river. The river (Bahr-el-abiad) is here of such breadth, that the features of a person standing on the other side cannot be distinguished, but the human voice is heard.—A number of trees is seen here to the W.

---

* The bearing of the road from Ril to Hellet Allais is reported to be generally E. with very small variation.

of the river, not to the E. Hellet Allais is altogether built of clay.—A large palm tree grows in the middle of the town.

On the eastern fide of the river is *Shillûk*—not far removed from it, being reported to be within fight of Allais.

Shillûk is a town of idolaters, built with clay. The inhabitants have no other clothing than bands of long grafs, which they pafs round the waift and between the thighs. They are all black; both fexes are accuftomed to fhave their heads. The people of Shillûk have the dominion of the river, and take toll of all paffengers, in fuch articles of traffic as pafs among them. The name *Shillûk* is not Arabic, and its meaning is unknown.—When afked concerning their name or country, the people reply *Shillûk*. When employed in tranfporting Mohammedans acrofs the ferry, they occafionally exhibit the importance which their fituation gives them. After the Mûflim has placed himfelf in the boat, they will afk him, " Who is the mafter of that river?" The other replies, as is ufual, " Ullah or Rubbani"—God is the mafter of it. " No," anfwers the Shillûk, " you muft fay that fuch a one (naming his chief) is the mafter of it, or you fhall not pafs." They are reprefented as fhewing hofpitality to fuch as come among them in a peaceable manner, and as never betraying thofe to whom they have once accorded protection. The particulars of their worfhip, as in moft other inftances where I have had my information from Mohammedans, have not been defcribed.

APPENDIX, No. II.

	Bearing.	Days.
From Shilluk to Dar Ruga	E. ¼ N.	1
From Dar Ruga to Waalia	E.	1
From Waalia to Shadli	E.	1
From Shadli to Sennaar		0½

Sennaar, *Medinet el Fuñ* or *Fungi*, is situated on the river which flows from Habbesh, which river is much smaller than the *Bahr-el-abiad*, and before the annual increase is fordable between Sennaar and Basboch.

The slaves who have usurped the government reside in *Terfeia*, on the opposite side of the river. Between them and the people of the city have been perpetual skirmishes for the last six years. (1794).

The Bahr-el-abiad suffers the same periodical increase and diminution as the Nile in Egypt.

From Sennaar to Gondár.

	Bearing.	Days.
From Terfeia to Rhad	E. N. E.	1
From Rhad to Dender	E.	1
From Dender to Béla	S. E.	1
From Béla to Teawa		1

Rhad is on the banks of a river of the same name. After passing Béla, the traveller leaves the river, and proceeds by a mountainous road to Teawa. The soil in the neighbourhood of Teawa is clay, and the town is built of that material. The people of the place use for bread the Mah-

riek,

APPENDIX, No. II.

	Bearing.	Days.

riek, (white maize,) which grows there luxuriantly.

| From Teawa to Râs el fil | S. E. | 1½ |
| From Râs el fil to Gondâr | E. S. E. | 7 |

The officer who governs Râs el fil is appointed by the king of Habbesh.—Inhabitants of Râs el fil called *Giberti*.

Road from Sennaar to Swakem.

From Sennaar to Teawa		4
From Teawa to Atbara, a town on that river	E.	1
From Atbara to Hallanga	N.	2

The people of Hallanga are Mohammedans, but use not the Arabic language generally. They are of an olive complexion. The *Mahriek* in their neighbourhood is said to grow so large, that the stem at bottom is seen of the size of a man's wrist.

| From Hallanga to Swakem | N. E. | 12 |

During great part of the way the road is mountainous and rocky. The space between the two last places is uncultivated, and inhabited only by wandering Arabs. These are of two races, Bijjé and Okoot. Both of them breed camels in great number, sheep, &c. Swakem is situated on an island, in which the governor and principal persons reside: but the greater number live on the main land.

Road from Sennaar to Mahas.

	Bearing.	Days.
From Sennaar to Herbajé	N. ¼ W.	3
From Herbajé to Halfeia	N.	5

At Halfeia is the confluence of the Bahr-el-abiad and Bahr el afrek.

From Halfeia to Chendi	} N. {	3
From Chendi to Birbîr		3
From Birbîr to Shaikié		3
From Shaikié to Dongola	N. W.	2
From Dongola to Mahas	N.	1

From Sennaar to Fazoglo.

From Sennaar to Dachala	E.	3
From Dachala to Emsirié	S. E.	1
From Emsirié to Louni	S.	3
From Louni to Gerbîn	S.	3

The people of Dachala are Mohammedans residing on the western bank of the Bahr el afrek.—Gerbîn is a mountainous place, which serves for confining malefactors under the government of Sennaar.

Mountainous—From Gerbîn to Fazoglo — S. 4

The mines of Fazoglo afford much gold: they belong to Sennaar.

APPENDIX, No. II.

From Gerbîn to Gondar.

	Bearing.	Days.
From Fazoglo there is no direct road. Having returned to Gerbîn,		
From Gerbîn to Hafsîb	E.	2
From Hafsîb to Beida	E. ¼ S.	2

Beida is the first town under the Abyssinian government, and is described as chiefly inhabited by fugitive slaves, who belong to persons within that empire.

From Beida to Kourmi		3
From Kourmi to Hasseb-ullah		3

This road is mountainous, circuitous, and abounds with springs of water. The civet cat is so common in this district, that in every house, it is said, there are fifteen or twenty tame ones.

From Hasseb-ullah to Gondâr	E.	10

Mountainous and difficult road.

Sundry routes of the merchants of Sennaar.

From Sennaar to Gebel-el-Moié	S. W.	1
From Gebel-el-Moié to Bahr-el-abiad	W. S. W.	1⅝
From Sennaar to Bahhadin	S. S. W.	0½
From Bahhadìn to Menâjel	S. W.	2
From Menâjel to the Bahr-el-abiad.	W.	2

Road to Gondar.

	Bearing.	Days.
From Sennaar to Terfeia	-	0½
From Terfeia to Subi-deleib	-	0½
From Subi-deleib to Wallad Midani	-	0½
From Midani to the Bahr-el-afrek	-	0½
From the river to Mendala	-	2
From Mendala to Kaila	-	1
Kaila is mountainous.		
From Kaila to Embutteik	-	1
Mountainous and deep sand.		
From Embutteik to Goze, or the sands	-	2
From Goze to the Atbara	-	3

This country is inhabited by the Bisharin Arabs, who are Mohammedans.

	Bearing.	Days.
From Atbara to Gebel Cuffa	-	3
From Gebel Cuffa to Gebel en Narr	-	3
From Gebel en Narr to Gondar	-	12

A Route which seems to be uncertain, and of which the bearings are not accurately given.

	Bearing.	Days.
From the Goze or sands of the Atbara, abovementioned, to El-Edd belonging to the Bijjé	-	3
From El-Edd to Swakem	N. E.	12

This road is filled with Arabs.

From Swakem to Gebel-el-Hellé	W.	3

From

APPENDIX, No. II.

	Bearing.	Days.
From Gebel-el-Hellé to Gebel-el-Sillah		2
From Gebel-el-Sillah to Gebel-el-beit	S. W.	2
From Gebel-el-Beit to Birbìr		6

All this road from Swakem to Birbìr is represented as rocky.—Birbir is situated in a clayey soil.

	Bearing.	Days.
From Birbìr to Wullad-el-Megedûb		2
From Wullad-el-Megedûb to Bìſharié	S.	2
From Bìſharié to Shûkûrié		3

Biſharié are a foreign race, but Shûkûrié ſpeak Arabic as their native language.

Arabs—From Shûkûrié to Hellalié		4
From Hellalié to Bahr-el-aſrek		1
From Bahr-el-aſrek to Em-uſhar		1
From Em-uſhar to Wullad-el-fûrûk		1
From Wullad-el-fûrûk to Hummûr		2

Clayey ſoil.

Mohammedans—From Hûmmûr to Senût-abûd		2

From Ibeit to Emdurmân and Halfeia, and return to Ibeit by another road.

	Bearing	Days
From Ibeit to Bahra	E.	1½
From Bahra to Emganatû	N. E.	2
From Emganatû to Shegeik	N. E.	1
From Shegeik to Gimmoyé	N.	2
From Gimmoyé to Emdurmân	N.	2

All this country is inhabited by Mohammedans, who ſpeak Arabic alone.—Gimmoyé and Emdurmân are both on the W. bank of the Bahr-el-abiad,

	Bearing.	Date.

and the latter is at the place of union between that river and the Abawi.—Returning W.

| From Emdurmân to Harraza, a mountain of difficult passage | S. W. | 3 |

Road desert and destitute of water.

The inhabitants of Harraza are idolaters, of mixed complexion, but most of them of a reddish hue.—They breed some horses, which they mount.

From Harraza to Abu-hadid	} S. W.	{ 1
From Abu-hadid to Zerawy		0¼
From Zerawy to Esherchar		1

Esherchar is famous for its salt, which is gathered by the Arabs, transported to other places and sold. The people of this last place are Arabs, but those of Zerawy, Harraza, and Abu-hadid, neither Arabs nor Mohammedans.

| From Esherchar to Bisherié | S. | 1 |

Road desert.

Bisherié is full of palm-trees.

| From Bisherié to Bahra | } S. S. W. | { 1 |
| From Bahra to Ibeit | | 1¼ |

Route from Ibeit to Sheibón, where are gold mines, and other places, returning to Ibeit.

From Ibeit to Bahra	E.	1½
From Bahra to Khûkjé	S. E.	4¼
From Khûkjé to Abu-jenûch	S.	1

From

APPENDIX, No. II.

	Bearing.	Days.
From Abu-jenûch to Seijé	E.	0½
From Seije to Tummara	S. E.	2

Between the two last places is a rocky road, with intervals of deep sand and clay.

From Tummara to Demîk	S. ¼ E.	1

The people from Abu-jenûch hither are idolaters, and destitute of clothing. The soil at and near Demik is clay.

From Demîk to Khéga	S. ¼ E.	1
From Khéga to Dibû	S. S. E.	0½

Mountainous and rocky.

From Dibû to Sheibôn	S. S. E.	1½

Clayey soil.

Near this place, in a deep glen or valley, much gold is found, both dust and in small pieces. The natives collect the dust in quills of the ostrich and vulture, and in that condition sell it to the merchants. They have a ceremony on discovering a large piece of gold, of killing a sheep on it before they remove it. The people are all black, as are those above mentioned from Abu-jenûch hither. They have some form of marriage, i. e. of an agreement between man and woman to cohabit. Women of full age wear a piece of platted grass on their parts. The younger and unmarried are quite naked. The slaves, which are brought in great numbers from this quarter, are some prisoners of war among themselves, (for their wars are frequent,) and some seduced by treachery and sold. But it is said to be a common practice for the father in time of scarcity to sell his children.

At Sheibôn are some Mohammedans, who live among the idolaters and wear clothing: it is not said whether Arabs or not.

The people above described are independent tribes of negroes, who have no other ruler than their respective chiefs, the authority of whom is very small, except in time of war. The Mecque of Sennaar used to claim some tribute from the people of Sheibôn, but received nothing regularly.

	Bearing.	Days.
From Sheibôn to Shurrû	} W. S. W.	{ 0½
From Shurrû to Luca		1

Luca is another place where resides an independent chief: it is also famous for its gold, which, as at Sheibôn, is the only medium of exchange among the inhabitants.

| From Luca to Koheila | W. | 1½ |

In Koheila are Arabs, not subject to any monarch of the country. Some idolaters also live among them.

From Koheila to Tlinga, a town	} W. ¼ W.	{ 1
People of Tlinga Mohammedans.—This country is called by the Arabs Dar Kinnana.		
From Tlinga to Gebel Sahd		0½

Gebel Sahd is within the dominion of Sennaar.

| From Gebel Sahd to Baha-ed-din | N. | 1 |

Still Dar Kinnana.

| From Baha-ed-din to Gebel-el-abid | N. N. E. | 1 |
| From Gebel-el-abid to Tumbûl | N. | 1 |

Tumbûl is under the government of the king of the Tuclawi.

APPENDIX, No. II.

	Bearing.	Days.
From Tumbûl to Seifabân		1
Seifabân is inhabited by Arabs alone.		
From Seifabân to Abdome		0½
From Abdome to Tuggala, capital of the king of Tuclawi	N.	0½
This diſtrict is called Sagurnié, country of the mountaineers.		
From Tuggala to Deir		1
From Deir to Gebel-el-deir		1
From Gebel-el-deir to Gebel-el-Bucclé	N. N. W.	1
From Gebel-el-Bucclé to Ibeit	N.	0¼

From Ril to Wara, capital of Bergoo.

From Ril to Gebel Marra, *deep ſand*	W.	2
Gebel Marra to Biſhara Taib	W.	2
Biſhara Taib to the confines of Fûr	W.	5

All this road is mountainous and rocky, and the inhabitants from Ril W. to the confines of Fûr are Mohammedans. The water on Gebel Marra, which is a lofty mountain, riſes with ſome remarkable circumſtances, and it is ſaid to be ſulphureous. The people there feed partly on wheat, which grows near the place, partly on Mahreik.

The people who inhabit the confines of Fûr W. are called *Túmúrkée*.

From the confines to Dar Ruma	W. ¼ N.	8
Deſert, ſand and clay, ſome water.		

	Bearing.	Days.
From Dar Ruma to Kibbéid		2
Kibbeid is situated on a hill or rock.		
From Kibbéid to Kajachsha		1
From Kajachsha to Bendala		1¼
Bendala is inhabited by the slaves of the Sultan of Bergoo.—The people of *Ruma*, and thence to Bendala are idolaters.	N. E.	
From Bendala to Wullad-el-Bucca		1
Bucca is a mountainous district.		
From Bucca to Dar Misselâd		1
From Dar Misselâd to Wara, the residence of the Sultan of Bergoo		2½

From Wara to Bahr-el-Gazalle.

	Bearing.	Days.
From Wara to Nimr, where the merchants reside, as at Cobbé in Dar-Fûr	W.	0¼
From Nimr to Battah		2
Battah is situated on a small river, which flows from the S. and then deviating to the W. falls into the Bahr el *Fittré*. Battah belongs to the Misselâd.		
From Battah to Dirota	W.	1
From Dirota to Dar Hummâr		0½
Road, clayey soil.		
From Dar Hummâr to Coseiât		1
Dar Hummâr rocky.		
From Coseiât to Shungeiât		1
Two towns of idolaters.		

	Bearing.	Days.
From Shungeiât to Dar Dajeou—*Caffres* Cooka, *Mohammedans*—From Dar Dajeou to Dar Cooka		1
		3
From Cooka to Muddago		2

In Muddago are Mohammedans, who are governed by a petty prince under the king of Bergoo.

From Muddago to Bahr-el-Fittré		1½
The people on the banks of Bahr-el-Fittré are called Abu-femmîn, and are Mohammedans. They use little boats for the purpose of passing from one place to another on the river.	N. W.	
From Bahr-el-Fittré to Bahr-el-Gazalle Road deep *sand*, *no trees*.		2

The neighbourhood of the Bahr-el-Gazalle is inhabited by Arabs, who feed camels and sheep, and some oxen.

Route from Khukjé to the Bahr-el-ada, and thence towards the Bahr-el-abiad.

From Khukjé to Baraka	S. S. W.	3

Baraka is inhabited by independent Arabs.

The greater part of this road is deep sand; the remainder, from *Baraka* by the Bahr-el-ada, is clay. The part of that river, which is here meant, is occupied by tribes of Arabs feeding cows and sheep; they are called Missicié. This part of the river is also frequented by wild and ferocious animals.

mals. The Missicié Arabs comb their hair back, twist it, and fasten it in the form of a scorpion's tail behind. They collect honey of the wild kind in great quantity, and hunt the elephant.

	Bearing.	Days.
From Baraka to Tûrrût	S. E.	4
From Tûrrût to Jungeión	S. E.	1

The people of Jungeión are tall and black; they have cows, sheep, and goats, and feed on the *Mabriek* or white maize. They collect the dung of the animals mentioned, dry it, roast it on the fire, and afterwards use it for a bed. These people are very numerous. The country in their neighbourhood is all a plain, and the soil clay. They have a practice, apparently superstitious, of milking their cows into a vessel with a narrow mouth, that the milk may not be seen, and never pour it into a dish or bowl; and any stranger who visits them is obliged to drink of the dugs of the cow, as do the calves.

| From Jungeión to Shäd | S. E. | 1 |
| From Shäd to Inigulgulé | N. | ¼ |

Route from Khukjé to the Bahr-el-ada, thence toward the Bahr-el-abiad, and returning to Ril.

The inhabitants of Inigulgulé are idolaters. They clothe themselves with a kind of cotton cloth.

From

APPENDIX, No. II.

	Bearing.	Days.
From Inigulgulé to the residence of the king of Ibbé	E. ¼ N.	1½
From said residence to the confines of Dar-Fûr	N. W.	4
From the confines to Tubeldié		2
From Tubeldié to Ril		8

All this road is sandy, but filled with many and large trees.

Road from Bahr-el-gazalle to Bornou.

	Bearing.	Days.
From Bahr-el-gazalle to the capital of Dar Baghermé	N. E.	3
From the said residence to Kottocom	N. ¼ W.	

The inhabitants of this district are Mohammedans. In the road two rivers are crossed by the traveller, one of which is called *Kitchena*. It runs from S. E. to N. W. — 18

From Kottocom to Bornou, the Imperial city — N. ¼ W.

The road lies in part through sand, in part through deep clay. There are many trees. The neighbourhood of the Bahr-el-gazalle seems by the description to be a forest.

The city Bornou is surrounded by a wall, in which there are four gates, opening E., W., N., and S. A small river runs near it, which falls into the Bahr-el-gazalle.

Bergoo is said to be fifteen days in extent from E. to W. and from N. to S. twenty days.—Bagarmé, in the former direction, twelve, in the latter, fifteen days.—Bagarmé has many troops, but Bergoo is estimated the strongest. The people of Bergoo are remarkable for their zealous attachment to the faith, and read the Korân daily.

Some description of Bergoo.

Within about a day's journey of Wara are said to be eight large mountains, the inhabitants of each of which use a distinct language. They are Mohammedans, and said to be brave, furnishing the armies of the Sultan of Bergoo with recruits as often as required. One of the mountains, called Kergna, is situated S. E.; another W. which is inhabited by a people called Wullad Mazé; Gebel *Mimi* N. Gebel Abſenûn E. Gebel Abdurrûg E.

Other mountains of Bergoo are, Gebel Tama, N. Gebel Kaſhimirié, W., each of them two days from Wara. Gebel Abu-hadîd, E. the same distance.

Three days W. of Wara is the river called Bahr Miſſelâd.

APPENDIX, No. II.

Route from Wara to Cubcabéa in Dar-Fûr, and another route from the laſt place back to Wara.

	Bearing.	Days.
From Wara to Abu-ſhareb	S. E.	5
From Abu-ſhareb to the confines of Fûr	E. ¼ S.	1½
From the confines to Emdokne	E.	1
From Emdokne to Dar Miſſeladîn	} E. ¼ S.	{ 1
From Miſſeladin to Cubcabéa	}	{ 3
From Cubcabéa to Gellé	N. W. ¼ W.	1
From Gellé to Gimmer	N. E. ¼ N.	4

The Sultan of Gimmer is ſubject to Fûr.—The people are Mohammedans. In the road is found water, and the ſoil is ſand and rock.

	Bearing.	Days.
From Gimmer to Zeghawa	E. ¾ N.	2

Mountainous.

The Sultan of Zeghawa is alſo dependent on Fûr.

	Bearing.	Days.
From Zeghawa to Tama	} N. N. W.	{ 2½
From Tama to the confines	}	{ 1
From the confines to Abu-ſenûn		2
From Abu-ſenûn to Wara	W.	8

A route ſometimes taken by the merchants of Bergoo.

From Wara to Emjûfûr		2
From Emjûfûr to Timé Degeou		1½

Another

Another route.

	Bearing.	Days.
From Wara to Jumbo	⎫	1
From Jumbo to Doreng		1
From Doreng to Dageou		2
Sandy road—Mohammedans.	N. with little variation E.	
From Dageou to Kergna		2
From Kergna to Ghannim		2
From Ghannim to Duida	⎭	2

This road is mountainous, soil sandy, many trees.

The people Mohammedans, under the government of Bergoo.

	Bearing.	Days.
From Duida to Bencia		1½
From Bencia to Dongata		3½
From Dongata to Bendala	W.	3½
Mountain.		
From Bendala to Bujid	S. S. W.	2½
From Bujid to Kibbeid		3½
Mountainous.		
From Kibbeid to Kajachsa		2
From Kajachsa to Baniân	S.	2½
From Baniân to Ain		3½
From Ain to Kuddano		1½
From Kuddano to Gizân	S. E.	2
From Gizân to Wara	S.	4

Another

APPENDIX, No. II.

Another route from Wara, and returning thither.

	Bearing.	Days.
From Wara to Middeisîs		2½
From Middeisîs to Beit-el-Habbûba		2
From Beit-el-Habbûba to Truanié	N. E.	2½
From Truanié to Gidìd		1½
From Gidid to Kuddano		2
From Kuddano to Wara		3

Another route.

	Bearing.	Days.
From Wara to Birket-el-Rumli	W. S. W.	4
From Birket-el-Rumli to Goze, *or the sands*	N.	2
From Goze to Dirota	E.	2½
From Dirota to Butta	E.	2
From Butta to Wara	E.	2½

Near Butta is a small river, of which my informer remembered not the name.—This road is full of a species of tree, whose leaves are described as white, and which bears a fruit, which, however, is not eaten, except by the camels which are fond of it; it is called *Culcul.*

Route from Cobbé to the copper mines of Fertit.

	Bearing.	Days.
From Cobbé to Cuffé		1
From Cuffé to Currio		1½
From Currio to Treiga		1¾
Sandy road.		
From Treiga to Beit Melek Eide		1
From Beit Melek Eide to Dar Miffelâd	S. ¼ W.	3
Rocky.		
From Dar Miffelâd to Dar Marra		1
Caffres—From Dar Marra to Dar Fungaro		3
One day and a half mountain, the remainder forest and clayey soil.		
From Dar Fungaro to Dar-el-abid-es-Sultan-Fûr		2½
From the latter to Dar-el-Nahâs		8½
Rocky road, earth where visible is red.		

The people wear a flight covering over the parts of generation, in other respects are quite naked.

From Dahr-el-Nahas to Bahr Taifha	E.	3
From Bahr Taifha to Bahr-el-abiad		4½

The former falls into the latter at a place called *Tenderni*, which is peopled by idolaters, called *Cufni*. This spot is full of palm trees, and another kind of tree, which by description would seem to be the cocoa.

Here it is seen that the distance between Cobbé and the copper mine is 23½ days, direction nearly S. and that the Bahr-el-abiad is 7½ days distant from that place, direction generally E.

Route

APPENDIX, No. II.

Route from Dar Bergoo to the sources of the Bahr-el-abiad.

From Abu Telfân South, ten days journey, is said to be the source of the Bahr-el-abiad: but the particulars of the route my informer was unable to give me, he not having travelled it. The place is called Donga, and is the residence of a chief or king of an idolatrous nation. The country there is very mountainous, and in the spot where the river rises are said to be forty distinct hills: these are called Kumri. From them a great number of springs issues, which uniting into one great channel form the Bahr-el-abiad. The people of Bergoo go thither sometimes to seize captives, but there is no trade between them and the natives. The people are quite naked, black, and idolaters. The place is said to be twenty days removed from the confines of Bornou. All the road thither is mountainous. From Donga to Shillûk 30 days.

APPENDIX.

No. III.
METEOROLOGICAL TABLE
FOR THE YEAR 1794.

Day of the Month.	JANUARY. Height of Therm. 7 A.M.	Height of Therm. 3 P.M.	Course of the Wind.	Day of the Month.	FEBRUARY. Height of Therm. 7 A.M.	Height of Therm. 3 P.M.	Course of the Wind.	Day of the Month.	MARCH. Height of Therm. 7 A.M.	Height of Therm. 3 P.M.	Course of the Wind.
1	58	76		1	62	69		1	73	83	
2	60	76		2	61	72		2	72	83	
3	59	75		3	58	74	No settled wind.	3	74	84	Westerly.
4	61	80		4	58	73		4	74	85	
5	60	79		5	52	70		5	73	82	
6	61	79		6	50	70		6	76	84	
7	57	78	Always Northerly.	7	54	73		7	80	83	
8	53	76		8	55	74		8	80	84	S.
9	58	78		9	53	71	N.	9	76	84	S.
10	59	80		10	56	76	N.	10	76	84	S.W. S.
11	56	75		11	60	78		11	72	85	
12	51	72		12	61	77		12	75	86	
13	53	73		13	65	81		13	73	84	
14	49	70		14	64	81		14	73	84	
15	50	70		15	61	80	S.W. and S.	15	74	86	S.W.
16	52	74	W.	16	63	82		16	76	86	
17	51	74	W. N.W.	17	62	80		17	77	86	
18	51	76		18	60	81		18	75	87	S.E.
19	53	78		19	58	76		19	78	87	S.
20	55	76	N.W.	20	58	75		20	80	83	S.E.
21	53	74		21	55	75	W. W.S.W.	21	79	86	
22	56	79	W.	22	56	75		22	80	81	S.E.
23	55	78		23	55	72		23	81	81	
24	51	72	W.S.W.	24	54	72	S.	24	79	87	S.
25	52	76		25	56	71		25	78	85	S.
26	58	80		26	53	70		26	77	85	S.
27	57	80	S.W.	27	54	75		27	79	85	
28	60	81		28	52	71		28	76	84	
29	63	82						29	79	86	
30	60	80						30	77	85	W.S.W.
31	61	81						31			

APPENDIX, No. III.

METEOROLOGICAL TABLE
FOR THE YEAR 1794.

	APRIL.				MAY.				JUNE.		
Day of the Month.	Height of Therm. 7 A.M.	Height of Therm. 3 P.M.	Course of the Wind.	Day of the Month.	Height of Therm. 7 A.M.	Height of Therm. 3 P.M.	Course of the Wind.	Day of the Month.	Height of Therm. 7 A.M.	Height of Therm. 3 P.M.	Course of the Wind.
1	80	97		1	85	89		1	80	94	N.W.
2	79	96		2	88	92		2	77	86	N.W.
3	79	97		3	88	94		3	82	90	N.W.
4	78	95	Generally N. or N.N.W.	4	86	95		4	83	94	N.
5	82	98		5	85	95		5	83	94	N.
6	80	96		6	84	94		6	84	94	S.E.
7	81	96		7	84	96		7	84	95	S.
8	79	95		8	84½	96		8	84	97	S.
9	80	94		9	85	97		9	82	90	N.W.
10	80	94½		10	86	97		10	81	90	N.W.
11	81	96		11	87	97		11	81	87	
12	82	96		12	87	98		12	83	89	N.W.
13	79	94		13	87	99		13	86	91	N.W.
14	80	95		14	82	94		14	87	95	S.E.
15	82	98	S.	15	81	94	South or South-easterly winds most part of this month.	15	87	95	S.E.
16	83	98	S.S.E.	16	82½	95		16	86	95	S.
17	83	98¼	S.	17	86	99		17	88	96	S.
18	83	99	S.E.	18	86	99		18	87	96	S.
19	80	97		19	85	97		19	82	89	
20	81	97	S.	20	86	96½		20	83	88	
21	81	96	S.	21	84	94		21	82½	88	
22	79	95		22	83	90		22	81	90	
23	80	94	N.W.	23	85	96		23	81	91	S.E. chiefly.
24	82	96		24	87	96		24	80	92½	
25	82½	98	S.	25	86	98		25	79	92	
26	82	98	S.	26	86	96		26	76	90	
27	84	100	S.	27	88	97		27	77	90	
28	84	101	S.	28	87	99		28	79	94	
29	83	101		29	87	100		29	80	97	
30	80	95	N.W.	30	85	98		30	81	97	
				31	84	98					

APPENDIX, No. III.

METEOROLOGICAL TABLE
FOR THE YEAR 1794.

Day of the Month.	JULY. Height of Therm. 7 A.M.	Height of Therm. 3 P.M.	Course of the Wind.	Day of the Month.	AUGUST. Height of Therm. 7 A.M.	Height of Therm. 3 P.M.	Course of the Wind.	Day of the Month.	SEPTEMBER. Height of Therm. 7 A.M.	Height of Therm. 3 P.M.	Course of the Wind.
1	82	93		1	79	90		1	82	94	
2	85	95		2	99	93		2	79	93	E. ¼ S.
3	85	98		3	82	93	S. E.	3	78	92	E. S. E.
4	85	94		4	80	91	S.	4	80	95	
5	83	94		5	80	91		5	81	95	
6	85	94½		6	84	96		6	80	94	E.
7	87	95		7	85	95		7	78	93	
8	86	97	S. E. or Calm, all this time.	8	82	94		8	83	94	S. E. E.
9	87	97		9	82½	93	N.	9	82	96	S. ¼ E.
10	88	97		10	83	94	N. N. W.	10	80	95	
11	87	95		11	84	94	E.	11	84	95	S. E. ½ E.
12	84	93		12	83	94	S. E.	12	84	93	
13	82	93		13	86	97		13	83	94	S. E.
14	82	90		14	84	92		14	81	92	
15	82	91		15	84	92		15	84	95	
16	81	92½		16	85	94		16	80	94	
17	83	94	N. W.	17	82	91	S.	17	79	90	E.
18	83	94	N.	18	80	92		18	80	91	E. N. E.
19	83	93	N. W.	19	75	92		19	80	92	N. E.
20	86	95	S. W.	20	80	93	N. W.	20	78	92	
21	85	96	W.	21	81	94	S. E. E.	21	82	94	
22	86	96	S. W.	22	81	94		22	82	93	
23	84	92		23	83	94		23	79	90	
24	80	92		24	84	97		24	80	93	
25	80	91	S. or S. E.	25	84	97	Generally S. or S. E.	25	79	94	Generally N. E.
26	81	93		26	80	92		26	78	92	
27	82½	94		27	83	92		27	80	92½	
28	82	94		28	82	93		28	82	94	
29	85	97		29	84	95		29	83	95	
30	85	98		30	85	95		30	80	92	
31	85	98		31	84	96					

APPENDIX, No. III.

METEOROLOGICAL TABLE
FOR THE YEAR 1794.

Day of the Month.	OCTOBER. Height of Therm. 7 A.M.	Height of Therm. 3 P.M.	Course of the Wind.	Day of the Month.	NOVEMBER. Height of Therm. 7 A.M.	Height of Therm. 3 P.M.	Course of the Wind.	Day of the Month.	DECEMBER. Height of Therm. 7 A.M.	Height of Therm. 3 P.M.	Course of the Wind.
1	78	90	} For the most part Northerly.	1	79	91	} W. and often S. W.	1	68	80½	N. W.
2	78	90		2	78	88		2	69	80	N. W.
3	77	91		3	78	88		3	71	81	
4	80	91½		4	79	87		4	73	82	N. N. W.
5	76	90		5	78	88		5	73	83	S. W.
6	77	92		6	78	86		6	72½	82	S. & E.
7	82	93		7	76	86		7	71	80	S. E.
8	82	93		8	74	85		8	73	83	
9	80	92		9	74	86		9	72	80	
10	79	92		10	75	85½		10	72	83	N. W.
11	78	90		11	73	84		11	69	80	N. W.
12	80	89		12	73	85		12	68	79	N. W.
13	81	90		13	73	86		13	68	81	N.
14	76	90	N. E.	14	76	86		14	68	82	N. ½ W.
15	76	88	N.	15	72	83½		15	67	81	
16	76	89	N.	16	74	84		16	66	82	} No settled wind.
17	79	91		17	74	82		17	66½	82	
18	78	90	N. N. E.	18	73	82	N. W.	18	67	81	
19	80	89		19	75	82	N.	19	67	81	
20	82	94		20	74	83		20	68	82	
21	82	93		21	72	81	N.	21	70	84	
22	79	93	N. W.	22	72	81½	N.	22	71	84	S. and S. E.
23	80	93		23	73	81½		23	70	84	
24	78	89	N.	24	73	82		24	70	82	
25	78	90	N.	25	72	83		25	70	81½	
26	80	91	N. W.	26	74	83½	N. or N. W.	26	66	80	
27	79	92		27	73	82		27	66	81	
28	77	90		28	73	81½		28	65	79	N. W.
29	77	89		29	72	82		29	67	79	N. W.
30	76	89		30	71½	83		30	67	81	
31	79	90	W.					31	68	81	

APPENDIX, No. III.

METEOROLOGICAL TABLE
FOR THE YEAR 1795.

Day of the Month.	JANUARY. Height of Therm. 7 A.M.	Height of Therm. 3 P.M.	Course of the Wind.	Day of the Month.	FEBRUARY. Height of Therm. 7 A.M.	Height of Therm. 3 P.M.	Course of the Wind.	Day of the Month.	MARCH. Height of Therm. 7 A.M.	Height of Therm. 3 P.M.	Course of the Wind.
1	59	75	} Generally N.W. or N. and very violent.	1	57	74	N.	1	65	81	} Very variable.
2	64	78		2	56	75	N.	2	66	84	
3	58	74		3	59	75	N.W.	3	66	80	
4	58	76		4	60	77	N.	4	66	82	
5	60	76		5	60	76		5	74	86	
6	61	76		6	61	76		6	72	90	
7	62	77		7	57	72	N.W.	7	74	90	
8	63	78		8	48	66	N.	8	74	91	
9	63	76		9	50	71	N.	9	69	88	
10	63	76		10	54	71		10	68	88	
11	60	75		11	52	74		11	68	90	
12	57	69		12	55	76	N. N. W.	12	71	90	
13	57	69		13	55	74		13	72½	92	
14	57	71		14	57	75	N.W.	14	73	92	S. W.
15	56	73		15	56	76		15	71	92	S. W.
16	56	73		16	59	76		16	70	91	
17	55	72½		17	59	76		17	72	91	W.
18	59	77		18	60	78	} Generally South.	18	74	92	
19	58	77		19	60	80		19	75	93	} S.
20	58	78		20	63	80		20	76	93	
21	60	81		21	64	81		21	75	93	
22	60	79		22	65	81		22	75	92½	
23	59	79		23	65	83		23	74	93	
24	60	79		24	65	82		24	72½	92	
25	58	80	} S. and S. E. or calm.	25	64	82½		25	71	92	S.
26	62	80		26	64	82		26	77	94	
27	60	81		27	66	83		27	74	91	
28	62½	81		28	66	84		28	76	90	
29	60	80						29	76	93	
30	61	80						30	73	92	
31	59	78½						31	70	91	N. W.

APPENDIX, No. III.

METEOROLOGICAL TABLE
FOR THE YEAR 1795.

Day of the Month.	APRIL. Height of Therm. 7 A.M.	Height of Therm. 3 P.M.	Course of the Wind.	Day of the Month.	MAY. Height of Therm. 7 A.M.	Height of Therm. 3 P.M.	Course of the Wind.	Day of the Month.	JUNE. Height of Therm. 7 A.M.	Height of Therm. 3 P.M.	Course of the Wind.
1	70	90	N. W.	1	77	93	N.	1	76	88	N. W.
2	72	90	N.	2	76	94	N.	2	76	92	
3	72	92		3	76	94	N.	3	78	93	N. N. W.
4	73	92		4	77	94		4	77	92½	
5	76	93		5	75	93	N. W.	5	80	90	
6	76	93		6	77	96	N. N. W.	6	78	91	N. N. W.
7	77	93		7	78	96		7	78	92	
8	77	94		8	78	96	S.	8	79	92	
9	77	94		9	76	95		9	81	98	
10	80	96		10	76	95		10	83	98	
11	80	96	S. S. E.	11	74	95		11	82	98	
12	76	92		12	73	92		12	81	97	S.
13	75	92		13	73	91	N. E.	13	70	97	
14	74	92		14	72	91	N. E.	14	79	95	
15	73	91		15	70	89	N. E.	15	76	94	
16	73	92		16	79	89		16	76	94	
17	75	93		17	71	89		17	77	93	
18	75	95		18	75	92	S. E.	18	77	94	
19	76	95		19	73	92	S. E.	19	80	95	
20	76	95		20	75	92½		20	80	94	
21	77	94	Variable.	21	74	95	S.	21	81	96	Generally South.
22	77	94		22	74	95	S.	22	78	92½	
23	76	94		23	76	95	S.	23	76	98	
24	74	93		24	78	100	S. E.	24	80	98	
25	74	93		25	79	98	S.	25	79	96	
26	72	93		26	78	98	S.	26	81	97	
27	73	95½		27	79	98	S. S. E.	27	82	97	
28	72	94		28	77	96		28	80	96	
29	73	94		29	77	95	N. W.	29	79	94½	
30	75	95½		30	78	96		30	82½	96	
				31	78	97					

APPENDIX, No. III.

METEOROLOGICAL TABLE
FOR THE YEAR 1795.

Day of the Month.	JULY. Height of Therm. 7 A.M.	Height of Therm. 3 P.M.	Course of the Wind.	Day of the Month.	AUGUST. Height of Therm. 7 A.M.	Height of Therm. 3 P.M.	Course of the Wind.	Day of the Month.	SEPTEMBER. Height of Therm. 7 A.M.	Height of Therm. 3 P.M.	Course of the Wind.
1	80			1	78	95		1			
2		96		2	78	94		2			
3				3	75	92		3			
4				4	74½	93		4			
5				5	73	92		5			
6		92	N. or N.W. during short intervals, but generally S. or S.E. or calm.	6	77	95		6			
7				7	78	97		7			
8	78	91		8	79	96		8	77	93	Always S.E. or S.
9	80	96		9	77	98	S.	9	80	95	
10	81	98		10	81	100	S.S.E.	10	81	95	
11	81	101		11	80			11	79	93	
12	80	97		12	79			12	78	93	
13	79	97		13	76	94		13	80	94	
14	80	96		14	78	94		14	77	92	
15	78	93		15	79	95		15	75	92	
16	77	93		16	78	95		16	74	90	
17	78	92		17	76	95		17			
18	76	92		18	79	96		18			
19	78	94		19	80	99	S.	19			
20		93		20	77	94		20			
21	76	91		21	76	94		21			
22	79	94½		22	75	94		22			
23	80	94		23	77	95		23			
24	80	93		24	77	93	N.W.	24			
25	81	95		25	75	93	N.W.	25			
26	77	92		26	76	94	N.N.W.	26			
27	78	92		27	75	92	N.	27			
28	78	94½		28	78	94		28			
29	79	96		29	80	96	S.W.	29	74	90	N.E.
30	79	94		30	78	95	S.	30	75	90	N.E.
31	80	99		31	77	95					

APPENDIX, No. III.

METEOROLOGICAL TABLE
FOR THE YEAR 1795.

| \multicolumn{4}{c}{OCTOBER.} | \multicolumn{4}{c}{NOVEMBER.} | \multicolumn{4}{c}{DECEMBER.} |

Day of the Month.	Height of Therm. 7 A.M.	Height of Therm. 3 P.M.	Course of the Wind.	Day of the Month.	Height of Therm. 7 A.M.	Height of Therm. 3 P.M.	Course of the Wind.	Day of the Month.	Height of Therm. 7 A.M.	Height of Therm. 3 P.M.	Course of the Wind.
1	76	90		1	70	83		1			
2	75	91		2	72	87	S.	2			
3	80	93	N.	3	71	86		3			
4	78	93		4	72	86		4			
5	77	92		5	73	87		5			
6	77	90		6	69	88		6			
7	77	91		7	69	82	N. E.	7			
8	76	91		8	70	82	N. N. E.	8			
9	78	92		9	69	81		9			
10	80	92		10	68	80		10			
11	75	90	N. W.	11	68	82		11			
12	74	87	N. N. W.	12	69	80		12	59	73	⎫
13	74	86		13	70	80		13	60	73	⎪
14	72	86	N. W. N.	14	68	79		14	62	79	⎪
15	72½	86		15	69	83		15	57	76	⎬ N.
16	73	84		16	72	86		16	57	77	⎪
17	75	86		17	72½	84		17	58	79	⎪
18	77	87		18	72	83½		18	57	78	⎪
19	76	87	N.	19	70	81		19	60	79	⎭
20	80	89		20	71	82	⎫	20	60	80	⎫
21	76	86		21	73	82	⎪	21	62	80	⎪
22	75	85		22	72	83	⎪	22	62¼	81	⎪
23	75	84		23	72	84	⎬ S.	23	61	81	⎬ S. W.
24	74	84		24	73½	86	⎪	24	57	80	⎪
25	76	84½		25	73	85	⎪	25	58	80	⎪
26	75½	86		26	72	85	⎭	26	56	74	⎭
27	74	84		27	74	82		27	60	76	
28				28	71	80		28	56	76	
29	72	81		29	70	80		29	57	76	
30	73	81		30	70	79		30	58	77	
31	72	81						31	57	76	

No. IV.

Some Observations on the account of Egypt given in the works of Savary and Volney.

Vol. i. p. 27. Savary says, Alexandria is only a village, containing scarcely six thousand inhabitants. The fall of Alexandria from its antient splendour has already been remarked; and how vague all computations of number must necessarily be, by persons who reside there only for a few weeks or months. But Alexandria alone furnished to the Imperial army and navy, in the war with the Russians, four thousand men able to bear arms. This, with other circumstances, might serve to prove that the population must greatly exceed the number mentioned.

He computes the people of Damiatt at eighty thousand, which appears no less extravagant on the other side, and is certainly at least double the real number.

Vol. i. p. 220. Savary's description of the topography of Memphis is characterized by an apparent error. He speaks of the small bourg *Menf*, antiently Memphis, a little to the South of the Pyramids. It is somewhat singular, that no one writer before him should have found a spot so remarkably coinciding in name with the antient capital. The writer of this inquired repeatedly for such a village, but always without effect; and *Olivier* and *Brugniere*, in the employ of the French Republic,

Republic, who passed several months in Egypt, nearly at the same epoch, were equally unsuccessful in their researches. So that it would seem fair to pronounce that no such place exists. The only town in Egypt which bears even a distant resemblance to the name of Memphis, is *Menûf*, which is many leagues to the North, and within the Delta.

P. 275. The story of Murad Bey discovering his father, it is somewhat surprising should have escaped all the merchants residing in Egypt, some of them almost half a century, and always eager for anecdotes of this kind. The inventive talent of the Greek servants is indeed often put in activity to amuse strangers with such tales, but Savary, who was so experienced in Egypt, should have had more discrimination than to blend *des contes de ma mere l'oye* with historic narration. The facts are wholly discordant.—The man is a labourer of the environs of Damascus, Murad Bey a native of Georgia.—To go from Damascus to Kahira he embarks at Alexandretta, seventeen days journey N. W. of Damascus, when he might have gone to Beirût, Seidé, Akka, or Yaffa, each of them four days. This labourer travels with the eccentricity of a comet; and even the French philosopher is lost in calculating his course. But Savary was writing on Egypt, and is not obliged to know the geography of Syria.

P. 288. J'ai tué plusieurs *Ibis* dans les marais près de Rossette. Ils ont les pattes longues, le corps mince, alternativement blanc et noir, et le col allongé. Ils vivent de poissons, de grenouilles et de reptiles.

Had

Had Savary given the Arabic name of this curious bird, that sups on so many different dishes, the extent of his own error might have been exactly known, by comparing the bird he means with the figure of the real *Ibis*. Others are contented with seeing one Ibis, but they have come in covies to welcome M. Savary, and he compliments them with a volley of small shot. S. should have known, that birds accustomed to feed on fish, do not commonly eat reptiles, and *vice versâ*.

Vol. ii. p. 59. The Ruin at Achmunein had before been fully described by Pococke; Norden passed it in the night, and therefore saw it not. Bruce has also mentioned it. What is described as gilding, however, on this and other monuments, I take to be yellow colour, never having seen any instances of gilding in the antient remains of Egypt. It might be curious to inquire of what materials these colours were composed, which have thus defied the ravages of time.

Vol. iii. p. 33. Savary speaks of the military corps of Assabs as still in being, but some years before his time that body had been dissolved, and no longer existed.

The Janizaries are still inrolled, to the number of about fourteen thousand; but the greater part of them are peaceable citizens, who never handle either sword or musket. From them are appointed the gate-keepers, a small garrison in the castle, &c. &c.

A body

A body of Janizaries was called out and maintained by Ali Bey, but since the time of Mohammed Bey Abu-dhahab I have not understood that they have been on active service. The Yenk-tcheri aga, or commander in chief of the Janizaries, ranks as a Bey, as do the *Kiabia* and *Ichawúsh*. These three are elected in the Divân of the Beys. The inferior officers are appointed by the *Shech-el-belad*, as are the officers of the city police.

Volney seems generally to hint that women are despised in Egypt, and says, they can possess no inheritance in lands.

They are exactly in the same predicament with the other sex as to inheritance of land, and receive possession by paying a fine to the government, from which none are exempted. In fact, their situation is in many respects better than that of men. Public opinion is in their favour, and their property is generally more respected, and they are treated more equitably than males. Their complaints, in case of injustice, sometimes carried even to intemperance, are heard with more patience.

A large portion of landed property having devolved to a widow at *Monfalut* in Said, Solyman Bey, Senjiak of Said, desired to purchase it at the price the widow might demand. She refused, and he afterwards married her to gain possession, though she was both old and diseased.

English

English edit. Vol. I. p. 216. Volney says, that when there are no ships at Suez, that town has no other inhabitants than the Mamlûk governor, and a garrison, consisting of twelve or fourteen persons.—In Suez are twelve or thirteen mosques, which could never have been designed for a garrison of so few persons. There are also several coffee-houses. In truth the inhabitants are not numerous, but there are four or five considerable merchants constantly residing there, who have their correspondents at Kahira, and in the towns of Arabia, and conduct the commerce between Egypt and India. There is consequently a proportionate number of their dependents, and persons who manage commercial affairs of a less considerable kind. There are ship-builders, and several other artificers; a large khan or okal where merchandize is lodged; some Greek Christians constantly residing there; Mohammedan ecclesiastics, and others; and a number of fishermen and people more immediately connected with the sea. The population is restrained by the difficulty of procuring water, scarcity of provisions, and other inconveniences; but invariably much exceeding the estimate here given.

P. 263. Volney remarks, that the horizon is every where flat, even in the Upper Egypt, and refers for a proof of his assertion to Norden's Plates, which demonstrate precisely the reverse. The fact is true indeed as to Lower Egypt, but from Kahira upward to Assûan there is only a very small space where the view is not terminated by the mountains, of various aspects, on each side.

Some

No. V.

Some remarks on the account of Egypt, contained in the recent correspondence of the French officers who accompanied Buonaparte to that country. The work referred to is intitled, PARIS, PENDANT L'ANNÉE 1798. *Par* PELTIER. *Vols.* xix. *and* xx.

VOL. 19, page 455. The distance from Cairo to the cataract is about 360 Geog. miles. The Nile is never an impetuous torrent, nor does it ever overflow its banks in the whole course from Assûan to Kahira, but is admitted at proper times into the transverse channels prepared for it.

P. 457. The Arabs, it is evident, would not build walls of much greater extent than the habitations they proposed to defend. A very small part of these being now filled, shews that the decay the city has undergone since the Turks became possessed of it, has even been greater than what it sustained from the time of Severus to the Saracenic conquests.

P. 459. Old Kahira is not Fostat, but Misr el attîké, further South.

Lettre de Boyer.

P. 475. I doubt whether any one of the towers about Alexandria would contain 700 men.

APPENDIX, No. V.

P. 475. The writer says every Mamlûk is bought; and yet there are Frenchmen among them.—Where are Frenchmen sold? It is probable no Frenchman would be found among them, unless perhaps two or three individuals who might have embraced Mohammedism, but who certainly never were sold. In an engagement, I believe, no one has more than a single piéton with him; for those inconsiderable officers, who are attended on ordinary occasions by numerous followers, when in the field, avoid as much as possible any shew of preeminence, which would only expose their persons to greater danger.

P. 476. A Mamlûk has rarely more than one fusil, which he discharges once, and then gives to his piéton, to reload if he find opportunity.—One pair of pistols is attached to the body, and the second pair is carried in holsters, never about the body.—Of the arrows in a quiver I have no knowlege; occasionally in engaging the Bedouins the Mamlûks use a light spear, about six feet long, or a *misdrâk*, which is often ten or twelve feet.—The former is thrown, the latter never discharged from the hand. But these are by no means part of their common arms.—One sabre is used most adroitly and with extraordinary effect, by every expert horseman, but never two—This part of the officer's account seems taken from the mouth of some Egyptian peasant, who, as usual, exaggerated.

P. 476. From Alexandria to the mouth of the Nile is not twenty leagues, but from twelve to fifteen.—The anecdote of the shech in the same page appears authentic.

P. 479. The Mohammedans in general, and the Egyptians in particular, of whatever order, are very far from being regardless of the children.—On the contrary, they are extremely anxious for their welfare. Perhaps their domestic government may in some degree afford an example of the happy medium between weak indulgence and unnecessary severity; and parents daily experience the benefit of this their moderation. Very few instances of ingratitude are seen in their children. Women offering to sell their children, it remained for Boyer to discover. If reduced to desperation they might have desired rather to see their offspring in slavery than pierced with bayonets; but not the most wretched of Egyptian mothers would ever have consented at any price to sell her child, even to Murad Bey. I rather imagine the writer mistaken as to this fact.

A moitié nuds. Would not men go half naked in Great Britain if the climate permitted it?—*La peau dégoûtante.* In the populace of no nation are fewer cutaneous diseases found, or the skin more smooth and healthy, than in the Egyptians. *Fouillant dans des ruisseaux,* &c. Are hedgers and ditchers in any country very polished and delicate?—None are found raking the muddy channels but those whose business it is to keep them clean. The houses of the Alexandrines are neat, and *comfortable* according to their ideas, though perhaps they would appear gloomy to a French or English man.

P. 480. This is not quite correct. On the West of the W. branch of the Nile, the arable lands are very narrow, but to the East

East they extend along the road to Bilbeis and Salehich. The villages indeed are ill built; yet a house is here of little use but as a shelter from the sun. One of our neat, snug, brick houses, covered with red tiles, would be absolutely intolerable in Egypt. They are poor because the government is oppressive, not because they are uninclined to labour. The muddy appearance of the Nile water is no motive for any Egyptian to abstain from drinking it; nor is any other circumstance attending it, except its being polluted. Water, according to their law, is not polluted by a camel, a horse, or an ox drinking of it; but it is by a dog's drinking, or a man washing his hands in it.

481. Boyer seems to have been too hasty in numbering the inhabitants—400,000 seems to me about one-fourth too much.

Ibid. The streets of Kahira are narrow, but inconveniences would attend their being wider. The houses are by no means without order: two long streets, as is seen in Niebuhr's plan, bisect the city longitudinally and parallel with the river. The streets are often rectilinear, though they are by no means rectangular.

The ecclesiastics all read, and many of them write. All merchants of any consequence read, and many write. Often their female offspring are taught to read. The Copts most of them read and write. Who then regards the arts of reading and writing with admiration? The soldiers, the peasants, and the laborious part of the populace are ignorant enough of reading and writing, but by no means wonder or are astonished at what they see daily practised.

Berthier's Letter, 2 Fructidor.

P. 536. All Egypt, according to this writer, is in submission to the French troops; but it appears the farthest post the latter have occupied is at four leagues from Cairo, where there is an entrenched camp; then there remain 130 leagues yet to subdue.

P. 599. It seems to me impossible that the old port could contain half the number of vessels here mentioned, viz. 300.

———. This place, whose name is so murdered, is spelled Jibbrîsh.

P. 603. In Julien's letter, I know not how the flag could be placed on the walls of *the celebrated city Thebes*, when all that remains of that city is the ruins of public buildings, that formed a part of its interior.—*Often join, &c.* There is one annual feast dedicated to the Prophet, called *Mewlet-en-Nebbi*, which lasts one day; and one feast also annual in honour of cutting the *Chalige*, which also lasts one day. How did the soldiers then often celebrate them?

604. The canal of Alexandria wanted nothing more than to be cleared of the sand which had accumulated in it, and to be defended by a dike against the incroachments of the sea, which

which the citizens of Alexandria refused to do for themselves, lest the repair of all other public works should be expected from them, and the Beys would not do it for them.

Dolomieu's Letter.

Vol. 20. p. 50. He says the Alexandria of the Greeks was situated on a tongue of land, formed by earth lately accumulated, when the city was founded.—He means, I suppose, that the sea had left it but lately. This is possible. The natural soil round the city is rock intermixed with sand. The vegetable mold appears to have been extraneous. If he suppose that district, like the Delta, to have been a deposition of the river, this seems utterly improbable; all the circumstances are at variance, which in such a case should be common to both. The land which divided the lake from the sea is a rocky ridge, which seems to have undergone no variation for a great length of time. The remark as to the column of Pompey is not new; but I cannot agree that the capital and base are of bad taste. The sharp relief of the foliage and mouldings is worn off by time, and it never was perhaps possible to exhibit on granite marble the finer strokes of the chissel, but the proportions, though not those of the later Corinthian, are strictly conformable to those of the purest age of architecture. What may have been discovered relatively to the obelisk by digging is uncertain; but from a comparison of this with the circumstances attending the obelisks at Thebes, it cannot be deduced that much is lost of its height. It must have been erected in the most flourishing state of the city, and while it remained in that state, it seems scarcely probable

probable that such multitudes of ruins should have existed as to raise other buildings on them. I am satisfied, from the position of the one that remains entire, and the broken one near it, they never underwent a second arrangement, but remain in their relative position, as at the gate of some public building. The obelisk is in a very low part of the city, (which indeed is all very low,) and very little above the level of the sea—how does this accord with the ruins of other buildings being yet found under it? Perhaps in this part a firm foundation was not found very near the surface, and the builders have formed an artificial one. The French antiquary may have mistaken this for the ruins of buildings.

P. 59. My measurement of the height of the pyramid was a few feet short of this, but does not very materially differ from the one here given.

P. 95. *El Maraboot* is a kind of fort, and the tomb of a saint, situated on a high ground in the neighbourhood of the Gulf of the Arabs, a good view of which it commands.

APPENDIX.

No. VI.

Explanation of the Plate facing page 286.

1. The principal inclosure, consisting of apartments exclusively appropriated to the use of the monarch.

2. Principal rukkûba, or place of public audience.

3. The large court where public audiences are given.

4. Two gates, the one of the interior, the other of the great court; at both stand slaves, to refuse admittance when the Monarch is not in the humour to do justice; and the chief of them, to strike the greater awe, is the public executioner.

5. Exterior court in which the public officers leave their horses, and thence walk barefoot to the presence of their master.

6. External entrance, fronting the market-place.

7. A court with some apartments in it for faquirs, guards, and slaves.

8. A wide court where are some horses tied.

9. Rukkûba at the other entrance, where the Sultan gives audience, principally in winter, and where he would be less public.

10. Small court surrounding that rukkûba or shed.

11. Outer court where a mob assembles, and horses and slaves are in waiting.

12. Outer gate, called *Bab-el-burrâni*, as the great one is called *Bab-el-Gebeia*.

13. A multitude of small apartments reaching almost the whole length of the palace, where slaves are kept in confinement,

ment, as a punishment for misdemeanors; they are chained and fettered, and kept to hard labour, as dressing and tanning leather, making spear heads, &c.

14. A large court of irregular form filled with a multitude of small apartments for the women; they pass through the two gates marked *w* to fetch water, but have no other outlet. Each of the principal women has a large apartment, surrounded by a number of smaller ones for her slaves; there are also apartments for cooking.

15. Granary, which is builded on a frame of timber, to prevent the accession of the *Termis* or white ant.

16. Gate by which the women enter the Sultan's apartment where that sex performs all offices.

17. Stable or court where the best horses are kept tied, and sheltered from the sun.

The Eunuchs live in the interior, to be always near the Sultan; male slaves, wherever they can find a place.

18. Are the slaves' apartments who guard the entrance.

19. A place where the faquirs read.

The officers immediately attached to the court live in small inclosures on the outside of the fence, as that marked 20.

The houses of the Meleks resemble this in miniature; those of inferior persons only of smaller size without divisions, and having fewer apartments.

The exterior is an hedge of dry thorns, about ten feet thick, and as many high.

THE END.